W9-ASQ-008

A12900 830445

Illinois Central College
Learning Resources Center

Hollywood As Historian

HOLLYWOOD AS HISTORIAN

American Film in a Cultural Context

Edited by PETER C. ROLLINS

THE UNIVERSITY PRESS OF KENTUCKY

ISBN: 0-8131-1486-1 cloth; -0154-9 paper

Library of Congress Catalog Card Number: 82-49118

Copyright © 1983 by The University Press of Kentucky

Scholarly publisher for the Commonwealth,
serving Berea College, Centre College of Kentucky,
Eastern Kentucky University, The Filson Club,
Georgetown College, Kentucky Historical Society,
Kentucky State University, Morehead State University,
Murray State University, Northern Kentucky University,
Transylvania University, University of Kentucky,
University of Louisville, and Western Kentucky University.

Editorial and Sales Offices: Lexington, Kentucky 40506-0024

This book
is dedicated to
ALVAH BESSIE
a man who has made history,
influenced Hollywood, and captured
human nature in his fiction.

Contents

Acknowledgments

Many writers in this collection have been encouraged in their work by the American Studies Association and the Popular Culture Association; in fact, numerous meetings at annual conferences of these professional organizations led to a special issue of the *American Quarterly,* 31 (1979). Devoted to film in American culture, the issue carried the essays in this volume by Vivian C. Sobchack, Thomas Cripps–David Culbert, Leslie Fishbein, Kenneth Hey, Charles Maland, and the bibliographical survey by Peter C. Rollins. The *American Quarterly* was also the source of the essays by Everett Carter (12 [1960], 347-357) and Thomas J. Knock (28 [1976], 523-542). The *American Quarterly* staff, to include Bruce Kuklick and Leila Zenderland, has been helpful through the many phases of this project.

The essay by Douglas Gomery is a complete rewrite of an article originally published by the *Quarterly Review of Film Studies,* 1 (1976), 315-330. Ira Jaffe's essay first appeared as part of a special issue of the *Journal of the University Film Association* devoted exclusively to Chaplin (21 [1979], 23-33). Leonard Leff's article is an expanded version of a piece which originally appeared in the *Cinema Journal,* 19 (1980), 41-55. Peter C. Rollins's article on New Deal documentaries was first published by the *Journal of Popular Film and Television,* 5 (1976), 125-146.

The authors, editors, and associations mentioned are thanked for permissions to use the articles which form this collection.

In years past, William Ferris, James Welsh, and Michael Marsden contributed their editorial expertise to the special film issue of the *American Quarterly.* In recent days, Leonard J. Leff, Kenneth Hey, Janet Rollins, Terry Hummer provided the editor with much needed administrative and stylistic assistance. The editor here offers his profound thanks.

Foreword

RAY B. BROWNE

IF A PICTURE, AS WE GENERALLY AGREE, IS WORTH A THOUSAND WORDS, then a *motion picture* or a movie, is worth millions of words because it is *words in action*. Pictures as history are exceptionally effective because, although words lie flat and dormant to some readers (indeed to a certain extent to *all* readers), it is difficult to miss messages carried in a motion picture as it explains a historical period or event—the historical message, the background, the setting, language, and incidental details. Most difficult of all to overlook is the power of the art. Indeed, the aesthetic power of a motion picture, historically correct or incorrect, is difficult to resist. Aesthetics in all artistic expressions is a great seducer, and must always be calmly surveyed, for it sells lies as well as truths, inaccuracies as well as accuracies. But then so do words; the only difference is that motion pictures propagate messages more massively, and effectively, and sometimes quite unexpectedly and surprisingly.

The literary critic Leslie Fiedler likes to tell a story of the time he was in Moscow and the State Department asked him to attend a showing of *The Birth of a Nation* (a film very capably discussed in this volume) and to explain its meaning—in other words, justify the distortions and historical inaccuracies presented in the movie—to a group of Communist officials. Expecting sharp condemnation of the film's blatant racism, Ku Klux Klanism, and distortion of history, Fiedler was surprised—indeed, devastated—to witness the Communists applauding at the wrong spots, the wrong episodes, exactly at the dramatic moments they should have been condemning the movie, America, Capitalism, etc.

Watching a movie, as Fiedler's anecdote illustrates, is a private and personal experience, although it is generally carried on in a theatre with a group of people. The Communists even in that setting could for a moment forget their doctrinaire philosophy and submit to the power of the work of art. Although nobody wants to meddle with the private and personal message of a movie, sometimes it is proper to bring a motion picture into public consciousness, at least as a beginning point for interpretation and understanding, and to free the work from the iron grip of aesthetics so that audiences will understand its cultural meaning. For this purpose, we need to return to the power of words, and realize that sometimes a word, properly chosen and used, can be worth a thousand pictures—to explain, to justify, to correct distortions, and inaccuracies, or simply to enrich. Judging from the millions of words printed yearly on the motion picture, there can never be too much said in conjunction with the experience.

And there can never be too many explanations of the significant and rich motion pictures discussed in this volume. In outlining the role of Hollywood as historian, although some readers might argue about the particular movies chosen to *exclude* (some, for example, might have insisted on the inclusion of *Gone With the Wind*), nobody could argue with the ones *included*. The individual essays will add greatly to our understanding of their place in history and of Hollywood as historian.

Introduction

PETER C. ROLLINS

HOLLYWOOD'S MYTHS AND SYMBOLS ARE PERMANENT FEATURES OF America's historical consciousness. In an obvious way, strictly historical films have recreated dramatic struggles—or revived historical personalities. For this collection, such films are represented by D.W. Griffith's *The Birth of a Nation* (1915) and Darryl Zanuck's *Wilson* (1944). Not satisfied with merely depicting the past, Hollywood has often attempted to influence history by turning out films consciously designed to change public attitudes toward matters of social or political importance. To illuminate this persuasive political role, classic New Deal documentaries are considered; in addition, this anthology includes a very detailed study of *The Negro Soldier* (1944), a wartime movie designed to promote racial understanding and pride. Without intending to act the role of historian, Hollywood has often been an unwitting recorder of national moods. In recent years, historians have used musicals, westerns, gangster films, and other escapist fare of the 1930s to decode messages about the Depression generation's hopes and fears. Films made to expose existing wrongs can yield more information about their times than was intended: *The Snake Pit* (1948) reveals unconscious attitudes of the postwar era; *Dr. Strangelove* (1964) gives access to a later period. With a constant eye on how each film text blends with its cultural context, this anthology attempts to show the multiple roles which Hollywood has played in relation to American history.

The essays in this anthology are arranged chronologically as an aid to teachers and students. The chronological sequence partially masks a basic goal of the collection: to present examples of superior interdisciplinary scholarship, each of which pursues a different approach to American film. Not every article addresses all the questions asked by the collection, but readers in search of the ideal method for studying American film in cultural context should take note of all the compass points. The remainder of this introduction will chart the major routes followed by *Hollywood As Historian: American Film in a Cultural Context.*

The Historical Film:
The Birth of a Nation and *Wilson*

The motion picture which demonstrated that film could be an art form was an epic attempt to interpret the historical meaning of the Civil War. *The Birth of a Nation* (1915) was a paradoxical blend of superior technique and self-serving racial theories; as Everett Carter observes, "Not only does significant motion picture history begin [with *The Birth of a Nation*], but most of the problems of the art's place in our culture begin, too."

Carter's investigation of *The Birth of a Nation* leads back to literary sources for the South's persistent myth, the "Plantation Illusion." In the antebellum period, novelists such as J.P. Kennedy and W.A. Carruthers portrayed an aristocratic leadership enjoying a fruitful land in harmony with a black underclass. As the Civil War approached, apologists such as George Fitzhugh borrowed neofeudal ideas from Thomas Carlyle to defend the southern way of life against northern detractors. At the turn of the century, followers of historian W.A. Dunning resumed apologetics for an old order. Although the historical notions of D.W. Griffith's film are foreign to Americans living decades after the passage of the Civil Rights Act, *The Birth of a Nation* was in harmony with the historical wisdom of its day. Such a fact will provide teachers and students much to discuss concerning the relativity of historical truths. That the President of the United States, himself a leading historian, greeted the film with unqualified praise tells volumes about the limits of American liberalism in the Progressive era. Certainly, contemporary black intellectuals such as W.E.B. DuBois and Monroe Trotter realized the *The Birth of a Nation* not only portrayed the past, but would serve to justify discrimination in the present. Screening *The Birth of a Nation* can still be a controversial campus event.

As a biographical film, *Wilson* (1944) focused on the life and accomplishments of the President who was so delighted by D.W. Griffith's Civil War epic. Producer Darryl F. Zanuck and his staff wished to highlight Wilson's fight for the League of Nations, hoping that an effective story would tilt American public opinion in favor of the United Nations, "clearing the path toward lasting peace for the new generations" after World War II. Like Griffith before him, Zanuck consulted the best historical sources available to him and—also like Griffith—Zanuck devoted himself to a feature-length production which would sway men's minds.

Thomas Knock's study of *Wilson* concentrates on historiographical issues while remaining attentive to such artistic elements of filmmaking as casting, set design, and story evolution. Subtleties of public response are explored with attention to the influence of *Wilson* on both elite and popular cultures. Unlike *The Birth of a Nation,* Zanuck's film has stood the test of time; on the other hand, *Wilson* was, very much like its predecessor, a powerful attempt by Hollywood to mold America's historical consciousness.

Film as an Influence upon History:
New Deal Era Documentaries and *The Negro Soldier*

During the 1920s and 1930s, Hollywood influenced the making of documentary films, if only by restricting its theatrical productions to escapism and irrelevance. *March of Time* newsreels, American Film Service documentaries, and Frontier Films productions attempted to address many social and economic issues of Depression America ignored by Hollywood. When war came to America, Hollywood professionals, under the general supervision of Frank Capra, were drafted by Washington to make films which would explain *Why We Fight*. The Depression and wartime experiments in documentary deserve more attention than they have received.

The March of Time (1935-1953) was a weekly newsreel begun under the auspices of Time, Incorporated. Louis de Rochemont and his team were devoted to investigative reporting, but—as an article by Peter C. Rollins demonstrates—the series was hampered from advocating fundamental reforms: "*March of Time* . . . wished for reform, but could not agitate for the radical changes required." For its persuasive purposes, the New Deal administration of Franklin D. Roosevelt attempted to reach American voters with such documentary films as *The Plow That Broke the Plains* (1936) and *The River* (1937). Because these New Deal films were more committed to influencing public opinion than *March of Time* weeklies, they more effectively exploited the dramatic potentials of music, voice, and editing. Finally, *Native Land* (1942) was an unusual persuasive feature-length production because—unlike either *March of Time* or the New Deal documentaries—it attempted to involve viewers emotionally. The varying relationships between politics and film language are explored in detail by Rollins' survey.

The Negro Soldier (1944) was one of a number of documentaries designed to explain to Americans why they must join a distant war. With painstaking attention to primary sources, Thomas Cripps and David Culbert reconstruct a story in which U.S. Army officials, Hollywood professionals, Black leaders, and social scientists worked cooperatively to produce a film that was a "watershed in the use of film to promote racial tolerance." The anticipated result was a product which would be important to black pride; an unexpected result came after the war. Hollywood professionals working on the project were so impressed with what they had wrought that they went on to produce unsponsored "message films" for peacetime distribution. Such thoughtful movies as *Pinky* (1949), *Home of the Brave* (1949), *The Defiant Ones* (1958), and *Guess Who's Coming to Dinner?* (1967) were all inspired in some degree by the success of *The Negro Soldier*.

Film as Historical Document:
Hollywood as Unconscious Historian

American films often tell more about their times than their filmmakers consciously intended. Leslie Fishbein, in her analysis of *The Snake Pit* (1948), and Charles Maland, in his study of *Dr. Strangelove* (1964), connect their films to important currents of surrounding history: Freudian theory in the first case and political thought in the second. Many other examples of the methodology used in these articles exist, but the care with which Fishbein and Maland relate Hollywood products to their times should serve as a model for those interested in exploring how Hollywood has served as unconscious historian.

When he made *The Snake Pit,* Anatole Litvak assumed that his film would help improve conditions at mental health institutions across the United States. Not only the director, but the actors on the film were very much committed to the reformist goals of the production. In her close reading of the film, Leslie Fishbein explains that popularized notions of Freudian psychoanalysis intruded themselves as *The Snake Pit* was adapted from book to screen. When released, the motion picture was hailed as a crusading production; yet, from later perspective, Fishbein identifies harmful messages embedded in the film. Rather than condemn society for thwarting the legitimate career goals of Virginia, the central character, the film condemns "feminine ambition as diseased." Virginia returns to sanity only when she gives up her dream of becoming a professional. Clearly, home and hearth were the places ordained by popularizers of Freud in the post-war years. Fishbein's ability to illuminate a film text with intellectual history makes her contribution a model for the student of American ideas.

Since the election of Ronald Reagan in 1980, rental requests for *Dr. Strangelove* have inundated distribution centers: prints of the film are in constant circulation, usually to college campuses, and there are few play dates available. Public awareness of nuclear hazards—so acute during the 1960s—has come back into focus with changes in technology, political leadership, and nuclear strategy. Charles Maland's study of *Dr. Strangelove,* although it addresses the obvious antinuclear theme, concentrates most of its attention on the film as a litmus test of evolving political attitudes. Stanley Kubrick—like his contemporaries—was unsure about how to explain the rationale of Cold Warriors: the ploy of comic treatment overtook him as he sifted through a great number of quasi-documentary strategies. Black comedy of the darkest kind supplied a needed detachment; for those who saw the movie when it was released in 1964, the manic laughter inspired by *Dr. Strangelove* seemed to be a useful step toward formulation of more constructive approaches to the nuclear age. Americans could feel themselves chortling their way out of a Cold War state of mind. Even though some of the comedy has paled with the passage of time, Kubrick's film continues to be an important evocation of a changing national mood.

Films as Part of Corporate and Institutional History

In addition to being works of artistic imagination, motion pictures have always been commercial products financed by American capitalism and therefore influenced by corporate, legal, and governmental pressures. A truly interdisciplinary study of film should explore the institutional dimension. In tracing such a web of relationships, Douglas Gomery's essay on how the Fox Film Corporation converted to sound is nicely balanced by Leonard J. Leff's narrative description of the demise of the Motion Picture Production Code: both essays indicate the wealth of insight available to cultural historians willing to pursue all relevant data.

Douglas Gomery's essay borrows a model of technological innovation from economic theory. Using court records, information from investment houses, and trade papers to supplement traditional sources, Gomery traces how sound started as an invention, became an innovation, and then grew to dominate the field of motion pictures. The essay is of special interest because of its stress on the importance of personality and vision on the business side of the film industry—a factor too often neglected. Gomery makes exciting the personal qualities of Theodore Case, Earl Sponable, and Lee DeForest; the collaborative efforts of these inventors within a competitive climate reads more like an adventure story than a historical narrative. The example provided by Gomery's essay is itself a persuasive argument that every major phase in film history should be examined from the corporate perspective.

In 1934, the Production Code Administration was put on notice to give a semblance of enforcement to the Motion Picture Production Code. There are a number of studies of the Administration's influence on Hollywood during the next thirty years, but Leonard J. Leff's research into the Code's demise is the first to profit from access to the files of the two most powerful groups responsible for American film censorship: the Code Administration and the Catholic Church's Legion of Decency. Leff traces the internal and external changes in attitudes which led to a limited approval by the Legion of such a controversial film as *Who's Afraid of Virginia Woolf?* (1966). Basing his study of internal factors on hitherto classified documents, Leff— like many of the other authors in this collection—discovered that history in close up is always a more tangled affair than history from long shot. Paradoxically, members of the Legion (many of them avid admirers of Federico Fellini, Ingmar Bergman, and other European film artists) were much more sanguine about the potential for motion pictures to deal with mature issues than members of the secular Code Administration's staff. As an external factor, court decisions related to the censorship of books introduced an additional vector to a complicated mode of change. Leff's study of the multiple institutional forces at work—corporations, churches, and government agencies—is an excellent example of conscientious research.

Film and the Other Arts: *On the Waterfront*

Economic institutions and censorship agencies are very careful to leave paper trails and—when access is granted—are perhaps more traditional sources for cultural historians than they might first appear. Very seldom are interdisciplinary students sufficiently familiar with a full spectrum of the arts to be able to note relationships among artistic forms. Kenney Hey's investigation of *On the Waterfront* (1954) is a rare exception, for his study speaks to both the political and the multiple artistic influences affecting a powerful movie.

The political and literary elements of the film were supplied by Elia Kazan (director) and Bud Schulberg (writer), both of whom had participated in radical movements during the 1930s, only to renounce their radicalism before the House Committee on Unamerican Activities in the late 1940s. In merging their concerns about the abuses of power and the importance of individual conscience in *On the Waterfront,* both artists tapped deep feelings of ambivalence: the project became an apology for their unpopular political actions. Kenneth Hey carefully identifies the intense peer pressures in Hollywood and New York affecting *On the Waterfront*'s creators and their film.

The theme of ambivalence, conceived by Kazan and Schulberg, was translated into visual images by Boris Kaufman, the cinematographer for *On the Waterfront.* A consistent and powerful tone pervades the film as a result of Kaufman's special skills with lighting, framing, camera placement, and synchronous sound. An additional layer of feeling was added by the score composed for the film by Leonard Bernstein: a variety of leitmotives enhanced verbal and visual messages. By successfully interrelating political, artistic, and genre elements, Hey has produced a study which shows how much a group of artists can accomplish in the collaborative art of film.

Aesthetics and Ideology: Three Chaplin Films, *The Grapes of Wrath,* and *Apocalypse Now*

It is a truism of aesthetics that form and content should reinforce each other if works of art are to be effective. For film studies, this can be translated to mean that elements of sound, sight, and editing should be compatible with the objectives of the artist. Unfortunately, students of culture interested in motion picture themes often forget this useful principle. The contributions by Ira Jaffe on three Chaplin films, by Vivian Sobchack on John Ford's adaptation of *The Grapes of Wrath,* and by William Hagen on the travails of Francis Ford Coppola to finish his study of the Vietnam war prior to the apocalypse of biblical prediction all devote considerable attention to matters of form in order to make significant statements about the philosophical or social or political messages of their films.

Charles Chaplin stubbornly continued to make silent films during a period when full sound technology was available. Ira Jaffe's study of *City Lights* (1931), *Modern Times* (1936), and *The Great Dictator* (1940) reveals that, at least in Chaplin's case, there were more than economic and technological dimensions to the sea change from silent to sound eras. Obviously, as "Charlie," Chaplin was committed to a screen *persona* who exploited the power of mime, but Jaffe reveals a more philosophical basis for Chaplin's resistance to new technology. The years of the Great Depression prodded the reexamination of many cultural traditions, including language. Chaplin was not alone in distrusting the capacity of existing vocabularies to cope with contemporary problems. Although the three films studied by Jaffe dealt with such basic issues as the class conflict, the problems of industrialization, the economic cycle, and the escalating international rivalries leading to World War II, Chaplin refused to use music, synchronous sound, or dialogue according to standard Hollywood conventions. Instead, for philosophical and aesthetic reasons, he devised a personal approach to film form and content.

The Grapes of Wrath (1941) is screened for countless history and literature classes across the country. The purpose of Vivian Sobchack's discerning essay is to call attention to the ways in which the visual style of the film conveys nonverbal messages of importance. In her efforts to repair the "visual neglect" the film has suffered, Sobchack explains how camera placement, tableau techniques, framing, lighting, and acting styles contributed to produce a film less radical than its literary original. Director John Ford translated the story of the Joad family into a sad tale of the eternal underdog rather than an indictment of the injustices of Depression America. In doing so, Ford created a cinematic world for the Joads "in which change is neither possible nor desirable." Sobchack's close reading of the visual language of *The Grapes of Wrath* explains how a message film could be so popular, yet so insignificant as a force for change.

Vietnam was America's first television war. William Hagen believes that the saturation coverage by television posed an aesthetic challenge for Francis Ford Coppola: how to produce a motion picture about Vietnam which could provide insight in a distinct visual and aural language. Coppola turned to *The Heart of Darkness,* Joseph Conrad's novella about imperialism and evil and, at least during the planning stages for *Apocalypse Now,* the literary model seemed to offer a useful pool of characters and themes to discuss underlying issues.

As Coppola's project matured, Conrad's themes turned out to be more problematic than helpful. For example, the theme of professionalism became confusing. As Noam Chomsky's *American Power and The New Mandarins* and Phillip Slater's *The Pursuit of Loneliness* have argued, many of America's problems in the 1960s stemmed from a misled faith in technology and professionalized knowledge. Hagen argues that Coppola's notorious aesthetic and production delays stemmed from his discovery of this dark paradox at the heart of American liberalism. By attending to three art forms—literature, television, and film—in two centuries, Hagen illuminates the complex relationship between aesthetics and ideology in an ambitious "failure."

The authors represented in *Hollywood As Historian,* while pleased with the collection, would be the first to admit that the study of film in a cultural context needs further refinement. Corporate and institutional dimensions are probably the least explored aspects of the Hollywood experience. The influences of other art forms on motion pictures have seldom been discussed because few cultural historians have been trained to address such connections. Tracing political ideology to aesthetic decisions also requires a rare balance of historical and artistic skills. Certainly more studies of individual feature films and important documentaries are needed, but researchers should avoid a strictly thematic approach. We hope that the essays of *Hollywood As Historian* will serve as models for those who wish to link American film texts to their broadest possible cultural contexts. And chapter 13 provides detailed bibliographical information for those ready to launch their own research projects.

CHAPTER 1.

Cultural History Written with Lightning: The Significance of *The Birth of a Nation* (1915)

EVERETT CARTER

ON FEBRUARY 20, 1915, DAVID WARK GRIFFITH'S LONG FILM, *The Clansman,* was shown in New York City. One of the spectators was Thomas Dixon, the author of the novel from which it was taken, who was moved by the power of the motion picture to shout to the wildly applauding spectators that its title would have to be changed. To match the picture's greatness, he suggested, its name should be *The Birth of a Nation.*[1] Only by a singular distortion of meaning could the film be interpreted as the story of a country's genesis; the birth it did herald was of an American industry and an American art; any attempt to define the cinema and its impact upon American life must take into account this classic movie. For with the release of *The Birth of a Nation* "significant motion picture history begins."[2] Its prestige became enormous. It was the first picture to be played at the White House, where Woodrow Wilson was reported to have said: "it is like writing history with lightning."[3] By January 1916 it had given 6,266 performances in the area of greater New York alone.[4] If we conservatively estimate that five hundred patrons saw each performance, we arrive at the astounding total of over three million residents of and visitors to New York who saw the picture, and forever viewed themselves and their country's history through its colorations.

1 Lewis Jacobs, *The Rise of the American Film* (New York: Harcourt, Brace & Co., 1939), p. 175.
2 Seymour Stern, "The Birth of a Nation in Retrospect," *International Photographer* VII (April, 1935), 4.
3 Jacobs, p. 175.
4 Stern, *International Photographer,* VII, 4.

And not only does significant motion picture history begin, but most of the problems of the art's place in our culture begin too. The picture projects one of the most persistent cultural illusions; it presents vividly and dramatically the ways in which a whole people have reacted to their history; its techniques in the narrowest sense are the fully realized techniques of the pictorial aspects of the motion picture; in the widest sense, its techniques are a blend of the epical and the symbolically realistic, and each part of this mixture has developed into a significant genre of cinematic art.

Griffith was a Kentuckian, a devout believer in Southern values, and these values, he was certain, were embodied in *The Clansman,* a sentimental novel of the Reconstruction which had appeared in 1905, had been widely read, had been seen in dramatic form throughout the South, and whose author had dedicated it "To the memory of a Scotch-Irish leader of the South, my Uncle, Colonel Leroy McAfee, Grand Titan of the Invisible Empire Ku Klux Klan."[5] In his introduction, Dixon went on to describe his theme: "How the young South, led by the reincarnated souls of the Clansmen of Old Scotland, went forth under this cover and against overwhelming odds, daring exile, imprisonment, and a felon's death, and saved the life of a people, forms one of the most dramatic chapters in the history of the Aryan race."[6] This strong suggestion that the South's struggle is a racial epic, involving all the people of one blood in their defense against a common ancestral enemy, became, as we shall see, a major influence upon Griffith's conception of his cinematic theme. And, in addition, the novel in so many ways served as what would later be called a "treatment" from which the story would be filmed, that we must examine the book closely before we can understand the significance of the film.

The Clansman told the story of "Thaddeus Stevens' bold attempt to Africanize the ten great states of the American Union . . ." It interpreted the history of the Reconstruction as the great Commoner's vengeance motivated partly by economics: the destruction of his Pennsylvania iron mills by Lee's army;[7] partly by religion: in his parlor there was "a picture of a nun . . . he had always given liberally to an orphanage conducted by a Roman Catholic sisterhood;"[8] but mainly by lust: his housekeeper was "a mulatto, a woman of extraordinary animal beauty . . ." who became, through her power over Austin Stoneman (the fictional name for

5 Thomas Dixon, *The Clansman* (New York: Grosset & Dunlap, 1905), Dedication, without page number.
6 *The Clansman,* Introduction, without page number.
7 *The Clansman,* p. 95.
8 *The Clansman,* p. 90.

Stevens) "the presiding genius of National legislation." [9] Stoneman was shown in private conference with Lincoln, whose words in his Charleston debate with Douglas were directly quoted: "I believe there is a physical difference between the white and black races which will forever forbid their living together on terms of political and social equality." [10] Stoneman's instruments in the South were all described as animals, demonstrating that the Civil War was fought to defend civilization against the barbaric and bestial. Silas Lynch, the carpet-bagger, "had evidently inherited the full physical characteristics of the Aryan race, while his dark yellowish eyes beneath his heavy brows glowed with the brightness of the African jungle." [11] The Negro leader, Aleck, had a nose "broad and crushed flat against his face," and jaws "strong and angular, mouth wide, and lips thick, curling back from rows of solid teeth set obliquely . . ." [12] The Cameron family of the Old South were the principal victims; Gus, a renegade Negro ravished Marion Cameron, the sixteen-year-old ". . . universal favourite . . ." who embodied "the grace, charm, and tender beauty of the Southern girl . . .;" [13] Silas Lynch attempted to violate Elsie Stoneman, the betrothed of Ben Cameron. The actual rape was a climax of a series of figurative violations of the South by the North, one of which was the entry of Stoneman into the black legislature, carried by two Negroes who made "a curious symbolic frame for the chalk-white passion of the old Commoner's face. No sculptor ever dreamed a more sinister emblem of the corruption of a race of empire-builders than this group. Its black figures, wrapped in the night of four thousand years of barbarism, squatted there the 'equal' of their master, grinning at his forms of Justice, the evolution of forty centuries of Aryan genius." [14] These figurative and literal ravishments provoked the formation of the Ku Klux Klan, whose like ". . . the world had not seen since the Knights of the Middle Ages rode on their Holy Crusades." [15] The Klan saved Elsie, revenged Marion, brought dismay to the Negro, the carpet-bagger and the scallawag and, in the final words of the book, ". . . Civilisation has been saved, and the South redeemed from shame." [16]

The picture followed the book faithfully in plot, character, motivation and theme, and became a visualization of the whole set of irrational

[9] *The Clansman*, p. 57.
[10] Paul M. Angle, *Created Equal?* (Chicago: University of Chicago Press, 1958), p. 235. *The Clansman*, p. 46 ff.
[11] *The Clansman*, p. 93.
[12] *The Clansman*, pp. 248-49.
[13] *The Clansman*, p. 254.
[14] *The Clansman*, p. 171.
[15] *The Clansman*, p. 316.
[16] *The Clansman*, p. 374.

cultural assumptions which may be termed the "Plantation Illusion."
The Illusion has many elements, but it is based primarly upon a belief
in a golden age of the antebellum South, an age in which feudal agrarianism provided the good life for wealthy, leisured, kindly, aristocratic
owner and loyal, happy, obedient slave. The enormous disparity between this conception and the reality has been the subject of Gaines's
The Southern Plantation[17] and Stampp's *The Peculiar Institution*.[18]
But our concern is not with the reality but with what people have
thought and felt about that reality; this thinking and feeling is the Illusion, and the stuff of the history of sensibility. The Illusion was embodied in Kennedy's *Swallow Barn* (1832), developed through Carruther's
The Cavaliers of Virginia (1834) and firmly fixed in the national consciousness by Stephen Foster's "Old Folks at Home" (1851), "My Old
Kentucky Home" and "Massa's in the Cold, Cold Ground" (1852), and
"Old Black Joe," songs which nostalgically describe a "longing for that
old plantation . . ." In 1905 Dixon summarized it in the assertion that
the South before the Civil War was ruled by an "aristocracy founded on
brains, culture, and blood," the "old fashioned dream of the South"
which "but for the Black curse . . . could be today the garden of the
world."

This was the image realized almost immediately at the beginning of
The Birth of a Nation. A scene of Southern life before the Civil War is
preceded by the title: "In the Southland, life runs in a quaintly way that
is no more." A primitive cart is shown trundling up a village street,
filled with laughing Negroes; there is further merriment as a few children fall from the cart and are pulled up into it; then appears a scene
of a young aristocrat helping his sister into a carriage; she is in white
crinoline and carries a parasol; the young Southerner helps her gal-
lantly from the carriage, and the title reads: "Margaret Cameron, daughter of the old South, trained in manners of the old school." With the two
levels of feudal society established, the scene is then of the porch of the
plantation house. Dr. and Mrs. Cameron are rocking; he has a kitten in
his arms, and puppies are shown playing at his feet. A pickaninny runs
happily in and out among the classic columns while the Camerons look
indulgently on; a very fat and very black servant claps her hands with
glee.

A corollary of this aspect of the Southern Illusion, one might even say
a necessary part of it, is the corresponding vision of the North as the land

17 F. P. Gaines, *The Southern Plantation* (New York: Columbia University Press,
1924), pp. 143-236.
18 Kenneth Stampp, *The Peculiar Institution* (New York: Alfred A. Knopf, 1956).

of coldness, harshness, mechanical inhumanity; expressed most generously, it is the description of the North as "Head" and the South as the warm human "Heart" which was Sidney Lanier's major metaphor in his Reconstruction poems. Although Lanier had called for the reunion of the heart and head, a modern Southerner, John Crowe Ransom, has scolded Lanier for preaching reconciliation when, Ransom said, what should have been preached was the "contumacious resistance" of the warm, agrarian South against the harsh industrialism and rationalism of the North.[19] *The Clansman* had emphasized the contrast between warm South and cold North by rechristening Thaddeus Stevens, "Thaddeus *Stoneman*"—the man of stone; the radical republican who is the obdurate villain of the picture. He has a clubfoot and moves angularly and mechanically; his house, his dress, are gloomy, dark, cold, as opposed to the warmth and lightness of the Southern planation garments and scene. In the novel, Dixon had identified him as the owner of Pennsylvania iron mills, and Griffith took the hint, giving him clothes to wear and expressions to assume which, in their harshness and implacability, suggest the unyielding metal. The sense of commercialism, combined with rigidity and pious hypocrisy is identified with the North, too, by showing the presumed beginnings of slavery in America. We see a Puritan preacher sanctimoniously praying while two of the elect arrange the sale of a cringing slave; the following scene is of Abolitionists demanding the end of slavery; the grouping of the two scenes, the dress and features of the characters in both, make the point strongly that these are the same people; the montage is a dramatization of Ben Cameron's assertion in the novel, that "our slaves were stolen from Africa by Yankee skippers . . . It was not until 1836 that Massachusetts led in Abolition—not until all her own slaves had been sold to us at a profit . . ."[20]

In these opening scenes, too, we have the complete cast of characters of the Plantation Ideal. The Camerons are shown as they go down to the fields to mingle with the happy and trusting slaves. A title tells us that "in the two hour interval for dinner given in their working day from six to six the slaves enjoy themselves;" then appears a view of slaves clapping hands and dancing. Ben Cameron places his hand paternally upon the shoulders of one, and shakes hands with another who bobs in a perfect frenzy of grateful loyalty: in several seconds a wonderful summary of a hundred years of romantic tradition in which "a beautiful felicity of racial contact has been presented, not as occasional but as constant; an

---

[19] John Crowe Ransom, "Hearts and Heads," *American Review*, II (March 1934), 559

[20] *The Clansman*, pp. 124-25.

imperious kindness on the part of the whites, matched by obsequious devotion on the part of the blacks." [21]

The Plantation Ideal had to explain the obvious fact that during the
war and Reconstruction, many Negroes fought with the Union and
greeted Emancipation with joy. The Illusion protected itself by explaining that the true, southern, fullblooded Negro remained loyal throughout and after the war. It expanded the truth of individual instances of
this kind into a general rule. In the Civil War sequences of *The Birth
of a Nation,* the Camerons' slaves are shown cheering the parade of the
Confederate soldiers as they march off to defend them against their
freedom. The fat Negro cook and the others of the household staff are
described as "The Faithful Souls"; they weep at Southern defeat and
Northern triumph; they rescue Dr. Cameron from his arrest by Reconstruction militia.

While the Illusion persistently maintained the loyalty of the true
slave, it premised the disaffection of other Negroes upon several causes,
all of them explicable within the framework of the Plantation Ideal. The
major explanation was the corruption of the Negro by the North. The
freed Negro, the Union soldier, is a monster of ingratitude, a renegade
from the feudal code, and only evil can be expected of him. The picture
shows The Faithful Soul deriding one such abomination; the title reads,
"You northern black trash, don't you try any of your airs on me." And a
little later, we see her lips saying, and then read on the screen, "Those
free niggers from the north sho' am crazy." The second explanation was
that the mulatto, the person of mixed blood, was the arch-villain in the
tragedy of the South. Stoneman, the radical republican leader, is shown,
as he was in the novel, under the spell of his mulatto housekeeper. A
scene of Stoneman lasciviously fondling his mistress is preceded by the
title: "The great leader's weakness that is to blight a nation." The mistress, in turn, has as a lover another mulatto, Silas Lynch, who is described as the principal agent in Stoneman's plans to "Africanise" the
South. This dark part of the Plantation Illusion is further represented
in the twin climaxes of the picture, both of which are attempted sexual
assaults on blonde white girls, one by a Northern Negro, and the other by
the mulatto, Silas Lynch.

The sexual terms into which this picture translated the violation of
the Southern Illusion by the North underscores the way in which the
film incorporates one of the most vital of the forces underlying the Illusion—the obscure, bewildering complex of sexual guilt and fear which
the Ideal never overtly admits, but which are, as Stampp and Cash and

[21] Gaines, p. 210.

Myrdal [22] have pointed out, deeply interwoven into the Southern sensibility. The mulatto, while he occasionally would be the offspring of the lowest class of white woman with Negroes, much more commonly was the result of the debasement of the Negro woman by the white man, and, not infrequently, by the most aristocratic of the characters in the plantation conception.[23] At the very least, then, the deep convictions of the Protestant South about the nature of sin would cause the Southern Illusion to regard a living, visible evidence of a parent's lust as evil in itself, and at the most, and worst, and most debilitating, as a reminder of the burden of guilt the white must bear in the record of sexual aggression against the Negro. *The Birth of a Nation* gives all aspects of these sexual fears and guilts full expression. Typically, the burden of guilt is discharged by making the mulatto the evil force in the picture, evincing both the bestial, animal sensuality of the unrestrained Negro, and the perverted intellectual powers of the white. And the full-blooded, but renegade, black justifies any excess of the Klan, by accomplishing that final most dreaded act of the sexual drama, the violation of the blonde "little sister." The book had made the rape actual: "A single tiger-spring," it narrated, "and the black claws of the beast sank into the soft white throat." [24] The picture shows us the little sister as she jumps off a cliff to escape dishonor; but a scene of Gus, kneeling blackly over the white-clad, broken body, makes the sexual point without the overt act. And this point is further reinforced by a description of Lynch's attempts to possess Elsie Stoneman, by a portrayal of the passage of the first law of the black Reconstruction legislature legalizing miscegenation, and by a scene of Negroes who carry signs reading "Equal rights, equal marriage."

The descriptions of Gus as "tiger-like" and of Stoneman's mistress as a leopard, brings us to the last element of the Plantation Illusion—the defense of the system on the basis of the essential non-humanity of the Negro. The book had been blatant in its statement of this position; the picture projects this attitude by its shots of the eyes of mulatto and Negro displaying animal lust and ferocity, and by its view of Gus as a slinking animal, waiting, crouching, springing.

As the record of a cultural illusion, then, *The Birth of a Nation* is without equal. Furthermore, it is the film to which, as the historian of the art declares, "much of subsequent filmic progress owes its inspira-

22 Stampp, pp. 350 ff., W. J. Cash, *The Mind of the South* (New York: Alfred A. Knopf, 1941), pp. 114-17. Gunnar Myrdal, *An American Dilemma* (New York: Harper & Bros., 1944), p. 562.
23 Stampp, p. 355.
24 *The Clansman,* p. 304.

tion." In order to understand its significance, one has to remind oneself of the nature of the motion picture art. It is not an art of external events and the people who perform them; it is an art of the camera and the film. Before Griffith, the camera was treated as a fixed position, much like the spectator of the drama. The interpretation was by the actors, by their bodies, by their faces, by physical objects and by the settings before which these performed. Griffith made the ordering and interpretation—the art, in brief—one of the location, the angle, the movement of the camera and of the juxtaposition of the images the camera records by means of cutting and arranging these images to bring out their significance. An example of the first technique—camera position—was the famous scene of Sherman's march to the sea. The camera shows the serpentine line of Union troops in the distance, winding over the landscape. War is distant; it is simply a move of masses over territory; the camera turns slowly until it includes, in the left foreground the figures of a weeping mother and child. Immediately a perspective is achieved; what was remote and inhuman becomes close and humanized; the human implications of such mass movements are illustrated clearly, sharply, poignantly simply by the perspective of the camera.

An example of the second aspect of the purely filmic technique was Griffith's juxtaposition of the two parallel scenes in the introduction to the Plantation Ideal: Negro cart and white carriage. Alone the first shot would be at worst meaningless, at best a bit of atmosphere; the second would serve merely to introduce two characters who might have been presented in an infinite variety of ways. Placed together, both scenes become significant forms because of the two elements they have in common: means of transportation, and the perfect fitness of each group of characters to that means; the juxtaposition thus serves to summarize the feudal theory—the rightness of each part of society in its place.

A second aspect of this editorial technique—the cutting and arranging of images—was also brought to its fullness of possibility in *The Birth of a Nation* after Griffith had experimented with it in earlier films. This was the intercutting of parallel scenes occurring at different locations in space, but at the same location in time, each of which has a bearing upon the other, with the meanings of both carefully interwoven, and with the tensions of either relieved only when the two are finally brought together. The famous example of this, an example which has been followed faithfully from then on, was the intercutting of shots of Lynch's attempted forced marriage to Elsie Stoneman with shots of the gathering of the Klan which will effect her rescue. A series of six shots of Lynch and Elsie is superseded by seven shots of the gathering of the Klan; then two single shots of the Klan and two of the attempted ravishment are quickly alternated; fourteen shots of Lynch and Elsie are followed by one of the Klan; a shot of long duration during which the Elsie-Lynch struggle becomes more intense is then followed by seven shots of the Klan's ride to the rescue; and so it goes until both sequences are joined in space when the Klan finally reaches Elsie. As an early critic described the meaning of this achievement: "Every little series of pictures . . . symbolizes a sentiment, a passion, or an emotion. Each successive series, similar yet different, carries the emotion to the next higher power, till at last, when both of the parallel emotions have attained the nth power, so to speak, they meet in the final swift shock of victory and defeat." [25] To these epoch-making achievements of camera placement, significant juxtaposition and intercutting, Griffith added the first uses of night photography, of soft-focus photography and moving camera shots, and the possibilities of film art were born.

And with it were born most of the problems of those of us who wish to take the art seriously. For what can we make of so awkward a combination of sentimental content and superb technique? We must admit, first of all, that the effect of the film's detachable content was pernicious. It served the ugliest purposes of pseudo-art—giving people a reflection of their own prejudices, sentimental at best, vicious at worst, and a restatement of their easy explanations of the terrible complexities of their history as Americans. It demonstrated how easily and how successfully the art could pander to the sentimentality of the public, how effectively and profitably it could transfer melodrama from the stage and false values from the novel. The enormous commercial success of the film at a time when men like Louis B. Mayer, later to become the head of the greatest studio, were starting their careers as exhibitors, cannot have but fixed the melodramatic, the cheap and obviously emotional, as the index to the potential economic success of a film.

But it showed, as well, two directions in which the film would move: one is in the direction of the epic, and the other in what may be termed "symbolic realism." Its move in the first direction, of course, was an immense and shocking perversion. Griffith apparently sensed the truth that great epics are involved with the destiny of whole races and nations, and had seized upon Dixon's hint that the South's struggle was part of an "Aryan" saga. The Klan was described in the book, and on the screen, as part of an "Aryan" tradition. The term is used again at a crucial point in the screen narrative, when a mob of Negro soldiers attack the em-

[25] Henry MacMahon, "The Art of the Movies," New York *Times*, June 6, 1915; section 6, p. 8.

battled whites. The battle of the Caucasians, the title on the screen tells us, is "in defense of their Aryan birthright." Griffith improved upon Dixon in emphasizing the "epical" quality of the story: before they ride, the Klansmen are shown partaking of a primitive barbaric rite; they dip a flag in the blood of the blonde white virgin before they go out to destroy.

The picture is no epic, but rather an epic *manqué*: partial, fragmentary and therefore necessarily inartistic; in attempting to be the saga of a shattered fragment of a nation, in attempting to erect upon false premises a series of racial responses reputedly instinctive, it was immediately self-defeating. An epic is justified in its radical simplifications, its stereotypes, its primitive terms, by its appeal to a real national unity of belief, and by its power to reinforce that unity. The oversimplifications of *The Birth of a Nation*, however, are not the controlled and ordering images of an art based upon a set of beliefs to which an entire people subscribe, images which emotionally order and control the world of that people's experience; instead it is the projection of images of disorder, an attack upon cultural and moral unity; the images of the film are the debilitating images of a false myth, a pseudo-epic.

The picture did, however, provide another cinematic genre with many of its basic situations. In 1908, with the "Bronco Billie" series, the Western setting had begun to be realized as particularly suitable to the enactment of the drama of simple primitive faiths and national aspirations. After *The Birth of a Nation*, its images of elemental struggle and black and white moral values, and its techniques for making these exciting and significant, were transferred to the "Western." The epic qualities of *The Birth of a Nation* were false and vicious because they impinge upon contemporary reality, and oversimplify both actual history and contemporary social circumstance; transferred to a realm of pure mythology—the Western scene of Richard Dix, *Stage Coach* and *High Noon,* and to the moral blackness of outlaw and moral whiteness of law, these simplifications, and the techniques for pictorializing them, have given us something much more artistically valid.

But more important, *The Birth of a Nation* pointed in the second, and the major direction of the motion picture art. This direction we can call "symbolic realism"—the apparent imitation of actuality which brings out the symbolic or representational meaning of that apparent reality. This "significant" or "symbolic" realism was demonstrated to be effective in the portrayal of either deep psychological or wide universal meanings. To take a rather titillating example in *The Birth of a Nation* of the first kind of surface realism arranged to illustrate unexpressed psychological truths: Lillian Gish plays an innocent love scene with the hero, returns to her room, and seats herself dreamily on the bed; the bed happens to be a four-poster each of whose posts is almost embarrassingly suggestive of masculinity; she dreamily embraces and caresses the bedpost. Some years later, Greta Garbo, as Queen Christina, after three days in bed with John Gilbert, used the bedpost in similar fashion. More significant, perhaps, is the way in which images were juxtaposed in this pioneering picture so as to bring out the universal significance of the concrete instance. The view of the army winding past the mother and child to symbolize the agony and displacements of war; the cart and the carriage as symbols of feudal levels of society; Stoneman's clubfoot representing the maimed wrathful impotence of the mechanical North; little sister adorning her coarse post-bellum dress with a bit of cotton rescued from the destroyed plantation fields—these were but a few of the large number of symbolic extensions of the surface, and they pointed the way toward the great documentary symbolic realism of Flaherty, and the imaginative symbolic realism of *The Informer, Sous les Toits de Paris, The River* and the whole run of wonderful Italian neo-realistic films: *Open City, Paisan, The Bicycle Thief* and *La Strada.*

A preliminary examination of a significant motion picture, then, has yielded some profit as well as some disappointment. The disappointment is largely in the failure of this pioneering picture to measure up to standards of artistic greatness: its failure to achieve that fusion of content and technique which together make up a great work of art. Its failure is doubly disappointing, because it involves an inversion and debasement of epic powers in which those powers pander to popular taste instead of attempting to reach a whole vision, sinewed with moral responsibility. But in this very failure lies some of its profit for us as students of American civilization; better than any other art work, it summarizes every aspect of the Plantation Illusion which is so vigorous a force in the history of American sensibility; for the student of the art form, it will demonstrate the beginnings of techniques which both rescue *The Birth of a Nation* from ugliness, and which, when used to embody more aesthetically malleable content, give us the possibilities of the art of the movie.

CHAPTER 2.

Problems in Film History: How Fox Innovated Sound

DOUGLAS GOMERY

THE COMING OF SOUND TO HOLLYWOOD, AND SUBSEQUENTLY TO THE REST
of the world, provides an important demarcation in the history of cinema.
Yet even with the addition of two recent books, film scholars still understand little of how this transition took place as an *industrial* transformation.[1] Questions concerning the introduction of sound as business history
continue to be ignored because of, we are told, a paucity of data. One significant example lies in the experience of Fox Film, the U.S. company which
innovated sound-on-film recording and reproduction, the process still used
for most prints and in most theatres today. Simply put, since Fox Film left
no records, scholars have emphasized its contribution far less than that of
Warner Bros., pioneer of the disc system. Overlooked for forty years, however, has been William Fox's penchant for becoming personally involved in
lengthy court fights. During the Great Depression, this movie mogul first
sought to claim all rights to two basic patents for sound-on-film recording.
He failed, and thus had to file for personal bankruptcy in 1936. Within
these cases are reams of documents containing testimony, correspondence,
contracts, and financial records concerning the Fox Film Corporation's activities during the coming of sound. Moreover, Fox Film secured much financial support for its innovation of sound through a Chicago investment
banking house, Halsey, Stuart. A recent examination of files in Halsey, Stuart's headquarters has revealed additional, detailed records of Fox's financial activities. Supplementing the above primary evidence are data from investigations of Fox's activities by agencies of the United States government,
and the fine coverage of its business affairs in trade papers such as *Variety,
Moving Picture World, Motion Picture News,* and *Film Daily.* This mass of

---

[1]The most recent work ignores questions of economics and business practice: Alexander
Walker, *The Shattered Silents* (New York: William Morrow, 1979) and Harry M. Geduld, *The
Birth of the Talkies* (Bloomington: Indiana University Press, 1975).

information furnishes the historian with more than enough evidence to construct a thorough re-evaluation of Fox's contributions regarding the introduction of sound-on-film technology.

Availability of primary evidence, however, hardly constitutes historical analysis. Here the methodology of the economic historian can contribute to the study of film history. In moving toward that goal, the economic theory of technological innovation deserves attention.[2] Profit maximization is assumed to account for the motivation of the owners and managers of an enterprise. The stages for change then include invention, innovation, and diffusion. First scientists must create the necessary inventions. Second, entrepreneurs determine how best to adapt this knowledge as a business investment for reducing costs, raising revenues, or both. Gradually the firms of an industry adopt the new technology, and the process of diffusion begins. This extension of neoclassical economics provides a powerful tool for organizing the new evidence concerning Fox Film's activities during the late 1920s, and demonstrates, I shall argue, just how important a role Fox played in this crucial transformation. Fox's contributions should rank equally with the efforts of Warner Bros., *The Jazz Singer,* et al.—currently the centerpiece for all accounts of the coming of sound.

Any process of innovation must be proceeded by the creation of new knowledge. Fox's sound-on-film system became available because of the efforts of two recluse scientists working in a private laboratory—still very much in a nineteenth century, pre-corporate research and development tradition. In 1913 an independently wealthy, eccentric, Yale-trained physicist, Theodore Case, opened a private laboratory in his hometown of Auburn, New York, a small city near Syracuse. Spurred on by recent breakthroughs in the telephone and radio fields, Case, and his assistant Earl Sponable, sought to improve the Audion tube, a device by which to amplify weak incoming radio waves. In 1917 Case and Sponable perfected the Thalofide Cell, a highly improved vacuum tube, and imediately the U.S. Navy Department contracted with Case to adopt this invention to improve ship-to-shore communication. But America's participation in World War I ended before the two scientists could complete their assigned task, and in 1919 the Navy ceased all funding.[3]

[2]I recognize there exist alternative approaches for analyzing technological change. Edward Brannigan compares four methods in his article, "Color and Cinema: Problems in the Writing of History," *Film Reader* IV (December, 1979), pp. 16-34. See also my comment on Brannigan's work, "Technological Transformation and Mass Media History: The Search for a Method," *Film Reader* V (December, 1980), (forthcoming).

[3]"Theodore W. Case, Honor Roll Award," *Journal of the Society of Motion Picture Engineers,* 48 (May, 1947), pp. 437-438; T.W. Case, ""Thalofide Cell": A New Photo-Electric Substance," *The Physical Review,* XV, Series II (April, 1920), no. 4, pp. 289-292: T.W. Case, "Infra Red Telegraphy and Telephony," *Journal of the Optical Society of America,* VI, no. 4 (June, 1922), pp. 398-406.

Case and Sponale returned to a pre-war goal—to integrate the Thalofide Cell into a system for recording sounds. As part of this work, in 1922 Case met with the even more individualistic Lee De Forest, inventor of the Audion tube, and presently at work on his Phonofilm system for recording sounds on motion picture film. For personal reasons—envy perhaps—Case turned all his laboratory's efforts to besting De Forest. Within 18 months Case Labs would produce a sound-on-film system, based on the Thalofide Cell. Naively, De Forest contracted to use the Thalofide Cell, while providing Case with all his knowledge of sound-on-film free of charge. As De Forest unsuccessfully attempted to market his Phonofilm system to Famous-Players, MGM, and other film industry giants, Case and Sponable continued to work quietly in upstate New York. In 1923 the pair developed an improved microphone, recorder, and amplifier. By August 1924 Case had constructed—with his own funds—a complete sound studio, and projection room adjacent to his laboratory.[4]

In 1925 Case determined he was ready to try to market his sound-on-film system. Case's skills as a businessman hardly matched his scientific acumen. First he attempted to form an alliance with De Forest, but that effort was doomed from the start. The temperamental De Forest partially blamed his own sales difficulties on Case, and the two broke all formal and informal communication in September of that year. Case then approached Edward Craft, vice-president for research at the American Telephone and Telegraph-controlled Western Electric, Inc. In December 1925 Case and two assistants visited the Case Laboratory, and saw and heard a demonstration film. Craft was impressed, but after some consideration, decided that Case's patents added no substantial improvements to the Western Electric sound-on-disc system—then under exclusive contract to Warner Bros. Pictures, Inc. Rebuffed, Case decided to imitate Western Electric's limited achievements, and diectly solicit a show business entrepreneur. He first approached John J. Murdock, the long time general manager of the Keith-Albee vaudeville circuit. Case argued his sound system could be used to record musical and comedy acts, and even the accompanying music of an orchestra, and present these sound motion pictures in Keith-Albee houses throughout the United States. Then the most popular performers could "appear" simultaneously all over the United States at greatly reduced costs. Earl Sponable attended those meetings with Case, Murdock, and other Keith-Albee executives, and later recounted the latter's reaction: They were "very much disturbed to think that [anyone] would dare bring up the sub-

---

[4]Lee De Forest, "Journal Notebook, Volume 21, 13 May 1923 and Volume 22, 10 February, 11 May, 29 June and 15 August 1924," Lee De Forest Collection, Library of Congress Manuscript Collection, Washington, D.C.; Earl I. Sponable, "Historical Development of Sound Films," *Journal of the Society of Motion Picture Engineers,* 48 (April, 1948), pp. 286-290; Lee De Forest, *Father of Radio* (Chicago: Wilcox and Follett, 1950), pp. 368-370.

ject of talking pictures to them again. They admitted that they had been
stung on the thing twice, once about fifteen years ago where they invested
considerable money in the stock of a talking picture outfit, and later in certain connections with the De Forest Company. The Vice-President of the
Keith Company [Murdock] stated positively that they were not interested in
talking motion pictures.[5] Executives from all the "Big-Three" motion picture corporations—Famous-Players, Loew's (MGM), and First National—
echoed Murdock's response.[6] None expressed the slightest interest in this
latest version of "talking motion pictures."[7]

Case moved to the second tier of the U.S. film industry—Producers Distributing Company (PDC), Film Booking Office (FBO), Warner Bros.,
Fox, and Universal. Each of these five firms controlled a national distribution network, but only the latter two owned theatres. In order to effectively
compete with the "Big-Three," all five needed to significantly expand, or
face an ever declining profit rate. (Indeed, by 1930, PDC and FBO would
become part of the Radio-Keith-Orpheum combine, Universal would shrink
into a minor enterprise, and Fox and Warner Bros. would develop into industry giants, to constitute the "Big-Five.") In 1926 Theodore Case cooper-
ated with Fox because Courtland Smith, president of Fox Newsreels, rea-
soned that with sound newsreels he could push that branch of Fox Film to
the forefront of the industry. In June 1926 Smith arranged a demonstration
for company owner, founder, and president William Fox. The boss was
pleased, and within a month, on 23 July 1926, helped create the Fox-Case
Corporation to produce motion pictures using the Case sound-on-film technique. Case turned all patents over to the new corporation, retired to the security of his laboratory in upstate New York state, and ordered Earl Sponable to supervise all engineering changes for Fox-Case. Cortland Smith assumed the presidency of the new enterprise.[8]

Initially, William Fox's approval of experiments with the Case technology began as only a small unit of a total plan to vault Fox Film back to pre-
eminence in the motion picture industry. During the 1910s the self-reliant,
often egotistical William Fox had successfully challenged the hegemony of
the Motion Picture Patents Trust. But then the company seemed to stagnate
during the early 1920s. Challenged again, William Fox and his advisors ini-

<hr>

[5]Sponable, "Historical Development," p. 297.
[6]The Loew's Corporation functioned as the parent company for its more famous subsidiary, Metro-Goldwyn-Mayer (MGM), a production unit.
[7]Sponable, "Historical Development," pp. 290-299; Lee De Forest, "Journal Notebook,
volume 22, 7 December 1924, and volume 23, 7 September 1925, 19 December 1925," Lee De
Forest Collection; De Forest, *Father of Radio,* pp. 394-395; Altoona Publix Theatres, Inc. et
al. v. American Tri-Ergon Corporation et al., 294 U.S. 477 (1935), Record, pp. 251-252.
[8]Paramount Publix Corporation v. American Tri-Ergon Corporation, 294 U.S. 464
(1935), Record, pp. 410-412; In the Matter of William Fox, Bankrupt, no. 24431 (New Jersey,
1936), Testimony of William Fox, pp. 117-146; Altoona Publix Theatres, 294 U.S. 477, Record, pp. 223, 240; *Film Daily,* 3 January 1926, pp. 1, 11; *Variety,* 22 September 1926, p. 5.

tiated an expansion campaign in 1925. By marketing six million dollars of
new common stock, they increased budgets for feature films, and enlarged
the newsreel division. (Courtland Smith was hired at this point.) Simultaneously Fox began acquiring and building a chain of motion picture theatres.
At that time Fox Film controlled only twenty, small neighborhood houses in
the New York City environs. In July 1925 a third interest in West Coast theatres was purchased, thus guaranteeing access to the best theatres in the
state of California. By 1927 the Fox chain included houses in Philadelphia,
Washington, D.C., Brooklyn, New York City, St. Louis, Detroit, Newark,
Milwaukee, and a score of smaller cities west of the Rockies. The flagship
became the Roxy—in the heart of Manhattan's Times Square. To finance
these sizable investments, William Fox at first utilized the services of several
Wall Street banking houses. Dissatisfied he ultimately developed close ties
with Harold Stuart, president of Chicago's Halsey Stuart, an investment
banking house. In financial circles Stuart's reputation as a renegade
matched William Fox's rapscallion image in the motion picture industry.
Not surprisingly, these two kindred spirits worked closely to supervise the
growth of Fox Film throughout the late 1920s.[9]

   As Fox, Stuart, and their assistants strove to produce a motion picture
colossus, Courtland Smith controlled a small, then quite insignificant subsidiary, the Fox-Case Corporation. In 1926 he initiated the innovation
phase of the Case sound-on-film technology. At first all he could oversee
were defensive actions designed to protect Fox-Case's patent position. On
September 23, 1926, exactly two months after incorporation, Fox-Case was
threatened by Lee De Forest who claimed Case had illegally acquired basic
De Forest patents. To defend Fox-Case, Courtland Smith acquired two options to purchase two million dollars of Phonofilm stock. Before the second
option expired, however, Smith learned De Forest did not possess complete
ownership of "his" patents. Fox-Case withdrew its offer; the matter was
dropped. The other major threat came from abroad. The German Corporation, Tri-Ergon A.G., controlled important sound-on-film patents developed by German scientists. Smith contacted Tri-Ergon executives and secured an option to purchase non-German (rest of the world) rights. For six
months Smith and his staff explored the potential value of signing a long
term agreement. Finally, after much investigation, William Fox paid fifty

   [9]W.R.K. Taylor, "Summary of a Detailed Study of Fox Film Corporation, September,
1927," pp. 6-14, Fox Folder 6; "Statement and Affidavit of Winfield R. Sheehan, 24 March
1930," pp. 26-27, Fox Folder 17; William Fox, "Answer of William Fox to 'Open Letter' of
Halsey, Stuart & Co. of 24 March 1930," pp 5-14, Fox Folder 17; "Fox West Coast Properties,
Supplementary Memorandum, 11 April 1927," Fox Folder 18; Prospects for Fox St. Louis
Theatre and Fox Detroit Theatre, 1927, Fox Folders 2 and 15, all Bache Halsey-Stuart Library,
Chicago, Illinois; John Sherman Porter (ed.), *Moody's Manual of Industrials—1931* (New
York: Moody's Investor Service, 1931), Record, p. 410; United States v. Fox Theatres Corpor-
ation et al., Eq. 51-122 (S.D.N.Y., 1929), Answer for Fox Film Corporation, pp. 27-28.

thousand dollars for the rights if only to check the minute potential for a suit by Western Electric, De Forest, or some other yet unanticipated rival.[10] Now Courtland Smith could move to supplement the Case technology by adding certain necessary amplification equipment. Smith first approached the chairman of the board of General Electric, Owen D. Young. GE had developed its own system of sound-on-film: variable area recording. Fox-Case employed the variable density method.[11] Initially Young noted some virtues in an alliance, but ever cautious, he would formalize nothing without the approval of David Sarnoff, then president of GE's commercial agent for broadcasting, the Radio Corporation of America (RCA). Seizing the moment, Sarnoff persuaded his superior that General Electric should compete with the smaller Fox-Case and Warner Bros., and extend GE (and RCA's) commercial arena to include motion pictures with sound.[12] Rebuffed, Smith turned to Western Electric. Its legal staff referred him to Warner Bros. because at this point in time that corporation held exclusive rights to all licenses of Western Electric patents. Warner's willingly granted Fox-Case a sublicense—on the last day of 1926. In return Fox-Case agreed to pay Vitaphone, Warner's subsidiary for sound film production, eight percent of all gross revenues against a minimum which would eventually rise to nearly one hundred thousand dollars per year. In addition Fox-Case cross-licensed all its patents with those of Vitaphone and Western Electric.[13]

At last Fox-Case could commence to assault the marketplace. Although Courtland Smith pushed for immediate experimentation with sound newsreels, William Fox, somewhat conservatively, ordered Fox-Case to imitate

[10]In the Matter of William Fox, Testimony of William Fox, pp. 155-176; Lee De Forest, "Journal Notebook, Volume 23, 7 October 1927," Lee De Forest Collection, Library of Congress; United Artists Collection. O'Brien File. Manuscript Collection. (Wisconsin Center for Film and Theatre Research, Madison, Wisconsin), Box 84-6, Letter, F.T. Woodward to Vitaphone Corporation, 3 December 1931; U.S. Federal Communications Commission. *Telephone Investigation Exhibits* (Pursuant to Public Resolution No. 8, 74th Congress), 1936-37, Exhibits 1794-1797; *Variety,* 13 October 1926, p. 5; Altoona Publix Theatres, 294 U.S. 477, Record, pp. 116-123; "Fox Loses," *Business Week,* 9 March 1935, p. 18.

[11]For an excellent discussion of the differences between the two sound-on-film systems see Raymond Spottiswoode, *Film and Its Techniques* (Berkeley: University of California Press, 1969), pp. 279-322.

[12]In the Matter of William Fox, Testimony of William Fox, pp. 129-131; Altoona Public Theatres, 294 U.S. 477, Record, p. 621; Paramount Publix Corporation, 294 U.S. 464, Record, p. 415; *New York Times,* 23 October 1926, p. 35; *New York Times,* 27 October 1926, p. 19; *New York Times,* 28 October 1926, p. 25; *Variety,* 27 October 1926, pp. 55, 62; Eugene Lyons, *David Sarnoff* (New York: Harper and Row, 1966), pp. 141-142; John A. Miller, *Workshop of Engineers* (Schenectady, N.Y.: Maqua, 1953), p. 21.

[13]U.S. Congress. House Committee on Patents. *Pooling of Patents. Hearings* before the Committee on Patents, House of Representatives, on H.R. 6250 and H.R. 9137, 68th Congress, 1st Session, pp. 1245, 1315-1349; General Talking Pictures Corporation et al. v. American Telephone and Telegraph Co. et al., 18 F. Supp. 650 (1937), Record, pp. 2732-2734; *Moving Picture World,* 8 January 1927, p. 1; *Moving Picture World,* 15 January 1928, p. 2; *Exhibitor's Daily Review,* 6 January 1927, pp. 1-2.

the innovation strategy of Warner Bros.: filming popular vaudeville performers. Warner's had begun in June, 1926; four months later, in October,
Fox-Case filmed a sound short starring the noted vaudevillian, Sir Harry
Lauder. Production continued on a regular basis during that winter. On
February 24, 1927 Fox executives felt confident enough to stage a widely-
publicized demonstration for the press of the newly christened Movietone
system. At 10:00 a.m. fifty reporters and photographers entered the Fox
studio near Times Square, and were filmed using the miracle of Movietone.
Four hours later these representatives of the U.S. and foreign presscorps
saw and heard themselves as part of a special private screening. In addition,
Fox-Case presented several vaudeville sound shorts: a banjo and piano act,
a comedy sketch, and three songs by the then popular cabaret performer,
Raquel Mueller. The strategy worked. Favorable commentary was unanimous; the future looked bright. Consequently, William Fox ordered sound
systems for twenty-six of Fox's largest, first-run theatres, including the recently acquired Roxy.[14]

Yet overnight the fad for talkies seemed to die. Ill-prepared Fox-Case
could offer no more demonstrations until August. Warner Bros. programs
of synchronized, scored silent feature films, and vaudeville shorts with
sound no longer attracted better than average crowds. Smith pressed William Fox to reconsider the original plan: newsreels with sound. Then, Smith
argued, Fox Film could provide a unique, economically viable alternative to
Warner Bros.' presentations. In terms of the economic theory, Fox-Case
would differentiate its product from that of Vitaphone, and move into a
heretofore unoccupied portion of the market for motion picture entertainment. Furthermore, sound newsreels would provide a logical method by
which Fox-Case could gradually perfect necessary new techniques of camerawork and editing, and test the market, at minimal cost. William Fox and
his top staff were convinced, and ordered Smith to adopt this alternative
strategy for technological innovation. This decision would prove more successful for Fox Film's overall goal of corporate growth than either William
Fox, or Courtland Smith imagined at the time.[15]

Smith moved quickly.[16] The premiere came on April 30, 1927 at the Roxy
in the form of a sound newsreel of cadets marching at West Point. Lasting
only four minutes, and despite the lack of any buildup matching the Feb-

[14]U.S. Congress. *Pooling of Patents*, pp. 1670-1672; *Moving Picture World*, 19 February
1927, p. 1; *Moving Picture World*, 26 February 1927, pp. 622, 677; *Variety*, 10 November
1926, p. 9; *Variety*, 23 February 1927, p. 7; *Variety*, 2 March 1927, p. 10.

[15]*Moving Picture World*, 5 March 1927, p. 20; *Variety*, 6 April 1927, p. 54; *Variety*, 13
April 1927, p. 9; *Variety*, 20 April 1927, p. 1; *Variety*, 4 May 1927, p. 4.

[16]In addition, Courtland Smith also helped Fox Film plan new theatres, open additional
distribution outlets, and increase the production of 'quality' films. For an analysis of how Fox
Film achieved the latter goal, see Robert C. Allen, "William Fox Presents *Sunrise*," *Quarterly
Review of Film Studies*, II, No. 3 (August, 1977), pp. 327-338.

ruary press demonstration, this first Movietone newsreel drew an enthusiastic response from the trade press and New York based motion picture reviewers. Soon after Smith seized upon one of the most important symbolic news events of the 1920s. On May 20, 1927 Charles Lindbergh departed for Paris at 8:00 a.m. That evening Fox Movietone News presented footage of the takeoff—with sound—to a packed house (6,200 persons) at the Roxy theatre. The throng stood and cheered for nearly ten minutes. The press saluted this new motion picture marvel and noted how it had brought alive the heroics of the "Lone Eagle." In June Lindbergh returned to a tumultuous welcome in New York City and Washington, D.C. Movietone News cameramen recorded portions of those celebrations on film, and Fox Films distributed a ten minute Movietone newsfilm to the few theatres equipped for sound.[17] Again press response proved overwhelming. Both William and Courtland Smith were now satisfied that the Fox-Case system had been launched onto a propitious path.[18]

That summer Smith sent cameramen to all parts of the globe. They recorded the further heroics of aviators, harmonica contests, beauty pageants, and sporting events, as well as the earliest sound film statements by public figures such as Benuto Mussolini, Alfred Smith, and Admiral Richard Byrd. Newspaper columnists, educators, and other opinion leaders hailed these latter short subjects for their didactic value, and wide appeal. Fox Film's principal constraint now became a paucity of exhibition outlets. During the fall of 1927, Fox Film did make Movietone newsreels the standard in all Fox-owned theatres, but that represented less than three percent of the potential market. To push toward more extensive profits, Fox Film moved to create a larger and larger chain of first-run theatres. In the meantime Courtland Smith established a regular pattern for release of Movietone newsreels—one ten minute reel per week. He also increased the permanent staff of cameramen, and laboratory employees, and developed a worldwide reticulation of stringers.[19]

Smith and William Fox also decided to again try to produce vaudeville shorts, and feature films with synchronized musical accompaniment. Before 1928, Fox-Case had only released one scored feature, *Sunrise*. The two executives moved quickly and by January 1, 1928 Fox had signed up a

[17]I use camera*man* because Fox Film did not hire women to operate newsreel cameras.
[18]*Variety,* 4 May 1927, p. 27; *Variety,* 11 May 1927, p. 80; *Variety,* 25 May 1927, pp. 9, 18; *Variety,* 1 June 1927, p. 25; *Variety,* 15 June 1927, p. 28; *Moving Picture World,* 7 May 1927, p. 28; *Moving Picture World,* 28 May 1927, P. 248; *New York Times,* 29 May 1927, VII, p. 5.
[19]Altoona Publix Theatres, 294 U.S. 477, p. 243; *Variety,* 7 June 1927, p. 26; *Variety,* 29 June 1927, p. 11; *Variety,* 17 August 1927, p. 12: *Variety,* 7 September 1927, p. 8; *Variety,* 21 September 1927, pp. 1, 20, 23; *Variety,* 2 November 1927, p. 21: *Variety,* 30 November 1927, pp. 18-19; *Moving Picture World,* 11 June 1927, p. 433; *Moving Picture World,* 23 July 1927, p. 1; *Moving Picture World,* 1 October 1927, p. 299; *Moving Picture World,* 5 November 1927, p. 10; *Moving Picture World,* 3 December 1927, pp. 12-13.

dozen major vaudeville artists (including Eddie Cantor), filmed ten vaudeville shorts, and even announced a part-talkie feature, *Blossom Time*. During the spring of 1928 these efforts, Fox's newsreels, and Warner's shorts
and feature films (one of which was *The Jazz Singer*) proved to be the hits
of the season. Thus in March 1928 William Fox declared that fully twenty-
five percent of the upcoming production schedule would be "Movietoned."
By May Fox was confident enough to raise that share to one hundred percent. Simultaneously Fox Film continued to wire, as quickly as possible, all
the houses in its ever expanding chain, and draw up plans for an all-sound
Hollywood-based studio. Fox's innovation of sound seemed near success;
colossal profits loomed on the horizon.[20]

The moguls of the film industry's giants—Paramount and Loew's
(MGM)—agreed. On May 11, 1928 both firms contracted with Western
Electric for sound recording and reproduction. Other members of the U.S.
film industry followed as quickly as possible. As the film industry raced toward complete diffusion of sound film technology, Fox and Warner Bros.
were positioned far ahead. Warners experiences are well known.[21] Fox continued to exploit its comparative advantage in sound newsreels. As competitors braved the switch to sound during the last seven months of 1928, Fox
Movietone News increased its weekly output to two "issues" per week. In
June it had twenty-seven Movietone units in the field; by October the number reached forty. In January 1928 there were fifty, with thirty-five for U.S.
news, and fifteen for the rest of the world. During the fall of 1929 Fox
reached its apex by releasing four separate newsreel editions each week, produced by seventy crews. The theatre division opened America's first all-
newsreel theatre, the Embassy, in the heart of New York's Times Square.
And most importantly for company profits, movietone demanded all theatres sign exclusive agreements for five years of Fox newsreels at rates double those for silent newsreel competitors. The dominant U.S. theatre chains
quickly acceded to these stiff terms. Only giants Paramount and Loew's
(MGM) possessed enough economic power to resist, and wait until their
own newsreel suppliers caught up with Movietone News.[22]

Fox wisely pressed its advantage in newsreels, because for the other motion picture forms—narrative, all-talking features, and vaudeville shorts—

---

[20] *Variety,* 30 November 1927, pp. 1-5; *Variety,* 28 December 1927, p. 5; *Variety,* 15 February 1928, p. 14; *Variety,* 22 February 1928, p. 9.

[21] For the classical account, see Arthur Knight, *The Liveliest Art* (New York: The Macmillan Company, 1957), pp. 150-159; for a revisionist thesis compare Douglas Gomery, "Writing
the History of the American Film Industry," *Screen* (U.K.) 17, No. 1, Spring, 1976, pp. 40-53.

[22] Electrical Research Products Inc. v. Vitaphone Corporation, 171 A. 738 (1934), Affidavit
of John E. Otterson, pp. 192-197; *Variety,* 16 May 1928, passim; *Variety,* 1 August 1928, pp.
16, 22; *Variety,* 22 August 1928, p. 28; *Variety,* 12 September 1928, p. 10; *Variety,* 26 September 1928, p. 17; *Variety,* 3 October 1928, p. 12; *Variety,* 28 November 1928, p. 22; *Variety,* 5
December 1928, p. 7; *Variety,* 20 March 1929, p. 7.

Fox quickly lost any leverage it possessed. Warner Bros. switched completely to all-sound features by September 1928; Fox did not release its earliest all-talkie feature film until four months later. By then, even Paramount
and MGM were producing all-talking features. The rest of the industry
trailed Warners, Fox, Paramount, and MGM by six months. For vaudeville
shorts, during the early months of the diffusion phase Fox was the only firm
with the facilities and technical staff to effectively compete with Warners.
Yet Fox quickly learned that in fact this segment of the market for all-sound
motion picture entertainment offered little profit potential. Warner Bros.
simply had the most popular vaudeville and musical performers under exclusive long-term contracts. Consequently Fox Film rapidly phased out the
production of vaudeville shorts, releasing its last in May 1930. It had produced only seven between September 1929 and May 1930. Only giants,
Paramount and Loew's (MGM), again commanded the economic power
necessary to challenge Warner Bros., and these three controlled the market
for vaudeville shorts well into the 1930s when that form began to lose its
special allure.[23]

Building on earlier expansionary investments, the popularity of sound
films rapidly thrust Fox Film toward the acme of the U.S. motion picture
industry. Aggressively William Fox reinvested all profits, and borrowed the
maximum available during the economic distention of the "Roaring Twenties." On October 28, 1928 Fox opened Movietone City, an all-sound studio
near Beverly Hills, California. This ten million dollar plant had taken only
four months to construct, because 1,500 persons worked three shifts,
twenty-four hours a day, seven days a week to build it. But the largest commitment of resources were allocated toward securing theatresm Fox took
over theatre chains in New England, New York, New Jersey, California,
Wisconsin, and the Pacific Northwest. Funds came from the Halsey, Stuart
banking house, and Western Electric. The latter knew that for every theatre
Fox acquired, Western Electric sound equipment, cross-licensed with Fox-
Case patents, would be installed. Western Electric and Fox Film worked
quite closely during 1928 and 1929. At the pinnacle in 1930 Fox Film enter-
prises controlled 532 theatres in the United States, and 450 overseas—second in size only to the Paramount-Publix chain.[24]

[23]For a complete discussion of the diffusion of sound see Douglas Gomery, "Hollywood
Converts to Sound: Chaos or Order?," in Evan W. Cameron, ed., *The Coming of Sound to the
American Cinema, 1925-1940* (Pleasantville, N.Y.: Redgrave, 1980), (forthcoming).
[24]U.S. Federal Communications Commission. *Staff Report on the Investigation of the
Telephone Industry in the United States.* (House Document 340, 76th Congress, 1st session,
1934), II, 474-79; "An Analysis of Fox Theatres Corporation, 2 August 1929," pp. 1-2, Fox
Folder 19, Bache-Halsey Stuart Library, Chicago, Illinois; *Variety,* 1 February 1928, pp. 5, 25;
Variety, 10 October 1928, p. 5; *Variety,* 27 June 1928, p. 51; *Variety,* 7 November 1928, p. 5;
Variety, 28 November 1928, p. 19; *Barrons,* 30 August 1928, p. 20; *Barrons,* 28 September
1928, p. 8.

The independent, egocentric William Fox now neared the top of an industry he helped found. In fact, events would momentarily push his enterprise past even Paramount to become the world's largest, and potentially most profitable film company. In 1927 the founder of Loew's (MGM), Marcus Loew, died. Soon thereafter the Loew family indicated its third interest of Loew's, Inc. was for sale at the current stockmarket prices: $28 million. That would prove to be too large a single investment for any entrepreneur in the U.S. film industry—except William Fox. Intoxicated by recent successes, Fox maneuvered to purchase the stock from the Loew family, as well as shares from top officers of the Loew's corporation, and even some shares on the open market. To secure the needed $50 million, the daring entrepreneur turned to Western Electric and Halsey, Stuart. After weeks of round-the-clock meetings, the initial financing broke down as follows: Western Electric supplied $12 million; Halsey, Stuart added $10 million more; and the two combined to underwrite $6 million from one of their bankers, the Chatham-Phoenix National Bank and Trust Company. Since William Fox sat as a director of Banker's Security Company of Philadelphia, he was able to secure a ten million dollar loan from that concern. The financial package now totaled $38 million dollars—$12 million short of William Fox's goal. To underwrite the necessary capital, Fox and Harold Stuart transferred stock among Fox's corporate subsidiaries, and further mortgaged the company's (and William Fox's personal) assets. On the verge of the biggest takeover in the history of the U.S. film industry, William Fox even secretly cleared the merger with the United States Justice Department. Officials guaranteed that no antitrust action would result if the takeover was consummated. On March 3, 1929 William Fox held a press conference, and announced the Fox-Loew's ammalgamation. Fox Film controlled the largest motion picture production-distribution enterprise in the world, owned more than 1,000 theatres in the best locations, and foresaw nearly unlimited profit potential. In five years Fox had pioneered a sound-on-film process, and parleyed that into the creation of the world's largest motion picture empire.[25]

Fox Film rested at the summit of the U.S. film industry for less than six months. By the spring of 1930 the fragile mesh of Fox Film's financial support had begun to come apart. Upton Sinclair and Glendon Allvine have vividly recounted the descent of the corporation and the man.[26] Unfortu-

[25]U.S. v. Fox Theatres, Eq. 51-122, Answer for Fox Film Corporation, pp. 25-26; *Variety,* 6 March 1929, pp. 5, 10; *Motion Picture News,* 12 January 1929, p. 82; *Film Daily,* 1 March 1929, p. 1; *Barrons,* 11 March 1929, p. 11; FCC, Staff Report, Volume II, pp. 475-478; William Fox, "Answer," pp. 18-19, Fox Folder 17, Bache-Halsey Stuart Library; *Motion Picture News,* 2 March 1929, p. 611.
[26]Upton Sinclair, *Upton Sinclair Presents William Fox* (Los Angeles: Privately Printed, 1933), and Glendon Allvine, *The Greatest Fox of Them All* (New York: Lyle Stuart, 1969).

nately the melodrama of William Fox unsuccessfully trying to save his empire from Wall Street wizards has overshadowed the importance Fox Film played in bringing sound motion pictures to U.S. movie screens. In fact, Fox innovated the system—variable density—which rendered Warner's disc obsolete by 1930, and proved as practical in the long run as RCA's variable area method. Indeed for an economic history of the American film industry Fox's pioneering efforts deserve to rank along with the activities of Warner Bros. Utilizing inventions from the Case Laboratory, William Fox, Courtland Smith and their assistants integrated the innovation of sound into Fox Film's goal of corporate expansion. Experimentation with sound newsreels provided a flexible, low cost alternative to Warner Bros.' concentration on vaudeville shorts. By the time the rest of the U.S. film industry began to adopt sound technology, Fox Film had originated many of the necessary new modes of camerawork, editing, and the manipulation of mise-en-scene. The transition to talkies was over, and the next chapter of an economic history of this important industry, the impact of exogenous forces set in play by this century's worst economic downturn, had begun.

CHAPTER 3.

Ideology and Film Rhetoric: Three Documentaries of the New Deal Era (1936-1941)

PETER C. ROLLINS

THE PRECEPT OF AESTHETICS THAT FORM AND CONTENT ARE INEXTRICABLY related also applies to the art of film. While all filmmakers are aware of this principle, very few film scholars have taken it seriously. For this reason, film scholarship could profit from more attention to a basic distinction between thematic and cinematic elements of film. The theme of a film is the central idea around which it is constructed. The themes of the Thirties documentaries here examined are readily stated: *The River* strives to show that uncoordinated industrial exploitation has so abused the ecological system of the Mississippi Valley that biennial floods have resulted; *Land of Cotton* stresses that the Old South's commitment to a single crop has led to an agricultural depression which affects both sharecropper and landlord; *Native Land* tries to convince workers and farmers to band together so that they may enjoy traditional American rights in the industrial era.

The cinematic elements of a film are the devices of film language which contribute to the distinctively filmic communication of the theme. Each cinematic factor is carefully selected by a director and then arranged by his editor to convey a unique message. In social documentaries such as *Land of Cotton, The River,* and *Native Land,* it would seem only logical that the differing political persuasions of the filmmakers would determine not only different contents for each film, but that different choices in film language would be made so that the rhetoric of each film would be consonant with the liberal Republican or New Deal or leftist persuasion of the filmmaker.

This article will attempt to contrast these three film rhetorics concretely. *Land of Cotton* (1938) is an episode from the famous *March of Time* newsreel series. Louis de Rochemont felt that *March of Time* was breaking new ground in the newsreel tradition because it attempted to go below the surface of events. Selected scenes from *Land of Cotton* will be analyzed to correlate *March of Time*'s cinematic language with the liberal Republican world view of Time, Inc. Moving somewhat leftward on the political spectrum, portions of a government-sponsored documentary, *The River* (1937), will be examined. Pare Lorentz justified the existence of his U.S. Film Service on the grounds that it took a needed additional step beyond the documentary insight provided by *March of Time*: not only were problems exposed to public view, but the New Deal's solutions to these problems were persuasively presented. Still further to the left, Leo Hurwitz and Paul Strand worked as independent filmmakers in order to carry the contribution of social documentary films beyond the mark established by Lorentz. These makers of *Native Land* had actually worked as cameramen for Lorentz during the making of *The Plow That Broke the Plains* (1936). As that project had progressed, Hurwitz and Steiner became increasingly unhappy with Lorentz's "arty" script. They drafted their own and presented it to Lorentz. As Lorentz recalled the ideological/production confrontation, "they wanted it to be all about human greed and how lousy our system was. And I couldn't see what this had to do about dust storms."[1] The rhetoric of *Native Land* (1942) reflects its leftist orientation. This article will first describe the orientation of these three documentaries of the New Deal era, and then relate their different rhetorical styles to the political ideologies of their makers and sponsors.

THE MARCH OF TIME (1935-51)

During the twenties, Louis de Rochemont rose from cameraman to vice president in the newsreel business. As a professional, he was disturbed that newsreels "never get behind the news . . . [never explain] . . . what has led up to a given event. What does it portend?" He boasted that "Someday I'm going to revolutionize the newsreel." In 1931 Time, Inc. gave him an opportunity to make good on his claims.[2]

Time, Inc. had already sponsored a thirty-minute radio program called *The March of Time,* a series which dramatized news events through reenactments. De Rochemont approached the program's producer, Roy Larsen, with a plan about adapting the program's format for the screen. Henry Luce was excited by the idea of using the powerful medium of film: he convinced his board of directors that a special corporation should be established to launch Time, Inc. into this "colossal" field.[3] Over $100,000 was

[1]Quoted in Robert L. Snyder, *Pare Lorentz and the Documentary Film* (Norman: University of Oklahoma Press, 1968), p. 31. Hereafter cited as Snyder, *Pare Lorentz.*
[2]A. William Bluem, *Documentary in American Television* (New York: Hastings House, 1965), p. 36. Hereafter cited as Bluem, *Documentary.*
[3]Robert T. Elson, *Time Inc.: The Intimate History of a Publishing Enterprise, 1923-1941* (New York Atheneum, 1968), p. 231. Hereafter cited as Elson, *Time Inc.*

spent during the trial period alone. The venture was richly rewarded, for one year after its premiere in 1935, episodes of *The March of Time* were playing before an international audience of some 15,000,000.

The March of Time was controversial enough to jar the sensibilities of those in the industry who considered film to be an innocuous diversion. Martin Quigley, oracle of the Motion Picture Code and an ardent believer in wholesome entertainment, cautioned theatre owners to maintain a censorial attitude toward the newsreel series: "The exhibitors of the country ought to tell *The March of Time* that it is welcomed when it behaves itself but only then. They should tell it . . . that they expect it to be mindful of the proprieties of theatrical presentation—that they do not want controversial political material which is calculated to destroy the theater as the public's escape from the bitter realities, the anguishes, and the turmoil of life."[4] Libel suits by the Reverend Gerald K. Smith (a crony of Huey Long), diplomatic protests by dictators Rafael Trujillo and Adolph Hitler attest that this New York based newsreel series could be controversial, especially on issues related to foreign affairs and the rather antediluvian injustices of Southern society.

Probably the most obvious novelty about *The March of Time* was that it made a profit. Although many felt that *The March of Time* was slick and commercial, some hoped that the series would cultivate an audience for headier stuff. English documentarian, John Grierson, was elated: "In no sense conscious of the higher cinematic qualities, it has yet carried over from journalism some of that bright and easy tradition of free-born comment which the newspaper has won and the cinema has been too abject even to ask for." Because of *March of Time*'s success, "The world, our world, appears suddenly and brightly as an oyster for the opening; for film people—how strangely—worth living in, fighting in and making drama about."[5]

Unfortunately, like its literary predecessor, *Time, March of Time* lacked a coherent, self-conscious political viewpoint. As the Thirties depression worsened, *Time*'s policy of "unbiased, objective journalism" came under increasing attack.[6] An in-house memo to Henry Luce by a *Fortune* editor attempted to highlight the limitations of *Time*'s much vaunted "objectivity" in a suffering world: "*Time* is ostensibly impartial but actually (perhaps unconsciously) right wing. Because its bias is unadmitted and perhaps even unrecognized by its editors, it is unable to allow for its prejudices."[7] *March of Time*'s "objectivity" often led viewers to come away from the series with

[4]Martin Quigley, *Motion Picture Herald,* February 5, 1938, p. 8.
[5]*Grierson on Documentary,* ed. Forsyth Hardy (Berkeley: University of California Press, 1966), p. 163.
[6]Elson, *Time Inc.,* p. 249.
[7]*Ibid.,* p. 251-52.

March of Time, "Sharecroppers" (Courtesy of Museum of Modern Art/Film Stills Archive)

entirely different impressions. An especially controversial episode, *Inside Nazi Germany—1938,* was so ambiguous that it was at once attacked as "a flaming pro-Nazi story," defended as "an editorial for democracy," and lauded for its impartiality.[8]

Both the opening and closing segments of *Land of Cotton* are full of similar equivocations. During the establishing shots which follow the main title, viewers become visually acquainted with a tenant shack in the middle of seemingly endless fields of cotton: laundry hangs on the front porch; barefooted men sit and smoke on the back seat of an automobile which serves as their porch glider. Only the most callous viewers could withhold sympathy from these impoverished people.

Instead of pursuing an examination of the plight of Southern sharecroppers, *Land of Cotton* re-enacts a disturbing dialogue between a representative landlord and his tenant. As in many other scenes of this film, the visual evidence contradicts the explicit oral statements of the people photographed: visually, a gap in the status of the two men is clearly established by

[8]This confusion is documented in detail by Raymond Fielding, "Mirror of Discontent: *The March of Time* and its Politically Controversial Film Issues," *Western Political Quarterly,* 12 (1959), 146-53.

their contrasting dress, posture, smoking devices. The sharecropper wears overhauls and sits on the front stairs of his shack. The landlord stands over him dressed in white. As the landlord speaks, he lights a cigar and throws the expended match at the feet of his tenant. The eyes of the unsmoking tenant involuntarily follow the flight of the match to the ground. What is most disturbing about this re-enactment is that it completely contradicts evidence later adduced about the intense struggle between landlords and tenants:

> LANDLORD: "I know times are hard and I know conditions are far from perfect. It's the system that's wrong. It's been handed down to us through generations. It can't be corrected over night. You don't think I'm getting rich, do you?"
>
> TENANT: [Abjectly] "No, seh. . . ."

A subtle, nonverbal element of film rhetoric is at work here to support a conservative interpretation of the Southern problem. The interview described above is strategically placed. It is preceded by shots of tenant suffering. The contrived interview then verbally asserts that landlords share that suffering. The shots which then follow the interview return to images of sharecropper poverty. The resulting effect upon the audience of this shot sequence is to arouse sympathy for all classes in the region. Significantly, the only villians identified are the long-dead generations who committed the South to a single crop.

Like the opening segment of *Land of Cotton,* its closing is edited in such a way as to muffle any implication that classes are in conflict. Words uttered again conflict with the information communicated by visual images. The narrator concludes that "only basic change can restore the one-time peace and prosperity of the Kingdom of Cotton," but the remedy suggested by cinematic language is far from radical. An establishing shot of a small rural chapel is followed by a close-up of the bell which summons the community to worship. The service inside is then quickly depicted by montage: a series of medium shots reveals that it is attended jointly by both members of the ragged sharecropper class and the white-shirted middle class. The entire society is united in song, the Episcopal hymn, "Holy, Holy, Holy." We are asked to conclude that all ranks of Southerners would be happy to continue living with their semi-feudal system if they could only obtain enough to eat. Good times will return with diversification. The rich will be less cruel; the poor whites and blacks will willingly return to their allotted places on the social ladder.

How can these conservative opening and closing scenes be reconciled with *Land of Cotton*'s revelations of evictions, beatings, lynchings by the dominant class in its effort to repress both black and white tenants? The editing choices can be explained only by *March of Time*'s curious liberal Republican ambivalence toward reform. On the one hand, *March of Time* (like its parent company, Time, Inc.) obviously wanted to generate an awareness of social and political issues. Yet, as "objective" (and unconsciously conservative) journalists, *March of Time*'s staff could not go so far as to incite action against any sector of society. The rhetoric of *Land of Cotton* thus reflected the liberal Republican dilemma: it wished for relief, but could not agitate for the radical changes required to effect the needed reforms. Contemporaries were exasperated by *March of Time*'s reticence about solutions. One critic, George Dangerfield, voiced the irritation of many: "I wish that the editors of *March of Time,* since they have at their disposal these fictions which excite and enrage people, would use them to some purpose—I wish they would say—outright, beyond question—that somebody was right or wrong. Then we would attack them or defend them, and they would be exciting their audience honestly."[9]

The unwillingness to incite audiences to action was clearly reflected in *March of Time*'s lack of attention to the expressive potential of film. Filmmakers are always aware of the difference between the informational and the compositional content of film. *March of Time* was characterized by its complete lack of attention to the compositional qualities of its footage. Shots were cut to keep up with the pace of narration rather than being arranged to suit their own natural lengths. This reliance on a narrative spine might be traced back to the radio origins of the series, but it seems more likely that *March of Time*'s lack of exploitation of film as an expressive medium can be explained by the unconscious conservatism of the series. Properly edited films might be inflammatory.

March of Time must also be faulted for its ineffective use of sound. While the series was famous—indeed, infamous—for its sepulchral "voice of doom" narration, the effect upon the viewer was often less than persuasive. All subtlety of feeling was lost. The music of the series relied more upon cliche and volume rather than the host of established commentative techniques that were utilized by Pare Lorentz and Leo Hurwitz. It seems clear that the rhetorical anemia of both the visual and the aural tracks reflected the ideology of the filmmakers: an effective film would violate the code of objectivity.

THE RIVER (1937)

Two of the first significant social documentary films produced in America, *The Plow That Broke the Plains* (1936) and *The River* (1937), were made by a thirty-six year old West Virginian who had never heard of the term "documentary film." As one critic reported in 1936, Pare Lorentz "knew in general the difference between the camera's tripod and its lens [but] his information stopped a little beyond this point."[10]

[9]*New York Times,* October 27, 1935.
[10]William L. White, "Pare Lorentz," *Scribner's,* January, 1939, p. 8. Hereafter cited as White, "Pare Lorentz."

The River (Courtesy of the Museum of Modern Art/Film Stills Archive)

By the early 1930's, Pare Lorentz had made his mark as a film reviewer who was unhappy with Hollywood's twaddle of "sin, sex, and six-shooters."[11] Lorentz believed that film should be used to clarify public perception of issues. In an especially trenchant review praising the work of King Vidor (*Our Daily Bread,* 1934), Lorentz pointed out that "a social revolution was

[11]C.M. Black, "He Serves America," *Colliers,* August, 1940, p. 38.

in progress and crying to be photographed while most studios ground out the same old escape stuff."[12] Since Lorentz believed that the movie was "America's greatest contribution to art," he hoped that Americans would be the first to explore this new potential for film.[13]

Simultaneously, the Roosevelt administration was exploring new avenues to communicate the message of the New Deal to the American people. This was an especially vexing problem because the most influential newspapers, radio, and film corporations were controlled by conservative Republicans with a bitter hatred for "That Man." As a result of this problem of media, Roosevelt and his administration experimented with alternate avenues of approach. Roosevelt himself created the now standard Presidential press conference with its intricate unwritten rules and restrictions. The President's famous "fireside chats" were an informal method of giving the American people a sense that their leader cared about their dilemma—an especially welcome relief after the silence and stolidity of Roosevelt's predecessors, Coolidge and Hoover. The Department of Agriculture, headed by Henry Wallace, made some noteworthy efforts to communicate the dilemma of the farmer to the nation as a whole. Under the leadership of Rexford Tugwell, the Resettlement Administration (later called the Farm Security Administration) sponsored an extensive photographic survey of rural poverty conditions "to educate the city dweller to the needs of the rural population."[14] The still photography work of Dorthea Lange, Walker Evans, and Arthur Rothstein in this effort have become very famous.

Wallace and Tugwell were also interested in using motion pictures to bridge the communications gap between government and the public. They called Pare Lorentz to Washington for an interview. Lorentz quickly convinced Tugwell and Wallace that a few "films of merit" should be made rather than a host of innocuous films "about such inspired subjects as the manufacturing of paving-brick and the love-life of the honey bee. Instead, the government should produce "films . . . good enough technically to bear comparison with commercial films and be entertaining enough to draw an audience."[15] Only by quality dramatization of the goals of the New Deal could government films win the minds (and the votes) of the American people.

Lorentz's films were received with great *éclat* by the aesthetes: among its many awards, *The River* was named as the best documentary film by the 1938 Venice International Film Festival. A man who knew something about language, James Joyce, observed for the press that the narration of *The*

[12]White, "Pare Lorentz," p. 8.
[13]Quoted in Snyder, *Pare Lorentz,* p. 17.
[14]Chief of the Resettlement Administration's photographic staff, Roy Stryker, as quoted by Snyder, *Pare Lorentz,* p. 23.
[15]Snyder, *Pare Lorentz,* p. 25.

River contained "the most beautiful prose I have heard in ten years."[16]
While stating its praise humorously, the *American Magazine* was not far
from a deep truth when it suggested that "Pare Lorentz has done for the
United States what Hollywood has done for its glamour girls."[17] All of the
major critics praised the film for its sensitive combination of pictures,
words, and music to create an aesthetic "rhythm which is irresistible, exciting, transparent."[18]

The films impressed some as potent political weapons. President Roosevelt himself saw the potential of both *The Plow That Broke the Plains*
(1936) and *The River* to impress the public with the need for soil conserva-
tion, relief for the South's sharecroppers, and regional planning. In the case
of *Ecce Homo* (1939) and *The Fight for Life* (1941), Roosevelt was not
above indicating to Lorentz that his films would soften up the public for
specific New Deal measures related to public works and health.[19] At lower
echelons, some prospective Democratic congressmen and senators found a
place for *The Plow* and *The River* in their campaigns for election.[20] In response, a cry of pain about government propaganda issued from the Republican camp. Lorentz had a ready answer to such charges: if Henry Luce
could have his popular *March of Time* film series shown in theaters around
the nation, "The United States government deserves to have at least thirty
minutes a month to explain in film the major problems which affect the
whole country, Republicans and Democrats alike."[21]

While Lorentz's argument may have carried the power of logic, the American people (especially after the World War I experience) were too fright-
ened of the word "propaganda" to make subtle distinctions. As one theater
manager reported, "It could be the greatest dramatic miracle of all time and
I wouldn't touch it if the government made it."[22] A particularly irritated
(perhaps even terrified) reviewer claimed that *The River* "is on the intellectual level of a voodoo ceremonial. Its aim is to win acceptance of a false-
hood."[23] Rep. Eugene Worley of Texas went so far as to threaten to punch
Tugwell in the nose for sponsoring a film that was "a libel on the greatest
section of the United States." After the drought recorded on film had
abated, many plains region legislators resented the image of their home
areas that *The Plow* perpetuated. Rep. Karl Mundt explained in 1939 that
the sovereign state of South Dakota had turned to greener pastures since the
drought, and that the continued circulation of *The Plow* was an insult to his

[16]White, "Pare Lorentz," p. 9.
[17]Rev. of *The River, American Magazine,* May, 1938, p. 109.
[18]Mark Van Doren, "The Poetry of Erosion," *The Nation,* October 30, 1937, p. 485.
[19]Snyder, *Pare Lorentz,* pp. 101-02.
[20]*Ibid.,* pp. 75-78.
[21]*Ibid.,* p. 144.
[22]Quoted in rev. of *The River, Literary Digest,* November 20, 1937, p. 34.
[23]Quoted in White, "Pare Lorentz," p. 9.

constituents. With the help of his colleaues, Mundt was able to have *The Plow* withdrawn from circulation in 1939, supposedly to have it revised in the light of "improved agricultural conditions." Funds for the revision were never appropriated, and *The Plow* did not become available to the public again until 1961.[24]

Unlike *Land of Cotton, The River* makes effective use of cutting to reinforce thematic messages. For example, during the section on lumbering, each shot is reduced in length to accentuate the mood of frenetic extractive activity. Later, slow pacing is used when the film returns to survey the disastrous results of exploitation. A series of long panning shots are linked together by dissolves. Because the composition of the shots matches so well, we seem to be examining an endless horizon of devastation. This matching of composition together with the slow pace from shot to shot yields a mood of involved reflection—a mood further intensified by Virgil Thomson's score.

In *The River,* Lorentz made extensive use of intellectual montage, a basic cinematic device entirely absent from *Land of Cotton.* The solution phase of *The River* contains one of the most impressive New Deal montages. The narrator explains: "We had the power to take the valley apart. We have the power to put it back together again." The following visual images were juxtaposed by Lorentz to evoke this idea:

LS: Explosion of dynamite.
MS: Steam shovel scooping tons of rock.
MS (Low Angle): Pneumatic drill operator with breathing mask.
LS (High Angle): Dam under construction from moving crane.
LS: Pouring concrete for dam.
LS: Controlled water flowing thunderously.
LS: Explosion of dynamite (as above).
MS: Pneumatic drill (as above).
LS: Explosion of dynamite (as above).
MS: Pneumatic drill (as above).
LS: Pouring concrete (as above).
LS (With dissolve transition): Before/after shots of gorge now blocked by the Norris Dam.

Sergei Eisenstein, the early advocate of intellectual montage, spoke of ideas as new creations generated in the minds of viewers as a result of the collision of images. In this example, the images and sounds were edited by Lorentz to evoke an idea about the relationship between machines and men. Early sections of *The River* demonstrated the misuses of technology. In harmony

---

[24]Rep. Karl Mundt deserves the credit for suppression of *The Plow* while Orville Freeman was responsible for its re-release. See Snyder, *Pare Lorentz,* pp. 76, 89-80. The up-beat New Deal conclusion to *The Plow* is still missing.

with New Deal thinking, this intellectual montage asserts that man is essentially a tool user despite previous excesses. What the nation needs is not a rejection of technology, but the intelligent guidance of planners who can coordinate its application. The controlled consumption of resources will yield a better life for all.

The soundtrack of *The River* was also designed to arouse the viewer. A series of roll calls announce the names of trees, rivers, cities, and dates of floods. While these roll calls obviously convey factual information, their main function is to evoke poetic feeling. Even the tone in which the narrator reads the names is varied to suit the mood of each section: for example, the roll call of trees is expansive during the scenes of exploitation, but the same words are uttered in an elegiac tone when the film returns to calculate the cost of denuding the Northern hillsides. The Whitmanesque repetition and metaphor exploited throughout the film establishes an effective verbal rhythm:

> We cut the top off the Allegheny
> and sent it down the river;
> We cut the top off Minnesota,
> and sent it down the river.

The musical component of the soundtrack subtlely reinforces thematic messages. Leitmotives are announced during the roll call sequences. Just as the narrator's voice is optimistic and dynamic during the first roll call of trees, so is the river theme which is played in the background. During the exploitation scenes, the leitmotive turns minor and brassy, reinforcing the dolorous second narrative roll call of trees. During the early lumbering sequence described above, we watch one-hundred year old trees race down a sluiceway. An orchestra which becomes increasingly larger plays the tune "Hot Time in the Old Town Tonight." The intended contrast between the vigorous industrial activity on the screen and the orchestrated barroom song evokes an obvious reflection in the minds of viewers—this exploitative intoxication will end in a very painful hangover.

Social documentaries often follow a problem-solution formula, and *The River* is no exception. What is unusual is the curious difference between the intensity of the problem phase and the confidence of the solution section. This difference in tone can only be accounted for by reference to the New Deal orientation of the filmmaker and his sponsor. The problem phase of the film is powerfully conveyed: our indignation is aroused at those who have misused the land and resources of the Mississippi Valley. But even as we view the widespread suffering that has resulted, viewers are never thrust into the scene. We are always concerned observers of a social problem rather than involved participants. The solution portion of the film confirms this observer status. The floods, the poverty, and the backwardness of the

South are being dealt with by the Roosevelt administration. Viewers need do no more than ratify the ongoing work of the New Deal. In sum, while *The River* works hard to arouse the feelings of its audience, film rhetoric does not promote a sense of participation, nor is personal action demanded.

NATIVE LAND (1942)

Native Land (1942) is generally acknowledged to be the best product of a short-lived American radical film movement in the Thirties. The first radical film group, the Workers Film and Photo League, worked closely with a leftist relief group known as the Workers International Relief Organization. Members of the League accompanied WIR representatives to textile mills in New England and coal mines in Harlan County, West Virginia, where the resistance of workers was recorded on film. Locally, the League filmed the protests by taxi drivers and tenement dwellers in New York City. The League felt a special calling for its labors because the bourgeois press simply left the labor story unreported. As one League member noted wryly: "There was no *March of Time* even to simulate the reality of the early thirties in film."[25] Until the mid-thirties, the League attempted to do little more than accumulate a visual record on celluloid. Tom Brandon's description of his own motives for participating communicates the basic spirit of the early days: "I didn't consider myself a filmmaker. I saw certain needs and I learned how to use a 35mm camera and I went and covered some important things because I knew nobody else was doing it."[26]

By 1935, some members of the League wanted to move on to more sophisticated projects, and these men founded a production group which they called Nykino (i.e., New York "kino" or film-eye). This group experimented with *March of Time* style re-enactments in *Sunnyside* (a story of New York evictions) and *The Black Legion* (a study of an American fascist group). *Pie in the Sky* tested the possibilities of improvisation for social documentaries. As Leo Hurwitz recalled, the more committed filmmakers of the League had been struck by "the necessity of expanding our ideas from simple coverage to something like an essay form that would have ideas and events, connectives and preparations, to show what was not necessarily visible or photographable."[27]

Frontier Films, an affinity group consisting of Leo Hurwitz, Paul Strand, Ralph Steiner, Jay Leyda and others, was an outgrowth of the

[25]Fred Sweet *et al.*, "Pioneers: An Interview with Tom Brandon," *Film Quarterly,* 26, No. 5 (1973), 12. Hereafter cited as Sweet, "Pioneers." It should be noted that President Roosevelt endorsed Lorentz's U.S. Film Service for similar reasons. The New Deal story was simply not being told.

[26]*Ibid.,* p. 22.

[27]Michael and Jill Klein, "*Native Land*: An Interview with Leo Hurwitz," *Cineaste,* 6, No. 3 (1975), 4. Hereafter cited as Klein, "Interview with Leo Hurwitz."

Nykino experiments. The filmmakers convinced such prominent intellectuals and artists as Ernest Hemingway, John Dos Passos, Archibald MacLeisch, and Lillian Hellman to contribute time, effort, or money to their cause. Some of the best films which resulted were on foreign crises: *Heart of Spain* (1937) and *Return to Life* (1937) were designed to raise funds for the Loyalist cause in the Spanish Civil War; *China Strikes Back* (1937) portrayed a unified people struggling against an imperial invader. Frontier Films also produced some excellent studies of domestic American conditions: the struggle of Detroit auto workers was intensely portrayed in *United Action* (1939); rural poverty (but also the pleasures of rural life) was explored in *People of the Cumberland* (1938). Finally, the epic of Frontier Film's seven year activities was *Native Land,* a film begun in 1938, but not issued until May, 1942.

Contemporary reviewers welcomed *Native Land* enthusiastically. *Time* called it "vitally American" even though it portrayed a bitter class struggle at work in America.[28] The *New Republic* was especially pleased that the civil rights issue had at last received filmic treatment: "a story which too long has been distorted through the mouths of congressmen and newspapers."[29] *Native Land* has been called "the most important U.S. independent thirties film," but it has been neglected by film scholarship.[30] The press of events worked against proper recognition of *Native Land.* Leo Hurwitz received the answer print from the laboratory the day after Pearl Harbor was bombed. With the United States at war, not even the Communist party was interested in distributing a film which could be construed as an attack on national unity.[31]

Native Land attempted to use specific incidents of civil rights violations as a means to evoke a general picture of repression in America. The efforts of little men to challenge the policies of "the big shots," "the interests," "powerful corporations" are shown to be fruitless if conducted on an individual basis. Sharecroppers, workers, small merchants must learn to work cooperatively in the industrial era. Freedom is the result of vigilance, not an automatic condition. As in his other films, Hurwitz worked hard in *Native Land* to develop a maximum number of intellectual and moral implications for the particular stories told.

Native Land closely examines eight civil rights violations. While only the second incident will be analyzed, its thematic content and rhetorical style are representative. The plot of the incident is extremely simple. A young girl is washing the windows of an urban apartment building. In the course of her duties, she discovers the unconscious body of one of the tenants, a man

[28]"The New Picture," June 8, 1942, p. 50.
[29]Manny Farber, "The Naked Truth," May 25, 1942, pp. 734-35.
[30]Tom Brandon quoted in Sweet, "Pioneers," p. 16.
[31]Klein, "Interview with Leo Hurwitz," p. 6.

Native Land (Courtesy of the Museum of Modern Art/Film Stills Archive)

who has been beaten for attempting to organize a union at a nearby factory.

The rich film rhetoric of this incident was organized in such a way as to thrust the viewer into the story of a participant. As the scene opens, we are swept down the street toward the girl by means of a moving camera. Involvement of the viewer builds through the use of subjective camera and reverse angles: as the girl sits in an apartment window cleaning the outside of a large lower pane, she turns to look down into the street. Through subjective camera, we see a boy below showing off his skill with a paddle ball. A reaction shot of the girl indicates that she has the same smile on her face that a responsive viewer has probably assumed. The camera angle is again reversed: we look up at the girl in the window through the boy's eyes. They are both obviously happy to be alive and active on this sunny day. Viewer attention is then humorously focused upon the girl's dog, a small mutt who frets over the safety of his mistress. Throughout the scene, a slightly operatic tune is developed.

Such an extended portrayal of persons apart from issues might at first seem irrelevant to the goals of a social documentary film. Certainly, neither *Land of Cotton* nor *The River* considers the private live of the people whose problems are reported. Yet such a slow beginning has a very necessary place within this leftist film. In part, it is a logical result of the egalitarianism of the Frontier Film group. But this close scrutiny of simple pleasures in the lives of the working class has a second purpose more closely linked to *Native Land*'s rhetoric of involvement. The invasion of an established fabric of existence will shock us all the more if we first become acquainted with the girl as an innocent young person rather than as a special problem (*March of Time*) or as a client of the government (*The River*). The ideology and rhetoric of this introduction are inextricably related.

Once viewer identification with the girl has been established, the scene progresses. She carries her pail upstairs to the second floor. The camera at the top of the stairs follows her movements in long, slowly paced shots. As she climbs the stairs and turns the corner, she continues to hum the tune which we heard during the charming opening scene. The little dog follows dutifully behind.

The girl knocks at the union man's door, but no one answers. At this point, many different elements of film language work in concert to develop a new mood: the light operatic tune shifts from violins to sour brass; the pace of editing accelerates; close-ups of details inside the room are intercut with shots of the girl's attempts to push her way in. Throughout this quickly-paced scene, camera angles change rapidly to further charge the atmosphere. Finally, she succeeds in pushing aside the dresser which barred the door. Although we learn of the harm done to the union organizer inside, viewer attention does not remain focused on the victim. Instead, we cringe because we anticipate the traumatic effect which this incident will have on the innocent young girl.

As the girl steps inside the room, we re-enter her point of view: through a subjective camera, we survey the damage. The soundtrack goes dead. This silence is especially effective because the brass has been playing the leitmotive with increasing volume and dissonance. We look up at the girl from a low angle. There is a delay in sound and expression as we observe the full effect of this brutal scene. Thematically, we are shown that large corporations can crush individuals who attempt to stand up for their rights. But this conceptual acknowledgment is informed by personal feeling. We have shared in the girl's painful discovery as participants in the scene rather than as concerned observers of a distant wrong.

The leftist persuasion of the filmmakers determined the conclusion of this representative incident from *Native Land*. *March of Time* would have assured viewers that a vigorous press was contributing to the eventual solution by exposing the abuses of power. *The River* would have softened the blow by pointing to President Roosevelt's growing moral and legislative support of the union movement. *Native Land* provides no such escape clause from personal responsibility. Because its creators assumed that both the press and the government of the United States too often bowed to money interests, *Native Land* requires nothing less than full participation by viewers. The narrator muses: "Again. It happened again. They say he was a union man. Nothing in the newspapers. . . . It wasn't on the radio. . . . Don't understand it. . . . New York, Chicago, Cleveland. . . ." The implication here, and at the close of the other eight incidents, is that the reader must come to conclusions on his own based upon the strength of the emotional involvement promoted by the rhetoric of the film.

SUMMARY

The different film rhetorics of *Land of Cotton, The River,* and *Native Land* can be related to the liberal Republican, New Deal, and leftist persuasions of the respective filmmakers. As we move leftward on the political spectrum, there is a greater appeal to our feelings and an ever-increasing pressure upon the viewer to become involved in the action. *Land of Cotton* rests on the principle that "exposure" by an objective, free press will generate discussion and—at some future date—action. Yet a number of obstacles were placed in the path of a concerned viewer: for every exposure of a social problem, there was a contradicting note about social harmony in the Kingdom of Cotton. The film rhetoric of *Land of Cotton* was not exploited fully because of this underlying ambivalence. In its ideological and rhetorical confusion, the cinematic monthly shared the weakness of Time, Inc.'s literary weekly: by its unwillingness to take a stand, it inadvertently supported the status quo.

The rhetoric of Pare Lorentz's *The River* is of pure New Deal vintage. During the problem phase of the film, every rhetorical device in the lexicon of film is employed to force upon the viewer a realization of the folly of our industrial exploitation. Editing, music, and narration are used to their fullest to arouse our indignation about the plight of those who would later be called the "Other America." Yet the solution segment allows viewers to sit back and watch rather than encourage them to help bring about a solution. We are assured that we can surrender our responsibility to government planners who will solve our economic and ecological problems for us. We are told that we are justified in giving planners such sweeping powers because the original problems to be solved were created through ignorance and lack of foresight rather than by any inherent human tendency to misuse power.

The film rhetoric of *Native Land* is as distinctive as its radical message. Viewers are never allowed to merely observe contemporary scandals (*Land of Cotton*), nor to trust in the benevolence of public officials (*The River*). By first introducing viewers to the wholesome lives of farmers, laborers, urban merchants and then dramatizing the disruption of these lives, *Native Land* elicits a deep emotional response. The mounting emotion which we feel at the end of these eight incidents is the pain of personal tragedy.

Henry James once described the American Dream as the pervasive desire of his countrymen to make so much money that they could stop caring. By their differing lights, "objective" journalist Louis de Rochemont, New Dealer Pare Lorentz, and leftist Leo Hurwitz attempted to counter the tendency of Americans to ignore the responsibilities of citizenship. The film rhetorics of *Land of Cotton, The River,* and *Native Land* are consonant with their differing demands for feeling and action.

CHAPTER 4.

Fighting Words: *City Lights* (1931),
Modern Times (1936), and
The Great Dictator (1940)

IRA S. JAFFE

"THE ART OF LIFE IS *FIRST* TO BE ALIVE," STRESSED Alfred North Whitehead, "*secondly* to be alive in a satisfactory way, and *thirdly* to acquire an increase in satisfaction."[1] Chaplin's artistic task, in part, was to keep faith with Whitehead's "threefold urge."[2] The tramp's first cause was his empty stomach and the physical effort to fill and appease it. But even when the immediate peril was to his spirit rather than to his body, the tramp was most eloquent when he expressed his need in terms of the materials of bare survival. "First to be alive" was the most compelling and least superfluous stimulus of his actions and his dreams.

This passionate urge Chaplin evidently brought to his consideration of the spoken word. According to his autobiography, he judged the word in terms of the survival of his tramp and his art, and he reacted with alarm and hostility. Canny reflection as much as instinctive dislike of the unknown made him regard the spoken word as an enemy: "Occasionally I mused over the possibility of making a sound film, but the thought sickened me, for I realized I could never achieve the excellence of my silent pictures. It would mean giving up my tramp character entirely. Some people suggested that the tramp might talk. This was unthinkable, for the first word he ever uttered would transform him into another person. Besides, the matrix out of which he was born was as mute as the rags he wore."[3]

While Chaplin may have enjoyed talking in his everyday life, at times he felt not just threatened but overcome by the talking motion pictures: "Another thought was that, if I did make a talking picture, no matter how good

---

[1]Alfred North Whitehead, *The Function of Reason* (Boston: Beacon Press, 1929), p. 8.
[2]*The Function of Reason,* p. 18.
[3]Charles Chaplin, *My Autobiography* (New York: Simon & Schuster, 1964), p. 397.

I was I could never surpass the artistry of my pantomime. I had thought of possible voices for the tramp—whether he should speak in monosyllables or just smile. But it was no use."[4] "There was no further incentive to stay in Hollywood. Without doubt silent pictures were finished and I did not feel like combating the talkies."[5]

According to his autobiography, the prospect of making *The Great Dictator* excited Chaplin precisely when it struck him as an opportunity to talk while preserving the silent identity of the tramp: "Then it suddenly struck me. Of course! As Hitler I could harangue the crowds in jargon and talk all I wanted to. And as the tramp I could remain more or less silent. A Hitler story was an opportunity for burlesque and pantomime."[6]

Chaplin's plan for the toxic word, then, was to place it in the mouth of the villain who would regurgitate it in storms of aggressive gibberish. Even when actual words rather than "jargon" emerged, the effect presumably would be that of malignant nonsense. The tramp would be "more or less silent," hence sensible and pure. But both the tyrant and the word would be exposed as witless conductors of incoherence. At last Chaplin's antagonism toward speech would be vented and vindicated, for the spoken word which had threatened his tramp and his art he would cast as the enemy of life itself.

Chaplin's severe plan almost certainly reflected a life-long quarrel with the word that had disturbed his personal as well as his professional existence. At age thirteen, he was scarcely able to read or write, and this deficiency he identified with ignorance and infirmity. He found knowledge and the word often synonymous, and he pursued both in order to survive: "I wanted to know not for the love of knowledge but as a defense against the world's contempt for the ignorant."[7]

Furthermore, if the world was inclined to employ the word as a weapon against Chaplin, he was determined to mock the word and disarm the world. He recalls in his autobiography a moment during a banquet for Pavlova at the Russian consulate which called for speech-making in honor of the great dancer:

> I believe I was the only Englishman called upon. Before my turn came to speak, however, a professor delivered a brilliant eulogy of Pavlova's art in Russian. At one moment the professor burst into tears, then went up to Pavlova and kissed her fervently. I knew that any attempt of mine would be tame after that, so I rose and said that as my English was totally inadequate to express the greatness of Pavlova's art I would speak in Chinese. I spoke in a Chinese jargon, building up

[4]*My Autobiography*, p. 420.
[5]Ibid., p. 410.
[6]Ibid., p. 425.
[7]Cited in Raoul Sobel and David Francis, *Chaplin: Genesis of a Clown* (New York: Quartet Books, 1977), p. 79.

to a crescendo as the professor had done, finishing by kissing Pavlova more fervently than the professor, taking a napkin and placing it over both our heads as I continually kissed her. The party roared with laughter, and it broke the solemnity of the occasion.[8]

In Chaplin's play, the professor's actions coalesced into a wondrous essence. If words were lost, their emotional import was not. If the spoken word was banished, a primitive impulse was released that enlivened the occasion. As Henri Bergson might have noted, a relatively rigid predicament suddenly achieved flexibility: ". . . as soon as we forget the serious object of a solemnity or a ceremony," said Bergson, "those taking part in it give us the impression of puppets in motion."[9] Perhaps Chaplin's action restored to the puppets that quality which Bergson called the "inner suppleness of life."[10]

There may be a related justification for Chaplin's displacement of the spoken word. His behavior at the banquet served to translate the professor's communication into the language of pantomime and burlesque through which Chaplin was known all over the globe. His performance at the banquet also enhanced his status by suggesting resemblances between his own art, which depended on physical movement and contact rather than words, and the art of the dancer Pavlova. More than once in his autobiography Chaplin calls attention to such affinities. He declares, for example, that in his films long before *Limelight* "violence was carefully rehearsed and treated like choreography";[11] and he proudly repeats, shortly before his account of the banquet for Pavlova, the compliment he received from Nijinsky: "Your comedy is balletique, you are a dancer."[12] A dancer might not use vocal gibberish as Chaplin had done at the banquet; certainly the pantomime artist would not. Such vocal displays belonged to burlesque and the tyrant of *The Great Dictator* more than to pantomime and the tramp. Yet it might be argued that Chaplin's "Chinese jargon" with its deliberate crescendo and emotional directness resembled music more than speech, and that consequently it was permissible in the worlds of dance and mime. In any case, Chaplin had made his point; the form and power of his own art were not so distant from the great dancer's that they did not deserve celebration at the same banquet.

Just as the word had been a challenge for Chaplin off the screen, it had meant trouble since his first days in the movies when he sought to forge a type of film comedy that would favor personality, and subdue the delirium

---

[8]*My Autobiography,* p. 208.
[9]Henri Bergson, "Laughter," in Wylie Sypher, ed., *Comedy* (New York: Doubleday Anchor, 1956), p. 90.
[10]"Laughter," p. 89.
[11]*My Autobiography,* p. 199.
[12]Ibid., p. 203.

of camera tricks and mechanical effects which he associated with the films of Mack Sennett. According to Chaplin, Sennett once told him that the chase was "the essence" of Keystone comedy. Chaplin was sorely dismayed; ". . . Personally I hated the chase. It dissipates one's personality: little as I knew about movies, I knew that nothing transcended personality."[13] Personality for Chaplin was a rich, expansive entity that greedily absorbed time and space in order to reveal the fantastic interplay of its multiple aspects. That time and space which Sennett dynamized in the chase Chaplin seemed to require for the free play of the tramp's battery of startled faces. Chaplin writes that he described these faces to Sennett as follows: "You know this fellow is many-sided, a tramp, a gentleman, a poet, a dreamer, a lonely fellow, always hopeful of romance and adventure. . . . He would have you believe he is a scientist, a musician, a duke, a polo player. However, he is not above picking up cigarette butts or robbing a baby of its candy. And of course if the occasion warrants it, he will kick a lady in the rear—but only in extreme anger!"[14]

Although Chaplin's debate with Sennett centered on personality or character, it was informed by the aura of the spoken word. For if Sennett's race of automatons ruled film comedy without serious challenge, one reason was the popular wisdom which held that complex characterization was the province of the word, hence of the novel and theater instead of the seditious movies. In *Chaplin: Genesis of a Clown,* Raoul Sobel and David Francis state the argument as follows:

> At the turn of the century in France, theatrical comedy was in the hands of authors . . . who relied almost entirely on a brilliant manipulation of language. It was thus inconceivable for the early film producers, steeped in theatrical tradition as they were, to consider the possibility of a comedy based on character or wit which did not contain dialogue. There seemed no alternative but to turn to low comedy for their raw material. The first screen clowns were therefore recruited from vaudeville or variety, burlesque and the circus, places where speech took second place to slapstick and where the main qualifications for work seems to have been a talent for tumbling and the stamina to perform for long hours at fever pitch."[15]

Perhaps because "the possibility of a comedy based on character . . . which did not contain dialogue" appeared slight, production schedules further discouraged the creation of complex screen personalities: "With a schedule of two or three films a week each clown was expected to summon up an instant character which would elicit an instant and uncomplicated response."[16] In their account of the development of early film comedy, Sobel

[13]Ibid., p. 146.
[14]Ibid., p. 150.
[15]*Chaplin: Genesis of a Clown,* p. 127.
[16]Ibid.

and Francis focus on French comedy. The question arises whether circumstances in the United States were substantially different. One answer is suggested by Ray L. Birdwhistell in *Kinesics and Context*: "I wish to stress the American emphasis on dialogue, on the words, as carrying the central meaning of an interaction. I think that we would have no difficulty in agreeing that this emphasis is not restricted to the stage. Radio, television, and movie performances seem to utilize the same convention."[17] Possibly the American environment was never encouraging to the development of personality through a silent art.

CITY LIGHTS

Yet the first moments of *City Lights,* Chaplin's first film of the sound era, reflect both a reluctance to employ the spoken word and an inclination to link human vocal utterance to basically sterile functions. The opening title declares *City Lights* to be "a comedy romance in pantomime." Then a stout man and lean spinsterish woman appear on a platform overlooking a crowd in order to donate, states a title, a monument called "Peace and Prosperity" to the people of the city. The title, along with the grand manner of the two dignitaries, serves to set them apart. The man and woman are not common citizens or their representatives, but condescending chieftains remote from both the faceless crowd and the covered monument. Each haughtily offers some vocal gibberish that mildly adumbrates the mad jargon which Chaplin was to assign the tyrant in *The Great Dictator*. But while Hynkel's babble would reflect the hysteria of a fractured soul, the boring, mechanical utterances of the donors suggested the complete dissolution of the human vocal apparatus.

As if in reply to their abrasive, machine-like jabber, the tramp is unveiled at the same instant as the monument. He wakes from his rest upon the lap of the monument's central figure, scratches his head and his leg, quickly surveys the situation, and aptly concludes that his presence is unwelcome. He begins to leave the monument, but the rear of his trousers is pierced by a sword held high by the monument's reclining figure. The spinsterish donor, her face like a frozen beak, stares at him, but she continues to ignore the bouquet of flowers in her arms. A policeman waves for the tramp to leave, but the music of the national anthem from an invisible source pointlessly intercedes. The donors, the policemen, the crowd, and even the tramp automatically assume respectful postures. When the anthem ends as abruptly as it began, the conflict proceeds. In the effort to escape, the unbidden tramp finishes effacing the monument with his body. He sits on the face of the male figure that holds the sword. He cautiously crosses over to another

---

[17]Ray L. Birdwhistell, *Kinesics and Context: Essays on Body Motion Communication* (Philadelphia: University of Pennsylvania Press, 1970), p. 55.

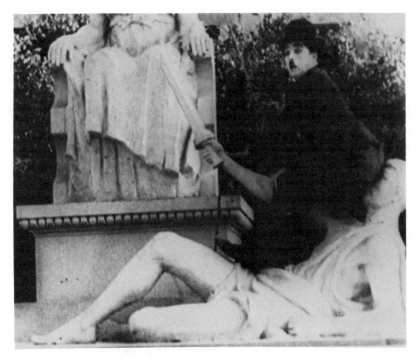

City Lights (Courtesy of the Museum of Modern Art / Film Stills Archive)

male figure whose stance is erect and genteel. The tramp sits upon this figure's upturned hand, and presses his nose to the thumb of the figure's second hand. The tramp steadily eyes the figure, makes a few silent, indignant
remarks, tips his hat to it, and climbs away over the fence.

If the tramp's behavior seems improper to the donors, it nonetheless in-
vests the ceremony with the unpredictable impulse of life, somewhat as did
Chaplin's actions at the banquet for Pavlova. The raising of the canvas to
reveal the monument has bared also a human being who has made tangible
use of both the canvas and the statue. While the monument may serve a
symbolic function that eventually will benefit human survival, the tramp
has made it serve needs for rest and shelter that are basic and immediate. He
has conferred practical value on the monument and, particularly in the
course of his escape, he has stressed tactile sensation in the void of a ceremony that seemed determined to resist both physical and spiritual contact.
The tramp's reclining and intimate fumbling upon the monument, even the
pressing of his nose against the statue's inflexible thumb, have brought the
formal, vapid event to life. For an instant they also have made human
touching rather than human talking the central, if subversive, action of the
film.

The tramp's movements upon the monument, moreover, may suggest the infant's tactile testing of his environment and even the effort to express human experience in sculptural form. In contrast, the donors and the crowd appear to have lost touch with the origins of their life. The gibberish of the donors suggests not the dawn of speech but a confused condition in which the spoken word is out of reach. These dichotomous circumstances seem utterly consonant with the balance of the film. For if *City Lights* makes a point, it is that the essential relations and truths by which life locates itself primarily involve not speaking and hearing, but touching and feeling.

The first encounter between the tramp and the blind girl may serve to demonstrate that it is literally by touch that lovers meet. After the tramp inadvertently knocks the girl's flower from her hand with his elbow, he picks the flower up and places it in her hand. This flower she places in the lapel of his jacket with her right hand, while her left hand rests gently for a moment upon his chest. Then the tramp puts the coin into her hand and, lightly holding her hand, he helps her sit down. Earlier the tramp has been stunned to discover that the girl cannot see, but the final import of the scene depends on the mutual discovery and balance of their tactile exchange.

If the first encounter between the two lovers develops out of the tramp's visual discovery of the girl's blindness as he observes her probe for the fallen flower she cannot see, the final encounter also proceeds from a moment of visual perception toward one of tactile recognition and adjustment. Probably sight does play a larger role in the final encounter than in the first, for at last both lovers can see. But the new visual contact between them, as they stare at each other through the glass wall of the flower shop, must be corrected and realized by touch. Through sight alone the girl meets only the waif-like admiration of a tramp beyond the window who holds a fragile flower he has picked from a pile of dust swept from the store. Through touch, however, the girl recognizes the person who has been her benefactor and friend, whose appearance she now must reconcile with the ideal vision she has formed of him. This reconciliation, like the recognition, she negotiates through touch. Perhaps afraid that the touch which united them now will bring rejection, the tramp tries to acquit himself without accepting the fresh flower which she emerges from the store to offer. Her movement arrests his, however, and although he successfully reaches to take the flower without touching her hand, she overcomes the distance when she presses the coin deeply into his hand. The tramp then holds the flower so near his mouth that it seems at moments fixed in his teeth. The girl moves her hand to his shoulder and then fingers the lapel where she left the flower at the end of their first transaction. He acknowledges that he is the person she remembers and he lets her draw his free hand to her chest, and directs at her from just above the flower a piercing grin.

In this final communion of the tramp and the girl, the spoken word and even natural sound have lttle place compared to that of touch and sight. The scandalous dancing and touching which were banished with the tramp from the dedication ceremony have captured the center of the stage. Similarly, the flower which in the form of a bouquet at the ceremony was peripheral and ignored, held but not grasped, has become central to the understanding at the end. In contrast, the mechanical, predictable jabber of the dedication ceremony has been supplanted by a tactful intimacy that affirms the implicit claim of the ballerina's question in *Limelight,* "What is more eloquent than silence?"

There exist today prints of short Chaplin films of the silent era such as *The Pawnshop* and *Behind the Screen* in which sounds other than music occur more frequently than they do in *City Lights.* While some of these sounds seem unnaturalistic, the majority suggest a naturalistic intent. The chirping of invisible birds which accompanies the tramp's dance in front of the store early in *The Pawnshop* constitutes a deliberate instance of unnaturalistic sound. Relatively naturalistic, however, are the sounds which accompany the tramp piling plates, sweeping the floor, and drilling into the clock. Yet more important for our purposes than the frequency of the naturalistic sounds in *The Pawnshop*[18] is that they exist outside a pattern set in *City Lights* whereby naturalistic sounds prmarily mark moments of physical and spiritual danger.

The first naturalistic, synchronous sound in *City Lights* occurs when the piano keys are struck by the faltering head of the drunken tramp as he slips further into the suicidal orbit of the millionaire. The second such sound, which quickly follows, is the shot from the millionaire's gun. The third prominent sound is that of the whistle which the tramp swallows at the party when a woman gaily slaps his stomach. Whistling hiccups convulse the tramp like earthquakes, and seem to choke his ability to eat, drink, and breathe. The hiccups do yield, however, the tramp's first audible utterances of the sound era; and it befits Chaplin's care for his character's silent identity that the utterances are alien and involuntary.

The gong over the boxing ring in which the tramp fights to pay for the blind girl's rent and the operation on her eyes is too big to swallow. But by the end of the bout the rope that hangs from the gong is coiled around the tramp's neck, and he is being choked again. Each time he falls to the canvas, the overly tight rope and the sound of the bell pull him up. When he reaches his corner before being hit, the rope again unites with the sound of

---

[18]Distributed by Kit Parker Films, Carmel Valley, California. This film, like all of the Mutuals, was not owned or controlled by Chaplin. *The Pawnshop* was distributed by Mutual until 1919 when it was picked up by Clark-Cornelius; in 1922, Chaplin-Classics released the film for three years, giving way to Export and Import Company. In 1932, the Van Beuren Corporation (a subsidiary of RKO) added sound effects and music and did some re-editing. It is the Van Beuren version which is now most widely available, and there is substantial documentation that Chaplin was not at all pleased with the tampering.

the bell to return him to the fray. Eventually the sounds of the bell proceed so rapidly that the tramp, as if in a nightmare, loses the ability to track their meaning. Each sound becomes a baffling double-command to fight and to stop fighting.

MODERN TIMES

Even though technical means existed to add human utterance, including speech, to the sparse gallery of sound in *City Lights,* the spoken word is resisted and mocked. In *Modern Times,* Chaplin is less stingy about the number of sounds, and he includes the spoken word. But his stylized use of the sounds, and of the words, again portrays them as largely hostile to human life. Indeed, their hostility in *Modern Times* becomes considerably more pervasive and systematic than in *City Lights.* The mechanical impersonality of the ringside gong and of the speakers at the dedication ceremony in *City Lights* develops into a sickening roar in *Modern Times* which finally must breed the lonely, authoritarian city of Hynkel in *The Great Dictator.*

The world of *Modern Times* is set in motion by the blast of the factory horn that is the twin of the gong at the boxing match in *City Lights.* Virtually every subsequent sound, both inside the factory and out, emanating from machines, time clocks, sirens, and guns, suggests the sacrifice of human need to mechanical or impersonal dictate. Predominant within the factory are sundry sounds, often grinding and crushing, of heavy metal. Even before the metal washers which the tramp will almost swallow are put on the plate of the feeding machine locked around him, unnatural metallic sounds accompany the passage of food into his mouth.

Whereas the music in *Modern Times* may connote hope as well as danger, the natural sounds adamantly stress the tramp's frustrations. The preference for sounds that accentuate forces inimical to the tramp is demonstrated succinctly during his brief stay with the gamin in the wooden shanty by the water. We easily hear the sounds of a board falling on the tramp's head, of a wooden table collapsing, of a chair sinking into the floor, and of the roof giving way. But no sound accompanies the tramp successfully forcing the roof back up with a wooden beam, or cheerfully entering his little paradise and shutting the door. The sound of a splash accompanies his unfortunate jump into shallow water, but his emergence and his return to the shack are conducted in silence.

The self-destructive impulses of the millionaire in *City Lights* are rampant in *Modern Times*; and one materialization of such human self-betrayal is the feeding machine mentioned earlier, which subverts the act of eating and humiliates the human spirit. Next to the eruptive sounds of this machine, the sound of gurgling which rises from the stomach of the minister's wife in the jail of *Modern Times* seems almost saintly. The smiling tramp, fearing only that he will shortly be set free by the warden, appears to find the gentle sound most tolerable. But the minister's severe wife becomes highly uncomfortable, and seeks to suppress the sound, as she would a loud pagan in church. As if contaminated by her shame, the tramp becomes extremely nervous. He finds the sound of gurgle-drowning seltzer shot into a glass by the minister's wife nasty and aggressive. Even the more benign sounds of *Modern Times* take on the harsh overtones of the gong in *City Lights.*

The spoken word in *Modern Times* occurs sparingly and within the conventions of the silent film. Most of the verbal communication is silent; words appear in the titles. The use of audible words in *Modern Times*, however, is worthy of a world in which human consciousness increasingly surrenders ideals of justice and beauty to pursue the speed and power identified with machines. Almost invariably in this film the spoken word, like the naturalistic sound, appears hostile to life. Almost invariably, spoken words assume the form of commands for greater industrial efficiency at the expense of the health of the human body and spirit. Thus the first articulate words uttered in Chaplin's cinema come from the owner of the factory who appears on a video screen to order a "speed . . . up" of all factory activity. His second utterance is not very different: "Section Five, More Speed, Four, Seven." Next the captain of industry appears in the immense screen on the wall of the factory lavatory, where the tramp is taking part of his work break. "Hey," shouts the captain to the tramp, "quit stalling. Get back to work." The voice of "the mechanical salesman" on the record that speaks for Mr. Billows, the inventor of the feeding machine who silently stands by the phonograph, appeals to the factory owner's obsession with dehumanizing efficiency. The voice warns him to "keep ahead of the competition" by utilizing the feeding machine's automatic soup plate, which cools soup without the aid of human breath, and its "low-to-high-gear," which shifts with a mere "tip of the tongue." Not least, the mechanical salesman stresses the sanitary saving of worker energy that is assured by the "automatic food pusher" and the "sterilized mouth cleaner." In short, the feeding machine will reserve for the owner's factory the energy which the worker ordinarily expends to touch, taste, and breath. The machine quickly breaks down, but as if still inspired by the credo of the mechanical salesman, the factory owner issues yet another command: "Give her the limit." Even the voice that speaks from the jail-cell radio, which the tramp turns on to overpower the gurgling sound, issues a notice of efficiency: "If you are suffering from gastritis, don't forget—." The tramp abruptly turns the radio off.

Yet another aspect of the spoken word in *Modern Times* is its indirectness. The speaker never addresses the listener in person, but through video, a record, or the radio. When the factory owner talks within physical reach of the tramp or Mr. Billows, his words are silent, inaudible, and occasionally they are followed by silent titles. Consequently, the audible word, perhaps even more than the silent word, becomes part of the distant impersonality that oppresses the tramp and his co-workers. The user of the audible word never permits the contact or instant feedback of human touch or breath.

When the tramp agrees to sing in the nightclub at the end of *Modern Times,* he promises not the first audible spoken words of the film, but the first audible vocal utterance which risks an intimate response. It is this fact along with the playful romantic theme of his song which distinguishes the performance the tramp promises from the previous utterances in *Modern Times* and from the jabber directed at the distant, faceless crowd at the ceremony initiating *City Lights.*

Before the moment arrives for the tramp to sing, however, the "singing waiters" at the nightclub incorporate audible words in their own song. Moreover, as if succumbing to an overwhelming current in the world of *Modern Times,* these words—like those of the captain of industry, the mechanical salesman, and even the radio voice—connote a form of exploitation: "In the evening, by the moonlight, you can hear those darkies singing," croon the white waiters. Perhaps it is because he fears the word as but one more exploitative tool that the tramp was so reluctant to sing when the club's owner first offered him the job. The tramp pointed helplessly to his throat, as if it lacked the larynx, and started to shake his head. But in desperate need of work and under pressure from the gamin, the tramp finally accepted the owner's offer of a "trial" in which he would not only wait on tables but also sing.

As the fateful moment approaches, the tramp mimes his song in the dressing room, while we hear from the club the surprisingly brittle lyrics of the singing waiters. For an eerie instant their words seem to emanate from the tramp's active lips. Then he complains to the gamin, "I forget the words," and she proceeds to write them down on the cuffs of his sleeves. His confidence increases, and when at last he emerges in front of the crowd that just moments earlier (prior to the song of the white chorus) found him supremely entertaining as the waiter whose roast duck was stolen and tosssed like a football, he appears almost ebullient. He launches into his seductive dance, his arms sail into the air, and the cuffs fly off. The volatile crowd stirs and murmurs for the song to begin. "Sing! Never mind the words," the gamin anxiously shouts to him from the wings.

He proceeds with his love rhapsody of coy gibberish and agile mime to pose an elegant reply to the scarcely human voices that preceded him in *City Lights* and *Modern Times.* In his rendering, the exact meaning of the sound complexes surrounding terms like "taximeter" which are identifiable in English seems unimportant. For as a whole the jaunty communication, including the loud kiss and the slap which constitute the first non-vocal sounds in

Modern Times (Courtesy of the Museum of Modern Art/Film Stills Archive)

Chaplin's cinema produced by the tramp's own body, feels wonderfully clear. As if to confirm this essential clarity, the audience in the club greets what appears to be the end of each stanza with hearty sounds of laughter and recognition, such as befit successful voyeurs and would-be accomplices. When Hynkel in *The Great Dictator* lapses into gibberish to tell Napaloni the famous Tomanian proverb, Napaloni has a good laugh, and then says, "That's very funny. I wish I understand it." The audience in *Modern Times* understands well enough.

Like the conclusion of *City Lights,* Chaplin's performance near the end of *Modern Times* suggests that significant human communication can occur without the spoken word. Furthermore, the most life-giving moments of *Modern Times* stem from the unleashed force of the tramp's non-verbal art. Perhaps the most brilliant instance occurs when the tramp emerges from his prostrate voyage along the giant wheels of the machine and erupts into his acrobatic dance against the machines and the machine-like people. With his ejaculating cans of oil, he appears to seek both their reduction and their emancipation. In contrast, the rigid, enslaving role of the spoken word in *Modern Times* merits it no privileged place in a hierarchy of the materials of human communication. Indeed, to the extent that the spoken word is a primary cause and not just a symptom of the dilemma of *Modern Times,* it deserves to be banished, as the tramp was from the opening ceremony in *City Lights.* Life will proceed through the straightforward immediacy of gesture, look, touch, and natural sound. Calvero virtually elaborates this view in *Limelight* when he tells Terry that "life is a desire, not a meaning . . . the meaning of anything is merely other words for the same thing." Calvero adds that the power of life—"moving the earth, growing the trees"—exists within each individual and requires no words to realize itself.

Yet Chaplin's films from *City Lights* through *Limelight* attest to the existence of forces of destruction and decay as penetrating as the power of life and equally independent of the word. Indeed, at one point Calvero seems able to suggest the power of life only by citing the power of death. "Life is as inevitable as death," he encouragingly tells Terry. And if, as he has Terry claim in his dream of their stage performance, life is "motivated by love," Calvero acknowledges also the hate composing our ruin: "We all despise ourselves—the best of us," he tells Terry.

THE GREAT DICTATOR

If the impulses of love and hate, like those of life and death, can advance without the spoken word, the word remains available to these impulses, as do the numerous non-verbal means of communication. At the start of *The Great Dictator,* the cooperation of the spoken word and non-verbal tools in the service of destruction emerges in a hail of commands not unlike the orders of *Modern Times.* "Fire," "Let 'em have it," "Prepare to attack," and "Forward" are among the imperatives which inaugurate the action during World War I on the Tomanian front, while the voice of the off-screen narrator authoritatively tells of the building of a Tomanian "war machine" that will "strike terror into the hearts of the enemy." Later in the film, at Hynkel's headquarters some twenty years after the end of World War I, the narrator speaks again of the burgeoning Tomanian "enterprise that would build the world's greatest war machine." Machinery and business enterprise, the divinities of *Modern Times,* reign again in *The Great Dictator.*

The machines have become undisguisedly aggressive, and the workers have grown apace. The rhythm of production has been perfected, so there is no waste. Garbitsch is just the name of a general. Destruction is an overwhelming hunger. People are spaghetti. The freshest nutrient is gas. Profits are measured in conquered lands and human deaths. The projections are for a new race—neither captains nor captives of industry, but machine men fueled by "the instinctive pleasure which youth finds in the power of engines."[19] The compass of these projections Erik Erikson estimated as fol-

[19]W.W. Backhaus, "Ueberwindung der Materialschlacht," *Das Reich,* Berlin, 13 July 1941. Cited in Erik H. Erikson, *Childhood and Society* (New York: Norton, 1963), p. 352.

lows: "It would be fatal to brush aside such Nazi mysticism. To defeat motorized Germany, the youth of other countries also had to learn like modern
centaurs to grow together with their fighting machines into new restless beings of passionate precision. Hitler tried to anticipate an age that would experience a motorized world as natural; and to fuse it with the image of a totalitarian 'state machine.'"[20]

Chaplin could not keep the tramp silent. He spoke almost the first instant he appeared on the Tomanian front line of World War I holding a
rope that tied him to the trigger of Big Bertha, the great new cannon. His
first words were "Yes, sir" in reply to the command to "stand by" to fire.
Then, following a second command, he pulled the rope; but already the
tramp was gone. Chaplin's prediction had been correct. The tramp's first
words transformed him. Indeed, his significance was such that they may
have seemed to transform the world. More likely, however, is that they dramatized a transformation that already had occurred and that now had to be
reversed. Furthermore, if spoken words were to help, they could not remain
servile to forces of hate and death. Hitler had written that "the power which
has always started the greatest religious and political avalanches in history
rolling has from time immemorial been the magic power of the spoken
word, and that alone. Particularly the broad masses of the people," he
added, "can be moved only by the power of speech."[21] Nevertheless, if
speech were to roll *back* Hynkel's avalanche, it required the cooperation of
gesture, touch, and the other tools of the tramp's masterful trade. No single
instrument would suffice to restore the power of life; all had been sub-
verted, and all had to retort in concert.

The power of life, perhaps always more fragile than Calvero would
admit, has become so diminished that the sun, the barber informs Schultz,
appears to be "shining upward . . . defying the laws of gravity." Humanity
may be mistaking darkness for light, cold for heat, and entertaining numerous other dangerous inversions and substitutions. Hynkel's warlike gibberish, for example, which supersedes the tramp's love song of *Modern Times,*
is being officially translated in English as an overture of peace. Yet the
sounds of Hynkel's murderous speech choke the dictator. They boomerang
as certainly as did the shell which turned against the barber at the Tomanian
front.

The tramp was a figure who existed at the edge of society, but his quest
for food, shelter, and love was so central to survival that it placed him at the
center of our attention. While his antagonists usually left his kind of quest
behind them, or out of sight, he remained an endangered species. It was not
this fact alone which distinguished him, however, but also the intensity of

[20]*Childhood and Society,* pp. 352-353.
[21]Adolf Hitler, *Mein Kampf,* trans. Ralph Manheim (Boston: Houghton Mifflin, 1971),
pp. 106-107.

The Great Dictator (Courtesy of the Museum of Modern Art/Film Stills Archive)

his desire, almost regardless of its object. As he demonstrated in *City Lights,* he had the gift of making a cigar butt or a flower seem as essential to survival as a morsel of bread. Yet in the expression of both his intense desire and its frequent frustration, references to good were plentiful even if the food was not. In *Modern Times* the feeding machine is one example. Another is the chicken that the tramp uses as a funnel through which to pour liquid for a fellow worker who is trapped in a machine. It is in a dining room, moreover, after his roast duck has been despoiled, that the tramp finally sings. Earlier in the film his fantasy of a home for himself and the gamin concluded as the two of them cut into a huge, juicy steak. In *The Gold Rush* his fantasy of love is expressed in the dance of the Oceana rolls. Another instance of a fantasy linked at least indirectly to food occurs in *City Lights.* During the boxing match, the trainer of the battered tramp dissolves into the consoling image of the blind girl while he rubs the tramp's stomach. In addition to their physiological funcions, the stomach and food were the stuff of the tramp's dreams.

Consequently, Hynkel's belligerence is not reduced when it is characterized as the most extensive assault against eating in all of Chaplin's cinema. Following Hynkel's first harangue, Herring warns that even worse is needed to "get the people's minds off their stomach." The warning summarizes the enormity of Hynkel's attack on human nature. The workers in Hynkel's factories are fed "synthetic food" and bread filled with sawdust. Perhaps because Hynkel offers tirades instead of food, he assumes at the military demonstration that Napaloni is talking when he simply is chewing peanuts. In Hynkel's feverish hands, spaghetti and bananas become human bodies and wills to be stretched and broken; sandwiches become bombs to hurl into bowls of punch. Wine and champagne are not for drinking, but for spilling on the eve of war. Coins fill the barber's pudding, and a metallic rattle rises from his stomach.

The tramp's art of mime and dance is transformed by Hynkel into a lethal, narcissistic ballet with the balloon globe. The tramp's playful, libidinal mouth which issued the boisterous kiss at the end of *Modern Times* has become a gnashing organ of hate.[22] Moreover, the endless dissolves between Hynkel and the barber finally have yielded a new creature with the voice of Hynkel, blasting like a machine gun into the street, and the body of the barber, faltering and scrambling backwards to the mad beat of the voice— which, after all, is his own. Yet it is the metallic rattle, symptom of the machine stomach, that justifies as much as do the other transformations in this film of destructive inversions and substitutions the creation of Chaplin on the pulpit, at last a prophet who can swallow and talk without choking.

"The hate of men will pass, and dictators die, and the power they took from the people will return to the people." This hopeful prophecy may not sound overpowering, but the speech may represent another transformation for Chaplin; an act of self-destruction perhaps, but also of growth. The step is difficult: "You must talk," Schultz says. "I can't." "You must." In a world where "only the voice of Hynkel was heard," Chaplin ascends, unmasks himself, and admits a stranger, the spoken word, into the structure

[22]See Weston LaBarre, *The Human Animal* (Chicago: The University of Chicago Press, 1954), pp. 163-165, for succinct comments on libidinal aspects of the human mouth.

The Great Dictator (Courtesy of the Museum of Modern Art/Film Stills Archive)

of his desire. "Don't give yourselves to these unnatural men—machine men with machine minds and machine hearts. You are men!" If the thought does not seem strikingly new, one reason may be that it was the subject of much of his cinema. "Words come to us from a distance; they were there before we were," writes Stanley Cavell in *The Senses of Walden*.[23] Perhaps Chaplin was admitting the spoken word into a meaning already present, and consequently it is enough if he spoke the words fully meaning them.

Chaplin hardly proposes in his films a comprehensive theory of the role of the spoken word in human development. Yet it appears that he would oppose theories, such as the following offered in 1923, which identify the advance of culture almost exclusively with speech: "In short, culture can probably function only on the basis of abstractions, and these in turn seem to be possible only through speech, or through a secondary substitute for spoken language such as writing, numeration, mathematical, and chemical notation, and the like. Culture, then, began when speech was present; and from then on, the enrichment of either meant the further development of the other."[24]

[23]Stanley Cavell, *The Senses of Walden* (New York: Viking, 1974), p. 63.
[24]A.L. Kroeber, *Anthropology: Culture Patterns & Processes* (New York: Harbinger, 1948), p. 33.

Possibly the apparent oversights of such a rigorous claim would encourage Chaplin to support an extreme stance against the spoken word, such as the following: "Since all real intentions and emotions . . . get themselves involuntarily expressed by gesture, look, or sound, voluntary communication, such as language, must have been invented for the purpose of lying or deceiving. People forced to listen to diplomatic jargon and political double talk will be tempted to agree."[25]

Along a similar line of argument, Chaplin might welcome the following assessment of the role of the spoken word in an American family: "They used words to drown out relevant information or as a place to store messages full of trivial information."[26] Finally, in a strife-beset world Chaplin might remember an old argument which associates the spoken word with human differences, and non-verbal communication with global unity. Ray L. Birdwhistell cites this argument which "saw 'verbal' communication as subject to (and responsible for) human diversification while 'nonverbal' communication provided a primitive and underlying base for (and was the resultant of) human unity."[27]

Yet Chaplin would be discouraged from asserting the universality of non-verbal communication by the following observation: "Insofar as I have been able to determine, just as there are no universal words, no sound complexes, which carry the same meaning the world over, there are no body motions, facial expressions or gestures which provoke *identical* responses the world over."[28]

Consequently, Chaplin might settle for a position which stresses the rich interdependence (or interchanneling) of the spoken word and the various non-verbal materials including gesture, look, touch, taste, and odor. Also, with speech no longer considered the only engine of culture, Chaplin might note that the organs of speech do not serve only, or even primarily, to produce the spoken word: "If we examine the functioning of the lips, the tongue and teeth, the palate, the esophagus, the larynx, pharynx, and lungs, we become quickly aware that to call these the 'organs of speech' is to disregard their continuous function as related to breathing and swallowing."[29] If we give thanks for the organs of speech because they enrich our life, we also may give thanks because they allow us life. The same range of gratitude possibly applies to the organs of gesture and touch vital both to survival and to the magic of the tramp's union with the blind girl in *City Lights,* his explosive dance in the factory in *Modern Times,* and his desolate ballet as Hynkel with the balloon globe in *The Great Dictator.* Finally, acknowledgment is

[25]Mario Pei, *The Story of Language* (New York: Mentor, 1965), pp. 25-265. Quoted is Pei's summary of a view he attributes to E.H. Sturtevant.
[26]*Kinesics and Context: Essays on Body Motion Communication,* p. 53.
[27]Ibid., p. 30.
[28]Ibid., p. 24.

due a principle that perhaps makes human survival and human enrichent interdependent, even inseparable, just as it unifies Whitehead's "three-fold urge." This principle and the variety of means for its realization Ernst Cassirer discusses as follows:

> The principle of symbolism, with its universality, validity, and general applicability, is the magic word, the Open Sesame! giving access to the specifically human world, to the world of human culture. Once man is in possession of this magic key further progress is assured. Such progress is evidently not obstructed or made possible by any lack in the sense material. . . . Human culture derives its specific character and its intellectual and moral values, not from the material of which it consists, but from its form, its archtectural sculpture. And this form may be expressed in any sense material. Vocal language has a very great technical advantage over tactile language; but the technical defects of the latter do not destroy its essential use. The free development of symbolic thought and symbolic expression is not obstructed by the use of tactile signs in the place of vocal one. If the child has succeeded in grasping the meaning of human language, it does not matter in which particular material this meaning is accessible to it. As the case of Helen Keller proves, man can construct his symbolic world out of the poorest and scantiest materials. The thing of vital importance is not the individual bricks and stones but their general *function* as an architectural form. In the realm of speech it is their general symbolic function which vivifies the material signs and "makes them speak." Without this vivifying principle the human world would indeed remain deaf and mute.[30]

[29]Ibid., p. 76.
[30]Ernst Cassirer, *An Essay on Man* (New York: Bantam, 1944), pp. 38-39.

CHAPTER 5.

The Grapes of Wrath (1940): Thematic Emphasis through Visual Style

VIVIAN C. SOBCHACK

SINCE ITS RELEASE IN 1940, THE FILM VERSION OF *THE GRAPES OF Wrath* has attracted enormous and enduring critical and popular attention.[1] Yet, in some ways it has also remained a neglected film, a film obscured by the shadow of its illustrious parentage (John Ford out of John Steinbeck) and by its generic absorption into that body of culturally significant art representative of and concerned with Depression America. Certainly, *The Grapes of Wrath* was and still is a highly visible film; its popularity as a "classic" is evidenced by its frequent appearance on prestigious commercial television series, at cinema club retrospectives, and in literature, film, and American Studies classrooms across the country. In addition, the film enjoys a wealth of critical consideration—as an adaptation of a work of fiction, as a cultural artifact which illuminates various aspects of popular American ideology and myth, and as part of the *oeuvre* of a major film *auteur*. Paradoxically, however, this widely considered film has suffered from visual neglect. Examined from several critical perspectives, *The Grapes of Wrath* has been more frequently looked *into* than looked *at*. Its visual surfaces have been hardly explored and mapped, its texture and tone have been rarely considered as functions of its imagery, and its dominant thematic emphasis has been only minimally related to its visual style.

The reasons for this literal and figurative oversight can be linked, of course, to the myopia demanded by focused and limited critical discourse. Adaptation criticism, for example, is practiced through a comparison of a novel and film. And, no matter how sophisticated and cinematically liter-

---

[1] John Ford directed *The Grapes of Wrath* for Twentieth Century–Fox.

ate such adaptation criticism is, its comparisons tend to gravitate toward the literary values and structures which supply common ground between the two art forms. Thus, whether the literature/film critic is ignorant of the complexity of a film's visual text or conversant with film aesthetics, the bulk of adaptation criticism seems to consider a film like *The Grapes of Wrath* almost solely in terms of the literary structures which dictate its narrative action, characterization, and thematic emphasis. George Bluestone's influential *Novels into Film* and Warren French's more recent *Filmguide to The Grapes of Wrath* spend the major portion of their discussion and analysis of the film dealing with its adherence to or departure from Steinbeck's parent work on the basis of dialogue selection, scene deletions or additions, characters maintained, dropped or synthesized, and the structural arrangement of narrative activity.[2] What the image *looks* like is neglected for a consideration of what *happens* in it. The subject matter is considered dominant to its visual treatment. Similarly, what happens next is considered more important than how the images happen next. Indeed, images are ignored as affective and cumulative units of meaning and texture which accrue to express the film's theme in conjunction with its verbal and literary devices. Rather, they are regarded as discrete particles of larger dramatic sequences and greatly subordinate in importance to what dialogue and action take place within and through them. Although both Bluestone and French describe various visual aspects of *The Grapes of Wrath,* they have difficulty in their respective methods integrating what they see with what the film says and means. In the final analysis, their differing conclusions about the thematic emphasis of the film and its relationship to Steinbeck's novel both derive from a primarily literary approach to the film text.

A similar approach is taken by those critics whose interest in the film is more cultural than aesthetic. *The Grapes of Wrath* has been praised for its courageous realism and its social relevance as well as damned for its conservatism and timidity in addressing the problems it pretended to tackle. It has also been analyzed and discussed as a cultural and social barometer, expressive of those "meanings and values that were a part of the dominant culture"[3] at the time the film was made and seen. If the cultural approach is not quite literary, it is often too literal in its response to the film's imagery. Content again is predominant and considered independently from its visual treatment. For example, at its release, the fact

[2] George Bluestone, *Novels Into Film* (1957; rpt. Berkeley: Univ. of California Press, 1973); Warren French, *Filmguide to The Grapes of Wrath* (Bloomington: Indiana Univ. Press, 1973).
[3] Charles J. Maland, *American Visions: The Films of Chaplin, Ford, Capra, and Welles, 1936–1941* (New York: Arno Press, 1977), 367.

that the film dealt with relatively contemporaneous subject matter, that it cinematically seemed to articulate the world and the plight of Dust Bowl migrants, and that the material content of its images bore a superficially strong resemblance to the physical world outside the theatre attracted far greater critical attention than did the film's stylized and abstracting treatment of its subject matter and physical content. Indeed, the film was initially reviewed and apotheosized more in terms of its relationship to actuality, to documentary realism, than treated as a successful adaptation of a novel or a work of cinematic fiction and art. *Life* magazine called it "bitter, authentic, honest,"[4] and Edwin Locke, a documentary filmmaker, compared the film favorably with the documentary films of Pare Lorentz and the Depression photographs of Dorothea Lange, saying it "set a precedent for contemporary and historical honesty in movie-making."[5]

Certainly in recent years cultural criticism of *The Grapes of Wrath* has moved far afield from measuring the film's social worth on the basis of its realism. Now the pendulum has swung the other way and the film's value as a cultural artifact is based on its relation to myth, to its expression of a popular social vision which Charles Maland, for example, sees conveyed through the construction of "a symbolic universe meant to present a pattern of values and meanings in a popular fictional form to a broad audience." But despite the increased sophistication of such cultural analysis, the notion of social vision is linked only rarely to actual vision, to the integration of the film's images and visual texture with the reading of its narrative and cultural content. Thus, while Maland may conclude that *The Grapes of Wrath* is one in a number of contemporaneous films whose concern for the American family "symbolically represents a larger shift in the American film industry at large from a social criticism to affirmation, another indication of the decline of radicalism between 1936 and 1941," that contention is never given the ample and cogent visual support the film could provide.[6]

One might expect that the literary emphasis of adaptation criticism and the literal emphasis of cultural criticism directed toward *The Grapes of Wrath* would be counterbalanced by the more visually-oriented attention of film criticism. Not bound through intent or academic discipline to compare the film to the novel or to investigate its place in a cultural and historical *gestalt*, cineastes might be expected to consider the film more

[4] French, 59.
[5] Edwin Locke, review of *The Grapes of Wrath, Films* (Spring 1940), rpt. in *American Film Criticism*, ed. by Stanley Kauffmann with Bruce Henstell (New York: Liveright, 1972), 389.
[6] Maland, ix, 169–70.

freely as an autonomous work of visual as well as verbal art. Unfortunately, such has not been the case. As Steinbeck's novel has obscured the less verbal aspects of the film from literary critics, and as the film's relationship to a particularly fascinating period of social and cultural history has narrowed the focus of cultural critics, so has John Ford's position as a pantheon *auteur* blurred the specific vision of film critics. Rather than being considered on its own merits and discussed on the basis of its aesthetic development and coherence, *The Grapes of Wrath* has been regarded primarily within the context of Ford's entire body of work. As such, it has been either seen as less than a major work and ignored, or discussed less visually than thematically as part of the director's continuing vision of what Andrew Sarris calls a "nostalgic" and "family level of history."[7] In the first instance, the film is often given short critical shrift because it is not a Western, because it was made at a mid-point in Ford's career which has garnered less attention than his work in the 1930s and after the 1940s, and because it is regarded as somehow less "pure" Ford for being an adaptation of a classic novel. (It is interesting to note that most of the close textual analysis of Ford films is practiced on those *not* adapted from literature, and that although Ford used literary sources for ten of his films, only *The Informer* and *Stagecoach* have merited nearly unanimous praise and attention from cineastes.[8]) In the second instance, that film criticism which has dealt with *The Grapes of Wrath* in any detail has done so in terms of its thematic concerns as derived from its narrative structure and its general resemblance to other Ford films. The film itself and its visual specificity have fallen victim to how a given critic feels about Ford. For someone like Sarris, the film's apolitical evocation of nostalgia through its "humanizing Steinbeck's economic insects into heroic champions of an agrarian order of family and community"[9] is clearly one of the film's chief virtues. On the other hand, in a negative "reassessment" of Ford, Michael Dempsey castigates the director and his work for political conservatism and easy sentimentality and says disparagingly of *The Grapes of Wrath*, "Ford the contemporary of Dreiser and Dos Passos and even Steinbeck gives us . . . a hollow celebration of that emptiest abstraction, The People, along with a cop-out analysis which avoids blam-

[7] Andrew Sarris, *The American Cinema, Directors and Directions 1929–1968* (New York: E. P. Dutton, 1958), 43–49, quote p. 44.

[8] The two most detailed textual analyses of specific Ford films are "John Ford's *Young Mr. Lincoln*," *Screen*, 13 (Autumn 1972) translated from the original in *Cahiers du Cinéma*, No. 223 (1970); and "*The Searchers:* Materials and Approaches," *Screen Education*, No. 17 (Autumn 1975). See also H. Peter Stowell, "John Ford's Literary Sources: From Realism to Romance," *Literature/Film Quarterly*, 5 (Spring 1977), 164–65.

[9] Sarris, *The American Cinema*, 45.

ing any individual or interest for the plight of the Okies."[10] These statements, however, whether for or against Ford as a film artist of merited
stature, are not backed up by careful consideration of the film's imagery.
Unfortunately, that imagery is too often assumed as a given by critics
anxious to get on with the job of dealing with Ford's themes. As Pierre
Greenfield notes, a great deal of such criticism presents "an exposition of
Fordian philosophy without any serious justification of it."[11] Film critics
are therefore as guilty as literary and cultural critics in their general neglect of the visual elements of *The Grapes of Wrath*.

This tripartite oversight needs some redress—not necessarily because
The Grapes of Wrath is a great work of film art (which is arguable), but
because it is a *film* and it is shown on a screen and has a *visual* presence.
The way we read and perceive it is as much a function of its visual
imagery as it is of its literary and dramatic and cultural content. Indeed, in
most cases the strength and immediacy of a film's visual imagery is at
least equal to if not far greater than its literary content—even if its power
is not acknowledged or articulated. Because of this power, a film's visual
imagery merits as much attention when it is supportive of literary and
cultural and thematic analyses as when it is more flamboyantly contradictory or quietly subversive. In the case of *The Grapes of Wrath*, the consensus of critical response has been nearly unanimous in its recognition
that Ford's film is different in tone and spirit from Steinbeck's novel and
that the film is a politically conservative and poetic work whose major
theme is the value and resilience of the American family. That consensus
was not arrived at merely by an examination of the film's structural relationship to the novel which was its source, or by a cultural analysis of its
place in a *gestalt* of populist art, or by its thematic echo of what its
principal creator expressed in his work both before and after it. That
consensus of critical response to *The Grapes of Wrath* was also generated
by the *seeing* of the film, by the intuitive integration of the film's imagery
into the critical act. The apprehension of that imagery and its function
needs both appropriate recognition and articulation.

It is agreed that Ford's transliteration of Steinbeck's book to the screen
restructures the values of an essentially realistic and political novel and
emphasizes those aspects of the parent work which are the most consistent with the filmmaker's own values and personal vision. Although both
Steinbeck and Ford do share a common bond in their focus on American
institutions and ideology, in their dramatic humanization of those institu-

---

[10] Michael Dempsey, "John Ford: A Reassessment," *Film Quarterly*, 28 (Summer 1975), 5.
[11] Pierre Greenfield, "Print the Fact: For and Against the Films of John Ford," *Take One*,
5 (Nov. 1977), 15.

tions and ideas through the medium of proletariat protagonists, and in their use of humor and folklore, their sympathies and interests are dramatically divergent. Steinbeck's novels emphasize the importance of the present, the harshness of reality, the potential of radical politics, and the need for social and political change. Conversely, Ford's films emphasize the values of the past and soften the harsher aspects of historical reality with nostalgia; his film worlds are apolitical and atemporal and his aesthetic evocation of America revolves around the harmony and established traditions of community. Indeed, his life's work reveals a reverence for those human values which are most simple and universal, a reverence which balks and trembles at the necessity for progress and change. As Andrew Sarris cogently indicates in *The John Ford Movie Mystery*, "Ford never lost his faith in the benign drift of American history . . . and intuitively redirected the pessimistic class conflicts in . . . Steinbeck . . . into relatively optimistic family chronicles." [12]

The novel, however, is less concerned about seven months in the life of the Joad family than it is about the relationship of men to land, about an untenable economic system, and about the inevitable awakening of a communal revolutionary consciousness in the oppressed and exploited. The Joad family is only a sharply-focused point from which the novel continually moves out far beyond the limited awareness of its main characters to deal with epic social and political issues, abstractions which—of dramatic necessity—must find embodiment in the concrete and specific, in characterization and action and the details of physical imagery. Although the Joad family takes on the bulk of this dramatic function in the novel, Steinbeck has structured the book in such a way that the reader cannot forget that the family is only one of many families, that it is part of a larger organism composed not only of families but also of land and plants and animals and weather. The Joads are constantly counterbalanced by the equal emphasis given in the intercalary chapters to larger issues than their immediate survival and on larger groups than the family. As a result, their family unit is not metaphorical in function; it is, instead, illustrative. Its importance in the novel is not in its mythic cohesion and endurance, but in its realistic specificity. The Joads comprise only half of the novel's emphasis, enjoy only half its attention. And the universal theme of family solidarity is greatly subordinate to the larger emphasis Steinbeck gives to a cry for the solidarity of men in a definite political and economic context. Indeed, as Warren French points out, the novel charts the progress of the Joads' "growing out of the narrow con-

[12] Andrew Sarris, *The John Ford Movie Mystery* (Bloomington: Indiana Univ. Press, 1975), 161.

cept of 'fambly' in the blood-relationship sense to a concept of membership in the entire 'human family.' '' [13]

As has been pointed out by many critics including those cited here, Ford is not particularly concerned with the Joads' integration into the family of man. Nor is he particularly interested in relating them to an economic or political milieu. Although there is a great deal of dialogue in the film which relates the family to the land, to a larger population, and to a political climate *verbally,* the visual interest of the film is on the Joads as an isolated and universal family unit which transcends the particularity and specificity of time and place. Certainly, the Joads on screen are specific and particular in their photographic realization; it is the nature of the medium to particularize "characters" and "place" far more exactly and idiosyncratically than written language. But the visual treatment of Henry Fonda's Tom, Jane Darwell's Ma, Charley Grapewin's Grampa, John Carradine's Casey, and John Qualen's Muley softens their physical individuality and resonates photographic specificity into expressive metaphor (see Figure 1). Because of the manner in which the major portion of the film has been visually conceived and shot, Steinbeck's multiple themes and simultaneous emphasis have been exchanged for a less epic but equally universal vision, for a scope at once smaller than the novel's in its reduction of politics and economics and social realities to the size of a single romanticized family, and yet also a scope larger than the novel's in its evocation of the survival and endurance of that family against a stylized background which is not limited by time and space. While Charles Maland suggests that Ford's emphasis on the Joads as a familial and communal unit can be linked to the director's natural affinity for Jeffersonian agrarianism, to his belief in independent ownership of land by industrious and hard-working families,[14] the Joads gain their universality from their being dispossessed of their land. Indeed, it is their lack of land (and its lack of photographic reference) which abstracts them into the generalized and poetic space of the montage sequences and places them in cramped close-ups and medium shots isolated in trucks and cars and tents far from communion with anyone but themselves.

Thus, where the novel *moves out* both structurally and imagistically from the Joads to continually emphasize the land, biological presence, and the crush of thousands of migrants on the move, the film's movement visually *closes in* on the Joads, at times to such a degree that they have only a minimal connection with either the land or the rest of society. The characters, of course, do pay lip service to that connection through the

[13] French, 27.
[14] Maland, 164–66.

Figure 1. The Joads and their friends often live out relationships in universalized space. The film visually softens physical individuality and instead emphasizes expressive metaphor. (All photographs of *The Grapes of Wrath* are courtesy of the Lester Glassner Collection.)

dialogue—so much so that a reading of the continuity script alone might result in the impression of a quite different film from the one actually realized on the screen. But that connection is not actually visible through a great portion of the film. Land is not as visible as what French calls "the fresh, temporary look of studio sets." [15] Most of the film was shot indoors or on the studio lot rather than on location in a landscape which might have matched the visual power and presence of the Monument Valley Ford used in so many of his Westerns. Though there are some brief long shots of authentic locations in some of the montage sequences, their open quality primarily serves as a striking reminder of the film's overwhelmingly closed visual construction. If one *looks* at the film's imagery, it seems rather off the mark to read *The Grapes of Wrath* as a land tragedy.

Some early critics noted this absence of land imagery in the film and remarked on Ford's departure from Steinbeck in this regard. Generally, these astute reviewers were filmmakers themselves, attuned to the visual

[15] French, 18.

qualities of film. Edwin Locke, for example, came to the film with a background as a member of the U.S. Film Service, a government agency whose films specialized in evoking the beauty of the American landscape:

> It is a pity that Ford's sense of environment has not come through as well as his sense of people. The opening of the picture is greatly weakened because he has given us no feeling of the country or the people's background. Where are the vast stretches of the dust bowl and the tiny houses as lonely as ships at sea? Where is the dust? It is hard to believe that Ford has ever seen *The Plow That Broke the Plains*. It is baffling to hear that a camera crew was sent to Oklahoma along Route 66; certainly but a few feet of their film was used. It is regrettable that the Joads were snatched across the beautiful and terrifying expanses of the country in a few pans and process shots; we could justly have expected more. We could have expected more of what it is like to be tractored off the land, more than the knocking over of a prop house by a Caterpillar roaming at large, more than a hackneyed montage of clanking monsters in abstract maneuvers. We might have all these things, and a richer picture, if Ford had followed a little further the documentary technique that is now being talked about in connection with his work.[16]

Similarly, Pare Lorentz, director of *The Plow That Broke the Plains* and *The River,* was disappointed by the lack of will to evoke the land and its moods:

> . . . he [Nunnally Johnson, the screenwriter] needed to think in terms of skies and brown land and, most of all, wind. He needed only to have written "drought" and then left it to the director to re-create the feeling of those dusty plains tilting from Oklahoma clear up to Canada, with their miserable huts and busted windmills. In fact, he needed only to have gone to the panhandle of Oklahoma and Texas and western Kansas and the Dakotas and eastern Colorado and said: "Photograph this—here is where they came from."
> As he did not, then Director John Ford (who, by virtue of going to Zion Park in Utah to photograph his outdoor sequences in *Stagecoach,* made a Western action picture into a thing of beauty) at least might have started his picture with the Great Plains instead of with scenes that, even though they were from the book, did not give you a feeling of the land.[17]

Less important for their recognition of how Ford's film broke a certain faith with Steinbeck's book or with natural history than for their recognition that the visual images of a film are crucial to its meaning, these

---

[16] Locke, 387–88. (*The Plow That Broke the Plains* was made in 1936 by Pare Lorentz for the U.S. Film Service.)
[17] Pare Lorentz, review of *The Grapes of Wrath* in *Lorentz on Film* (New York: Hopkinson and Blake, 1975), 184.

comments indicate the closed quality which permeates Ford's work, his visual *choice* which omits wide-open spaces and panoramic vistas of either parched earth or pastures of plenty. Indeed, until Ford brings the Joads into Hooverville—halfway through the film—the camera isolates them, disconnects them, perhaps even protects them from larger forces and larger movements which give the novel an epic quality.

The general composition of *The Grapes of Wrath* is consciously controlled and tight. For the most part, the action occurs in visually limited space—limited either by its actual spatial parameters and tight framing or by the amount of it we are allowed to see by virtue of the given illumination. Right from the beginning—after one brief long shot—we move inward. Tom hitches a ride and we are confined for the first of many times in the cab of a truck, cramped in its interior or looking in close-up through the windshield at Tom and the driver. While Maland's comment that the film "consists almost entirely of the Joads riding in their ramshackle truck"[18] is an exaggeration, it is true that the characters are usually cramped into a cluttered screen and limited space (see Figure 2). Not only is a good deal of the Joads' odyssey confined and isolated in automotive interiors, but a large share of the dramatic action is also confined indoors: in cluttered or darkly oppressive rooms, tents, or shacks, all of which close in the characters. Out of the 50 "scenes" French describes as comprising the units of the film, a total of 25 are shot (entirely or in part) within the Joad truck or within an oppressive interior.[19]

Those compositions which occur in "open space" are also chafingly contained and limited by their cardboard and set-like quality and by the relative lack of internal movement of both the camera and the characters. Although, for example, Tom's initial encounter with Casey takes place in an "open" field punctuated by an overly-aestheticized willow tree, the camera stays in one spot and the characters stand immobile except for occasionally and uncomfortably shifting their weight from foot to foot. Containing their physical movement in such a way, Ford contains the frame as well. The visual effect is that there is no field outside the limits of the camera's vision, no land—rather, there is a non-space, or a studio set covered with false and aestheticized earth. The long long shot which concludes the sequence shows Tom and Casey silhouetted against the darkening sky as they set out for the Joad homestead. But the shot—however long and panoramic—is more closed than open, more memorable for its composed quality and artful lighting and static vision than it is for an evocation of a real world with real earth and dust which is really

---

[18] Maland, 154.
[19] French, 38–56. (I have not included those scenes shot in brightly lit interiors.)

Figure 2. The Joad family is often abstracted from context through framing.

blowing away. Uncle John's farm yard is no more open spatially than a stage setting which pretends to realism. And both the Keene Ranch and the Wheat Patch government camp seem patently artificial in their respective evocations of squalor and darkness and spanking clean brightness. The effect of this spatial closure on the film is not necessarily negative, but it does communicate the visual message that the world which the Joads inhabit is less than real and vital. *Their* vitality against the cardboard settings, the Edward Hopper skies and contrived grimness and beauty, makes them more important than the problems they face—for they are physically present and dramatically highlighted while the Depression and the land blowing away and the rest of the world are shown as an abstracted stage set or ignored altogether.

The static compositions, the tableaux-like posturing of the characters, and the pattern of the editing also add to the visual elements which lift the Joads out of connection with things immediate and specific and create of their struggle and endurance something universal and iconic. The camera rarely moves, preferring for the most part to look at its subjects from eye-level and mid-distance. This point of view produces images which look at times like the same view of the action one would get watching a stage production or historical tableau; the entire human figure is seen in the frame and so the image does not extend itself imaginatively out into the world, and the relative immobility of the camera creates a sense of the characters entering and exiting from wings as opposed to the camera's seeking them out. The one literally jarring exception to the general pattern of composition and camera and subject movement is the visual treatment given to the Joad's entrance into Hooverville, and to the fight which occurs in that tent city. The subjective camera which moves as a member of the Joad family through the street visually opens up the film as it, paradoxically, limits its objectivity. Both the subjective vision and the camera movement are more jolting than the supposedly shocking content presented, as is the later fight sequence which contains so much more movement and randomness than we have seen before. Indeed, generally the dramatic activity or stage "business" within the frame is rarely spontaneous or random, and the relative lack of physical movement by the characters when someone has something important to say (a "speech" such as Casey's on not being a preacher, or Muley's on being "touched," or Ma's on Tom's not becoming mean) makes the dialogue denser than it might otherwise be if lightened by some random motion. Instead, such speeches are met with stillness, are photographed as tableaux removing the characters from a peopled and physically present environment into the realm of archetype and iconography. The settings of the Joad farm, of Uncle John's farm, of the cabin in the pickers' camp, in the tents of Hooverville, in the neat exteriors of the government camp—not one of them has the uncontrolled and extraneous quality of realistic and immediate art or document. Not a chicken stirs, and every object seems to exist for dramatic and atmospheric rather than natural purpose. As a result the social and political and economic problems which the characters face seem far more dramatic than real, far more aesthetically and narratively functional than immediately pressing.

The way in which the film is edited further stresses the archetypal and iconic aspects of the Joads by creating stylized temporal relationships between shots. The Joads exist in montage time, for example—shots linked together rhythmically or superimposed so as to convey the passage of time without really being specific. As well, the Joads exist in what might be called "tableau time"—that is, they are seen in set pieces, in scenes which are not dynamically connected or visually continuous to others. Warren French has derogatorily commented about the perfunctory nature of the editing, criticizing not only the narrative puzzles it presents with the disappearance of Noah Joad or Rosasharn's baby, but also with the use of "sharp breaks between scenes" and the lack of associational editing, the "switch from one scene to another by cutting from an object in one scene to a similar object in another." He also notes that Ford "apparently preferred to break the picture into a series of discrete episodes by the use of sharply delineated fadeouts and fadeins." These editorial devices add to the film the "compensating universality" French sees as a substitute for the bite and timeliness of Steinbeck's novel. The lack of simultaneity through cross-cutting, the abstractness of the montages, the measured and highly theatrical fades, and even the one flashback sequence in which Muley "tells" what happened to the land— all are stylistic choices which serve to abstract the Joads.[20]

Whereas the average viewer might not notice the abstracting qualities of the film's composition and editing, it is nearly impossible not to notice that the film is dark. French points out that "almost exactly half the action takes place at night or under dimly lit conditions,"[21] a proportion which might allow one to also argue that almost exactly half the film takes place during the day or in brightly lit conditions. The dramatic weight of the film, however, falls on the dark side, for if one compares those scenes which occur in varying degrees of darkness with those which take place in relatively bright light it becomes obvious that the former are more important to the narrative and more intense in their emotional content than the latter. Casey and Tom's reunion is marked by the dimness of approaching dusk. The long and highly dramatic scene in the deserted Joad cabin is shot in candlelight as Casey and Tom are joined by Muley who relates in the dark present and in the punctuating brightness of a flashback what has occurred to the farmers and their land. Ma Joad's brief but powerful review of her life's souvenirs occurs in the dimness of the stripped house. The Joads' first stay in a campground with other migrants and their encounter with the man who tells them about the false promise of the handbills is at night. The Joads' desert crossing in which Granma dies is also dark. And nearly the entire 22 minutes of the Joads' sojourn at the Keene Ranch is played in the dusky interior of the filthy cabin or at night—as is the important dramatic sequence under the bridge in which both Casey and Tom and their companion strikebreakers fight the Keene guards, a fight which leaves Casey dead and Tom hurt and guilty of murder. Finally, even the climactic scene in the Wheat Patch camp occurs at night; despite the celebratory nature of the Saturday night dance and its triumphant drama in which the migrants form a cohesive and persuasive group to oust their enemies, the sequence is dark—as is the related scene in which Tom says goodby to Ma and delivers his "I'll be ever'where" speech before

[20] French, 35, 33, 38.
[21] Ibid., 34.

disappearing into the blackness. The drama and narrative impetus in the daylight scenes are anecdotal compared to the force of the night scenes. And, again, it is only in Hooverville that Ford provides a marked exception.

The chiaroscuro lighting of a major portion of the film does more than merely supply atmosphere and support the thematic darkness of the Joads' odyssey. It also functions as a technique which is abstracting, which again brings a sense of closure to the screen image by obscuring the connection between various objects in the frame and turning the viewer's attention inward toward the Joads. The shadows spatially blot out the rest of the world much of the time and are, as well, oppressive and confining. Consider, for example, the sequence in the Joads' abandoned farmhouse near the beginning of the film. Composed quite statically and shot in darkness punctuated only by candlelight and flashlight, the images curl into themselves rather than extend outwards to the corners of the frame and to a consciousness of a physical world in motion beyond its confines. The camera's emphasis is on faces, faces which become not quite real in the semi-darkness, faces which are isolated in cinematographer Gregg Toland's "web of shadows and night" visually reinforcing, for instance, "Muley's belief that he is just 'an ol' graveyard ghos'."[22]

Either through the actual proximity of close-ups or the masking effect of darkness in the medium shots, the abundance of expressionistic cinematography which emphasizes the pale faces and glistening eyes of the characters (see Figure 3) is not really counterbalanced to any great degree by an equivalent insistence on realistic and clearly-defined imagery. Indeed, the personal intensity and attention of the camera on the faces of the Joads is never matched in kind by equally intense or emphatic shots of the people they meet or the land they supposedly revere—with one exception. Muley's flashback sequence is as stylized and intense and visually compressed as any in the film. The land as a force is *visually* acknowledged in such a manner that it is made as transcendent and universal as the Joads. In one stylized and uncharacteristic high angle shot, Muley squats on his land, alone and in dark contrast to the barren lightness of the earth around him. And in another, the final shot of the sequence, the camera moves from Muley and his family to isolate their shadows upon the ground marked with the destructive tracks of the caterpillar tractor. The confluence in the frame of the men's shadows, the trail of destruction, and the land itself is as expressive and compressed as Charles Maland suggests in his analysis of the sequence.[23] But the expres-

---

[22] Stowell, 167.
[23] Maland, 156–59.

Figure 3. This production still demonstrates the effect of chiaroscuro lighting used throughout John Ford's rendering of *The Grapes of Wrath*.

sive weight and metaphorical force of the flashback's visual articulation is diluted by its early and singular placement in the film. The same is true of the visual style and brighter illumination in the sequence in Hooverville. It is only in Hooverville that Ford connects the Joads visually with a context which unites them with other people. The tent city is teeming with spontaneous humanity. It is more concretely physical in its presence than any other location in the film—a world of dirt and dust and texture which Ford let Toland photograph in daylight. The images of Hooverville are less moody, less artfully shadowed and expressionistic than elsewhere in the film; the viewer is allowed to see and thereby experience the texture of material things, the gray and grainy images effectively evoking the feel of grit and dust. Because there is more light, the composition seems freer and the boundaries of the frame seem larger and more potentially extendable; our attention is not directed inward to the center of the frame as it is through a great deal of the rest of the film. Because of the relatively bright illumination, because there is more random movement of more characters who are visually seen in contiguity with the Joads, and because there is a selection of more spontaneous visual detail (it is hard to control the flapping of clothes drying on a line), the episode in Hooverville is singular in its attempt at documentary realism. Although it is memorable, it is also jolting in its contrast to the film's predominant visual style, a style acknowledged by both Ford and Toland for its "blackness."[24] That blackness is less grim than abstracting, less harsh than protective; the Joads and the viewer are removed from a visually urgent and engaging context and the result is a predominant imagery which seems highly aestheticized, staged, and framed.

The lighting in *The Grapes of Wrath* and its abstracting effects derive from the *chiaroscuro* practiced by the German Expressionists in their nightmare paintings and films and, indeed, practiced by Ford himself in two highly expressionist and stylized works which rank among his personal favorites—*The Informer* (1935) and *The Fugitive* (1947). The visual ambience created by the lighting in *The Grapes of Wrath* evokes the vague outlines of night and dream rather than the harsh specificity of daylight and Depression America. In a brief but cogent discussion of the film's lighting, French concludes that through the lighting "Ford converted what could have been a nerve-wracking social protest . . . into an artful product that resolves all transient violence in a serene meditation."[25]

That serene meditation is, of course, on the Joads' "coherence as a family . . . not as a class,"[26] and the film's appeal and emotional force derive from the simplicity and directness of Ford's focus. Indeed, Maland

---

[24] John Ford speaks of this in Peter Bogdanovich, *John Ford* (Berkeley: Univ. of California Press, 1968), 78.
[25] French, 34–35.
[26] Sarris, *The John Ford Movie Mystery*, 96.

points out the film's ability to satisfy "the intense desire of many Americans to be involved, through their sentiments at least, in the human problems caused by the depression."[27] But one might amend Maland's observation by suggesting that Ford's film was so satisfying precisely *because* it involved the contemporaneous viewer primarily on the level of sentiment, because its transcendent vision of the Joads as an archetypal family freed the viewer from the responsibility for specific social action. It is not only the lighting (as French suggests) but the whole visual style of the film which lifts the Joads from specificity and immediacy, which elevates them far from spatial and temporal urgency. Indeed, the film is most powerful in its use of what might be identified from today's perspective as the visual shorthand of a Depression iconography. Through its images it evokes the softened and popularized form of the Depression—its outline—without assaulting the viewer with the harsh demands of actual content.

Although he sometimes confuses the content of the imagery with its softened treatment, George Bluestone senses the iconic visual quality of *The Grapes of Wrath:*

> Behind the director's controlling hand is the documentary eye of a Pare Lorentz or a Robert Flaherty, of the vision in those stills produced by the Resettlement Administration in its volume, *Land of the Free . . .*, or in Walker Evans' shots for *Let Us Now Praise Famous Men. . . .* Gregg Toland's photography is acutely conscious of the pictorial values of land and sky, finding equivalents for those haunting images of erosion which were popularized for the New Deal's reclamation program and reflected in Steinbeck's prose.[28]

While Bluestone seems off the mark in his efforts to prove how the film and novel share a common tone or evoke similar land imagery, he is to the point in noting the film's visual resemblance to the documentary poetry of both Robert Flaherty and Pare Lorentz. Both of these filmmakers dealt in a kind of generalized imagery which has given their work universal qualities. Man's struggles against the landscape of Flaherty's *Nanook of the North* and *Man of Aran* are as primal and timeless as they are physically concretized in specific geography, and the editing techniques of Lorentz combined with his use of abstracting close-ups of water and land and objects give to both *The Plow That Broke the Plains* and *The River* a temporal and spatial vagueness which is powerful and iconic. Indeed, despite Lorentz' criticisms of the absence of land imagery in *The Grapes of Wrath,* Ford's visual abstraction of the Joads parallels in style and effect that documentary filmmaker's timeless and aspatial treatment of the ecological problems of the Middle West. On the other hand, Bluestone displays a visual insensitivity to style when he equates Ford's film and the

---

[27] Maland, 161.
[28] Bluestone, 161.

photography of Walker Evans. The hard-edged clarity, sharp focus, and unsentimental asceticism of Evans' work is removed in both sensibility and style from Flaherty, Lorentz, and John Ford. *The Grapes of Wrath* only superficially resembles the always specific and unsparing definition in either Evans' or Dorothea Lange's Depression photography; if there is a likeness it is in content rather than style. A visual counterpart to the general effect of the film's imagery can be more readily found in the work of a fine artist who tempered the realistic subject matter of his content with a softening of focus, a rounding off of hard edges and sharp contrasts; *The Grapes of Wrath* looks more like the blunted vision of Edward Hopper than the acutely-detailed vision of the Depression's most acclaimed photographers.

Indeed, the film derives much of its emotional and aesthetic power from its generalized quality, its use of what Bluestone calls "popularized" images which are neither realistic nor documentary as Bluestone's aligning them with documentary filmmakers and photographers would suggest. They serve mythology and metaphor rather than social realism, and while they may often tug at the heartstrings with their sentimental appeal, they rarely incite the viewer to serious thought; they are equivalent not to the harsh prose of Steinbeck's work or the clarity and asceticism of Evans' photographic style, but rather to the emotional appeal of poster art. Thus, much as Ford in his Westerns has used the temporally and spatially circumscribed and compressed world of object and landscape to evoke a mythology which creates its own contained time and space and which owes little to actual history, he has also used the temporally and spatially circumscribed iconography of the Depression to create softened and blunted images which evoke the Depression but which continually contain it in the realm of art. The film abounds with material objects and landscapes which simultaneously concretize and yet abstract the political, economic, and social realities of Steinbeck's chapters about the Joads into poetic and emotional shorthand: the slouched and soiled hats, the caps, the floral print dresses and the haphazardly buttoned sweaters which have come to clothe our emotional associations with the Depression; the static posturing of family groups, stiffly posing for the future with a fascinating self-consciousness which keeps them rigidly facing the camera while they secretly avert their eyes from it; old trucks and jalopies whose geometry is top-heavy as an inverted pyramid—falling apart, choking, and bursting at the seams with material goods gathered together with old clothesline, familiar mattresses, and old kitchen chairs; gas stations and gas pumps somehow evocative of both ordered corporate power in a technological society and the migratory movement of an agricultural people no longer in harmony with the land; industrial machinery glorified by the power conferred by the closeup and low angle, biting into the earth like prehistoric carnivores. The visual imagery of Ford's film uses all this emotional

Figure 4. Ford's tableau compositions draw from Depression iconography.

iconography which has come to us generalized out of specific and harsher pieces of Depression art and life (see Figure 4).

In the final analysis, the film projects the images of a ritualized world, a world in which change is neither possible nor desirable. Instead, survival and endurance and the continuation of traditional values are apotheosized by the Joads and their odyssey through "a timeless world that cages men, while allowing them the freedom of movement to dignify and humanize their lives through action and comedy."[29] This is certainly not the world of John Steinbeck. Rather, the film is the result of the legitimate aesthetic choices made by a director with a reputation at least equal to the novelist's whose work he has translated. By choices, Ford's film is powerful in its realization of "Family." His style is not miscalculated or unconsidered. And it is not merely derived from the changes made in the literary elements of the film. The static compositions and camera placement, the artificiality of the studio set, the non-dynamic editing, and the chiaroscuro lighting and its resultant softening of harsh contrasts and hard edges, coupled with Ford's neglect of a concrete political and social context and his omission of those sequences which would make the family less attractive than it is—all serve his emotional exploration of the endur-

[29] Stowell, 169.

ing dignity and value of American family life. Rather than choosing to follow Steinbeck's alternation of the abstract with the concrete (something which film is quite able to do despite its constant dependence on material reality), Ford has chosen to make a film equivalent in tone with the intercalary chapters of Steinbeck's novel. That tone, however, is applied to the stuff of Steinbeck's more concretely realized chapters: the Joads. If Ford's film is so enclosed, so reluctant to include the visual feel and evocation of humanity found in Walker Evans' or Dorothea Lange's Depression photographs so alive with sweat and dirt and particularity, it is consistent with Ford's lack of interest in the specificity of history and politics and social problems. It is no accident that the film's visual style neglects real estate and agriculture for people. We never see the Joads work the land they speak of. At the Keene ranch, when the men and children go off to pick fruit the images stay behind with Ma and Rosasharn. The only work we see Tom do that has any connection with earth and dirt is laying pipeline. And there isn't a single peach in the film.

Asked by Peter Bogdanovich what attracted him to the novel, Ford answered: ''The whole thing appealed to me—being about simple people—and the story was similar to the famine in Ireland, when they threw the people off the land and left them wandering on the roads to starve. That may have had something to do with it—part of my Irish tradition—but I liked the idea of this family going out and trying to find their way in the world.'' [30] The family as the basic unit of community is crucial to Ford's work. Thus, as Warren French notes, the director aims at ''abstracting the Joads from any particular context and treating them as ageless figures of dispossessed wanderers.'' [31] The film image hardly leaves the Joads for more than a few moments. Tom's final speech to Ma about his metaphorical omniscience everywhere articulates his and his family's own position within the context of the film. And Ma's final affirmation (''We'll go on forever, Pa. We're the people.'') is less an assertion of social consciousness than of the indomitability of the family. With respect for what it achieves in its own right as well as for its artistic coherence and its place in a larger body of acknowledged work, Ford's *The Grapes of Wrath* clearly and *visually* evidences his main interest and main thematic emphasis on the Joads as a family unit—and not as Steinbeck emphasizes them in the novel as a family of Man. Although the same conclusions about the film can be arrived at through careful consideration of the film's literary elements and its place in the culture of a specific period, those conclusions deserve the support of an equally careful visual analysis.

[30] John Ford in Bogdanovich, 76.
[31] French, 38.

CHAPTER 6.

History with Lightning:
The Forgotten Film *Wilson* (1944)

THOMAS J. KNOCK

WOODROW WILSON LOVED THE MOVIES. ONE OF THE FIRST HE EVER SAW
was D. W. Griffith's momentous Civil War epic *Birth Of A Nation* (1915),
which supposedly drew from the President the remark, "It is like writing history with lightning." Thereafter, Wilson went to the motion picture theater
occasionally, sharing a pastime which became increasingly popular with
Americans during his administration. In the last months of his presidency,
while recovering from a paralytic stroke, he saw movies in the East Room as
part of the diversionary therapy which his doctors prescribed.[1] As he sat
convalescing, broken by the strain of the "Great War for Democracy" and
his failure to convince the Senate and the American people that the United
States should join the League of Nations, Wilson could hardly have guessed
that the story of his life and his crusade for world peace would be resur-
rected upon the screen during a second world war which he had prophesied.

Many motion pictures about the country's favorite historical figures,
including several presidents, have been produced over the years. But of the
many sweeping pageants emanating from Hollywood, none approached the
multilevel political and historical significance of the screen story about the
twenty-eighth president. Heralded by its promoters as "The Most Important Event in Fifty Years of Motion Picture Entertainment," this 1944
production of Darryl F. Zanuck and Twentieth Century-Fox, a fervent
mission on behalf of international cooperation, was the most talked-about
picture of the year, receiving more critical praise and journalistic coverage
than any other up to that time, with the possible exception of *Birth Of A Nation* and *Gone With The Wind* (1939). *Wilson* has been neglected in histories
of the motion picture and in writings on American popular culture, but it was

[1]Lewis Jacobs, *The Rise of the American Film: A Critical History* (New York: Teachers
College, 1939), 175; Gene Smith, *When The Cheering Stopped* (New York: Morrow, 1964),
137–39.

enormously significant—mainly because, along with *Birth Of A Nation, Intolerance* (1916), *All Quiet On The Western Front* (1930), and *Citizen Kane* (1941), it was among the first few American films which attempted to raise public political consciousness. Released just as World War II was coming to an end, during a period when over half the American population went to the movies each week, *Wilson* was pregnant with meaning for its audiences because of its theme of peace and its implied plea for the future United Nations; one New York review headlined *Wilson* as "The Movie To Prevent World War Three."[2]

Yet as the overwhelming majority of observers claimed that the film represented "Hollywood at the crossroads . . . of mature responsibilities"[3] there nevertheless were partisan voices calling for its censorship. The charge that *Wilson* was "Fourth Term Propaganda" for Franklin Delano Roosevelt created consternation for the United States Army and the Senate; and it elicited an act of Congress before the matter was settled. *Wilson* is of historical interest for other reasons. In addition to being one of Hollywood's best screen biographies, the film is also notable because it parallels the Wilson historiography of the day, which concentrated favorably on Wilson's career at Princeton University, and as president during the war, the Paris peace negotiations, and his fight for the League of Nations. On a vast popular scale the film enhanced the image of Wilson and his administration, which had fallen into disrepute in the 1930s. It also stimulated the rebirth of interest in both the President himself and in books published about him in the mid-forties.

Then too, few "behind the scenes" stories of the making of a historical motion picture are as fascinating as *Wilson's*. Mounting a huge production that required restaging the 1912 Democratic National Convention, building facsimiles of White House and Capitol Hill interiors, and designing thousands of period costumes, all photographed in Technicolor, constituted a tremendous technical challenge. No less difficult were those challenges of research and preparation for the screenplay, and selecting a cast to play highly sensitive, demanding roles.

*   *   *

That a major feature film about the life and times of Woodrow Wilson should be produced at all was essentially the idea of Darryl F. Zanuck. Zanuck had always been interested in making entertaining and educational movies about the lives of great people in history and had successfully

---

[2]*New York Times,* July 30, 1944, VI, 38 (full-page advertisement); *1945 Britannica Book of the Year* (Chicago, 1945), 460; *PM*, Aug. 3, 1944, 2.

[3]*Time,* Aug. 7, 1944, 84.

produced several before *Wilson*, including *Disraeli* (1929), *The House of Rothschild* (1934), *The Story of Alexander Graham Bell* and *Young Mister Lincoln* (1939). But he was most devoted to recent biography and politics. His political attitudes were contradictory: Zanuck had voted for Alf Landon in 1936, then became a close friend and frequent dinner guest of Franklin Roosevelt; yet in 1940 he campaigned for Wendell L. Willkie, his best friend in politics, who became chairman of the board of Twentieth Century-Fox in 1942.[4]

The producer conceived the idea for *Wilson* while working on an outline for a film about Samuel Gompers. Such a film, he believed, might help ameliorate current tensions between labor and management. While examining the part that Wilson played in Gompers' career it occurred to him that in the President there existed a subject of cinematic potential. The draft of a Wilson script was begun but Zanuck shelved it and the Gompers project when the United States entered the war.[5]

As a colonel in the Army Signal Corps, Zanuck served in the Aleutians and North Africa in 1942 and 1943. Like many others (including Roosevelt and Willkie) Zanuck believed that World War II was an outgrowth of the thwarting of Wilson's attempt to establish the League of Nations; that as the war was nearing an end, it seemed that history was repeating itself; that Wilson had, indeed, been a prophet. After the Office of War Information turned down his offer to make a documentary about Wilson and the League (because it was too ambitious and contained too many political traps), Zanuck returned undaunted to Hollywood in 1943 to film "The Woodrow Wilson Story." By explaining in stimulating pictorial terms America's failure to follow Wilson's lead, Zanuck hoped to vindicate the late President's counsel and thus help clear the path toward lasting peace for the new generation. He wanted to produce a full-length feature that provided entertainment along with an urgent message; in Hollywood terms: " . . . the story of a family [that became] the drama of the world!"[6]

To delineate the complex personality and career of Woodrow Wilson and interweave an issue of international concern into a palatable screen story was a task of Wilsonian proportions. Lamar Trotti, a seasoned writer with a flair for biography, took on the assignment. Trotti spent more than two years reading all the biographies and memoirs about Wilson in order to draft his screenplay. He also interviewed Josephus Daniels, Wilson's Secretary of

---

[4]Zanuck's best-known films include *The Grapes of Wrath* (1940), *Gentleman's Agreement* (1947), *All About Eve* (1950), and *The Longest Day* (1962). Mel Gussow, *Don't Say Yes Until I Finish Talking: A Biography of Darryl F. Zanuck* (New York: Doubleday, 1971), xv and 115–16.

[5]John Gassner and Dudley Nichols, eds., *Best Film Plays, 1943–44* (New York: Crown, 1944), "Preface to *Wilson*," by Darryl F. Zanuck, 1–2.

[6]Ibid.; Gussow, *Don't Say Yes*, 118; *New York Times*, July 30, 1944, VI, 38.

Navy, Miles McCahill of the Secret Service, and others who provided different perspectives. Eleanor Wilson McAdoo, the President's daughter, served as an informal counselor on family activities and other matters. Trotti also studied the collections of the Woodrow Wilson Foundation and the Library of Congress, where he consulted with Katherine E. Brand, Special Custodian of the Wilson Papers.[7] But the screen writer's chief source was Ray Stannard Baker and his eight-volume biography *Woodrow Wilson, Life and Letters* (1927–1939) which had won the Pulitzer Prize in 1940, and which, despite many weaknesses in critical analysis, is still used by students and scholars. The leading authority on Wilson during the thirties and forties, Baker was skeptical at first, but he read the lengthy preliminary script and was pleased. Although he made many corrections and notations, he was impressed by the quality of the writing and with the serious "homework" Trotti had done. Several revisions followed, each reviewed by Baker who became an inspired adviser, captivated by the idea of conveying "to perhaps ninety million people Woodrow Wilson's essential message." In October of 1943 the 74-year-old journalist-historian travelled from his Amherst, Massachusetts, home to Hollywood, where he worked as a consultant for five months.[8]

Mrs. Wilson, whose own courtship would be reenacted on the screen, also studied each version of the script. Like Baker's, all of Mrs. Wilson's suggestions were incorporated into the text. Before actual filming began, she wrote to Baker that "the motion picture stands approved," words welcomed by all concerned. Later she wrote to Zanuck, "Needless to add, my hopes for the success of the picture are deeper than your own."[9]

With the script near completion, Zanuck sought a director and cast. One of Fox's leading directors, Henry King, a favorite of Zanuck's, at first tried to discourage the project. Many of Zanuck's associates believed that any story about Wilson, which necessarily included the saga of the League of Nations, must unavoidably take a position on a current political issue—isolationism versus internationalism. This, coupled with the problem of presenting the Democrats as "the good guys" and the Republicans as "the bad guys," rendered the Wilson story far too controversial, especially during an election year; in any circumstances it seemed, at best, a great financial risk.

[7]Lamar Trotti to Ray Stannard Baker, Feb. 2 and July 15, 1943, Ray Stannard Baker Papers, Library of Congress; Dean Francis B. Sayre, Jr., Washington National Cathedral (Wilson's first grandchild), to author, telephone interview, Feb. 25, 1974; Miss Katherine E. Brand to author, telephone interview, Dec. 8, 1975; *Washington Post*, Sept. 6, 1944, B-8.

[8]Baker to Trotti, Mar. 10, May 17, June 6, and July 19, 1943; Trotti to Baker, Feb. 23, June 11, and July 25, 1943; Baker to Jason S. Joy, Sept. 16, 1943, Baker Papers; see also Robert C. Bannister, Jr., *Ray Stannard Baker, The Mind and Thought of a Progressive* (New Haven: Yale Univ. Press, 1966), 303.

[9]Mrs. Wilson to Baker, Nov. 8, 1943 and Feb. 5, 1944, Baker Papers; Mrs. Wilson to Zanuck, Nov. 19, 1943, Edith Bolling Wilson Papers, Library of Congress, hereinafter cited as Wilson Papers.

Plate 1. Reception at the White House. Left to Right: Robert Lansing (Stanley Logan); Wilson (Alexander Knox); Edith Wilson (Geraldine Fitzgerald); William Gibbs McAdoo (Vincent Price); Colonel House (Charles Halton); Prof. Henry Holmes (Charles Coburn). (Courtesy of the Museum of Modern Art/Film Stills Archive)

Zanuck was not dissuaded and insisted that King read the script. King offered criticism, but liked it, and began directorial research by travelling to Princeton and Washington, D. C.[10]

Gathering the right cast for *Wilson* was difficult (see Plate 1). The role of Woodrow Wilson was monumental. The character would appear in 294 scenes and deliver 1,124 lines, including 338 speeches (verbatim excerpts from Wilson's own addresses). Casting the most suitable actor in the longest male role in screen history was crucial; Zanuck agreed with Mrs. Wilson that "it must be someone worthy of it!" The producer considered William Powell and Ronald Colman but soon decided not to seek a "star" name; he wanted an actor who would make a believable Wilson.[11] Alexander Knox, a 37-year-old Canadian actor had heard about the project and made a taping of the dialogue. His interpretation "proved so moving and dramatic . . . "

    [10]Zanuck to Mrs. Wilson, Nov. 15, 1943, Wilson Papers; S. A. Israel to Baker, Feb. 11, 1945, Baker Papers; Gassner and Nichols, *Best Film Plays,* "Preface to *Wilson,*" 2–3; *New York Times,* July 2, 1944, II, 3.
    [11]Mrs. Wilson to Baker, Nov. 8, and Baker to Wilson, Nov. 13, 1943, Baker Papers; Zanuck to Wilson, Nov. 15, 1943, Wilson Papers; *Collier's,* July 22, 1944, 47.

that Zanuck gave him the part. Unknown at the time, Knox became famous almost overnight as Wilson. Curiously, like Wilson, he was of Scotch-Irish ancestry, the son of a Presbyterian minister, and as a youth, like Wilson, had privately studied elocution. To prepare for the part, Knox became an ardent student of Wilson, attempting to bring both intellectual and artistic understanding to his portrayal.[12]

To play Edith Bolling Wilson, the strong-minded widow whom Wilson married sixteen months after the death of his beloved first wife, Ellen Axson (Ruth Nelson) in August 1914, Zanuck chose Geraldine Fitzgerald. "She's an independent young lady," said Mrs. Wilson approving of the choice, "and she will do for the part." In order to bring a dimension of humanness to their relationship, Fitzgerald, after reading Mrs. Wilson's autobiography, decided to treat the character of "Woodrow" not as the President, but as her husband, her lover, who happened also to be a great man.[13]

Sir Cedric Hardwicke played Henry Cabot Lodge of Massachusetts, Wilson's famous archenemy who chaired the Senate Foreign Relations Committee. Trotti constructed the character primarily from the Brahmin's own work, *The Senate and the League of Nations*, from the transcripts of the signal three-hour meeting of August 19, 1919, between Wilson and Lodge and the Committee during the League controversy, and from Mrs. Wilson's autobiography. In *Wilson* Lodge bears the blame for the failure of the United States to enter the League. Despite the villain-like profile, Lodge's namesake grandson felt that the characterization reflected his grandfather's viewpoint honestly, and consented to the portrayal.[14]

With permission secured from the heirs of 96 historical figures, and with a total of 148 speaking parts cast, including Thomas Mitchell as Joseph P. Tumulty and Vincent Price as William Gibbs McAdoo, production of *Wilson* commenced. As Zanuck made preparations, he worried that the picture might be dubbed "for 'highbrows' only." He thought that in order to be successful at the box office entertainment values would have to be underscored. Hence, his and director King's conception became a lavishly designed, Technicolored spectacle. The riotous Baltimore convention of 1912 (where Wilson was nominated for President on the forty-sixth ballot), for example, took place full-scale for entertainment's sake at the Los Angeles Shrine Au-

[12]Gassner and Nichols, *Best Film Plays,* "Preface to *Wilson*," 5; James Hilton, "Alexander Knox, A Rather Remarkable Man," *Photoplay* (February 1945), 42–43 and 94–95; see also "Introductory Remarks—Wilson Film" (speech by Baker at Winter Park, Florida, Feb. 27, 1945), Baker Papers.
[13]Edith Bolling Wilson, *My Memoir* (Indianapolis: Bobbs-Merrill, 1939); *New York Times,* July 30, 1944, II, 3.
[14]Henry Cabot Lodge, *The Senate and the League of Nations* (New York: Scribner's Sons, 1925); Trotti to Zanuck, Nov. 9, 1943, copy of memorandum in Baker Papers; *Newsweek,* Aug. 14, 1944, 72; *Collier's,* July 22, 1944, 47.

Plate 2. The Democratic National Convention as recreated by cinematographer Leon Shamroy. (Courtesy of the Museum of Modern Art/Film Stills Archive)

ditorium. Alive with cheers and marching bands, the scene required six filming days, 34 trucks filled with electrical equipment, and banners, placards,
and 1912-style seersuckers, and over 1,500 conventioneers (see Plate 2). To
backdrop other events in Wilson's life 126 sets were built, including re-
productions of the House of Representatives Chamber, the East, Blue, and
Oval Rooms, the Hall of Mirrors at Versailles, and hundreds of replicas of
White House set pieces. After the scores of players said their lines and an
additional 16,000 extras passed before the cameras during 90 days of shooting, Zanuck and his film editor worked for weeks to put the pieces together.
The extravaganza cost more to make than Fox had ever grossed on any previous production; at the then unheard-of price tag of $5,200,000, it became
the most expensive motion picture in history.[15]

Zanuck had devoted two years of his life to supervising all aspects of the
venture while overseeing other Fox efforts. His concern and expectations for
Wilson were boundless. "It was the *only* time I saw him on . . . [any] set,"
said Henry King. *Wilson* had become Zanuck's personal crusade for world
peace, in the belief that it would serve a great purpose for the country. Yet
with so much corporate money at stake, he had also to think about his stock-
holders. Consequently, Zanuck launched the publicity "campaign of the
century" to insure a healthy return on the record investment, and, ever the
man with a social conscience, the popular dissemination of the principles of
Woodrow Wilson. Illustrated features and full-page advertisements were
published in so many national magazines that their combined circulation
covered the entire American population. Across the nation 3,280 spot radio
announcements were broadcast during a four-week period. "*Wilson* Is Coming" in a 50′ × 75′ montage decorated the Fifth Avenue side of the Roxy
Theater; 32,000 smaller billboards advertised it from coast to coast. For the
gala August 1 premiere Zanuck summoned the cast members and other
movie people, presidents of major corporations, leading newspaper
publishers, prominent politicians, surviving members of the Wilson family
and Cabinet, and 200 members of the Woodrow Wilson Foundation. George
Jessel, master of ceremonies for the publicity broadcast carried by eight
New York radio stations, greeted Mrs. Wilson, Eleanor Wilson McAdoo,
Ray Stannard Baker, Bernard Baruch, and Josephus Daniels, as well as
Wendell Willkie, Sumner Welles, Henry Luce, Henry Morganthau, Jr., and
many others.[16] At that point Zanuck felt he had created a masterpiece, "the
most significant film . . . since *Birth Of A Nation*," but grimly quipped that

[15]Ibid., 18; Gassner and Nichols, *Best Film Plays,* 4–5; *New York Times,* Mar. 5, 1944, II, 3,
and Mar. 26, 1944, VI, 18–19; *Time,* Aug. 7, 1944, 84 (fn.). The budget included a million for
promotion; *Gone With The Wind* had cost $4,250,000 to produce.
[16]*Motion Picture Herald,* July 29, 1944, 35–37, and Aug. 5, 1944, 20; *Box Office Digest,* July
18, 1944, 10; *Motion Picture Daily,* July 24, 1944, 1 and 6; *Hollywood Reporter,* Aug. 2, 1944, 1
and 11.

Plate 3.   Wilson addressing the Joint Session of Congress.   (Courtesy of the Museum of Modern Art/Film Stills Archive)

unless *Wilson* was "successful from every standpoint, I'll never make another film without Betty Grable." And so, with "the eyes of the world . . . on the premiere," the epic story of *Wilson* unreeled publicly for the first time.[17]

The picture opens upon Woodrow Wilson, President of Princeton University, when the New Jersey political boss calls on the professor to offer him the Democratic gubernatorial nomination. After Wilson ultimately crosses 1600 Pennsylvania Avenue, the death of his wife, the outbreak of war in Europe, Cabinet debates over the sinking of the Lusitania and American neutrality, and Wilson's marriage to Edith Bolling Galt are all sketched episodically.

His reelection triumph over Charles Evans Hughes, based on the slogan "He kept us out of war!" is followed by the German resumption of unrestricted submarine warfare as of February 1, 1917. Wilson's ringing war message (a condensed version taken from Wilson's April 2, 1917 address) portends the solemn purpose of the remainder of the film. "For Democracy . . . for a universal dominion of right by such a concert of free peoples as shall bring peace and safety to all nations and make the world itself at last free," Wilson asserts, are America's reasons for entering the conflict. After months of war to end all wars, the announcement of the Fourteen Points brings about the Armistice, whence Wilson's overwhelming European reception and the Battle of Versailles are encapsulated in "March of Time" newsreels, intercut with reenactments of the deliberations of the "Big Four." Wilson returns home with the League of Nations, which he believes can maintain peace in the world. But Senatorial opposition to the treaty, led by Henry Cabot Lodge, stands in the way. The President feels compelled to stump the country, to tell "the people" what is at stake, and rally them behind the cause. He declares that America's isolation has come to an end and warns the people of a more dreadful war to come if the League is discarded. Soon after the strenuous campaign he suffers a stroke, and with Harding's election, the League is lost. On Inauguration Day at the Capitol, Wilson, a semi-invalid, defeated but resolute, assures his Cabinet that the ideals of the League will never die, conceding to Providence that "it may come about in a *better* way than we proposed." With that, as Edith takes his arm, "Wilson walks out of the room—into history."[18]

Wilson received a standing ovation at the Roxy. The story does not seem as significant and unusual today as it did then. But nothing like *Wilson* had ever before been seen on the screen. Before and during the Second World

[17]Zanuck to Mrs. Wilson, July 13, 1944, Wilson Papers; Gussow, *Don't Say Yes,* 115; *Motion Picture Herald,* July 29, 1944, 40.

[18]Gassner and Nichols, *Best Film Plays* (*Wilson* by Lamar Trotti), 86; Caption attached to *Wilson* still, Motion Picture Section, Library of Congress.

War the staple American film diet consisted mainly of light comedies, action–adventures backdropped by the war, musicals, love stories, and other
kinds of escapist fare. *Wilson* was different. Presented on a spectacular
scale, it was the first American film ever to assay the deeds of actual
politicians still living or of recent memory. To its initial audiences *Wilson*
was thought-provoking and timely. An unusual motion picture, ostensibly
intended for the purpose of entertainment, it interpreted recent events in
world history, and promoted a controversial solution to the tragic problem of
global war.

The critical response to the film was unprecedented. Leading publications
throughout the country observed its advent with a sense of excitement and
urgency. *Life* magazine typified the tidal wave of praise with a cover story
about *Wilson*, calling it "one of the best pictures Hollywood ever made."
Newsweek magazine reported that "Darryl F. Zanuck scores one of Hollywood's rare triumphs. . . . " *Time* described the film as "extremely absorb-
ing, significant, and entertaining" and declared that "Millions are likely to
be excited and moved by it." The *Washington Star* described it as "intellectually stimulating," and "proof of what the movies can do when guided
by intelligence," after *Wilson* opened in the nation's Capitol amid much
pomp and hoopla. And the *Washington Post* regarded it as "one of the most
distinguished films in the whole history of the cinema."[19]

Commentators stressed two major points—the image of Woodrow Wilson
created by the film, and the political and moral question, one of grave conse-
quence to the America of 1944, posed by the film. Recognizing the limits
placed on a 2½-hour-long movie, Knox managed to define a credible, sympathetic hero, an intellectual, professorial man possessing warmth, wit, integrity, and courage. Humanizing the image of Wilson was vital to the film's
success if audiences were to accept its thesis. Within Trotti's dramatic
construction Knox builds favorable sentiment in intimate scenes emphasizing Wilson's devotion to his family, his enjoyment of football, golf, and
vaudeville, his grief at his wife's death, and his happiness when he remarries.
Convincing the audience not only of Wilson's goodness but his greatness as
well, Knox's interpretation of Wilson as President makes the personality
study most impressive. The reading of the war message, for instance, in
a reenactment replete with a Joint Session of Congress, is dramatic and
portentous, underscored by Knox's brilliant elocution (see Plate 3). And the
restrained emotion he brings to the speech of "mortification and shame" at
Pueblo, Colorado, conveys the sense of epic tragedy of the end of Wilson's

[19]*Life*, Aug. 7, 1944, 53–56; *Newsweek*, Aug. 14, 1944, 72; *Time*. Aug. 7, 1944, 84–88; *Washington Star*, Sept. 8, 1944, B-12; *Washington Post*, Sept. 8, 1944, 16; *New York Daily News*,
Aug. 2, 1944, 35; *Los Angeles Times*, Aug. 11, 1944, 12; *San Francisco Examiner*. Aug. 30,
1944, 8; *Boston Globe*, Sept. 29, 1944, 19.

career. Bosley Crowther of the *New York Times* characterized the critical opinion: "Much of the film's exceptional quality is due to the performance of Alexander Knox. . . . It is good to hear speeches spoken—especially Wilson's—with a clear and resonant voice. The casting of Mr. Knox . . . in this role was truly inspired."[20]

The portrayal drew comment from Wilson's friends and family. Former Navy Secretary Josephus Daniels exclaimed that, although Knox's Wilson was not perfect, his lines were "delivered so impressively that one . . . felt he was living over again those tense days." Mrs. Wilson, very pleased, wrote to Zanuck, "Every detail is perfect. . . ." The rest of the family in general did not think that Knox actually sounded like Wilson or resembled him strikingly (the make-up consisted of little more than nose putty, hair oil, and pince-nez eyeglasses) but liked his performance and the film "fairly well"[21] (see Plate 4).

Of far greater importance than the quality of Alexander Knox's rendering of Wilson, and overshadowing the production values of the motion picture, was its examination of internationalism and isolationism. Before *Wilson* was completed Lamar Trotti had written to Ray Stannard Baker that

> It is our earnest hope that the men and women who see this picture . . . [will understand] that here was a great man who fought and died for a great ideal . . . a world united for peace through a League of Nations and that they will be awakened to the issues at stake, to the dangers of indifference, isolation, and reaction, so that the tragedy of the present war which the Wilson dream might have prevented, may never again be permitted to occur.

The point was lost on no one in the press. Marshall Field's *PM Daily*, which serialized the screenplay, considered it "without question, the most important picture of its time" because "*Wilson* may help to break the tragic pattern, to learn from the past . . . to save a new generation. . . . " Arthur Sweetser, president of the Woodrow Wilson Foundation, wrote in *Changing World* that *Wilson* was perhaps "the most important single contribution to the education of the American public regarding America's place in world-life that has ever been made. . . . " *Springfield Republican* columnist David Lawrence, who had authored *The True Story of Woodrow Wilson* in 1924, stated that *Wilson* represented "a milestone . . . in the teaching of American history to the people of this country." *Saturday Review* paid special tribute to *Wilson* by breaking its twenty-year-long policy of *not* reviewing movies; the editors strongly recommended the film, "convinced that this picture is a document of the first importance."[22]

[20]*New York Times*, Aug. 2, 1944, 18.

[21]Josephus Daniels, *Raleigh News and Observer*, Aug. 6, 1944, 4; Wilson to Zanuck, Sept. 9, 1944, Wilson Papers; Sayre to author, Feb. 25, 1974.

[22]"Mr. Trotti's Memorandum," undated copy, Baker Papers; *PM*, Aug. 2, 1944, 20, and Aug. 3, 1944, 2–9; *Changing World*, Sept. 1944; *Springfield Republican*, Sept. 13, 1944, 13; *Saturday Review*, Aug. 12, 1944, 23–24.

Plate 4. Wilson signs the Treaty of Versailles. (Courtesy of the Museum of Modern Art/ Film Stills Archive)

Nor did Wilson scholars ignore the film. Baker, of course, was delighted with it (like Mrs. Wilson) and agreed with the journalistic responses. Other historians, however, later noted several distressing oversights and inaccuracies. Thomas A. Bailey, for example, author of *Woodrow Wilson and the Lost Peace* and *Woodrow Wilson and the Great Betrayal*, pointed out aptly that Hollywood glossed over Wilson's personal shortcomings, and oversimplified and fictionalized some details of the Wilson-Lodge feud, Wilson's dismissal of Count von Bernstorff, the German ambassador, and the campaign for the League.[23] Arthur S. Link, the dean of the Wilson scholars, noted in the first volume of his definitive multivolume biography of Wilson that the film erroneously credited William Jennings Bryan with securing the presidential nomination for Wilson at Baltimore. Both historians felt that Knox was effective but regretted the film's distractingly recurrent expositions of the Wilson family singing around the piano and the blaring of popular songs and marching bands.[24] Because the production spent so much

    [23] *Woodrow Wilson and the Lost Peace* (New York: Macmillan, 1944); *Woodrow Wilson and the Great Betrayal* (New York: Macmillan, 1945); Wilson to Zanuck, Sept. 9, 1944, Wilson Papers; Baker to Trotti, Aug. 29, 1944, Baker Papers; Thomas A. Bailey, *Woodrow Wilson and the Great Betrayal,* vi and 114; Bailey to author, Mar. 2, 1974.
    [24] Arthur S. Link, *Wilson: The Road to the White House* (Princeton: Princeton Univ. Press, 1947), 463; Link to author, interview at Princeton University, Nov. 25, 1975. Professor Link told me that he looked upon the film favorably. Regarding it as one of the better Hollywood biographies, and as an effective propaganda piece for the United Nations, he nonetheless found its inaccuracies regrettable.

time on entertainment and spectacle, historical omissions were inevitable. Partly because all of the primary research sources were not then open to the public, and especially because the politics of Wilson's era merged with the politics of the 1940s, a penetrating examination would hardly have been likely.

Despite the film's historical oversimplification, its main thrust—Wilson's vain, yet courageous, crusade for the League of Nations—carried dramatic force. Most contemporary writers, albeit not scholars, were satisfied with the essentials of the film and agreed with Bosley Crowther that *Wilson* was evidence of "the widening scope of Hollywood," and was bound to shake "some cobwebs loose from the 'safety first' policies" of Hollywood.[25]

The film also drew *editorial* comment from major newspapers. The *New York Post* opined that "This fine movie can play a great and important part in that long fight [for world peace], into which we have twice poured so much hope and so much blood." The message editorialized by the *Post,* and the *Nation,* the *Christian Science Monitor,* the *Chicago Sun-Times,* the *Philadelphia Record,* the *Atlanta Constitution,* and others, was that all America should see *Wilson.* Reflecting such assessments in the press, columnist Lee Morris, overwhelmed by the film, proclaimed on the front page of the *Philadelphia Record* that *Wilson* was "the motion picture that may conceivably change the history of the world."[26]

As the film began its peace march throughout the movie palaces of America, notes of partisan criticism and suppression were sounded. A month before Wilson's general release the *Washington Times-Herald,* an anti-New Deal paper, attacked Zanuck's production for being part of an alleged Hollywood–White House scheme to reelect Franklin D. Roosevelt for a fourth term. The paper asserted that *Wilson* would be "counted on heavily by some of the more enthusiastic New Dealers to swing public sentiment behind FDR. . . ." Released at the beginning of the Roosevelt-Dewey contest, *Wilson,* which glorified FDR's first political mentor (Roosevelt had served as Wilson's Assistant Secretary of Navy) and promoted his fourth-term peace platform, acquired a new meaning. Following the *Times-Herald* broadside, the conservative *Washington Daily News* accused Zanuck in an editorial entitled "Franklin Delano Wilson" of subtly modeling his Wilson characterization after Roosevelt in order to swing the election, and suggested that the Democratic National Committee ought to subsidize Twentieth Century-Fox.[27]

A registered Republican, Zanuck dismissed the charge as ridiculous. The so-called underlying political purpose of the film, he countered, could just as

[25] *New York Times,* Aug. 6, 1944, II, 1.
[26] *New York Post,* Aug. 3, 1944, 21; *Philadelphia Record,* Sept. 9, 1944, 1.
[27] *Washington Times-Herald,* July 13, 1944, 14; *Washington Daily News,* Aug. 3, 1944, 20.

easily be interpreted as propaganda for many leading liberal Republicans like Zanuck's close friend Wendell L. Willkie. An adamant anti-isolationist, Willkie in 1943 had written *One World*, a best-selling tract which recounted his recent global travels and called for international organization. Furthermore, Governor Dewey, the 1944 Republican nominee, had promised in his campaign speeches to uphold the social legislation of the New Deal and pursue an internationalist policy. *Wilson* was therefore "damned nonpartisan" according to Zanuck.[28]

Many publications sympathetic to the film and Zanuck's reasoning (*Time* and *Newsweek*, for example) nevertheless made at least passing note of the pro-Roosevelt charge. *PM*, which gave *Wilson* extensive coverage, did the film damage when it cumbrously topped a rave review with "*Wilson* Wartime Wisdom May Help Win For FDR." Shortly, the headline appeared on the front page of the *New York Times* that the "Army Bans *Wilson* As Film For Troops." The Morale Services Division of the War Department announced that the film would be banned in all troop camps in the United States and abroad because it contained material which might be construed as violating the Soldiers' Voting Act, a law which prohibited the distribution on military bases of motion pictures, radio programs, and periodicals of partisan political content.[29]

It was not long before Secretary of War Henry L. Stimson collected a stack of telegrams protesting the ban. The League of Nations Association wired Stimson that the censoring of *Wilson* only "would be expected in the German and Japanese armies." The CIO War Relief Committee, the National Maritime Union, and individuals including Senator A. B. Chandler of Kentucky and Spyros Skouras, president of Twentieth Century-Fox, protested to Stimson that the ban was unfair, that it amounted to "tyrannical censorship to be expected only from the most reactionary . . . government." A number of newspapers editorialized against the ban, and New York City Mayor Fiorello LaGuardia told reporters that the army's opinion of the film "simply did not make sense." Senator Theodore F. Green, Rhode Island Democrat, called the whole affair "foolishness . . . by Republicans," while even Senator Taft of Ohio admitted that the army interpretation of the law was "silly."[30]

The original purpose of the Soldiers' Voting Act, according to Taft, was to prevent standing administrations from using their communications monopoly to disseminate politically biased information to the armed forces. As he

[28]*Collier's*, July 22, 1944, 47.
[29]*PM*, Aug. 2, 1944, 2; *New York Times*, Aug. 10, 1944, 1 and 15.
[30]League of Nations Association to Stimson, Aug. 11, 1944, Arthur Sweetser Papers, Library of Congress; *New York Times*, Aug. 10, 1944, 1 and 15, and Aug. 11, 1944, 7, and Aug. 12, 1944, 1; *Los Angeles Times*, Aug. 11, 1944, II, 4.

explained on the floor of the Senate, after reading into the record the *Washington Daily News* attack, the trouble with *Wilson* arose because under the existing legislation the Army ruled that publications and films and the like sold or distributed within troop camps somehow made them *government-sponsored* publications and films. The open-ended regulations had created similar minor problems in the past, but with the Morale Division's "unnecessarily restrictive interpretation" of *Wilson* the deficiencies in the law were laid bare. Responding quickly to the numerous complaints, Taft and Green co-sponsored successful amendments to the Soldiers' Voting Act. The changes provided for the unhampered circulation within the armed forces of all "entertainment material as generally presented to the public in the United States."[31]

While *Wilson* influenced legislative deliberations on Capitol Hill it also made history at the box office. During its record-breaking run at the Roxy Theater more than 20,000 crowded in line daily to see the film; after five weeks in circulation over one million people (in New York, Los Angeles, and San Francisco) had paid to see it. By February of 1945 an estimated ten million people had seen *Wilson* in hundreds of theaters at advanced prices.[32]

Although it is impossible to precisely determine the real effect that *Wilson* may have had on its audiences, it contributed to the climate of internationalism. The film commanded the greatest numbers as World War II drew to its climax, and as discussions at Dumbarton Oaks, succeeded by the United Nations San Francisco Conference, took place during a period when the name of Woodrow Wilson echoed irresistibly from the past. As the Woodrow Wilson Foundation pointed out, *Wilson* "carried unmistakable parallelism to the eyes of millions throughout the country who might not have been reached by the printed word." Several contemporary observations substantiate this assertion. Josephus Daniels, for example, wrote that he felt that the opening night audience in New York "left the theater with the feeling that this generation must repair the errors which made possible the present holocaust." Convinced that *Wilson* was "going to have a great effect throughout the country," Arthur Sweetser wrote to Ray Stannard Baker and to Undersecretary of State Sumner Welles of the audience in Washington, D. C.: "Certainly people seemed deeply moved, reflective, even saddened" by the film. After a private showing at the White House President Roosevelt wrote to Sweetser that *Wilson* "is excellent and will have a splendid effect." Years later Secretary of State Cordell Hull recorded in his memoirs that he reminded the American delegation of the contemporary lesson which the film dramatized during an impasse in negotiations at Dumbarton Oaks. Darryl F. Zanuck received more letters

[31]U.S., Congress, *Congressional Record,* Senate, 78th Cong., 2nd sess., Aug. 15, 1944, 90, pt. 5: 6936–39; House, 6983 (Senate Bill 2050).
[32]S. A. Israel to Baker, Feb. 11, 1945, Baker Papers; *New York Times,* Aug. 10, 1944, 15, and Sept. 10, 1944, II, 1.

about *Wilson* than Twentieth Century-Fox usually received in response to any other half dozen pictures. From all over the world he gathered hundreds of notes from soldiers, sailors, and civilians, and even avowed isolationists who admitted that the film had impressed them. Similarly, Mrs. Wilson wrote to Baker that the film "does seem to have done a real service and my mail reflects that every day."[33]

No organized survey was ever conducted to determine the degree of influence *Wilson* wielded over its audiences. However, the *New Republic* reported that some curious interviewers questioned patrons who had just seen the film and found "a definite increase in cooperative spirit among the movie-goers." During the ban controversy *PM* asked servicemen outside the Roxy what they thought of the film. "I believe in the United Nations. I think everyone should see this picture," answered a 20-year-old sergeant who typified the responses regardless of the individuals' political affiliations, "so we won't make the mistake again that we made in 1920. That's what I am fighting for." The *New York Times'* Bosley Crowther later conducted his own survey. Many people he spoke with came out of the theater in tears; some said it was the most inspiring film they had ever seen. Regardless of age or occupation, all of the people he interviewed left the movie endorsing the philosophy of the League. Crowther related his findings to a poll taken in 1943 to ascertain the effects of the pro-Russian film *Mission to Moscow*, a semi-documentary Warner Brothers release based on the memoirs of Ambassador Joseph E. Davies, which "raised pro-Soviet sentiment . . . among those who saw it." He suggested that the residual power of *Wilson*, and its message of "It must not happen again," would be greater and more widespread, that millions would leave the film in "an anti-isolationist frame of mind."[34]

Public opinion polls tell us that a tremendous shift of opinion in favor of U. S. participation in some kind of world organization took place among Americans throughout World War II. As one historian has pointed out, Americans realized gradually that they had been given perhaps their last "second chance." The new public profile was formed by the experience of a second war (and the events surrounding it), changing government policies regarding international cooperation, and a variety of media. A measurable example of the latter was Wendell L. Willkie's *One World*, considered "the most influential book published during the war," and which "both reflected

<hr/>

[33] *Woodrow Wilson Foundation Annual Report, 1944–45,* 3; *Raleigh News and Observer,* Aug. 6, 1944, 4; Sweetser to Baker, Sept. 8, 1944, Sweetser to Welles, Sept. 11, 1944, Roosevelt to Sweetser, Sept. 6, 1944, Zanuck to Sweetser, undated typescript, Sweetser Papers; *The Memoirs of Cordell Hull* (New York: Macmillan, 1948), vol. II, 1703; Israel to Baker, Feb. 11, 1945, and Wilson to Baker, Dec. 25, 1944, Baker Papers.

[34] *New Republic,* Sept. 11, 1944, 295; *PM,* Aug. 10, 1944, 3; *New York Times,* Sept. 10, 1944, II, 1; see also Melvin Small, "Buffoons and Brave Hearts: Hollywood Portrays the Russians, 1939–1944," *California Historical Quarterly* (Winter 1973), 326–337.

and helped to create" the turn away from traditional isolationism.[35] Yet, as *Wilson* was seen by so many people—several times the 1.5 million that bought *One World*—one can reasonably conclude that despite the fact that it has been neglected as such, the film was just as important as Willkie's book or any other single major factor during the final stages of American popular conversion to active internationalism. Thus, the motion picture became the most widely circulated and the single most influential propaganda piece on behalf of the United Nations of the entire decade.

There was another distinctive development attributable to *Wilson*. During the war, for obvious reasons, allusions to the President and consequent scholarly examinations of his administration burgeoned as his stature as a great world statesman grew. The major literary works included Thomas A. Bailey's volumes, mentioned previously, Herbert C. F. Bell's *Woodrow Wilson and the People*, *The Economic Thought of Woodrow Wilson* by William Diamond, Dexter Perkins' *America and Two Wars*, and Gerald W. Johnson's picture biography, *Woodrow Wilson: The Unforgettable Figure Who Has Returned to Haunt Us*. More than 600,000 pamphlets, additionally, were published by the Wilson Foundation pertaining to Wilson and the prospects for world organization, not to mention countless newspaper and magazine articles. Ray Stannard Baker told H. C. F. Bell in late 1943 that he believed that Zanuck's *Wilson* would be of "the greatest value in reviving interest" in the subject. Ruth Cranston, author of *The Story of Woodrow Wilson*, informed Baker that Charles Scribner's Sons, for one, realized the potential. "We expect to publish in August [1945] about the time the Wilson picture is released to second run movie houses," she wrote. Scribner's also saw opportunity for a reissue of Baker's biography, originally published by Doubleday. Baker wrote a new preface to Scribner's "Potomac Edition" of *Life and Letters*, published at the end of 1945, which cited the picture as the primary factor responsible for the new public interest in Wilson. Within one year Scribner's had sold nearly as many sets of the books as Doubleday had in ten years.[36]

[35] *Public Opinion Quarterly* (Fall 1943), 498; (Summer 1944), 301; (Fall 1944), 454. Of the American public 26% favored American participation in some kind of international peace-keeping organization in 1937. In 1941, 38% were in favor; 72% supported the idea by 1944. See also Robert A. Divine's perceptive study, *Second Chance: The Triumph of Internationalism in America During World War II* (New York: Atheneum, 1967), particularly 103–07 and 167–71. Samuel Eliot Morison, Henry Steele Commager, and William E. Leuchtenburg, *The Growth of the American Republic* (New York: Oxford Univ. Press, 1969, 6th ed.), vol. II, 603.
[36] Herbert C. F. Bell, *Woodrow Wilson and the People* (Garden City: Doubleday, Doran, 1945); William Diamond, *The Economic Thought of Woodrow Wilson* (Baltimore: Johns Hopkins Univ. Press, 1943); Dexter Perkins, *America and Two Wars* (Boston: Little, Brown, 1944); Gerald W. Johnson, *Woodrow Wilson: The Unforgettable Figure Who Has Returned to Haunt Us* (New York: Harper, 1944); Ruth Cranston, *The Story of Woodrow Wilson* (New York: Simon and Schuster, 1945); *Wilson Foundation Annual Report, 1944-45,* 7–10; Baker to Bell, Nov. 26, 1943; Cranston to Baker, May 30, 1945, Wilson to Baker, Jan. 1, 1945, and Baker

Earning about three million dollars (an outstanding gross in 1944–45) on
its road show and second run engagements, *Wilson* succeeded magnificently
as a Hollywood documentary-feature on three levels: it composed effective
propaganda for the United Nations, promoted a heroic image of Woodrow
Wilson, and provided for its audiences a general, if simplistic, education in
early twentieth-century American history. However, as commercial entertainment, Zanuck judged his work a failure, based on the amount of money it
cost to make compared to what it earned, and his criterion of complete success—acceptance by "the widest audience possible." When the film left the
big cities on the east and west coasts to tour middle America and the hinter-
lands, it lost all of its momentum. At a time when most people went to the
movies solely for relaxation, to see their favorite stars and escape into lands
of adventure and romance, *Wilson*, a history lesson fraught with controversy, was not everybody's idea of what constituted entertainment. Zanuck believed, probably correctly, that his film failed in cities like Minneapolis, St. Paul, Kansas City, Denver, Cleveland, and St. Louis because of
the native conservatism of many regions of the country where the seeds of
isolationism persistently grew and the support for international organization
was not as vigorous. In October of 1944 Zanuck brought a print back to his
hometown of Wahoo, Nebraska, for a special showing which the entire town
attended. In nearby Omaha the *Wilson* premiere was sold out. The next day
only 75 people out of a population of a quarter million came to the theater.
"Why should they pay seventy-five cents to see Wilson on the screen," asked
Zanuck's old family doctor, succinctly explaining the regional antipathy,
"when they wouldn't pay ten cents to see him alive?" Although it was among
the highest grossing films of the year, by the end of its national run it
registered a net loss of two million dollars.[37]

Another disappointment befell Zanuck and his associates. *Wilson* was
nominated for ten Academy Awards, including best picture of the year. Of
all the nominees on "Oscar Night" in March 1945, the real contest was
between *Wilson* and *Going My Way*, an enormously popular and sentimental film, also nominated for ten awards. *Wilson* won a total of five for
editing, sound recording, interior decoration, cinematography, and screen

to Wilson, Jan. 9, 1945, Baker Papers; *Life and Letters,* "Potomac Edition" (New York:
Scribner's, 1946), vol. 1, xviii; Mrs. Margaret Maher of Doubleday's Inventory Control Office
and Mrs. Maria Noreika of Scribner's Reference Department kindly provided comparative
sales statistics.
    [37] Zanuck to Sweetser, Nov. 7, 1944, Sweetser Papers; Frederick W. Williams, "Regional At-
titudes on International Cooperation," *Public Opinion Quarterly* (Spring 1945), 49. (Records of
box office receipts for *Wilson* are no longer available at Twentieth Century-Fox; my estimate is
based on 33 reports published in *Motion Picture Daily* from Aug. 3 to Dec. 22, 1944, and in *Motion Picture Herald,* Oct. 26, 1944, 48.) Gussow, *Don't Say Yes,* 119–120; *Time,* June 12, 1950,
65.

writing, before the last three categories were named. But King the director, Knox the actor, and *Wilson* the film lost to Leo McCarey, Bing Crosby, and *Going My Way.* Zanuck was mortified. He remained unswerving in his belief in the film and its subject. He donated $5,000 toward the purchase of the new Wilson Foundation headquarters and later $50,000, in Mrs. Wilson's name, for the restoration of Wilson's birthplace in Staunton, Virginia. *Wilson* was listed on the *New York Times'* annual Ten Best list and Alexander Knox's performance was voted the best of the year in a national poll of newspaper, magazine, and radio film reviewers. Nonetheless, Zanuck was embittered. Three years later, while accepting the 1947 best picture citation for *Gentleman's Agreement,* he glared at the Academy gathering and said, "Many thanks, but I should have won it for *Wilson.*" He has never changed his mind.[38]

After the ordeal of *Wilson,* Twentieth Century-Fox shied away from any further expensive experiments and abandoned Zanuck's plans to produce a film based on Willkie's *One World* as a kind of internationalist sequel to *Wilson.* The Wilson Foundation published a special booklet about the critical reception to the film and proposed that it be shown annually in theaters throughout the world. Shelved away for years after 1946, the film was never to be re-released until the 1960s when it was circulated on television in a truncated black and white version.

Wilson is one of the unique film biographies in American popular culture. Like its subject, ironically, its ascendance was as spectacular as its ultimate failure. Yet, the film is a noteworthy celluloid reflection of the past generation, revealing contemporary attitudes toward the problems of peace and war, as well as toward Wilson and his era. In an ostentatious but tasteful manner *Wilson* attempted to remind Americans of the global responsibilities they once shirked but would have to accept in a new, postwar world. Woodrow Wilson, who won the war, ironically gained increased fame for a lost peace. Therein lies his great personal tragedy, and, perhaps to some extent, therein lies his greatness. In the most recent major study of Wilson, Lord Patrick Devlin wrote of Wilson and his abortive world mission: "He is and will always be historically great because he was the first to try."[39] Much the same might be said of Zanuck's special experiment, despite its artistic shortcomings, because of what his film singularly tried to do.

In the thirty-odd years since *Wilson's* first exhibition historians have rendered a more balanced, realistic judgment of the subject. They have ex-

[38]Robert Osborne, *Academy Awards Illustrated* (Los Angeles: ESE, 1966), 122 and 128–29; Alden Hatch, *Edith Bolling Wilson* (New York: Dodd, Mead, 1960), 270; *New York Times,* Jan. 9, 1946, 21; Gussow, *Don't Say Yes,* 120.
[39]Lord Patrick Devlin, *Too Proud to Fight: Woodrow Wilson's Neutrality* (New York: Oxford Univ. Press, 1975), 679.

plored more critically the internal and external forces which motivated him
and have exposed the numerous chinks in the idealistic Wilsonian armor. Although the motion picture is marred by many oversights and gloss, it is
basically an honest film, commendable in its intent, inspiring in the ideals it
professed. Its overview of Woodrow Wilson is not at variance with that of
any of the President's most respected biographers—from Baker to
Link—for their works have in part been predicated upon the principle of doing honor to the memory of a great man. Countless ambitious historical
spectacles have been produced since *Wilson*. But because of the nature of
the moment, none of them have flashed their history as imposingly as
Wilson—if only for awhile—or told so many stories at the same time,
generated so much praise and controversy, and spurred so many passionate
expectations.*

*I am grateful to Professors Andrew Buni, Janet Wilson James, and R. Alan Lawson of
Boston College, and Professor Jack T. Kirby of Miami University (Ohio), and to M. Francesca
Nudo and my aunt, Dorothea M. Knock, whose encouragement and critical suggestions made it
possible for me to complete this essay. An uncut 35mm. Technicolor print of *Wilson* is available
at the UCLA Film Archives. All photos are courtesy of the Museum of Modern Art, Film Stills
Archive, 21 W. 53rd Street, New York City.

CHAPTER 7.

The Negro Soldier (1944):
Film Propaganda in Black and White

THOMAS CRIPPS and DAVID CULBERT

AFTER YEARS DURING WHICH BLACKS AND POLICE ENGAGED IN PITCHED
battles in small Southern towns and large Northern cities, Nicholas Kat-
zenbach, Attorney General under Lyndon B. Johnson, termed television
"the central means of making a private moral conviction public, of impel-
ling people all over to see and confront ideas they otherwise would turn
away from." Black activists considered television, in the words of a network producer, "the chosen instrument of the black revolution."[1] But
television was not the first electronic medium used to further social
change. The United States Army's orientation film, *The Negro Soldier*,
released in January 1944, is one of those rare instances which allows the
historian of mass media to speak confidently about conception, execution, and—to a degree—results both intended and unintended, of a
specific controversial film. The uses eventually made of the Army's motion picture illustrate the difficulty of gauging in advance the impact of
mass communication on social change.

During World War II the Army was officially committed to maintaining
existing patterns of segregation. But the liberal rhetoric of official war
aims proved fatal to thoughts of maintaining the *status quo* at home.
By inducting 875,000 Negroes into a fighting force of some twelve million,
the Army discovered that it was operating a social relations laboratory.[2]

---

[1] Quoted in Thomas Cripps, "The Noble Black Savage: A Problem in the Politics of
Television Art," *Journal of Popular Culture*, 8 (Spring 1975), 687–95.

[2] See Ulysses Lee, *The Employment of Negro Troops: Special Studies* (Washington, D. C.:
Office of Chief of Military History, U.S. Army, G.P.O., 1966), a volume in the official
series, *The United States Army in World War II;* see also.Richard M. Dalfiume, *Desegrega-
tion of the United States Armed Forces: Fighting on Two Fronts, 1939–1953* (Columbia,
Mo.: Univ. of Missouri Press, 1969); and Alan M. Osur, *Blacks in the Army Air Forces
During World War II: The Problem of Race Relations* (Washington, D. C.: Office of Air
Force History, G.P.O., 1977).

In spite of the wishes of many whites, the Army became a half-way house for those who believed that wartime should bring substantial racial progress.

The relationship between racial tensions and film can best be explained by a metaphor. The biologist defines symbiosis as an association of two different organisms which live attached to each other and contribute to each other's support. This article will describe the making and distribution of *The Negro Soldier* as an example of social symbiosis, for the idea did not come from one person, but emerged from a coalition of four wary interest groups which came together in antagonistic cooperation. The film offered important lessons to those who made post-war Hollywood "message" films, while black pressure groups discovered a new way to further social change through the distribution of motion pictures.

In retrospect, the four groups and their aims are easy to identify. First is the Army itself. By the time of Pearl Harbor both civilian and military leaders in America recognized motion pictures as a significant propaganda medium; they believed film could instill in citizens a spirit of patriotism and a will to fight.[3] Chief of Staff George C. Marshall believed that film should play a major military role in wartime.[4] Convinced that lectures about patriotism and recent history generally made no impact on draftees, he concluded that film could present serious material in a lively and interesting fashion. Thanks to Marshall, the Army chose Hollywood's Frank Capra to head an elite film unit assigned to make feature-length morale films intended to build enthusiasm for official war aims. To Marshall the key to morale for the educated soldier was to give a reason for fighting.[5] Capra's *Why We Fight* series, mandatory viewing for every

---

[3] Roger Manvell, *Films and the Second World War* (South Brunswick, N. J.: A. S. Barnes, 1974); David Culbert, "Walt Disney's Private Snafu: The Use of Humor in World War II Army Film," in Jack Salzman, ed., *Prospects: An Annual Journal of American Cultural Studies,* 1 (Dec. 1975), 80–96, and Richard Dyer MacCann, *The People's Films: A Political History of U.S. Government Motion Pictures* (New York: Hastings House, 1973).

[4] For an introduction see Richard Griffith, "The Use of Films by the U.S. Armed Forces," in Paul Rotha, *Documentary Film* (3d ed.; London: Faber and Faber, 1952), 344–58; on Marshall see Forrest C. Pogue, *George C. Marshall: Organizer of Victory 1943– 1945* (New York: Viking, 1975), 91–92; Frank Capra, *The Name Above the Title: An Autobiography* (New York: Macmillan, 1971), 325–70; and three official histories from *The United States in World War II*: Dulany Terrett, *The Signal Corps: The Emergency (To December 1941)* (Washington, D. C.: Office of the Chief of Military History, U.S. Army, G.P.O., 1956), 78–82, 223–30; George Raynor Thompson et al., *The Signal Corps: The Test (December 1941 to July 1943)* (Washington, D. C., 1957), 387–426; and George Raynor Thompson and Dixie R. Harris, *The Signal Corps: The Outcome (Mid-1943 Through 1945)* (Washington, D. C., 1966), 540–79.

[5] There is a vast literature about morale and its importance. See Wesley Frank Craven and James Lea Cate, eds., *Services Around the World,* vol. VII of *The Army Air Forces in World War II* (Chicago: Univ. of Chicago Press, 1958), 431–76, for a good introduction to the

soldier, defined official war aims in a way no other medium could match. Marshall hoped that a Capra-unit film about the Negro would provide a reason why racial tolerance was necessary to a unified military effort.

Capra's credentials for his assignment were considerable. A Sicilian immigrant, he began his Hollywood career by working on comic short subjects. Every film he made in the 1930s showed the "little guy" as eventually triumphant, a message bound to find a sympathetic reception in hard times. Above all, Capra's name became synonymous with the box office: no other Hollywood director could match his unbroken string of hits: *It Happened One Night* (1934), *Mr. Deeds Goes to Town* (1936), *Lost Horizon* (1937), *You Can't Take It With You* (1938), *Mr. Smith Goes to Washington* (1939), and *Meet John Doe* (1941). Capra was living proof that the American Dream did come true; to him patriotism was a high calling, though he masked his ardor with a deft comic touch. Capra's War Department film unit quickly attracted many of Hollywood's most talented cutters, scriptwriters, and directors. When the unit's first *Why We Fight* film, *Prelude to War*, appeared in November 1942, Capra's preeminent position in military filmmaking was assured.[6]

The second group is the blacks themselves, who saw World War II as a time to bring an end to longstanding discrimination. To black America, Franklin D. Roosevelt's Four Freedoms—freedom of speech, freedom of religion, freedom from fear, and freedom from want—were totally incompatible with segregation. The desires of black America must not be measured by the standard of today's activist rhetoric. In World War II most Negroes sought "racial tolerance" as a first step. Though there was violence, particularly race riots in Detroit and Harlem, the National Association for the Advancement of Colored People (NAACP), headed by Walter White, looked to the courts, and to white liberals, to bring about gradual change.

Earlier government films relating to blacks suggested progress more glacial than gradual. In World War I official Signal Corps footage used

---

problem. The scientific study of morale was an outgrowth of World War I. See Edward L. Munson, *The Management of Men: A Handbook on the Systematic Development of Morale and the Control of Human Behavior* (New York: H. Holtand Co. 1921); Munson's son became Capra's superior in I&E; he too wrote a widely used guide to morale: Colonel Edward Lyman Munson, Jr., *Leadership for American Army Leaders*, in *The Fighting Forces Series* (rev. ed.; Washington, D. C.: The Infantry Journal, 1944).

[6] Production files for "Prelude to War" are located in 062.2 ocsigo, Box 1, Records of the Chief Signal Officer, RG 111, Film Section, National Archives, where a viewing print may also be found [hereafter FS-NA]. See also 062.2 ocsigo, Box 12, A52-248, Washington National Records Center, Suitland, Maryland, for additional production material [hereafter WNRC-Suitland]. Concerning the optimism of Capra's films see Robert Sklar, *Movie-Made America: A Cultural History of American Movies* (New York: Vintage Books, 1976), 205–14.

Negroes for comic relief. During the 1930s, Pare Lorentz's conservationist films, *The Plow That Broke the Plains* and *The River*, contained only a few black faces. The first two years of the war saw little change. Blacks were patronized in the few films with specific Negro themes released by federal agencies, either by overpraising Jim Crow schools (*Negro Colleges in Wartime*), or by celebrating "safe" heroes such as George Washington Carver.

Henry Browne, Farmer, a Department of Agriculture film, failed to convince anyone that racial tolerance was desirable. Browne was the perfect obedient Negro: possessor of forty acres, some chickens, a son in the black 99th Pursuit Squadron, and a willingness to grow peanuts because his country needed their oil. To make matters worse, a low budget made the entire enterprise look second-rate. The Negro journalist who originally suggested the idea termed the finished product "an insipid little story far from our original purpose."[7]

Something more substantial was needed because the 1940 Selective Service Act prohibited racial discrimination. The Army looked to Negro manpower. At the same time, military compliance with segregation somehow did not, as the approved Army manual phrased it, "endorse any theory of racial superiority or inferiority."[8] The resulting situation was made worse by a pervasive hostility toward Negro soldiers, who tended to score lowest on the Army General Classification Tests. Deputy Chief of Staff Joseph T. McNarney voiced a prevalent Army attitude: "there is no use having colored troops standing by and eating their heads off if their lack of aptitude is such that they can never be used overseas."[9]

[7] Claude A. Barnett, head of the Associated Negro Press, to Victor Roudin, copy, March 26, 1953, in Barnett MSS, Chicago Historical Society, Chicago, Ill. As one black critic suggested, "Is there only one Negro family in the war and is the only thing they are doing farming?" William Ashby, Springfield [Ill.] Urban League, to Elmer Davis, Box 1431, entry 264, RG 208. Prints of both films are located in FS-NA. An official OWI analysis of *Negro Colleges in Wartime* is located in Box 1490, entry 271, RG 208; the script is in Box 1569, entry 302, RG 208; Box 1571, entry 302, RG 208, has nearly fifty photographs "taken for Negro Colleges but scenes not included in film"; stills from *Henry Browne, Farmer* are in Box 1569, entry 302, RG 208; the lack of appeal of *Negro Colleges in Wartime* is discussed in "Distribution of and Use of OWI Non-theatrical Films in April 1943," Box 1483, entry 268, RG 208, where only one film of all in OWI distribution had fewer bookings per print. All in WNRC-Suitland.

[8] [Donald Young], *Leadership and the Negro Soldier*, Manual M5 (Oct. 1944), 4. In keeping with wartime practice the author's name is not given. Culbert interview with Donald Young, Macungie, Pa., February 13, 1977. A copy of Manual M5 is located in Box 1011, Records of the Assistant Secretary of Defense, Manpower Personnel & Reserve, Record Group 330, Modern Military Records, National Archives, Washington, D. C. [hereafter MMR-NA].

[9] Secret Minutes, Meeting of General Council, May 31, 1943, 3-4, 334 cos, Box 30, Records of the Office of Chief of Staff, RG 165, MMR-NA.

Bitter racial prejudice did not distinguish among aptitude scores. Lacking an effective means of mass persuasion, the Army could only place "excessive faith in the effectiveness of hortatives" as a means of encouraging black and white soldiers to fight together for democracy. This approach was not enough. Secretary of War Henry L. Stimson's Civilian Aide for Negro Affairs, William Hastie, collected a file of outrageous racial incidents in which black soldiers, trained for the most part in the South, had been beaten by local rednecks. Such incidents, reported in the black press, offered a compelling reason for Negroes to reject official pleas for wartime unity.[10]

A group of leading social scientists employed by the Army's Information and Education Division (I&E) felt that scientific research could identify precisely what kind of film might bring white and black America closer together; these civilians made up the third group, and they wanted a documentary film about the Negro.[11] The idea for using motion pictures for persuasion was greatly aided by the fact that Capra's unit and the Research Branch worked side-by-side in I&E.

Brigadier General Frederick H. Osborn headed the Division. A wealthy New Yorker without prior military service, Osborn had family connections and a flair for administration. His father was one of Stimson's close friends, and an uncle, Henry Fairfield Osborn, had been largely responsible for bringing New York's Museum of Natural History to international prominence. Osborn, a board member of the Social Science Research Council (SSRC), had a scholarly study of eugenics to his credit. He came to the Army persuaded that morale could be determined by scientific means, and that traditional morale boosters—sports, camp songfests, "decks of cards and dice and tonettes"—belonged to a bygone era.[12] Osborn's advocacy, together with the support of both Marshall and Stimson, proved crucial to the military's adoption of both film and social science research.

Osborn was in an ambivalent position. Personally interested in statistical research, he headed a division concerned more with practical education and morale services within the Army than matters of sampling technique. I&E represented an unstable alliance between Capra's faith in film as entertainment, and faith in film as pedagogical tool, the latter the

[10] Lee, *Employment of Negro Troops*, 330.
[11] For a fine discussion of I&E see Neil Minihan, "A History of the Information and Education Division," manuscript loaned to Culbert. Also helpful is "Study of I&E Activities in World War II," typewritten, copy in Box 1, Francis Spaulding MSS, Archives of Harvard University, Cambridge, Mass.
[12] Interview with Donald Young, February 13, 1977; telephone interview with Frederick Osborn, November 5, 1976; telephone interview with Paul Horgan, November 10, 1976; Osborn, *Preface to Eugenics* (New York: Harper, 1940).

attitude of Samuel Stouffer, the University of Chicago sociologist who
headed the professional staff of the Research Branch.[13]
At the same time, everyone in I&E shared an ardent belief in salesman-
ship. Wartime was no time for recondite speculation. Ideas were measured by their practical value. Capra needed no instruction in sales
techniques: since the days of *Mr. Smith Goes to Washington* (1939) he
had been selling democracy in his feature films. Less familiar, however, is
the hucksterism of the social scientists. The Research Branch published
its findings in *What the Soldier Thinks*, where numerous graphs and charts
promoted the technique of "scientific" sampling along with practical results assured by asking questions incapable of complex answers.[14]
The social scientists realized that a morale film about race relations was
a perfect place to test ideas about social engineering.[15] This outgrowth of
behaviorial psychology argued that human behavior could be manipulated
towards socially desirable goals. Critics of industrial societies had long
complained that as technology spread its benefits, it also eroded traditional values. Stouffer and Donald Young, the War Department's official
expert on race relations, believed that a "humane" or "liberal" use of
film could reaffirm the values of a democratic society.[16] They also accepted a doctrine employed by most American propagandists in World
War II—the "strategy of truth" or "propaganda of fact."[17] One was
scrupulous about that which supported one's side while passing over the

[13] Culbert interview with Donald Young, February 13, 1977; letter of Young to Culbert,
December 27, 1976.
[14] Stouffer publicized his attitude surveys in *What the Soldier Thinks*, complete copies of
which are found in RG 330, MMR-NA, along with supporting unpublished data. In summary
form they appear in Samuel A. Stouffer, et al., *Studies in Social Psychology in World War
II: Vol. I, The American Soldier: Adjustment During Army Life; Vol. II, Combat and Its
Aftermath; Vol. III, Experiments on Mass Communication; Vol. IV, Measurement and
Prediction* (Princeton, N. J.: Princeton Univ. Press, 1949-50). The methodology of these
surveys is brilliantly attacked in Jacques Ellul, *Propaganda: The Formation of Men's Attitudes* (New York: Vintage, 1973), in particular 259-302.
[15] A good discussion of social engineering is found in Robert K. Merton, *Social Theory
and Social Structure* (rev. ed; Glencoe, Ill.: Free Press, 1957), in particular chapter 16,
"Science and Democratic Social Structure." See also Alvin M. Weinberg, "Can Technology Replace Social Engineering," in Albert H. Teich, ed., *Technology and Man's Future*
(New York: St. Martins, 1972), 27-35. For the origin of the term see H. S. Person, "Engineering," in Edwin R. A. Seligman, et al., eds., *Encyclopedia of the Social Sciences*,
volume V-VI (New York, 1931), 542.
[16] For Young's pre-war work see his *Motion Pictures: A Study in Social Legislation*
(Philadelphia: Westbrook, 1922); he also edited two special issues of the *Annals of the
American Academy of Political and Social Science: The American Negro*, 90 (1928) and
Minority Peoples in a Nation at War, 223 (1942).
[17] For a good discussion of the problem see Paul F. Lazarsfeld and Robert K. Merton,
"The Psychological Analysis of Propaganda," in *Writers' Congress. The Proceedings of the
Conference Held in October 1943 under the Sponsorship of the Hollywood Writers' Mobili-
zation and the University of California* (Berkeley, Cal., 1944), 362-80.

rest in silence. The result often sounded like a lawyer's brief pretending to objectivity.

The fourth group was the Hollywood film community. The fact that Capra's unit was staffed with regulars from the major studios, and that the films were actually made in Hollywood, meant that military filmmaking was followed on a daily basis. *The Negro Soldier* played a significant part in furthering a dramatic shift in the kinds of roles blacks received in feature films; after 1945 the era of the "message" film was at hand. Only *The Negro Soldier*, of all wartime films depicting blacks, actually tried to weave the Negro into the fabric of American life; this characteristic made the Army's film a model for filmmakers wishing to break through in-grained industry stereotypes.

Before 1939, virtually every black role was intended as comic relief.[18] The War Department's officer's training manual, *Leadership and the Negro Soldier*, described this stock figure vividly: "When the Negro is portrayed in the movies, or elsewhere, as a lazy, shiftless, no-good, slew-footed, happy-go-lucky, razor-toting, tap-dancing vagrant, a step has been taken in the direction of fixing this mental picture of the Negro in the minds of whites."[19] The NAACP's Walter White went to Hollywood twice in 1942 to urge a better future for blacks in feature films.[20] White, according to producer Darryl F. Zanuck of Twentieth Century-Fox, wanted Negroes "used as often as possible in the more heroic roles—in the positions which they occupy in real life."[21] In *Sahara* (1943), a black even acted as spokesman for democratic values. But such roles, however well-intentioned, were but more sophisticated versions of earlier attempts which overpraised Negro colleges.

To understand *The Negro Soldier* as a product of Hollywood technique and social science prescriptions, it is necessary to follow the evolution of the script. In March 1942 Frank Capra asked the Research Branch to draw up a list of "do's and don'ts" regarding the cinematic depiction of blacks. Sociologist Donald Young, who had devoted his pre-war career to the study of racial minorities and the impact of motion pictures, prepared a memorandum filled with well-meaning cautions, the ideas of a liberal who above all sought racial tolerance: avoid stereotypes such as the Negroes' alleged affinity for watermelon or pork; also avoid strong images of racial identity ("play down colored soldiers most Negroid in appearance" and

[18] Thomas Cripps, *Slow Fade to Black: The Negro in American Film, 1900–1942* (New York: Oxford Univ. Press, 1977).
[19] *Leadership and the Negro Soldier*, 4.
[20] Cripps, *Slow Fade to Black*, 375–76.
[21] Zanuck to screenwriter Eric Knight, July 22, 1942, Eric Knight MSS, Quakertown, Penna.

Figure 1. *The Negro Soldier* was directed by Stuart Heisler, shown here at left. Copy in Stuart Heisler MSS, Theater Arts Library, UCLA. (Courtesy of UCLA)

omit "Lincoln, emancipation, or any race leaders or friends of the Negro"). Young also favored intraracial politesse: "Show colored officers in command of troops, but don't play them up too much. The Negro masses have learned that colored men who get commissions tend to look down on the masses."[22]

The first script for *The Negro Soldier* was prepared by Marc Connelly. As writer for *Green Pastures* (1930) he had a reputation for sympathetic treatment of Negro themes.[23] Connelly began working in Washington in May 1942 and followed Capra to Hollywood when the unit moved there in June. The script, which has disappeared, was deemed "too dramatic" for the Army's tastes. A second draft, prepared by Ben Hecht and Jo Swerling, was also rejected because I&E continued to insist that the Negro film be "documentary"—i.e., an example of the "propaganda of fact."[24]

During script revisions, Capra gave little attention to the project; in fact, he planned to assign the film to his friend William Wyler, but the latter "got a better offer from the Air Force." In the fall of 1942 Capra chose Stuart Heisler, a comparatively young director (see Figure 1).[25] Heisler already had extensive experience as a studio technician and seemed knowledgeable about racial matters after having made *The Biscuit Eater*, a 1940 film shot on location in Georgia with an interracial cast. Heisler immediately accepted the offer, asking only that Capra provide him with "somebody that *really* knows the background of the Negro."[26]

As a result, Carlton Moss, a black writer, was pressed into service. Moss had attended Columbia University and had worked for the Federal Theater Project under John Houseman, who in turn recommended him to Capra. According to both Heisler and Moss the two "hit it off like magic." Moss remembers working on his version of the script in Washington at the Library of Congress, but not because it put him near the books he needed. It was hard to write about racial harmony while eating in Jim Crow restaurants; the Library's cafeteria was an unsegregated "oasis."[27]

[22] "Suggested Motion Picture of the Negro in the U.S. Army," n.d. [Mar. 1942], copy in Young to Culbert, December 27, 1976; the final memorandum is discussed in Lee, *Employment of Negro Troops*, 387; Culbert interview with Donald Young, February 13, 1977.
[23] Capra, *Name Above the Title*, 337.
[24] Carlton Moss to Donald Young, August 26, 1942; Box 224, Records of the Civilian Aide to the Secretary of War (Hastie File), RG 107, MMR-NA.
[25] Cripps interview with Frank Capra, La Quinta, Cal., December 31, 1976; Axel Madsen, *William Wyler: The Authorized Biography* (New York: Crowell. 1973), 224–25.
[26] Cripps telephone interview with Stuart Heisler, February 17, 1977.
[27] Cripps interviews with Carlton Moss, Hollywood, Cal., June 1970; Boston, Mass., April 1973; Iowa City, Iowa, July, 1974. Moss attended Morgan State College and wrote radio scripts for Dr. Channing Tobias, head of the black YMCA.

Shooting began in January 1943. Heisler, Moss, Research Branch representative Charles Dollard, and a camera crew travelled the United States, visiting nineteen Army posts, virtually every location where black troops trained in large numbers. In Philadelphia, Donald Young arranged for added scenes to be shot at the homes of prominent Negroes. Heisler prepared a number of sequences in which black officers directed the training of soldiers. Most of this footage never appeared because the final version relied more on a docudrama than a documentary style.

The finished film, 43 minutes long, received official approval in January 1944.[28] *The Negro Soldier* (OF 51) unfolded in classic studio style, with a narrative spinning out a flashback device, flawless lighting, and technically perfect optical effects punctuating the sequences. To black audiences, in particular, this technical quality was especially significant. Never before had a film purporting to document black American achievement been made with such professional competence. At the same time, the movie served the Army as propaganda for both black and white troops and as a teacher of comradely regard across racial lines without explicitly violating Army policy toward racial segregation.

A summary of the film's visual content shows how this was accomplished. Neat, clean, orderly, responsible, patriotic: these are the middle-class values which the film presents in image after image. Following the opening credits, a wide establishing shot places us in a splendid stone Gothic church. From the point of view of the congregation we see a black soldier, in uniform, singing a solo; we hear a chorus of extraordinary ability. As the last notes fade away a handsome young preacher (played by Carlton Moss) turns from his prepared text to introduce representative soldiers in the pews.[29] The camera cuts to a sailor, a soldier, even a beautiful light-skinned WAC, "Private Parks, First Class." "First class, indeed," says the preacher with undisguised pride.

The well-dressed, attentive congregation, full of servicemen in uniform, inspires Moss to reflect on the achievements of black Americans: newsreel clips show Joe Louis with his "American fist" recovering the heavyweight championship from Max Schmeling; black athletes defeat Nazi Germany's best at the 1936 Berlin Olympic games. It seems that black America is showing the world what democratic competition can do, and what happens when a Negro gets a fair chance to compete on equal terms. Moss reminds his congregation that the war is being fought to

---

[28] A copy of the original version of OF 51 is found in FS-NA.

[29] A complete copy of the final photographic scenario, May 31, 1943, plus an earlier version dated September 17, 1942, may be found in proj. 6022, 062.2 ocsigo, Box 12, A52-248, WNRC-Suitland. Moss ended up playing the preacher himself only after rejecting a succession of Hollywood Negroes who seemed tied to traditional black acting styles.

defend the American way of life. A Nazi training film shows Schmeling learning to be a parachutist; more newsreel footage shows Joe Louis, in uniform, going through Army basic training. Moss produces a copy of *Mein Kampf* and reads a passage in which Hitler describes the futility of teaching a "half-ape" to be a doctor or lawyer. The congregation looks appropriately shocked to learn what the Nazis really think about Negroes (see Figure 2).

Moss then reflects upon the heroism of blacks in earlier American wars. To recreate historic battles, Heisler used neither complete reenactment nor mere reproduction of old paintings and engravings. The shooting script called for transparencies or "glass shots" made from contemporary illustrative materials, while black and white actors dressed as soldiers passed in the foreground carrying powder and shot to their cannons.[30] The "glass shots," intercut with interracial closeups for emphasis, illuminated the black role in earlier wars, along with the settlement of the West. To Negroes the very idea of any black past other than slavery was for the most part a complete surprise. Here was visual proof that America owed its freedom to its entire population. This lesson in race pride made an indelible impression on those whose education included virtually no mention of black history.

For events after 1898, it was possible to use newsreel footage. Flickering images drawn from archival film allowed audiences to see documentary evidence of Negroes in Cuba and laborers digging the Panama Canal. A wonderful character ("Hi, I'm Jim"—who looks old enough to have fought in 1898) is superimposed over the documentary footage. He tells us about "cleaning up" in Cuba and digging the canal. He sounds so matter-of-fact that we are swept along into accepting the unspoken message: patriotic, dependable blacks have been working to keep America safe all along. For World War I there is footage of the 369th National Guard in the uniform of the French Army. The historical account ends with a staged sequence featuring a black sailor, sure to be taken for Dorie Miller, a steward in the segregated Navy who had taken up a fallen gunner's weapon at Pearl Harbor and became the first black in World War II

---

[30] The script's shooting instructions for achieving this result are instructive: "(NOTE: This scene will be used as a transparency to work in two or three Negro soldiers with white soldiers passing in the foreground carrying shot and powder for cannons.)"; "(NOTE: Beginning with the Revolutionary period, down through all the wars, including World War I IMPRESSIONISTIC CLOSEUPS—white and Negro—mostly recognizable Negro faces—will be shot for dressing up and emphasizing that there were Negro soldiers in all of these wars.)" Script, May 31, 1943, p. 12, A52-248, WNRC-Suitland. The official production budget under the heading "Bits and Extras" called for "Battle of New Orleans. 5 Negroes 1 day at $10.50 a day." Copy in 333.9, ig, Box 1160, Records of the Inspector General, RG 159, WNRC-Suitland.

Figure 2. Carlton Moss, holding a copy of *Mein Kampf*. Moss not only wrote the script but also starred as the minister. (Courtesy of the *American Quarterly*)

to fire at the enemy. The Japanese attack provides Moss with an opportunity to make another point: "And there are those who will still tell you that Japan is the saviour of the colored races," thereby suggesting the opposite—neither Hitler nor Hirohito have anything but contempt for Negroes.

The film now makes an abrupt transition from past performance to present opportunities. Mrs. Bronson, a handsome middle-aged woman wearing a suit and small fur stole (a scrupulous middle-class image in keeping with Donald Young's prescription), stands up in church to read a letter from her son who has just become an Army officer. As she reads the letter, the film cuts to scenes of basic training. Young Bronson is the very picture of light skinned, muscular leadership. He drills in the snow, goes to a segregated dance, meets a nice young girl, and back at camp, is introduced to the poetry of Langston Hughes. After soldiering all week Bronson heads for church on Sunday. The camp chaplain offers a pep talk describing improbably broad opportunities for blacks to get into Officer Candidates School and even West Point; Army units are shown as eager to accept black recruits (see Figure 3). The film ends back in Mrs. Bronson's church as the congregation rises to sing "Onward Christian Soldiers" which segues into "Joshua Fit' de Battle ob Jericho," over which we see a montage of marching men and women. The songs and images combine in a final emotional appeal for wartime unity.

At first, *The Negro Soldier* was intended solely for black troops. Donald Young wrote an official manual, *Leadership of Negro Troops*, to be used by the white officers who commanded black units in World War II.[31] But even before the film was released, two of the four groups, the social scientists and the blacks, began to agitate for wider military and civilian distribution.

Such talk resulted in an extraordinary amount of official debate. The film's director, Stuart Heisler, remembers representatives of more than fifty federal offices screening the rough cut and reading revisions of the script.[32] Nobody seemed sure what the impact of the film might be on black soldiers. To learn if the film would encourage rioting by Negro troops, Heisler, Moss, and Charles Dollard, the Research Branch representative, took their product to a "Negro camp outside of San Diego." The commander, who "knew" his men, insisted that the film would provoke violence. He brought in a special unit of nearly one hundred military police to prevent trouble. The result was hardly what the commander expected. Enthusiastic black recruits threatened to riot unless *all* Negro troops on the post saw the film.[33]

White soldiers offered a different problem. Here another group, the Army leadership, took a direct hand to ensure that the final product would be safe enough to appeal to the widest possible audience. Anatole Litvak, Heisler's superior in the Capra unit, hand-carried the completed "answer print" of *The Negro Soldier* to the Pentagon in October 1943. Marshall, Stimson, Osborn, the head of the Army's Bureau of Public Relations, General A. D. Surles, and Assistant Secretary of War John J. McCloy

---

[31] Osur, *Blacks in the Army Air Forces*, 80–81, notes opposition within the Army to issuing Manual M5. The foreword to *Leadership and the Negro Soldier*, p. iv, specifically suggests that *The Negro Soldier* be shown as part of the course of instruction, "preferably the second meeting," and also suggests, p. 64, that one of the Capra *Why We Fight* films, *Divide and Conquer*, be shown to combat racial "hate" rumors within the United States. Gunnar Myrdal's *An American Dilemma: The Negro Problem and Modern Democracy* (New York: Harper, 1944), is given particular emphasis in the manual's list of suggested readings, p. 101.

[32] Cripps telephone interview with Heisler, February 17, 1977; *The National Film Board News Letter*, February 4, 1944, 2, reported that "in Washington there are about sixty different bureaus or sub-bureaus of the U.S. Government concerned with either the production, distribution, or utilization of films." Copy in Box 1486, entry 269, RG 208, WNRC-Suitland.

[33] Cripps interview with Heisler, February 17, 1977.

Figure 3. Location footage of black troops revealed a wide range of military specialties and roles of blacks along with continuing segregation. (Courtesy of the Museum of Modern Art/Film Stills Archive)

personally viewed the film. On November 1, after much discussion, Litvak received a detailed memorandum outlining specific changes intended to make the film more factually accurate and to mollify racial sensibilities of audiences.[34] Heisler had already been ordered to cut the footage showing men "under the command of Negro officers."[35] War Department officials insisted that a section of the film dealing with World War I include "a small amount of footage which would show that Negroes did something other than engage in combat in the front line." Emphasis on black combat experience in the current war also had to be "toned down" since it "would give an erroneous conception of the overall job of the Army." Finally, every nicety of customary racial etiquette was to be preserved. For example: "The sequence showing a [white] nurse or physiotherapy attendant massaging the [black] soldier's back will be eliminated."[36] This momentary visual breach of racial and sexual taboos

[34] Munson to Litvak, November 1, 1943, 062.2 cos, Box 304, Records of the Chief of Staff, Troop Information & Education, RG 319, MMR-NA.
[35] Cripps telephone interview with Heisler, Feb. 17, 1977.
[36] Munson to Litvak, Nov. 1, 1943, Box 304, RG 319, MMR-NA.

could not be shown though the Army did use white staff to treat injured black soldiers.

In January 1944 the Army agreed to use the film in basic orientation for Negro troops, while continuing to debate further distribution.[37] The Research Branch conducted a "scientific" survey to see what statistics might say about wider reception. This was the wartime pattern: what individual commander's prejudice could compete with the scientifically measured opinion of the entire Army? The survey reported that almost ninety percent of black soldiers questioned wanted the film shown to white soldiers as well as black. Almost eighty percent thought civilians should see it. The surprise came in the white response, for almost eighty percent of those questioned favored showing the film to both black and white troops; nearly eighty percent wanted the film shown to white civilians.[38] Still, some military leaders insisted that the film be accompanied by printed material designed to blunt the message of racial tolerance. The Research Branch, particularly through the efforts of Donald Young, successfully insisted that the film stand alone.[39] In spite of itself, and in opposition to the wishes of some military leaders, the United States Army had a film based on social engineering precepts to teach racial brotherhood.

In the end, OF 51 became "mandatory" viewing for all troops at replacement centers within the United States.[40] Between February 1944 and August 1945, when the order was rescinded, almost every black in the Army and Air Corps saw this film; millions of white soldiers also viewed it as part of I&E's standard orientation program.[41] Though overseas combat zones could not enforce mandatory viewing for all soldiers, the Army still used the film late in 1946. Harry Truman's 1948 desegregation order marked the end of OF 51's official usefulness.[42]

The film had been made for military audiences. What would happen if it joined the ranks of a few other Army orientation films (including *Prelude to War* and *The Battle of Russia* from the *Why We Fight* series) and found

[37] Karl Marks to John Hubbell, Jan. 12, 1944, copy in OF 51 production files, 062.2 ocsigo, Box 14, RG 111, FS-NA.

[38] Report B-102, "Reactions of Negro and White Soldiers to the film *The Negro Soldier*, April 17, 1944. 439 blacks and 510 whites at Camp Pickett, Virginia, previewed the film. In addition almost 91 percent of the whites described it as "very good." Copy in Box 992, RG 330, MMR-NA.

[39] Memorandum, Maj. Gen. Ray Porter, Assistant Chief of Staff G-3, to Osborn, May 4, 1944, 413.53 ag, Box 3241, Records of the Adjutant General, RG 407, MMR-NA; Karl Marks to ocsigo, Apr. 15, 1944, 062.2 ocsigo, Box 44, A45-196, WNRC-Suitland.

[40] War Department Circular 208, May 25, 1944, 413.56 ag, Box 3241, RG 407, MMR-NA.

[41] War Department Circular 283, September 19, 1945, 413.53 ag, Box 3237, RG 407, MMR-NA.

[42] Brig. Gen. C. T. Lanham, Director, I&E Div., to Karl Korter, June 6, 1946, 062.2 cos, Box 374, RG 319, MMR-NA.

commercial distribution to movie theaters all over the United States? Would white patrons pay regular admission to see a film about racial tolerance? Distributors felt sure the answer was no. Blacks thought otherwise; they recognized that the official nature of the film would make it an effective weapon in the struggle for civil rights if it were widely seen by civilians.

The first step was official approval from Elmer Davis, head of the Office of War Information (OWI).[43] He and several members of his staff screened *The Negro Soldier* and demanded yet a few further changes. Davis concluded that the film "probably would be perfectly passable in any theatres whatever in the North; and that the only risks . . . would be attendant upon showing it in, say, Atlanta, or some such Southern center." One member of his staff introduced a new area of possible opposition—whether or not "the Negro press" might consider the film "just icing."[44]

OWI fears led in January 1944 to a private showing at the Pentagon for nearly two hundred black journalists. Frank Capra, though he had little to do with the film, arrived in Washington to show "his" production. Most of the audience wrote favorable—even glowing—reviews, passing over the omission of slavery and the realities of discrimination. Activist groups such as the NAACP and the National Negro Congress praised the film as "the best ever done" and called for its widespread distribution.[45] In April 1944 the Army officially released the film to civilian audiences.

It was one thing to make the film available to civilians, another to have it seen. From April 1944, the fate of *The Negro Soldier* increasingly turned on the activities of blacks, in particular Carlton Moss and Truman K. Gibson, now Stimson's Civilian Aide for Negro Affairs. Both proved adept at rallying Hollywood opinion in the film's favor, and overcoming a mixed critical response. Bosley Crowther of the *New York Times* thought the film "questionable" because it "sugar coats" and "discreetly avoids the more realistic race problems." James Agee, the Southerner who covered cinema for the liberal *Nation*, termed the film "pitifully, painfully mild" although he recognized that blandness made it more saleable. Few white critics shared Agee's insight into black attitudes toward the film. "Straight and decent as far as it goes," he wrote, it "means a good deal, I

[43] A good introduction to the OWI is Allan M. Winkler, *The Politics of Propaganda: The Office of War Information, 1942–1945* (New Haven: Yale Univ. Press, 1978); for Davis' pre-war radio experience see David Holbrook Culbert, *News for Everyman: Radio and Foreign Affairs in Thirties America* (Westport, Ct.: Greenwood, 1976), 125–52.

[44] Paul Horgan to Lyman Munson, Nov. 6, 1943, 062.2 cos, Box 304, RG 319, MMR-NA.

[45] Capra, *Name Above the Title*, 358-62. Mabel R. Staupers, NAACP, to Maj. Gen. A. D. Surles, February 25, 1944; and telegram, National Negro Congress to Surles, February 19, 1944, RG 107, MMR-NA.

gather to most of the Negro soldiers who have seen it.'' Moss agreed, telling a *Time* reporter that the movie would ''mean more to Negroes than most white men could imagine.''[46]

Civilian distribution depended on resolving a longstanding debate between the Army and the War Activities Committee (WAC), the group representing commercial distributors in negotiations for circulation of government films.[47] *The Negro Soldier*, at 43 minutes, or roughly half of normal feature length, would remain unpopular with bookers because no matter what its merits, the film required a change in the standard length of programs.[48] To combine an educational film of ''excessive'' length with OF 51's subject seemingly restricted viewing to black theaters.[49] But Army enthusiasm prevailed over WAC opposition. *The Negro Soldier* was released to those theaters which requested it from a national total of 16,203 ''pledged'' commercial houses. Accurate attendance records, kept in part to stave off possible government regulation, revealed that in calendar year 1944 the film was a commercial bust. It played in only 1,819 theaters in contrast to most OWI shorts which played in more than 13,000 theaters, or the Air Corps combat film *Memphis Belle* (in Technicolor), seen in over 12,000 theaters the same year.[50] Because of its awkward length, fears of resentment of its special pleading, and the normally low grosses generated by slack summer attendance, OF 51 in its first run seems to have done more poorly than any other film released by the government for commercial distribution.

Leading Hollywood producers, urged on by Moss and Gibson, tried another way of beefing up attendance. Litvak and Heisler re-cut the film to a 20-minute two-reeler, enabling the Army to offer two lengths of

---

[46] *The New York Times*, Apr. 22, 1944; *Nation*, March 11, 1944, 316; *Time*, March 27, 1944, 94, 96.

[47] For an excellent discussion of how the WAC functioned see mimeographed analysis of theater booking practices prepared for War Manpower Commission, n.d. [July 1944] in Taylor Mills to Francis Harmon, July 22, 1944, Box 1488, entry 269, RG 208; see also Mills to Truman Gibson, May 1, 1944, Box 1484, entry 268, RG 208, both in WNRC-Suitland.

[48] War Activities Committee, *Movies at War 1945* (New York: War Activity Committee, 1945), 42, copy enclosed in Francis Harmon to Culbert, January 26, 1977; information about exact bookings of OF 51 in each of thirty-one exchanges is found in Box 1485, entry 269, RG 208, WNRC-Suitland.

[49] Peter Noble. *The Negro in Films* (New York: Arno Press, 1970), 99–100 lists numbers of black theaters by state.

[50] Telegram, Lehman Katz to Lyman Munson, n.d. [June 19, 1944]; unsigned memorandum, n.d. [June 28, 1944], both in proj. 6024, 062.2 ocsigo, Box 12, A52-248, WNRC-Suitland. The short and long versions were both made available to commercial distributors in July 1944. Publicity release WAC, July 21, 1944, copy in Box 1, Albert Deane MSS, Museum of Modern Art Film Library, New York, N. Y. A print of Of 24 is available from the Army Training Support Center, Tobyhanna, Pa.

the same film to civilians, beginning in July 1944.[51] As OF 24, but with the same title, the film is virtually identical to OF 51, though omitting entirely Mrs. Bronson and her son's experience at Officer Candidates School. At the end a few added shots of black pilots and black construction workers in India helped give a wider visual sense of Negro involvement in the war. Only *The Negro Soldier*, of all films produced by the military during the war, was available in two versions at the same time. Moss estimated that possibly 5,000 theaters eventually showed the shorter version.

Civilian distribution still faced one last hurdle, a lawsuit from a white Jewish filmmaker who had also made a movie about race pride. Jack Goldberg, president of The Negro Marches On, Inc., for years had produced "race movies," a genre of cheaply mounted productions for distribution in Negro neighborhood houses. He sued in federal court to restrain the WAC from booking *The Negro Soldier*, claiming that it competed unfairly with his own film, *We've Come a Long, Long Way*, which dealt with roughly the same subject (see Figure 4). Goldberg's film possessed a certain credibility in black circles owing to its sponsorship by Elder Solomon Lightfoot Michaux, a radio evangelist well-known to Negro listeners.[52]

At this point the NAACP entered the controversy. Roy Wilkins helped Truman Gibson assemble a "confidential" list of white liberals to "assist distribution," including Nelson Rockfeller, Fiorello La Guardia, Cardinal Spellman, and the *New Yorker's* Harold Ross. NAACP special counsel Thurgood Marshall joined Gibson in filing an *amicus curiae* brief, insisting that the WAC provided "the only available medium" for circulating a film that "proceeded on the premise that racial prejudices which divide our population will have their effect minimized by the dissemination of facts." Marshall and Walter White then prodded the liberal Hollywood Writers' Mobilization into endorsing the film as a "real contribution to national unity" and a repudiation of "racist lies."[53] Gibson and Moss arranged for

[51] "Weekly Report on Film Production Activities," Lehman Katz to Paul Horgan, May 3, 1944, 319.1 cos, Box 370, RG 319, MMR-NA. Specific suggestions from the producers are quoted in Gibson to Anatole Litvak, Apr. 14, 1944, proj. 6024, 062.2 ocsigo, Box 12, A52-248, WNRC-Suitland.

[52] The Goldberg film was based on the OWI pamphlet *Negroes and the War*. Jack Goldberg to Francis Harmon, February 28, 1944, Box 1488, entry 269, RG 208.

[53] Wilkins to Gibson, January 3, 14, 15; February 1, 3, 1944; Wilkins to Maj. Homer B. Roberts, February 9, 1944; United States District Court, Southern District of New York, *Negro Marches On*, Plaintiff, v. War Activities Committee, Defendants, copy, n.d.; Gibson, *amicus curiae* brief, 2 pages, n.d.; Thurgood Marshall to Pauline Lauber, executive secretary, Hollywood Writers' Mobilization, May 2, 1944; Robert Rossen to Frank Capra, March 30, 1944, all in Box 277, Records of the National Association for the Advancement of Colored People, Manuscript Division, Library of Congress, Washington, D. C. [hereafter NAACP Records].

Figure 4. *The Negro Soldier* diverted attention away from Jack
Goldberg and Elder Lightfoot Soloman Michaux's *We've Come a
Long, Long Way,* one of the last "race movies" that seriously
challenged Hollywood's version of the Negro. (Advertisement in
NAACP Records, Library of Congress; courtesy of the *American
Quarterly*)

gala Hollywood receptions in May and June 1944 to drum up support for
both versions of "their" film. Black actress Lena Horne praised the film
and major Hollywood producers provided blurbs, most more convincing
than that offered by Columbia's Harry Cohn: "the greatest War Department Picture ever made."[54]

The NAACP, which had nothing to do with the making of OF 51, now
promoted the film as if it were its own. "NAACP Deplores Legal Action
Against Film *The Negro Soldier,*" declared a press release which
claimed that Goldberg's film was "insulting to Negroes," in contrast to
The Negro Soldier's "enormous potentialities for good in stimulating the
morale of American Negroes and in educating white Americans." White
also persuaded liberal Jewish groups to repudiate Goldberg, thereby avoid-

[54] Quoted in Gibson to Anatole Litvak, April 14, 1944, proj. 6024, 062.2 ocsigo, Box 12,
A52-248, WNRC-Suitland.

ing the appearance of a "Jewish vs. Negro situation." Goldberg was termed a longtime exploiter of black audiences. In the end Goldberg lost in court and settled for a few days' "clearance" to allow his film a brief run and give him a chance to get back part of his investment.[55]

The Negro press continued its campaign to gain wider distribution. It urged the National Council of Negro Women "to rally the public and force the special film, *The Negro Soldier*, to be released in full to audiences of both races." In Los Angeles press support led to a preview under the auspices of the mayor's Civic Unity Committee at a leading hotel.[56] Educators invoked the arguments of the scientific sample to promote the film. They tested OF 51 as a tool for teaching "inter-cultural education" and "living together," and ranked it third in effectiveness out of seventeen films studied.[57]

The campaign soon included plans for distributing the film to civilian audiences outside the commercial circuit. The coming of age of 16 millimeter film (at the time still called "substandard" film) proved a major means for spreading government information throughout the country. Indeed World War II marked the apogee of non-commercial distribution of films in the United States.[58] The OWI and the Army's Public Relations Bureau waged a tedious administrative battle over distribution. In April 1944 the OWI won the right to distribute the long version (OF 51) nontheatrically to a network of film departments in public libraries, schools, and colleges in every state.[59] The Film Library of the Museum of Modern Art in New York, which developed educational distribution of "classic" films in the late 1930s, helped promote *The Negro Soldier* by including it

[55] Goldberg to Congressman Andrew J., May, April 1, 1944; Goldberg to White, May 25, 1944; Ralph Cooper to White, June 8, 1944; Julia E. Baxter to Wilkins, November 4, 1943; press release dated April 27, 1944; White to Marshall, May 4, 1944; all in Box 277, NAACP Records.
[56] Clippings from black press; and invitations to Moss from the Civic Unity Committee and Charles U. Shellenberg, Los Angeles YMCA, April 24, 1944, in personal files of Moss, copies sent to Cripps; trade paper clippings in Stuart Heisler MSS, Theater Arts Library, UCLA.
[57] Discussed in Leonard Bloom, *California Eagle*, March 16, 1944; and Esther L. Berg, "Films to Better Human Relations," reprinted from *High Points* (New York: Brooklyn Jewish Community Council, n.d. [1945]), copies from personal files of Moss sent to Cripps.
[58] RG 208 has the extensive records of OWI's Non-theatrical Division of the Motion Picture Branch. See also Film Council of America, *Sixty Years of 16mm Film 1923-1983: A Symposium* (Evanston, Ill., 1954), 148–59.
[59] Curtiss Mitchell to Stanton Griffis, April 12, 1944, Box 1484, entry 268; Taylor Mills to Edgar Baker, June 8, 1944, Box 1486, entry 269; methods of distribution are discussed in C. R. Reagan to Congressman Louis Ludlow, June 10, 1944, Box 1581, entry 305; all in RG 208, WNRC-Suitland.

in a special series of Capra-unit films shown in New York to capacity audiences in July 1944.[60]

Black groups throughout the country were soon enthusiastic over "their" film and eagerly booked it for church and civic functions.[61] *The Educational Film Guide for 1945*, a standard guidebook for users of documentary film, praised OF 51's technical quality: "good photographs, a nice variety of scene, some flashes of humor and excellent musical background."[62] The film's superb technical quality made it the hit of the season in nontheatrical distribution. The film bureau of the Cleveland Public Library, for example, indicated frequent requests for the film in its monthly reports to the OWI, listing such groups as the "Woodbridge School & PTA" and the "Zion Methodist Church."[63] Not every report indicates attendance figures—nor are such figures capable of verification—but yearly estimated attendance at OWI films distributed nontheatrically numbered over 7.5 million, and that represents only domestic distribution.[64] The film was also used extensively in Latin America, particularly in Haiti, with its predominantly black population.[65]

With the release of OF 51, Moss lobbied for a second film, eventually called *Teamwork* (OF 14), a more self-conscious advocate for racial integration. The motion picture shows blacks in combat against the Nazis. A sequence shot on a Hollywood back lot has Nazi cannoneers shell black troops with a flurry of leaflets reminding them of the "lousiest" jobs and housing awaiting them at the war's end. The blacks toss aside the flyers, as they advance under fire. The narrator grants that "nobody thinks the United States is perfect."[66] Joe Louis is quoted as saying "there's

---

[60] Iris Barry, Curator, Museum of Modern Art Film Library, to Rudolph Montgelas, Bureau of Public Relations, n.d. [Aug. 1944], War Dept. folder, Central Files, Museum of Modern Art Film Library, New York, N. Y. 3,250 persons saw OF 51 (from July 24-30, 1944).

[61] Not every group had a choice: "Mr. E. J. Welch, D. C. Reformatory, Lorton, Va., is anxious to obtain the film, THE NEGRO SOLDIER, for a showing at the reformatory." Catherine Preston, to Joseph Brechsteen, September 13, 1944, Box 1483, entry 268, RG 208, WNRC-Suitland.

[62] Dorothy E. Cook and Eva Rahbek-Smith, compilers, *Educational Film Guide* (New York, W. W. Wilson, Co., 1945), 152. This annual compilation first appeared in 1936.

[63] "OWI Monthly Report of Government Film Showings for October 1944," Cleveland Public Library, Box 1640, entry 362, RG 208, WNRC-Suitland. Boxes 1624–1647 cover every state with varying degrees of completeness on a monthly basis.

[64] C. R. Reagan stated that he distributed 138 of his 150 16mm prints for 15,600 showings with an estimated total audience of 3,220,000 between June 15, 1944 and January 1, 1945. Reagan to Gibson, January 4, 1945, Box 224, RG 107 (Hastie File), MMR-NA.

[65] In June 1945 OF51 had been shown 69 times to 43,025 persons in Haiti. See monthly "16mm Films-Latin American Program-Summary by Title," Copy in Box 218, central files 3, Records of the Coordinator for Inter-American Affairs, RG 229, WNRC-Suitland.

[66] There is a print in FS-NA. The Script and production records are found in proj. 11, 015, 062.2 ocsigo, Box 19, A52-248, WNRC-Suitland.

nothing wrong with America that Hitler could fix!" A timid, much less elaborate production than OF 51, *Teamwork's* modest "message" about integration nevertheless alarmed some in the Army. The film received belated military release only in January 1946, thanks in part to the efforts of the NAACP. Roy Wilkins attended a sneak preview of the film at the Signal Corps Photographic Center on Long Island. Wilkins lobbied for release and the NAACP felt the film could "do much to promote racial unity *now and for the future.*" By the summer of 1946, *Teamwork* also went into civilian distribution.[67]

What in retrospect can be concluded about the direct and indirect impact of *The Negro Soldier* on postwar American race relations? We believe this film represented a watershed in the use of film to promote racial tolerance. *The Negro Soldier's* influence can be seen in three areas: promotion, production, and the demise of "race films."

1) Promotion. Black pressure groups learned that film was a tool for social change. The Army did not recognize how much the technical quality of the film suggested to viewers a military commitment to equality of opportunity. The existence of such a film indicated change within the Army— why not also in the civilian world? Carlton Moss, handsome and eloquent, was the educated preacher who moved his listeners with facts and force of logic. Mrs. Bronson, in her suit and fur, seemed to prove that a black mother was the same as other middle-class women, save for a slightly darker skin color. Moreover, the Army considered Mrs. Bronson's son a valuable asset and trained him thoroughly. His hard work paid off in an officer's commission. Was not this visual evidence of equality of opportunity? How about Private Parks, First Class—wasn't she attractive and competent no matter what her racial background? And that fine church and all those well-dressed people who took their civic responsibilities seriously—all America could see these were valuable citizens. Such images provided visual proof of why racial equality was not just morally but logically justified. Why not everywhere? As Moss put it, he set out to "ignore what's wrong with the army and tell what's right with my

---

[67] Wilkins to Surles, August 22, 1945; White to Marshall, Harrington and Wilkins, April 17, 1946; White to Arthur Mayer, May 21, 1946; White to Robert Patterson, May 9, 1946; Jeannette E. Samuelson, public relations director, Arthur Mayer and Juseph Burstyn Theatres, to "Friend," mimeographed, July 11, 1946; Ida Long, 20th-Century Fox to Fred S. Hall, December 27, 1944; Hall to White, December 29, 1944; Wilkins to Maj. Homer B. Roberts, January 2, 1945, all in Box 277; White to Wilkins, Marshall and Harrington, April 24, 1946; Wilkins to Julia E. Baxter and Harrington, October 21, 1946; White to Patterson, April 24, May 9, 1946, all in Box 274; all in NAACP Records. Samuelson to W. W. Lindsay, Army Pictorial Service, June 12, 1946, proj. 11, 015, ocsigo, Box 19, A52-248, WNRC-Suitland.

Figure 5. Goaded by NAACP pressure in support of wartime calls for "unity," "toler-ance," and "brotherhood," Hollywood movies sometimes included blacks in the ranks of the peoples fighting against fascism, as here in the case of Alfred Hitchcock's *Lifeboat* (1944), fea-turing Canada Lee. (Courtesy of the Museum of Modern Art/Film Stills Archive)

people," which, he hoped, would cause whites to ask "what right have we to hold back a people of that calibre?"[68]

The NAACP now understood how potent indirect messages in films could be. It produced a brochure promoting "audio-visual aids" for "teaching democracy." It formed a new national committee to deal with matters of film propaganda and encouraged film distributors to circulate inventories of films urging "tolerance" and "brotherhood" such as *Teamwork* and *Americans All,* produced by *The March of Time.* The National Conference of Christians and Jews joined what promised to be a new movement, discussed in journals with titles like the *16mm Reporter.*[69] Getting films off of shelves and before commercial and non-commercial audiences was a specific goal capable of fulfillment by any number of black pressure groups. The NAACP could echo the sentiment of an earlier enthusiast for social experimentation: "I have seen the future and it works."

[68] Moss clipping file, March 1944, in personal files of Moss, copies sent to Cripps.
[69] Press clippings in Box 274, NAACP Records.

Figure 6. The trend of wartime liberalism exemplified by *The Negro Soldier* persisted into the era of the so-called "message movie" such as Elia Kazan's *Pinky* (1949), a story of "passing" from black to white, starring Ethel Waters and Jeanne Crain. (Courtesy of the Museum of Modern Art/Film Stills Archive)

2) Production of "message films." A black journal's headline at the time of OF 51's release makes the point: "Army Shows Hollywood the Way." [70] The postwar era of feature films with "messages" about racial liberalism can be traced directly to the humane, natural realism of *The Negro Soldier*, though it would be simplistic to insist that a single film was the sole cause of every "message" motion picture produced after 1945. A number of examples demonstrate the connection.[71] Jester Hairston arranged the choral parts for *The Negro Soldier*. After 1945, Dimitri Tiomkin, who wrote OF 51's score, used Hairston for entire films, a startling change from "before the war [when] the studios only called us when they had 'Negro music' to be sung."[72] Stuart Heisler, director of *The Negro Soldier*, went on to make *Storm Warning* (1950), a harsh indictment of the Ku Klux Klan. Ben Maddow came from a background in wartime documen-

[70] *Negro*, II (Sept., 1944), 94, Johnson MSS.

[71] The tendency is described in Samuel Goldwyn, "How I Became Interested in Social Justice," *Opportunity*, 26 (Summer 1948), 100–01.

[72] "Movie Choir," *Ebony*, 4 (Oct. 1949), 25–27.

tary film to write the screenplay for Faulkner's *Intruder in the Dust* (1949), an urgent plea for mutual respect across racial lines in the South. Carl Foreman, who began the war by writing the Dead End Kids' *Spooks Run Wild*, worked for Frank Capra's film unit. Afterwards he wrote *Home of the Brave* (1949), in which the black hero was named "Mossy" as a tribute to a wartime friendship with Carleton Moss. Stanley Kramer, the producer of *Home of the Brave*, had worked at the Signal Corps Photographic Unit on Long Island during the war. His entire postwar career was devoted to "message" films, including *The Defiant Ones* (1958) and *Guess Who's Coming to Dinner?* (1967), both vehicles for Sidney Poitier and racial liberalism (see Figure 6).[73]

3) The demise of "race movies." The failure of Jack Goldberg's suit signalled an end for the "race movie." When feature films began to depict blacks as human beings, there was no longer a need for third-rate films designed especially for Negro audiences. After 1945 it was soon hard for anyone, black or white, to remember when as a matter of course separate-but-unequal "race movies" were a staple of the American scene. The humanity of *The Negro Soldier* had done its work well.

The historian is always interested in cause and effect, but perhaps a sense of irony is essential in understanding the impact of *The Negro Soldier*. Who would have thought that the Army, officially committed to segregation, would end up with a film which symbolically promoted the logic of integration? Who would have predicted that a documentary-style film about black history and opportunities for military advancement would spawn a generation of feature films calling for racial tolerance? Who would have thought that a military orientation film would make black civilians glow with pride? Minority pressure groups cannot help appreciating such ironies. Merely to show a film is no guarantee of anything, but screening a "message" film for a variety of audiences clearly can achieve results not originally conceived of. This is arguably the symbiotic potential of all mass media, a potential realized in the midst of total war, when the Army used film to show not just Hollywood but all America that civil rights was not only a moral but also a logical necessity. Such conclusions led Walter Fisher, one of a handful of black officers assigned to I&E, to remember this pioneering film a third of a century later. Although "we knew . . . the day of jubilee had not arrived," he considers *The Negro Soldier* "one of the finest things that ever happened to America."[74]*

[73] Cripps telephone interview with Carlton Moss, July 8, 1977; Cripps telephone interview with Stanley Kramer, July 11, 1977; Cripps telephone interview with Carl Foreman, July 12, 1977.
[74] Culbert and Cripps interview with Walter Fisher, Washington, D. C., July 12, 1977.
* We would like to thank the Woodrow Wilson International Center for Scholars, Smithsonian Institution, Washington, D. C., for support in preparing this essay.

CHAPTER 8.

The Snake Pit (1948):
The Sexist Nature of Sanity

LESLIE FISHBEIN

IN THE DECADE FOLLOWING THE FIRST WORLD WAR, FREUDIANISM HAD
become virtually pandemic as psychoanalysis was applied to literature,
the arts, the law, education, history, and social criticism. Grace Adams
insisted: "Psychoanalysis, which had begun its existence as a method of
curing neurosis, was becoming in America a veritable psychosis itself."
But psychoanalysis lacked a vocabulary with which to explain or cure the
profound economic crisis America experienced during the Great Depression. As a result, public interest in psychology, as measured in a survey of
the *Readers' Guide to Periodical Literature,* fell as dramatically as
economic output. The failure of the Freudians to predict the economic
debacle belied psychology's claim to being a full-fledged modern science,
and there was a corresponding loss of public faith in the discipline's
powers.[1]

Freudianism was revived in the late Forties in response to the exigencies
of the postwar world. Women who had experienced paid employment
outside the home during the wartime emergency often had difficulty re-
adjusting to a more restricted domestic role. Whereas during the war it had
been women's patriotic duty to contribute to the nation's economic life,
afterward there was scant cultural support for women who did not wish to
be fulltime homemakers. If anything, there was a proliferation of anti-
feminist tracts which consciously or unconsciously invoked the Freudian
dogma that "anatomy is destiny" to buttress their argument that women
were static creatures, impervious to historical change, whose very na-
tures would be violated if they were diverted from reproduction and nur-

[1] Grace Adams, "The Rise and Fall of Psychology," *Atlantic,* 153 (Jan. 1934), 85–87,
90–92.

turance to the "masculine" realms of intellect and career.[2] As Betty Friedan noted in *The Feminine Mystique* (1963), Freudianism served to buttress a mystique of feminine fulfillment that cajoled women into abandoning their jobs to returning veterans in order to find satisfaction as wives and mothers. The problems of love and sex diverted attention from the more difficult problems of atomic rivalry, communism, poverty, and discrimination: "There was a kind of personal retreat, even on the part of the most farsighted, the most spirited; we lowered our eyes from the horizon, and steadily contemplated our own navels."

Intellectual and career women became the *bêtes noires* of popularizers of Freudianism in the late forties. The preliminary findings of the Kinsey report seemed to indicate that between 50 and 85 percent of the college educated women polled never had experienced sexual orgasm, while less than one-fifth of the high school educated women reported the same difficulty; only a decade later was the full report published and the unrepresentative nature of the earlier sample evident. In fact, Kinsey's 5,940 case histories of American women demonstrated that the more educated the woman, the more likely she was to achieve orgasm. "But," Friedan noted, "the mystique nourished by the early incorrect figures was not so easily corrected." In addition, there was a proliferation of case histories and statistical studies of children abandoned and rejected because their mothers worked. Lest their children suffer the psychic scars of neglect, American women embraced a feminine mystique that turned motherhood into a full-time career and stifled their ambitions for achievements apart from domestic ones.[3] In fact, the appearance of Dr. Benjamin Spock's *Pocket Book of Baby and Child Care* (1946), according to Nancy Pottishman Weiss, marked a shift away from the practicality and concern for the needs of the mother which characterized the Children Bureau's popular childrearing manual, *Infant Care*, first published in 1914. Despite an ostensible desire to encourage natural motherhood and spontaneity, Spock's manual actually fostered maternal insecurity based upon the endless need to attend to the child's emotional, as well as physical, development and upon the nagging fear that improper mother love could harm the child. Hence the child-centeredness championed by Spock implied an apolitical mother without social involvements beyond her home, a woman devoted almost exclusively to nurturance who would eschew outside work in favor of eternal attentiveness to the needs of her child.[4]

[2] William Henry Chafe, *The American Woman: Her Changing Social, Economic, and Political Roles, 1920–1970* (1972; rpt. New York: Oxford Univ. Press, 1974), 199–210.

[3] (1963; rpt. New York: Dell, 1965), 174–78, 185–96.

[4] Nancy Pottishman Weiss, "Mother, the Invention of Necessity: Dr. Benjamin Spock's *Baby and Child Care*," *American Quarterly*, 29 (Winter 1977), 519–46. See especially pp. 520, 531–34, 543.

The late Forties was an era of growing awareness of social problems which had been submerged in wartime unity, not the least of which was the nagging unrest among women. Popularizers of Freudianism were not loathe to blame feminism for social turmoil: if women would renounce their unnatural desire to behave like men, national stability would be restored. Yet it was not only those who explicitly espoused Freudianism who touted its merits as a panacea for social ills. Popularized Freudianism had achieved such widespread acceptance that its language and assumptions pervaded many aspects of critical thought. Even Hollywood, attempting to grapple with the social problems it largely had ignored in the thirties, was not immune, as an examination of the 1948 film *The Snake Pit* reveals. *The Snake Pit* contains an essential paradox. Conceived by its makers and touted by reviewers as an exposé of dehumanizing and overcrowded conditions in the nation's mental hospitals, the film, in fact, offers a solution which celebrates the efficacy of psychoanalysis in restoring its heroine to mental health. Why did this film espouse a costly, time-consuming, highly individualized therapy as a plausible solution for what was clearly a social problem affecting masses of people? *The Snake Pit* will be examined in terms of the tensions between its efforts at social criticism and its commitment to a Freudian therapeutic.

The Snake Pit was released in late 1948 to a chorus of praise from film critics delighted that Hollywood had chosen to treat seriously the plight of the insane in American state mental institutions. Noting that the film "documented insanity with terrifying precision," New York *Herald Tribune's* Howard Barnes argued that *The Snake Pit* stood alone "in a field of subject matter which has been skirted warily by Hollywood, except for a few notable predecessors such as *Private Worlds*, or *The Lost Weekend.*"[5] *Time* praised the film for its willingness to do "what Hollywood has rarely done before: look harsh reality in the eye."[6] Philip T. Hartung of *Commonweal* found the film worthy of applause for conveying to the public "the idea that patients, even those as sick as its central figure, do recover."[7] *The New Republic* hailed the film's courageous exploration of insanity itself and the care provided for the great bulk of our insane as proof of Hollywood's continued vitality: "Hollywood may be moribund, as charged, but when it produces a film of this quality it is not dead."[8] A number of critics made reference to Albert Deutsch's newspaper articles and recently published book *The Shame of the States*,

[5] Howard Barnes, "*The Snake Pit:* Lunacy Dramatized" in "On the Screen," New York *Herald Tribune*, Nov. 5, 1948, 20.
[6] "Shocker," *Time*, Dec. 20, 1948, 44.
[7] Philip T. Hartung, "Associate Freely," *The Commonweal*, Nov. 12, 1948, 118.
[8] "Movies: *The Snake Pit*," *The New Republic*, Nov. 8, 1948, 28.

which had served to expose the squalor, filth, and overcrowding of the nation's mental institutions.[9] In fact, *The New Republic* reviewer wrote: "The picture these movie people have made is not overdone; if you think it is, have a glance at Albert Deutsch's forthcoming *Shame of the States,* in which the facts are documented by name and date and photograph."[10] While some critics faulted the film's artistry, most of the major reviews commended the social responsibility of the filmmakers. Jane Lockart advised her readers in *Rotarian* that *The Snake Pit* had avoided sensationalism to enlighten the public on the subject of mental illness: "Not for those seeking escapist entertainment, but to those concerned that the movies sometimes carry out their responsibility to comment constructively and dramatically on the varied facets of human living, a reassurance."[11]

Producer Anatole Litvak asserted that the film was not conceived with the intention of pandering to morbid curiosity in dramatizing the plight of the insane and the scientific processes used in their rehabilitation. His purpose in making the film, apart from his fascination with the dramatic possibilities of the theme, was to "awaken public interest in this vital matter, to reassure people that mental disorder is an illness which can be cured, and to direct attention to the facilities now available in our institutions." Considering Hollywood's previous treatment of psychiatric themes for their melodramatic convenience, Litvak had to exercise great persuasive power to enlist professional aid in fleshing out Mary Jane Ward's novel *The Snake Pit* (1946).[12]

The Snake Pit was based on the author's eight-and-a-half months' experience in a state mental hospital.[13] The novel's heroine, Virginia Stuart Cunningham, was an aspiring young writer with leftist sympathies who had accompanied her husband Robert from Evanston, Illinois to Greenwich Village, where they shared the burden of his economic failure. The pressure of financial insecurity proved too great for Virginia and led to her emotional collapse. The book chronicles Virginia's experiences in Juniper Hill Hospital from the heroine's point of view. It is a remarkably simple and realistic study of the institutional world of the mentally ill.[14] The

[9] "Shocker," 44; "Movies: *The Snake Pit,*" 28; "Good Case Work" in "The Current Cinema," *The New Yorker,* Nov. 13, 1948, 129.
[10] "Movies: *The Snake Pit,*" 29.
[11] June Lockart, *"The Snake Pit"* in "Looking at Movies," *Rotarian,* Jan. 1949, 53.
[12] Thomas M. Pryor, "Of Litvak and the 'Pit,'" *The New York Times,* Nov. 7, 1948, II, 5. Also, cf. Irving Schneider, "Images of the Mind: Psychiatry in the Commercial Film," *The American Journal of Psychiatry,* 134 (June 1977), 613–19, an article brought to my attention by Lawrence J. Suid.
[13] "Sound and Fury," *Newsweek,* Nov. 8, 1948, 92.
[14] Mary Jane Ward, *The Snake Pit* (New York: Random House, 1946).

novel's verisimilitude forced the author to state that although "based on personal experience and observation," the story was not autobiographical and that both characters and settings were fictitious. In fact, the resemblance between author and heroine was striking. Like Virginia, Mary Jane Ward was the author of two novels which had met with limited literary and financial success; both had accompanied their husbands from Evanston to the Village, sharing several lean years before succumbing to nervous collapse and institutionalization.

The novel evoked a chorus of praise from reviewers for its authenticity and realism.[15] Orville Prescott in *The New York Times* praised Ward's virtuosity in limning Virginia's madness, crediting not only her technical skill but her critical restraint:

> Her ability to make the plight of a patient in an insane asylum seem not just horrible or pitiful, but natural and understandable, is remarkable. The cause of Virginia's mental collapse is never revealed. Psychiatry cannot always discover the cause. Recoveries are sometimes made anyway. "The Snake Pit" might have had greater interest and force if Virginia's malady had been neatly explained. But it might also have seemed too pat and so less convincing. Miss Ward has wisely left to others the dangerous mantle of psychiatric omniscience.[16]

It was the author's capacity for understatement which most impressed reviewer Frederic Wertham, director of the Psychiatric Service of Queens General Hospital and president of the Association for the Advancement of Psychotherapy: "Juniper Hill, the hospital, is far above the average. That makes this novel as a document even more telling."[17] And for once Ward's critical success was matched by financial success: the book her agent had found so dubious that he declined to circulate it was made a dual selection by the Book-of-the-Month Club, reprinted in part in *Harper's Bazaar,* condensed in *Readers Digest,* and disseminated in foreign editions in English, Dutch, French, Swedish, Danish, and Spanish. The book earned over one hundred thousand dollars in its first month, proof of its instant popularity.[18]

The book's film adaptation had followed a tortuous course. The author of five previous novels, only two of which—*The Tree Has Roots* and *The Wax Apples* — had reached publication, Ward faced rejection of *The*

[15] "Ward, Mary Jane," *Current Biography, 1946,* 622–24.
[16] Orville Prescott, "Books of the Times," *The New York Times,* Apr. 5, 1946, 23.
[17] Frederick Wertham, "Pit without Pendulum," Review of *The Snake Pit,* by Mary Jane Ward, *The New Republic,* Apr. 8, 1946, 484–86.
[18] "Ward, Mary Jane," 622–24; "*The Snake Pit:* A condensation from the book by Mary Jane Ward," *Reader's Digest,* May 1946, 129–68; John K. Hutchens, "People Who Read and Write," *The New York Times,* Apr. 14, 1946, VII, 42.

Figure 1. Mary Jane Ward, author of *The Snake Pit,* discusses production of the best selling novel with star Olivia de Havilland, producer Robert Bassler, and director Anatole Litvak. (All stills courtesy of the Museum of Modern Art/Film Stills Archive)

Snake Pit by several publishers and her own literary agent. She independently submitted it to Random House, where it was published as a "prestige" item with an expectation of only limited sales. In May 1945, while *The Snake Pit* was still in galley form—long before it became the Book-of-the Month Club selection in April 1946 and before it exceeded a million sales—Bennett Cerf allowed his friend Anatole Litvak, still an Army colonel, to read the proofs. Litvak not only decided instantaneously to film the book but also convinced Olivia de Havilland to play the title role. He then persuaded Daryl Zanuck, chief of Twentieth Century-Fox, to buy the film rights from him. Litvak and Robert Bassler co-produced the film, with Litvak serving as director as well. All three producers and Miss de Havilland herself felt that the cinematic treatment of the novel would mark "the first authentic film study of a mental case and a mental hospital" [19] (see Fig. 1).

---

[19] "Vital Statistics on *The Snake Pit,*" a studio promotional release, p. 1, in Museum of Modern Art, Film Study Center, New York City. Hereafter referred to a MOMA/FSC.

Nevertheless, the film marked a significant departure from the novel. While the book strictly maintains the point of view of the heroine, Virginia Cunningham, providing a first person interior study of mental illness, director Litvak avoided montage and impressionistic photography, which might have evoked her state of mind, and instead had much of the action photographed from the vantage point of the psychiatrist, Dr. Kik, played by Leo Genn. According to Litvak, the camera would record merely the outward manifestations of the disorder from the viewpoint of realistic sanity.[20] While the reviewer in *Newsweek* mistakenly believed that "as in the book, Juniper Hill Hospital and everyone in it, including Virginia herself, are seen through Virginia's eyes," in fact, the film used the sound track alone as a conventional means of translating Ward's stream-of-consciousness technique for describing her heroine's disordered mind.[21] As a result, the disparity between the doubts and delusions of the sound-track and the portrait of reality recorded by the camera eye leads the viewer to distance himself from the heroine and to question the veracity of her perceptions. D. Mosdell in *Canadian Forum* remarked on the lesser efficacy of the cinematic technique:

> The impact of the original novel is more personal and immediate than that of the film, because from the beginning the points of view of the patient and of the reader are as nearly identical as the author's considerable talent allowed. The film audience's point of view is almost entirely that of the spectator, surveying the patient, the sagacious fox-terrier face of the psychiatrist, and the gyrations of the hopelessly lost—all from a point well outside the action.[22]

This shift from the subjective to an objective mode not only isolates the viewer from the heroine, but also implies the existence of a truth external to the situation, in this case supplied by professional expertise.

The novel left the heroine's illness and its treatment largely undefined.[23] The elaborate Freudian case history is a subsequent invention of the filmmakers. The narrator of the novel has been married to Robert much longer than her film counterpart and is already a mother. Hence she is portrayed as having a richer psychic life as an adult whereas the film heroine had been wed only a few days before her breakdown. The film also seems to condemn Virginia for her initial failure to accept her maternal destiny whereas in the novel she was, in fact, a mother, but one incapacitated by her illness from raising the child properly. In the book Virginia is presented as the author of two published novels, *Afternoon of a Faun* and *A Little Night Music*, itself set in a mental institution. Thus

[20] *"The Snake Pit,"* *Variety,* Nov. 3, 1948.
[21] "Sound and Fury," 92.
[22] D. Mosdell, "Film Review," *Canadian Forum,* Feb. 1949, 255.
[23] "Shocker," 45.

she is viewed as an accomplished human being, much like the author herself, rather than as the untested literary novice depicted in the film. Her work plays a far more significant role in the literary version of her collapse. Ward's heroine is torn between the need to work on her book and the emptiness and fatigue of her housewife's lot. While Ward does allude to Virginia's guilt over the death of her fiancé Gordon, a man who had mocked her ambitions to study medicine, her husband Robert is portrayed as supportive of her writing and intellectual development. Virginia's accomplishments and her husband's respect for her add to her credibility as a witness to her own plight and to her credentials as a social critic. In the novel her breakdown appears to be founded in part on her husband's failure to earn a decent living, forcing them to dip ever downward into dwindling savings. Her worries seem reasonable; it is Robert who seems incapable of fulfilling his traditional masculine role. His failure as a provider seems as potent a catalyst for her collapse as any guilt over her fiancé's death.

Moreover, the book makes scant reference to psychoanalysis and lacks the film's enchantment with its efficacy as cure. Ward emphasizes the private nature of the therapeutic and the central role played by patient rather than physician. In Ward 33, in the midst of those truly mad, Virginia experiences a dark night of the soul that will restore her to psychic health. Her recognition that she would recover comes as a result of a shock treatment far more primitive than any offered by modern medicine:

> Long ago they lowered insane persons into snake pits; they thought that an experience that might drive a sane person out of his wits might send an insane person back into sanity. By design or by accident, she couldn't know, a more modern "they" had given V. Cunningham a far more drastic shock treatment now than Dr. Kik had been able to manage with his clamps and wedges and assistants. They had thrown her into a snake pit and she had been shocked into knowing that she would get well.[24]

In the novel this snake pit experience and her own private invention of Thinking Therapy (T.T.), as opposed to the insipid Occupational Therapy (O.T.) offered by the institution, help restore her to normal functioning. In contrast, the film preserves the snake pit sequence, probably for its dramatic value, but makes psychoanalysis the *sine qua non* of her recovery (see Fig. 2).

Ward mentions psychoanalysis only briefly and in an offhanded manner. It is Robert who has to inform Virginia that she has been psycho-

[24] Ward, 9, 12–13, 59, 77, 79–80, 217, 240–42, 273.

Figure 2. Olivia de Havilland as Virginia Stuart Cunningham surrounded by frenzied inmates in snake pit sequence.

analyzed, an obvious violation of the analytic norm that the patient be a voluntary and fully conscious participant in the procedure. Moreover, Robert notes skeptically that the procedure is supposed to last several years whereas Kik had spent only a few months analyzing his wife. Nor does Virginia concur with Dr. Kik's diagnosis, as she does in the film. She views Gordon's death, now seventeen years in her past, as "the sort of thing that would be nice in a book," but hardly as a plausible explanation for her recent breakdown. She shares her husband's skepticism regarding Kik, noting the doctor's youth as a possible exculpation of his failure to understand their feelings about Gordon. Thus Ward's novel does not portray Kik as the wise avuncular figure we see in the film. Nor is Virginia the impressionable young woman barely past the threshold of matrimony. Ward's Virginia is far less interested than the one portrayed by Miss de Havilland in the inner recesses of her mind. She blithely informs her husband: "Well, the hell with my subconscious. What I'm interested in is getting the old conscious to working again." Her primary interest is in escaping from the asylum to the outside world. When it becomes oppor-

tune to disparage Dr. Kik's diagnosis to Dr. Gifford, the physician who
will determine her ultimate fate, Virginia does not hesitate to declare her
belief that Dr. Kik was mistaken. No longer a pawn of her physicians,
Virginia has learned to manipulate the institution for her own ends. She
relies not on the opinions of her doctors, who fail even to provide a
common diagnosis, but on her own good sense.[25] Ward's novel provides
no ammunition for the ardent Freudian.

In contrast, the film provides an elaborate case history missing in the
novel and makes psychoanalysis vital to Virginia's recovery. A number of
critics objected to the highly schematic nature of the case material ("the
girl's story sounds more like a case history out of a textbook than like real
life") or to its lack of dramatic appeal, but the inclusion of analytic material had not been intended merely to flesh out the novel for the screen.[26] It
involved a conscious choice on the part of the filmmakers. The film's
three producers bypassed other noted screenwriters to arrive at what they
considered an unorthodox choice: Frank Partos, for sixteen years at the top
of his profession in Hollywood, and Millen Brand, a famed novelist/poet
whose sensitive portrait of an escaped mental patient in his 1937 Book-of-
the-Month Club novel, *The Outward Room*, was responsible for his assignment. The two men agreed that their first task was to provide the
heroine with a proper case history. After composing a 123-page detailed
treatment, they went east for five weeks with producers Litvak and
Bassler to have professional criticism, suggestion, and approval for every
phase of their case structure.[27] At studio request, three prominent psychiatrists—Dr. Carl A. Binger, Associate Professor of Clinical Psychiatry
at Cornell University; Dr. M. Ralph Kaufman, chief psychiatrist at Mount
Sinai Hospital and during the war chief of all Army neuropsychiatric
activities in the Pacific; and Dr. Sidney Tamarin, supervising psychiatrist
at a New York mental institution—agreed to give scenarists Brand and
Partos the benefit of their technical advice to preserve the clinical accuracy of the film.[28] The psychiatrists, in fact, provided the writers with a
conventional Freudian analysis of the heroine, an element absent from
the novel.

Reflecting the concurrent popular vogue of Freudianism, screenwriters
Partos and Brand provided the heroine with a case history conforming to
classic analytical patterns. *Variety* even noted that the photoplay had

[25] Ward, 255–57, 270–71, 274.
[26] Mosdell, "Film Review," 255; "Shocker," 45; "Sound and Fury," 92; "Good Case
Work," 129; "Movie of the Week: *The Snake Pit*," *Life*, Nov. 29, 1948, 71.
[27] "Vital Statistics on '*The Snake Pit*,'" 2.
[28] Pryor, "Of Litvak and the 'Pit,'" II, 5.

established a father-fixation as fully as the Production Code would allow.[29] In flashback Virginia is portrayed as a child whose Oedipal relationship with her father has thwarted her impulse toward femininity. In "Some Psychical Consequences of the Anatomical Distinction Between the Sexes" (1925), Sigmund Freud had posited that the only successful resolution of the castration complex and penis envy in a girl involved the renunciation of any possible competition with the opposite sex: "She gives up her wish for a penis and puts in place of it a wish for a child: and *with that purpose in view* she takes her father as a love-object. Her mother becomes the object of her jealousy. The little girl has turned into a little woman."[30] Virginia, in fact, has reached this stage, expressing overt hostility toward her mother, jealously demanding exclusive possession of her father, and lavishing affection on a baby doll, symbol of her wish for a child.[31] Virginia tells Dr. Kik that she loved her father except when he took her mother's part, as in the instance when he wanted her to give the baby doll back to her friend Janie. In flashback we see her father coming out onto the porch and squatting besides his pouting daughter: "Virginia, how many times did I tell you to be nice to your mother now? You know you're going to have a little sister pretty soon, and your mother is sick and nervous these days." Virginia replies fretfully: "She's just sick so that you'll be nicer to her. That's all." The physician provides the orthodox Freudian interpretation of this episode. We hear Dr. Kik's voice on the soundtrack: "You wanted to have a baby of your own, so your father would be as nice to you as he was to your mother." Virginia's voice implicitly confirms his diagnosis: "He was nice to me always . . . until Mother told him about her baby."

These Oedipal conflicts are symbolized by dolls. Freud in "Femininity" (1933) distinguished two stages in a girl's play with dolls. In the initial stage the girl identifies with her mother with the intention of substituting activity for passivity: "She was playing the part of her mother and the doll was herself: now she could do with the baby everything that her mother used to do with her." Virginia's mother attempts to arrest her daughter in this stage, forcing her to play with a doll named Queenie, who represents a girl child like Virginia herself. Virginia pointedly ignores this doll, as in the scene in which she has left it propped on a side chair in the dining room so that her parents can be conscious throughout dinner of her rejec-

[29] *"The Snake Pit," Variety.*

[30] Sigmund Freud, "Some Psychical Consequences of the Anatomical Distinction Between the Sexes" (1925), rpt. in Jean Strouse, ed., *Women and Analysis: Dialogues on Psychoanalytic Views of Femininity* (1974: rpt. New York: Dell, 1975), 34.

[31] All references to the film version of *The Snake Pit* will be to the print, FCA 3434-FCA 3437, in the Motion Picture Section of the Library of Congress, Washington, D. C.

Figure 3. Damian O'Flynn as Mr. Stuart, Lora Lee Michel as Virginia (age 6), and Natalie Schafer as Mrs. Stuart in dinner scene in which Mrs. Stuart complains to her husband because Virginia has rejected her doll Queenie, propped in the chair at rear.

tion of the doll (see Fig. 3) Instead, Virginia prefers the baby doll she received from Janie in exchange for Queenie, proof that Virginia has arrived at the second stage of play described by Freud: "Not until the emergence of the wish for a penis does the dollbaby become a baby from the girl's father, and thereafter the aim of the most powerful feminine wish."[32] However, Virginia's steady march toward femininity is thwarted by her father's rejection of her imperious demands for exclusive affection and his support for her mother. As a result, her love for him erupts into hatred and sadism as she smashes the doughboy doll who symbolizes her father as love object.

It is Virginia's rejection of her father, and her subsequent guilt at his death, which account for her inability to transcend her Oedipal attachment and progress toward femininity. She renounces interest in males as an adolescent, escaping into the "masculine" realm of the intellect.

[32] Sigmund Freud, "Femininity" (1933) in Strouse, ed., *Women and Analysis*, 107.

Again, her case conforms to the Freudian canon: "When the girl's attachment to her father comes to grief later on and has to be abandoned, it may give place to an identification with him and the girl may thus return to her masculinity complex and perhaps remain fixated in it."[33] Virginia's initial choice of a love object is conditioned upon her Oedipal attachment in true Freudian fashion. Gordon represents the patriarchal, punctual, authoritative elements in her own father. He embodies an infantile wish fulfillment, and her choice of him is proof of her continued immaturity. Freud wrote: "The determinants of women's choice of an object are often made unrecognizable by social conditions. Where the choice is able to show itself freely, it is often made in accordance with the narcissistic ideal of the man whom the girl had wished to become. If the girl has remained in her attachment to her father—that is, in the Oedipus complex—her choice is made according to the paternal type." Feminine ambivalence toward the mother, who had been the girl's first love object but was rejected for having failed to provide her daughter with a penis, may threaten the young woman's choice of a man patterned after her father as a mate: "The woman's husband, who to begin with inherited from her father, becomes after a time her mother's heir as well. So it may easily happen that the second half of a woman's life may be filled by the struggle against her husband, just as the shorter first half was filled by rebellion against her mother. When this reaction has been lived through, a second marriage may easily turn out very much more satisfying."[34] Virginia's initial choice of Gordon, a man in the paternal mold, as a love object violates deeply rooted taboos in audience and heroine alike. Gordon's first appearance on screen evokes horror in the viewer because of his striking physical resemblance to Virginia's father, a likeness compounded by the similarity in personality as well. Obviously her love choice is doomed because it evokes in her profound hostility to infantile fixations, a hostility demonstrated in her physical revulsion at Gordon's proposal. Her subsequent choice of a love object in Robert, who shares her father's compassion and warmth but not his patriarchal qualities, is upheld by Dr. Kik as proof of her maturity: she has grown up and learned that husbands and fathers cannot be the same thing. Her ability to resume marital relations, to love a man other than her father, will be the litmus test of her psychic health.

   The Snake Pit was no mere recapitulation of Freudian theory or clinical result. The film pervaded the personal as well as professional lives of those who made it; it absorbed their energies on screen and off. Not only

---

[33] Freud, "Some Psychical Consequences of the Anatomical Distinction Between the Sexes," 34.
[34] Freud, "Femininity," 111–12.

were the participants in the enterprise dedicated to achieving clinical accuracy on screen; they also set out to observe actual institutional life to guarantee authenticity. The writing of the screenplay was begun only after Partos, Brand, and Litvak had spent three months observing patients and hospital routine at public and private institutions in New York, New Jersey, and California. Heroine Olivia de Havilland and Leo Genn, who portrayed her psychiatrist, spent several weeks simply visiting asylums and studying conditions. Litvak's passion for authenticity extended even to the extras who had to agree to observe actual types of psychotic behavior before being assigned to their roles.[35] In particular, Miss de Havilland assumed the full burden of her role, engaging in painstaking research to perfect her performance. According to Susie Berg, "the actress visited countless mental hospitals on the West Coast, traveled east to visit more, consulted at least a dozen psychiatrists on the abstruse points of Virginia's illness. She even deliberately lost weight in order to look convincingly ill and undernourished." Her heroic efforts to replicate the experiences and emotions of the insane produced a result "effective as only the clinically exact and real can be."[36] In fact, Miss de Havilland's personal life at the time reflected the film's celebration of the values of marriage and domesticity. In 1946 the thirty-year-old actress had startled Hollywood by her abrupt abandonment of her "fluttery, bachelor-girl days" to wed author Marcus Goodrich, a man eighteen years her senior. *Time* reported: "With him, Olivia has emphatically settled down." Goodrich provided his new wife with strict but tender patriarchal control, and she responded as deferentially to his opinions of her as Virginia had to the views of Dr. Kik in the film: "Goodrich's own view of his wife (he discusses her at length and objectively in her presence, while she listens meekly) is that she needs a firm hand. He watches over her, keeps an eye on her business and social engagements, sees that she gets enough sleep, discourages overwork."[37] Thus both on screen and off Miss de Havilland became an emblem of the new feminine mystique. And, as if to underline the cast's commitment to domesticity as an ideal, the studio announced that Mark Stevens, the young actor who played Virginia's understanding husband, "took his reel-husband role seriously, for, during the filming of 'The Snake Pit,' he became reconciled with his real-life wife, pretty Annelle Hayes Stevens, in time to celebrate the first birthday of their son

[35] Pryor, "Of Litvak and the 'Pit,' " II, 5.
[36] Susie Berg, "Bedlam and Back," *Kirkeley Hotels Magazine*, Jan. 1949, in MOMA/FSC.
[37] "Shocker," 50–51.

Mark Richard, together.''[38] Seldom have reel life and real life coalesced with such studio effusion.

The Freudian emphasis of the film is not a natural corollary of its social concerns. While Dr. Kik may be able to achieve success by treating every patient as if she were the only one, Dr. Curtis' pedantic list of statistics makes only too obvious the incredible overcrowding of patients both at Juniper Hill and in the nation's mental institutions at large. Virginia is cured only after an expensive and time-consuming treatment involving electroshock therapy, narcosynthesis, and psychoanalysis, a procedure too costly for widespread application. Even if one accepts the film's suggestion of narcosynthesis as a therapeutic short cut, one which most Freudians would reject because it violates the analytic norm that patients must be fully conscious throughout the procedure, the subsequent need for psychoanalysis would render the treatment still too costly and individualized for use in state mental institutions (see Fig. 4). A Canadian reviewer noted the incongruity of posing an individual answer for a social problem: "Judging by *The Snake Pit,* the outlook for any mental patient who is not, so to speak, Olivia de Havilland, and who cannot afford individual treatment outside a state institution, is none too bright; yet the fact remains that without a sufficient sum of money, no alternative is possible.''[39]

Why would *The Snake Pit* suggest a Freudian remedy that clearly is inappropriate to the social problem, namely the overcrowding and inhumane conditions in mental hospitals, that it seeks to correct? Here the film's espousal of the feminine mystique seems far more energetic than its commitment to social reform. During the 1940s, in part as a result of expanded work opportunities available to women in wartime, women faced a bewildering variety of role choices. In particular, educated women in the postwar world were buffeted by competing pressures toward homemaking and career ideals. Studying undergraduate women in 1942 and 1943, Barnard sociologist Mirra Komarovsky noted the incompatible sex roles imposed by American society upon college women who were urged simultaneously to be feminine ("not as dominant, or aggressive as men," "more emotional, sympathetic") and to be modern by demonstrating the same behavior, virtues, and attitudes that would be expected of men of a corresponding age. Komarovsky recognized that the source of inconsistency lay with society itself and not with the individual women analyzed in her study; the remedy for their situation lay not in individual therapy, but rather in social reconstruction: "The problems set forth in

---

[38] "Vital Statistics on *The Snake Pit,*" 4–5.
[39] Mosdell, "Film Review," 255.

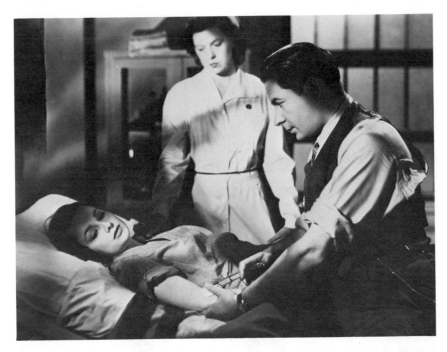

Figure 4. Leo Genn as Dr. Kik injecting Virginia in narcosynthesis sequence intended to provide a shortcut in her therapy.

this article will persist in the opinion of the writer, until the adult sex roles of women are redefined in greater harmony with the socioeconomic and ideological character of modern society. Until then neither the formal education nor the unverbalized sex roles of the adolescent woman can be cleared of intrinsic contradiction.''[40]

Rather than locate the source of feminine tension in society at large, *The Snake Pit* locates it within the heroine herself, a predilection shared by the era's popularizers of Freudianism. As noted earlier, the film ignores the pressures experienced by the literary heroine in trying to combine housework and writing and in coping with her husband's failure to fulfill the traditional male role of breadwinner, instead concentrating upon her Oedipal past. Similarly, such popularizers of Freudianism as social historian Ferdinand Lundberg and psychiatrist Marynia Farnham in *Modern Woman: The Lost Sex* (1947) viewed women themselves as a social problem. Recognizing competing impulses toward femininity and career

[40] Mirra Komarovsky, ''Cultural Contradictions and Sex Roles,'' *The American Journal of Sociology,* 52 (Nov. 1946), 184–89.

Figure 5. Lela Bliss as Miss Greene ordering Virginia off the rug in Ward Twelve.

analogous to those described by Komarovsky, the authors viewed the resulting tension as a neurotic response by women seeking fundamentally to be men; rather than propose societal accommodation to women's new needs, they suggested that the women themselves were in need of therapy:

> The effect of this "masculinization" on women is becoming more apparent daily. Their new exertions are making demands on them for qualities wholly opposed to the experience of feminine satisfaction. As the rivals of men, women must, and insensibly do, develop the characteristics of aggression, dominance, independence and power. These are qualities which insure success as co-equals in the world of business, industry and the professions. The distortion of character under pressure of modern attitudes and upbringing is driving women steadily deeper into personal conflict soluble only by psychotherapy.[41]

It was this social problem caused by the tensions of modern womanhood rather than the crisis in mental health care which most deeply engaged the makers of *The Snake Pit*.

The portrayal of the Juniper Hill nurses reveals that professional women are treated most kindly when they display the nurturant qualities associated with true womanhood; they are condemned when they identify more strongly with institution or career than with this nurturant role. Miss Sommerville, the nurse-turned-inmate as a result of her distress at overcrowding, and the young nurse who eases Virginia's adjustment to Ward One evoke audience sympathy because of their genuine concern for patient welfare. In contrast, the nurses who maintain greater professional distance from the patients are portrayed as masculine, clumsy, cold. Chief nurse Miss Davis, with her dour face and chaste bun, loses control when Virginia suggests that this otherwise icy woman might be in love with Dr. Kik; the mere hint of emotionality is enough to disrupt Miss Davis' chill professional efficiency. These more professional nurses lack a primary commitment to patient nurturance. For example, in Ward Twelve when Virginia seats herself on a huge rug in an otherwise barren room while other inmates march dully around its perimeter, the nurse Miss Greene orders Virginia off, saying that the rug is new and clean and that she wants to keep it that way. Virginia slyly asks her why she doesn't hang it on the wall, but the nurse fails to appreciate her patient's humor or the irony of preserving the rug at the expense of the inmates' comfort. Miss Greene orders Virginia to keep her big feet off the rug. "My big feet?" thinks Virginia, looking at the nurse's own clodhoppers, a subtle index of the

---

[41] Ferdinand Lundberg and Marynia Farnham, *Modern Woman: The Lost Sex* (New York: Grosset and Dunlap, 1947), 1, 235–36.

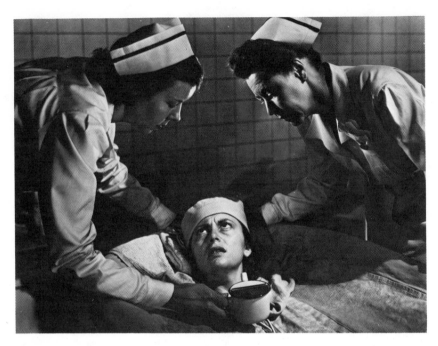

Figure 6. Nurses attempting to feed Virginia during her immersion in the therapy tub.

latter's lesser femininity (see Fig. 5). Similarly, in the tub sequence in which two nurses pontificate in pig Latin, insensitive to the emotional needs of their patient, Virginia interrupts their callous conversation: "It's not nice to call a person utsnay in this place." When the nurse calls her a "society lady," Virginia insists that she is Mrs. Cunningham and asks the nurse's name. "Jones," the woman replies. "Miss?" Virginia queries. "Don't rub it in" is the woman's sour response as she proceeds to feed Virginia forcibly until Dr. Kik intervenes (see Fig. 6). Thus *The Snake Pit's* treatment of nurses as professional women indicates that women who dedicate themselves to a career often lose the warmth and compassion of women who find fulfillment in marriage and motherhood.

In a similar fashion, the film ignores Virginia's conflicts as a frustrated writer and later briefly as a full-time housewife to concentrate on her psychopathology. Even Dr. Kik's personalized treatment does not go beyond giving Virginia the opportunity to type an hour a day, a kind of occupational therapy that wins the resentment of Miss Davis, who believes that it will merely enhance Virginia's sense of superiority over the other ladies because she is a writer (see Fig. 7). Neither the benevolent Kik nor the malevolent Davis has any appreciation of the rhythms or

Figure 7. Helen Craig as Miss Davis, head nurse in Ward One, skeptically administering Dr. Kik's orders that Virginia be allowed one hour a day as writing therapy.

needs of the serious writer; for them writing is the literary equivalent of *macramé*. Also, Virginia's criticisms of social institutions, despite the shrewdness of their warped insight, are stripped of any ultimate signifi- cance because they are the musings of a madwoman. To a lesser degree than in the novel, the film portrays Virginia as a social critic able to penetrate surface reality. Her tendency to view the asylum as a prison (see Fig. 8) and her own electroshock therapy as electrocution receive visual confirmation on screen, and we share her fear that Juniper Hill is an institution dedicated more to coercion and control than to any form of rehabilitation. But her dazed responses and the official memoranda which indicate that Virginia is unable to function realistically serve to remind us that, after all, she is mad and not to be trusted either as social critic or even as personal observer. Thus when on visiting day Virginia suggests to Robert that he divorce her: "You must divorce me. Yes, you must. It's not fair for you to be tied to me. You must have your freedom."—her proposal seems a bizarre response to the insanity surrounding her, in particular to the giggling woman who rouges her nose to greet the boy- friend who turns out to be the husband from whom she wishes a divorce. Robert insists that his freedom consists of the few hours he spends with Virginia. The film uses his sane reaction as proof that true freedom is to be

Figure 8. Virginia's view of Juniper Hill as inmates return from their outdoor rest period.

found within the marriage bond, not outside of it. Freudian analyst Edmund Bergler took a similar approach in his work *Unhappy Marriage and Divorce* (1946):

> Is, then, the institution of marriage as such to blame for marital unhappiness? This would be an erroneous conclusion. The institution of marriage is psychologically the most deeply rooted and the most ineradicable component of our society. At various times and under a variety of external circumstances, attempts have been made to replace marriage with something different, or even to modify it in principle. All such attempts have met with complete failure. It is not marriage that is to blame for the individual unhappiness of those who seek divorce, but rather their particular neuroses. It is not a myth that good marriages exist. The fact is that neurotics are unfit for good marriages. By a very convenient unconscious process of displacement, the neurosis is overlooked and the institution of marriage as such is indicted.[42]

Since the only two inmates who leave Juniper Hill are Margaret and Virginia, both of whom are portrayed as willing and able to resume their conjugal responsibilities, the film implicitly equates mental health with domesticity.

[42] Edmund Bergler, *Unhappy Marriage and Divorce: A Study of Neurotic Choice of Marriage Partners*, with an introduction by A. A. Brill (New York: International Universities Press, 1946), 12.

Any deviation from the cult of true womanhood is judged to be a violation of this morality of mental health. *The Snake Pit* undermines Virginia's genuine radicalism, her ability to discern the fundamentally coercive nature of seemingly benevolent institutions, by portraying it as a symptom of disease. In the novel Virginia is depicted as a fellow traveler active in leftist movements and as someone sensitive to the evil of racial discrimination as practiced at Juniper Hill. She recognizes the rigidity of the institution (e.g., the head nurse of Ward One, Miss Davis, is portrayed as more abnormal than the patients themselves), the genuine spirit of cooperation and generosity of the inmates in Ward Eight, and the return of selfishness which is supposed to herald her return to sanity. In contrast, in the film's dance sequence, Virginia's resentment at having a fellow inmate take all three of her remaining cigarettes is treated as a kind of healthy selfishness that merely demonstrates her restored future orientation. Both novel and film at times blur the distinction between normality and disorder, suggesting that sanity might be a dubious, even a reactionary, norm. In Ward's novel the nurse Miss Vance concludes that there can be only one result of the increased overcrowding of the hospital: "I'll tell you where it's going to end. When there's more sick ones than well ones, by golly the sick ones will lock the well ones up." [43] Virginia is given virtually identical lines in the film. [44] But both genres choose Miss Sommerville, the dedicated nurse driven to madness by her overwhelming obligations to the sick, to embody the blurred distinction between normality and disease. Since heightened social consciousness led to disorder in her case, both novel and film imply the need to dull one's ardor for reform lest madness ensue. [45]

Just as the film undercuts Virginia's radical critique of the institution that imprisons her, so does it undermine all her professional aspirations, attributing all personal anxieties to traumas in her past. Her unhappiness, whether as writer or wife, derives from unresolved Oedipal conflicts in her childhood. The film's analysis parallels that of the works of popularized Freudianism in the era. Lundberg and Farnham also attribute adult accomplishment to rejection by hostile mothers: "Their children, ever striving for maternal approval that never comes, may be converted into notable achievers in the world; may become persons alternately striving to achieve and repeatedly giving up in dejection; or persons making no attempt whatever to achieve anything, knowing it is useless to try to win approval (love). For them love must always be won. It is never something freely bestowed." In *The Snake Pit* Dr. Kik informs Virginia that her

[43] Ward, 20, 110–11, 192, 204–05, 248–49, 272, 277–78.
[44] "I'll tell you where it's going to end, Miss Sommerville. When there are more sick ones than well ones, the sick ones will lock the well ones up," *The Snake Pit,* 1948, Library of Congress print.
[45] Ward, 260.

Figure 9. Virginia cradles a rag doll as Dr. Kik observes her.

illness may have begun with lack of sufficient affection from her mother even while Virginia still was an infant. In seeking to be a writer, an identity that Virginia retains during her institutionalization even while she may deny being a wife, she has chosen an avenue of accomplishment that denies femininity and domesticity. Farnham and Lundberg also claim that women who value worldly achievement have taken the male road of exploit rather than the female road of nurture. The truly healthy woman is one who responds passively to male energy, accepting dependence upon the male to achieve the final goal of sexual life—impregnation; all other feminine striving for achievement is dismissed as mere penis envy.[46] In *The Snake Pit* Virginia's recovery is marked by her recognition that she is Robert's wife and by her admission that she shares the universal feminine desire for motherhood. When Miss Davis mistakenly accuses Virginia of

[46] Lundberg and Farnham, 173–74, 235, 237, 306.

having stolen a rag doll, Dr. Kik finds the alleged offender cradling the doll and rocking it in her arms (see Fig. 9). The following dialogue ensues:

> Dr. Kik: Are you a good mother?
> Virginia: But I'm not a mother. I never had a baby.
> Dr. Kik: Did you want to have one?
> Virginia: Every woman wants to have one, I guess.

Dr. Kik allows her to keep the doll and later is pleased to have her accept its unraveling into rags between her fingers, a symbolic indication that the child that she wants is real.

The Snake Pit also rejects feminine ambition as diseased. The film dismisses Virginia's period of avoiding males in adolescence as neurotic rather than as a necessary period of preparation for a career. Helene Deutsch in *The Psychology of Women: A Psychoanalytic Interpretation* (1944) attributes hostility toward men in puberty to the resentment felt by a girl that her father could not by his strength and love save her from dependence on her mother. The child Virginia in *The Snake Pit* also resents her father for failing to interpose his strength between her and her mother and in adolescence comes to reject males. Deutsch contends that intellectual women have been masculinized: "Only exceptionally talented girls can carry a surplus of intellect without injuring their affective lives, for woman's intellect, her capacity for objectively understanding life, thrives at the expense of her subjective, emotional qualities." For women intellectuality represents a direct betrayal of their fundamental feminine nature: "All observations point to the fact that the intellectual woman is masculinized; in her, warm intuitive knowledge has yielded to cold unproductive thinking." Thus women's worldly achievements are portrayed as unnatural; their protests derive from neurotic dissatisfaction with their ordained lot: "Women are often prone to expressions of the most active indignation. They often participate in violent anonymous protests and join revolutionary movements. Most of the time they are unconsciously protesting against their own fate. By identifying themselves with the socially oppressed or the nonpossessing class, they take up a position against their own unsatisfying role."[47]

The Snake Pit also depicts Virginia's revolutionary ardor as part of her deranged protest against her feminine role. It is only when she comes to accept femininity and domesticity as they are embodied in the institution of marriage that she is pronounced cured. Bergler argues in *Unhappy Marriage and Divorce* that neurosis based on infantile disorders causes neurotic partners in marriage to displace their own inner conflicts onto

[47] Helene Deutsch, *The Psychology of Women: A Psychoanalytic Interpretation*, Vol. I: Girlhood (1944; rpt. New York: Bantam, 1973), 124, 146, 280–81, 298.

Figure 10. Released from Juniper Hill, Virginia is supported by her loving husband Robert, played by Mark Stevens.

their mates. Healthy people are capable of love, neurotics of transference only, at times mistaking transference for true love.[48] When Virginia recognizes her relationship to Dr. Kik as one of transference rather than love, thus freeing herself from immature dependence upon her analyst, the audience knows that she is restored to health and ready to be reunited with her husband. When Virginia is released from Juniper Hill, her face is clouded until Robert reassures her that he has kept her wedding ring for her (see Fig. 10). The final proof of her sanity is her desire that her husband restore the marriage ring to her finger, a token of her willingness to renew the marital bond that her madness had put asunder. Femininity and mental health are equated in the final frames as Virginia is reunited with her husband to the strains of the song "Going Home." Thus, while *The Snake Pit* won public acclaim for its realistic treatment of the theme of mental illness, its more central concern was the crisis in modern womanhood which popularized Freudianism had promised to solve by its parallel equation of femininity and mental health.

[48] Bergler, 11–12, 13, 36, 38.

CHAPTER 9.

Ambivalence as a Theme in *On the Waterfront* (1954): An Interdisciplinary Approach to Film Study

KENNETH R. HEY

THE STUDY OF FILM IN AMERICAN CULTURE POSES SOME INTERESTING challenges to the person using an interdisciplinary method. First, as an historical document, film has contextual connections with the contemporary world. The people who make a film bring to the project their own interests and attitudes, and these various perspectives, when added to the collaborative process, forge a product which resonates in some way with society. Second, as a work of art, film requires textual analysis similar to drama, photography, painting, and music. But as an aesthetic object which combines different artistic media into a single experience, film requires an analytical method which considers all contributing disciplines. Finally, as an art historical object, film stands at the intersection of ongoing traditions in the medium's own history and of theoretical interests alive at the time the film is made. To single out one feature of the film (e.g., its historical context or a self-contained meaning in the text) is to sacrifice the film for something less. To avoid examining the relative contributions of all the major participants is to miss the unique feature of this collaborative art form.

As an example of the collaborative film process and as an object of cultural significance, *On the Waterfront* (1954) has few competitors. Bringing together some of the best and most innovative artists in their respective media, the film was an attempt to weave together the threads of two contemporary events with the strands of aesthetic themes derived from several different artistic media. Unlike many intriguing films which lose their appeal as society changes, this twenty-five-year-old film continues to evince the intended moral outrage from viewers ignorant of its

Figure 1. The dockside establishing shot includes most of the objects which play a prominent role in the film—the cross, the looming ships, the mobsters' dingy shack—and several of the visual motifs which reappear throughout the story—diagonal lines leading to foreshortened spaces, tension between positive and negative spaces, and protruding, unbalanced vertical lines. (Courtesy of the Museum of Modern Art/Film Stills Archive)

historical background and to receive harsh criticism from detractors aware of the film's origins.[1]

On the Waterfront tells of Terry Malloy (played by Marlon Brando) who begins as an ignorant and complacent member of a corrupt gang that controls the longshoreman's union. Terry previously boxed profession-ally for the mob and obediently took "a dive" so the mobsters could win big on the opponent. He now contents himself with a "cushy" dock job and a "little extra change on the side." The mob, headed by Johnny Friendly (played by Lee J. Cobb) with the assistance of Terry's brother, Charley "the Gent" (played by Rod Steiger), applies "muscle" discipline where necessary; when a dissident member breaks the "D and D" rule ("Deaf and Dumb") and talks to the Crime Commission, the mobsters have him killed. Edie Doyle (played by Eva Marie Saint), sister of the film's first murder victim, Joey Doyle, tries to unravel the mystery of union corruption, hoping to uncover the identity of her brother's mur-derer. Joined by Father Barry (played by Karl Malden), she soon concen-trates her attentions on Terry, whose basic philosophy ("Do it to him before he does it to you") clashes with the Christian morality ("Aren't we all part of each other") she has absorbed at a convent school. Terry's indifference to Edie's pleas eventually leads to the murder of "Kayo" Dugan (played by Pat Henning), whose violent death extracts an emotional eulogy from Father Barry. After the mob kills Charley for protecting his brother, the younger Malloy seeks revenge. Father Barry convinces Terry to vent his anger in open testimony before the State Water-front Crime Commission. But the impersonality of formal testimony fails to appease Terry's desire for vengeance, and he confronts Johnny Friendly directly. Although he loses the ensuing fist fight, he seems to win a "battle" by circumventing Friendly's authority and personally leading the men back to work. (See Figure 1.)

The following study will seek to explain how and why *On the Water-front* came to be. As a method of explaining the film's origins and mean-ing, each collaborator's career, point of view, and major interests will be discussed briefly and fitted into the evolving product. When all of the artists' efforts are considered as part of the whole, a single theme pre-dominates: ambivalence. The film argues openly that injustice can be remedied through existing political institutions; but it grafts onto this basic liberal position the suggestion that individuals are frequently casual-ties of the conflict between right and wrong in society and that the indi-vidual's response to the clash of absolute moral standards is ambivalent. In the film, the "thesis" of evil (Johnny Friendly) is confronted by its

---

[1] For example, see Roger Tailleur, "Elia Kazan and the House Un-American Activities Committee," *Film Comment,* 2 (Fall 1966), 43–59.

"antithesis" of good (Father Barry and Christian morality); the new "synthesis" (Terry Malloy) miraculously fuses selfishness and selflessness, but as an individual staggering beneath the burden of moral decisions, he remains unconvinced of the rightness of either extreme.

The idea for a waterfront drama came from a person who had nothing to do with the final product. In 1949, Arthur Miller, flushed with the success of two Broadway plays (*All My Sons*, 1947; *Death of a Salesman*, 1949), directed his considerable talent toward the social struggle then being waged on the Brooklyn docks. His play, *The Bottom of the River* (also titled *The Hook*) told of the misadventures of Peter Panto who in the late 1930s tried to organize dissident longshoremen in Brooklyn's Red Hook district. According to the longshoremen with whom Miller talked, mobsters feared Panto's rapid rise to popularity and had him killed, dumping his body in the East River. In 1951, when the first script was finished, Miller contacted colleague Elia Kazan, suggesting that they work jointly on the film.[2]

Kazan, after completing his studies at the Yale School of Drama in 1932, had joined both the innovative Group Theatre and the energetic Communist Party, but his radical fervor soon waned and he severed Party affiliations because of a conflict over artists' prerogatives and freedoms. From his 1930s experiences in dramatic art and radical politics, Kazan developed an aesthetic theory which favored optimistic realism and assumed a political posture "left of center and to the right of the Communist Party."[3] A deft creator of dramatic tension on stage, Kazan usually directed Broadway plays that projected his liberal ideas. From his work on the Group Theatre's *Golden Boy* to his direction of Tennessee Williams' *A Streetcar Named Desire* (play, 1947; film, 1951) and of Arthur Miller's *All My Sons* and *Death of a Salesman*, Kazan had helped shape studies of inhuman exploitation, bestial degradation, and aimless materialism, as well as statements concerning moral responsibility. But the pessimism which often infused these social dramas was not wholly suited to the optimism of a scrapping and successful immigrant like Kazan. In *On the Waterfront*, he would resurrect Clifford Odets' "golden boy" and make his own "original golden warrior," Terry Malloy, rise from his beating and depose momentarily his corrupt adversary. Kazan would also revive Tennessee Williams' characters from *A Streetcar Named Desire*. In the play, Kazan had directed Vivien Leigh to play

    [2] Arthur Miller, "The Year It Came Apart," *New York* (Dec. 30, 1974–Jan. 6, 1975), 42. For Peter Panto's story, see Allen Raymond, *Waterfront Priest* (New York: Henry Holt, 1955), 65–66.
    [3] Elia Kazan, cited in Michel Ciment, *Kazan on Kazan* (New York: Viking, 1974), 20; quote in following paragraph, 71.

Blanche DuBois as "an ambivalent figure who is attracted to the harshness and vulgarity" surrounding her at the same time she fears and rejects it. For the waterfront drama, Kazan would transfer the character ambivalence to Terry Malloy, converting Blanche DuBois into an effective Edie Doyle, and the befuddled Mitch into a forceful Father Barry (both played by Karl Malden). Stanley Kowalski and Terry Malloy (both played by Marlon Brando) would share several characteristics—an inability to express themselves clearly, an incapacity to control or even comprehend their situations and actions, and a vulnerability which belies a certain sensitivity. But unlike Kowalski, Terry Malloy would be permitted to grow and change. Kowalski's bestial drives mixed with brute strength would give way, under persistent moral preachings, to Malloy's survival instincts tempered with human indecisiveness.

Kazan's successful Group Theatre experiences, his fleeting glance at radical politics, his personal rise from immigrant boy to Broadway's "gray-haired" wonder, and his early Hollywood popularity (*A Tree Grows in Brooklyn*, 1945; *Boomerang* and *Gentleman's Agreement*, both 1947) led him to believe in the value of his own work and in the real possibility of reform. But Kazan stopped short of naive idealism. When confronted with large, historical forces, the individual becomes a victim who may, despite a heroic character, flinch and recoil, as did Emiliano Zapata when offered the reins of the Mexican government (*Viva, Zapata!*, 1952). Thus, by the time Arthur Miller contacted Kazan about a waterfront film, the two Broadway collaborators had shared several artistic experiences, but Miller's clearly defined goods and evils, so evident in *All My Sons*, did not blend well with Kazan's admixture of optimism and moral ambivalence.

Despite this difference in perspective, the two authors collected Miller's completed script and headed west to seek financial backing. After feelers to Kazan's studio, Twentieth Century-Fox, proved unsuccessful, the two appealed to Harry Cohn, president of Columbia Pictures. Cohn, who showed interest in the project, contacted Roy Brewer, whose advice on labor affairs Cohn considered essential. Brewer headed several Hollywood unions and served on the Motion Picture Alliance for the Preservation of American Ideals, an organization of conservative filmmakers who fought communism in Hollywood by aiding the House Committee on Un-American Activities (HUAC). He supplied union workers and projectionists for films he considered politically acceptable and made it impossible for filmmakers disdainful of HUAC to secure a crew in Hollywood.[4] Cohn and Brewer suggested that the authors convert the water-

---

[4] Robert Sklar, *Movie-Made America: A Cultural History of American Movies* (New York: Random House, 1975), 258–59.

front mobsters into communists. When Miller and Kazan refused, Brewer retorted that the creators were dishonest, immoral, and un-American.[5] The power behind this hardline position must have seemed ominous to Kazan in 1952 when he received a subpoena from the House Committee on Un-American Activities to testify concerning his knowledge of communist activities in the 1930s.

According to Kazan, *On the Waterfront* was "partly affected" by his two appearances before the celebrated House Committee on January 14 and April 9, 1952. "I went through that thing," he later admitted, "and it was painful and difficult and not the thing I'm proudest of in my life, but it's also not something I'm ashamed of."[6] No doubt, Kazan confronted his unfortunate role as friendly witness with the perspective that he was trapped between two opposing and irreconcilable forces of evil, neither of which deserved his allegiance. However, he also must have seen that the federal government and the strong pro-HUAC sentiment lodged in Hollywood could destroy his career. The general "good" he perceived in the exposure and criticism of the American Communist Party's activities could be easily fused with the individual "good" of his personal success. "It is my obligation as a citizen," he told the committee, "to tell everything."[7] Like "golden boy" Joe Bonaparte, Willy Loman, and even Blanche DuBois, Kazan saw himself as another victim of social and political forces which corrupt even the most honorable intentions.

With the committee as audience, Kazan read a carefully prepared statement which contained three clearly framed sections. First, he admitted and repudiated membership in the Communist Party. "I was a member of the Communist Party from some time in the summer of 1934 until the late winter or early spring of 1936, when I severed all connection with it permanently. . . . I had had enough anyway. I had had a taste of police-state living and I did not like it." Second, he explained the depth of his complicity by describing his mission and by listing people with whom he had worked.

> For the approximately nineteen months of my membership, I was assigned to a "unit" composed of those party members who were, like myself, members of the Group Theatre acting company. . . . What we were asked to do was four-fold: 1) to "educate" ourselves in Marxist and party doctrine; 2) to help the party get a foothold in the Actors Equity Association; 3) to support various "front organizations" of the party; 4) to try to capture the Group Theatre and make it a Communist mouthpiece.

[5] Miller, "The Year," 43.
[6] Elia Kazan, interview, "Cinema Grand Illusions," *The Real Paper* (May 30, 1973), 24.
[7] Elia Kazan, testimony, *Hearings Before the Committee on Un-American Activities,* House of Representatives, 82d Cong., 2d sess., Apr. 10, 1952, 2408. All quotes in the following paragraph, 2408–13.

All the people Kazan named had previously been named, and thus he did not actually lengthen the HUAC list. But he gave legitimacy to the Committee's witch hunt, and—not insignificantly—insured his future employment in Hollywood.

In the third section of his dramatic presentation, Kazan defended his career since leaving the party and tried to show that his artistic activities were in no way un-American. "After I left the party in 1936 except for making a two-reel documentary film mentioned above in 1937 [*The People of the Cumberlands*], I was never active in any organization since listed as subversive." In characterizing his artistic efforts since 1936, Kazan described *Death of a Salesman* as a story which "shows the frustrations of the life of a salesman and contains implicit criticism of his materialistic standards"; he called *Viva, Zapata!* "an anti-communist picture." He labored to show how even the most critical works were essentially American in intent, purpose, and effect. Depicting himself as a staunch defender of democracy, Kazan asserted that concern for the social problems of the 1930s had drawn him to the Communist Party but that the Party's preoccupation with political subversion had actually harmed real social reform.[8]

Prior to his second appearance before the House committee, Kazan wrote a lengthy letter to the editor of *The Saturday Review*, defending the anti-communist message of *Viva, Zapata!* In explicating the democratic theory behind the film's action, Kazan described Zapata (played by Marlon Brando) as "no communist; he was that opposite phenomenon, a man of individual conscience."[9] The true reformer was an individualist who fought for the same ends as did the Communist Party, but consulted his conscience rather than ideology when making political decisions. Kazan submitted his entire letter to the House committee as part of his formal statement. In the same issue of *The Saturday Review,* Norman Cousins delineated the essential differences between a communist and a liberal. "A Communist, although he pretends to be independent, always takes his order from above; a liberal makes up his own mind. A Communist, because he takes orders from above, is sometimes trapped by an overnight change in Party policy; a liberal can change his mind but he does so slowly, painfully, and by his own volition."[10] Three days after

[8] For a broader study of this point, see Daniel Aaron, *Writers on the Left* (New York: Avon, 1961, 1969), 388–407.

[9] Elia Kazan, "Elia Kazan on *Zapata!*" *The Saturday Review* (Apr. 5, 1952), 22–23. For a longer study of *Viva, Zapata!*, see Paul J. Vanderwood, "An American Cold-Warrior: *Viva, Zapata!* (1952)," in John E. O'Connor and Martin R. Jackson, eds. *American History/American Film: Interpreting the American Image* (New York: Ungar, 1979), 183–201.

[10] Norman Cousins, "Can an American Be Trusted?" *Saturday Review* (Apr. 5, 1952), 20.

testifying, Kazan purchased advertising space in the amusement section of *The New York Times*. In the two-column, page-long "Statement," Kazan defended his actions before the Committee and called upon other liberals to come forward. "Secrecy," he wrote, "serves the communists." In May 1952, Clifford Odets, whom Kazan had named as a former member of the Communist Party, appeared before the Committee and reiterated the emerging liberal theme. "One must pick one's way very carefully through the images of liberalism or leftism today," he told the subcommittee, "or one must remain silent."[11] Odets, Kazan, and others like them had evidently changed their minds "slowly, painfully and by [their] own volition" because they chose, as Terry Malloy would choose, not to remain silent.

Yielding to political hysteria on the right did not appeal to all liberals. Kazan's performance before the committee incensed his associate, Arthur Miller, and the two embarked on an artistic duel which lasted into the 1960s. Miller fired the first round with *The Crucible* (1953), an apparent study of witchcraft in Puritan Salem. According to Miller, "the witch-hunt was a perverse manifestation of the panic which set in among all classes when the balance began to turn [away from communal unity and] toward greater individual freedom."[12] Miller tried to link the Salem witch-hunts with Washington red-baiting. While hoping to avoid spurious connections between witchcraft and communism, he did seek to explore hysterical and oppressive responses to individual acts of conscience. Kazan's return volley in the artistic duel, *On the Waterfront*, made mobster control over the waterfront analogous to Communist Party control over the individual. But the film did not confuse communism *per se* with gangster racketeering; it sought to explore two forms of oppression. Miller and Kazan, the liberal duellists, were firing at each other by firing in opposite directions. Standing back to back, Kazan fired at the political left while Miller fired at the right.

Kazan's role as a "friendly witness" before the House Committee on Un-American Activities and Miller's efforts to capture the "witch-hunt" in dramatic form left undeveloped their ideas for a film on waterfront crime. After testifying, Kazan contacted author Budd Schulberg. Son of a famous Hollywood producer, B. P. Schulberg, the young writer had grown up surrounded by famous people and great wealth. After graduating from Dartmouth College, he returned to his hometown, wrote

[11] Clifford Odets, cited in Lately Thomas (pseud.), *When Even Angels Wept: A Story Without a Hero* (New York: William Morrow, 1973), 175. Elia Kazan, "A Statement," *New York Times* (Apr. 12, 1952), 7.
[12] Arthur Miller, "The Crucible," in *Arthur Miller's Collected Plays* (New York: Viking, 1957), 228.

extra dialogue for various studios, and released his first novel, *What Makes Sammy Run?* (1941). This searing critique of money-hungry executives in the film industry not only singed the coats of all capitalists, it also avenged his father's premature ouster from Paramount Studios. His second novel, *The Harder They Fall* (1947), updated and expanded Odets' *Golden Boy*, detailing the moral failings of comfortable and dependent employees of a corrupt boxing syndicate. Schulberg followed this cynical blast at complacent self-interest with *The Disenchanted* (1950), a partially autobiographical novel which simultaneously traced the demise of Manley Halliday (known to be F. Scott Fitzgerald) during the filming of *Love in Ice* (Walter Wanger's *Winter Carnival*) and the slow disenchantment of a fresh, young screenwriter (Shep/Schulberg) with 1930s socialist thought.[13]

In each of these novels, Schulberg created a powerful character whose success depended upon pitiable humans who cowered before the very force that exploited them. While exploring the curious dynamics of a social structure which propelled the most vicious hoodlums to the top, the three works recorded the slow and agonizing incapacitation of a lone victim struggling to maintain dignity in a hostile environment. From his first novel, which condemned ambitious Hollywood capitalists, to his third, which followed the demise of an "artist" in Hollywood's film factory, Schulberg sketched a debased and graceless society which protected and rewarded the powerful for trouncing upon the weak.

Shortly after his third novel appeared on the market, Schulberg's attention was diverted to the New York waterfront. In 1949, Joseph Curtis, an aspiring film producer with Hollywood connections, had founded Monticello Film Corporation for the sole purpose of converting to celluloid Malcolm Johnson's *New York Sun* articles on union corruption. In 1950, the articles, which won Johnson a Pulitzer Prize, appeared in book form. With this popular momentum, Curtis convinced Robert Siodmak to direct the film and asked Schulberg to write the script. Despite his original hesitancy to return to an industry he had lacerated mercilessly in his fiction, Schulberg agreed. Measuring the distance between successful people and social rebels, Schulberg explained his fascination with the film's subject matter. "The epic scale of the corruption and violence intrigued me. Only a few blocks from Sardi's and Shor's and other places where itinerant social philosophers assemble to discuss the problems of the day, guys who said 'no' to industrial-feudalism were getting clobbered

[13] Budd Schulberg, *What Makes Sammy Run?* (New York: Random House, 1941); *The Harder They Fall* (New York: Random House, 1947); *The Disenchanted* (New York: Random House, 1950).

and killed."[14] Invigorated by the importance and scale of the project, Schulberg investigated, planned, and finished *Crime on the Waterfront* by the spring of 1951, but due to grievous errors in the financial planning, the script was languishing in production limbo when the House Committee on Un-American Activities summoned the author to Washington.

As a disillusioned ex-member of the Communist Party, Schulberg chose to obey the subpoena. Testifying on May 23, 1951, he admitted Party membership, explained Party methods of controlling dissident writer-members, and named former associates. He argued that the limited choices available to the 1930s reformer matched with the urgent need to do something made Party membership seem reasonable. "I joined," he told the committee, "because at the time I felt that the political issues that they seemed to be in favor of, mostly I recall the opposition to the Nazi and Mussolini and a feeling that something should be done about it, those things attracted me, and there were some others, too."[15] He separated offenders into those who joined the Party to advance basically humanitarian causes and those who wished to manipulate the humanists to advance totalitarian ends. Ideological fanatics within the Party exploited socially credible writers who sought to study society's ills. Irritated over the Party's attempts to regulate his own writing, Schulberg left the organization. In his testimony, he contended there were communists and innocent communist dupes, and the "innocents" were really solid democrats fighting for legitimate causes.

In 1952, with the Curtis project still in financial trouble, the rights to *Crime on the Waterfront* reverted to Schulberg. Shortly thereafter, Kazan, who was interested in making a film on corrupt judicial processes in an eastern city, contacted Schulberg. Because they had both been involved in aborted film projects concerned with waterfront crime, they quickly agreed to develop a realistic story based on mobster control of longshore unions. Drawing upon personal investigations, two previously completed scripts, and Johnson's *Crime on the Labor Front*, the two collaborators familiarized themselves with the details of waterfront conditions.[16]

From 1946 to 1951, the docks in New York and New Jersey were rampant with illegal activities. Attempts at reform, as demonstrated by the ill-fated effort of Peter Panto, proved fruitless. After a wildcat strike in

---

[14] Budd Schulberg, "*Waterfront*: From Docks to Film," *New York Times* (July 11, 1954), II, 5. Also, "Suit Seeks Profits of *On the Waterfront*," *New York Times* (Oct. 19, 1954), 24.

[15] Budd Schulberg, testimony, *Hearings Before the Committee on Un-American Activities*, House of Representatives, 82d Cong., 1st sess., May 31, 1951, 583–84.

[16] Malcolm Johnson, *Crime on the Labor Front* (New York: McGraw-Hill, 1950). For a broader view of waterfront crime, see Daniel Bell, *The End of Ideology: On the Exhaustion of Political Ideas in the Fifties* (New York: Free Press, 1960, 1962), 197–205.

1945 focused national attention on the waterfront, William F. Warren, the workers' popular leader, reportedly "fell and hurt himself" on the job, and before reappearing on the docks, made a public "confession" that he had been "a dupe" of the Communist Party. In 1948, a second major strike reached its peak soon after the New York Anti-Crime Commission subpoenaed mobster John M. Dunn, who while awaiting execution in prison promised to name the man known as "Mr. Big"—called "Mr. Upstairs" in the film. While most workers assumed "Mr. Big" to be financier millionaire William "Big Bill" McCormick, dockworker speculation thought New York City's Mayor, William O'Dwyer, better suited the description. But Dunn reneged on his threat, the strike was settled with force, the Anti-Crime Commission recessed, and Mayor O'Dwyer ran for reelection.

By November 1952, when Kazan and Schulberg started writing their story, the New Jersey harbor, the specific location for the film, was the setting of frequent assaults, firebombings, beatings, and mobster activities. With the year coming to a close, the New York State Crime Commission (the Commission in the film) made known its findings. With a sweep of media sensationalism, the Commission charged the obvious: the docks were battlefields for entrenched corruption. Workers were forced to take extortionary loans for guaranteed work, and illegal strikes were called to extract larger fees from shippers. Union leaders abused elections, bookkeeping practices, and pension systems; and shippers, to insure against loss, remained silent. Drawing upon this vast cityscape of corruption, Kazan and Schulberg ran through eight different scripts, each of which exposed illegal activities on the New York waterfront while providing the authors an opportunity to explain their position on analogous contemporary events of seemingly greater national significance.

The themes which emanated from Kazan's and Schulberg's HUAC testimonies—the beguiled innocent manipulated for unwholesome purposes; individual responsibility to the democratic whole; preference for individual morality over ideological fanaticism—were literary in nature and religious in tone, and they helped the authors shape the raw material of waterfront crime. Likewise, the testimonial ceremony, which included confessing anti-social activities, identifying associates and theories responsible for those misguided endeavors, and recommending more desirable ways of expressing social concern, suggested dramatic form. The three stages of their testimony became the three major steps of Terry Malloy's conversion. The first segment of the film exposes Malloy's associations with the corrupt gang; a second segment depicts his discovery of corruption as well as the depths of his own guilt; the final segment shows him battling for his own "rights."

Each segment has a ritualized scene which summarizes the action. The "shape-up" scene discloses the dehumanizing conditions fostered by union corruption. A union leader throws "brass checks" on the ground where longshoremen wrestle to retrieve their guarantee of one day's work. Terry, shown separated from the central scramble, is given a "cushy" job as a reward for setting up Joey Doyle for "the knock-off." A "martyrdom" scene in the middle of the film includes Father Barry's oration over the dead body of "Kayo" Dugan. The "waterfront priest" pleads with the men to come forward and speak because silence only serves the mobsters. A "testimonial" scene at the Crime Commission hearings completes the trilogy. The legal institutions receive reinforcement, and Terry confesses to society his complicity. The state's principal investigator thanks Terry profusely, explaining that his actions "have made it possible for decent people to work the docks again." This speech echoes the one Representative Francis E. Walter addressed to Kazan after his HUAC appearance: "Mr. Kazan, we appreciate your cooperation with our committee. It is only through the assistance of people such as you that we have been able to make the progress that has been made in bringing the attention of the American people to the machinations of this Communist conspiracy for world domination." [17] In the film, confession and reassurance release Terry from his past transgression and enable him to reclaim his "rights."

The first two ritual scenes—the shape-up and the martyrdom—were borrowed from Johnson's *Crime on the Labor Front*. The prize-winning reporter for the *New York Sun* characterized the longshore working conditions "as not befitting the dignity of a human being," a theme consistent with the testimonies and previous creations of both Schulberg and Kazan. The city's district attorney claimed that the abject conditions on the docks were "a direct result of the shape-up system." [18] Johnson's description of the typical dockside call for workers—the morning shape-up—was to fit neatly into the Kazan-Schulberg script:

The scene is any pier along New York's waterfront. At a designated hour, the longshoremen gather in a semicircle at the entrance to the pier. They are the men who load and unload the ships. They are looking for jobs, and as they stand there in a semicircle their eyes are fastened on one man. He is the hiring stevedore, and he stands alone, surveying the waiting men. At this crucial moment he possesses the power of economic life or death over them, and the men know it. Their faces betray that knowledge in tense anxiety, eagerness and fear. They know that the hiring boss, a union man like themselves, can accept

[17] Kazan testimony, *Hearings*, 2414.
[18] Johnson, *Labor Front*, 137.

them or reject them at will. . . . Now the hiring boss moves among them, choosing the man he wants, passing over others. He nods or points to the favored ones or calls out their names, indicating that they are hired. For those accepted, relief and joy. The pinched faces of the others reflect bleak disappointment, despair. Still they linger. Others will wander off inconsolately to wait another chance.[19]

The potency of this scene in the film results from camera positioning. When Big Mac (played by James Westerfield) blows his whistle to call the workers, the camera stands behind him, permitting his large figure to obscure the huddled longshoremen. During the scramble for tags, the camera is low to the ground, capturing facial expressions; character movement is downward, and the camera seems to press the viewer against the dirty dockside surface. When Edie, who has come to the "shape-up" to study the causes of union corruption, tries to retrieve a tag for her father, she comes in contact with Terry Malloy. He overpowers her and recovers the contested tag for his friend, suggesting that muscle prevails on the docks. But when Terry learns that his female adversary is the sister of the kid whom he "set-up for the knock-off," his "conscience" convinces him to surrender the tag to her. Thus, the conflict between muscle and morality is established. During this encounter, the camera first frames Edie and Terry's contest in the foreground with the longshoremen's struggle in the background. When the scramble gives way to moral considerations, the camera changes position, isolating their conversation and making a special case within the generally demeaning environment. The moral "conscience" which Edie embodies alters the situation. For the scene as a whole, the camera presents the viewer with the facts of the story (a sense of viewing a "real" event in the workers' daily lives), the filmmakers' opinion about the story (Mac and his associates have the power; the workers are oppressed and unorganized), and Terry's special relationship to the depicted waterfront conditions. Through camera positioning, the scene establishes conflicts to be explored as the film progresses.

To Kazan and Schulberg, the discipline within the communist "unit" of the 1930s depended upon similar insults to personal dignity. "The typical Communist scene of crawling and apologizing and admitting the error of my ways,"[20] as Kazan described the practice, degraded human intelligence, and the film's "shape-up" scene was intended to capture such dehumanization. After Mac throws the last tags on the ground, exasperation leads to pushing, which eventually leads to chaos. In the film,

[19] Ibid., 133–34.
[20] Kazan testimony, *Hearings*, 2410–11.

Figure 2. Terry Malloy, emerging from the church and the omnipresent fog, tries to catch Father Barry and make a private confession. Even though the "fog" never lifts completely, Terry's confession soon becomes public. (Courtesy of the Museum of Modern Art / Film Stills Archive)

this central expository scene attempts to highlight the hopelessness and futility of longshoremen in a place "which ain't part of America."

Johnson's portrait of waterfront conditions also contained a model for the film's moral catalyst, Father Barry. As associate director of the St. Xavier School (Manhattan), Rev. John M. Corridan, the "waterfront priest," delivered sermons, held meetings, contributed advice to troubled longshoremen, and exhorted the dock workers to strike and rebel. On the violent New Jersey docks, where the film was actually shot, Corridan delivered a virulent attack on union corruption. His sermon, "A Catholic Looks at the Waterfront," was reproduced in Johnson's book:

> You want to know what's wrong with the waterfront? It's love of a buck. . . . Christ also said "If you do it to the least of mine, you do it to me." Christ is in the shape-up. . . . He stands in the shape-up knowing that all won't get work and maybe He won't. . . . Some people think the Crucifixion took place only on Calvary. . . . What does Christ think of the man who picks up a longshoreman's brass check and takes 20 per cent interest at the end of the week? Christ goes to a union meeting . . . [and] sees a few with $150 suits and diamond rings on their fingers.[21]

As his words make clear, Corridan applied the moral teachings of Christ to waterfront unionism, and this unadorned social gospel reinforced the dualism between brutality and innocence which had figured prominently in previous works by Kazan and Schulberg. Because of the familiar set of visual symbols attached to Christian mythology as well as the moral authority and political safety of such a conservative institution, the filmmakers expanded and made essential Father Barry's role in convincing Terry Malloy to testify (see Figure 2).

The filmmakers, both former members of the Communist Party, used Father Barry's funeral oration to air their rejuvenated ideology and to challenge silent liberals to speak out against past totalitarian activities. The emotional speech introduces the idea of shared guilt and encourages action to combat and defeat the mobsters. As the shrill accusations resound through the ship's hold, the forces of chaos (the "mugs" who throw cans and tomatoes) are silenced (Malloy punches Tillio on the chin). With the camera searching high overhead to find Friendly and Charley, it is obvious that the power relationships have not changed. But the men begin to realize that their silence only serves their oppressors.

While Father Barry speaks, the shadow of a cross-like form rises on the wall behind him. After the speech, Dugan's body ascends from the worker's hell (the lower depths of the ship) accompanied by Father Barry and

[21] Johnson, *Labor Front*, 223.

Pops, two saintly escorts for the workingman's martyr. The men stand
with their hats off, unified at least momentarily by this ritual. Whereas the
shape-up belittled the workers, this affirmative scene "resurrects" their
self-image. The action of the men at the shape-up was downward to the
ground; here it is upward toward the sources of oppression.

A "testimonial" session with the Crime Commission, the third ritual
scene in the film, completes the film's structural argument. Corruption
and human indignity, exposed in the shape-up and then condemned
over a martyr's body, are finally made public before a tribunal which
seeks to punish those responsible. In the Commission hearing room,
mobsters, newspapermen, commissioners, and interested citizens have a
designated place in a physically ordered environment where legal processes are conducted in the open for all to see. Unlike the dreary alleys and
dingy asylums of waterfront criminals, the brightly lighted and crowded
room encourages photographers and reporters to publish what they hear.
Investigators doggedly pursue the illegality hidden behind unions without
accounting books and without elections. The degraded competition between workers in the shape-up has become a fair and open contest
between equal adversaries made possible by a legal system which insures
individual "rights." Totalitarian irreverence is supplanted by democratic
dignity.

*   *   *

In the spring of 1953 with the script completed, Kazan and Schulberg
went to California to seek studio backing. After several rejections, Twentieth Century-Fox purchased the rights, and then immediately released
them. A foreign-born producer was staying in the hotel room across the
hall from the anxious screenwriters, and casual conversation led to an
agreement whereby Sam Spiegel assumed all production responsibilities
for Horizon Pictures. Spiegel had arrived in Hollywood in 1938 and soon
started producing minor films under the name S. P. Eagle. His unsteady
career gained stability in 1947 when he and John Huston founded Horizon
Pictures. Although Spiegel rarely intruded forcefully into a film's creation, he usually selected stories which concentrated on the dignity of
human beings (e.g., *African Queen,* 1951). Thus, his decision to back *The
Golden Warriors,* the film's new working title, was consistent with his
other Hollywood investments.[22]

[22] Archer Winsten, "Reviewing Stand," *New York Post* (July 6, 1953), 22; James F. Fixx,
"The Spiegel Touch," *Saturday Review* (Dec. 29, 1962), 13–14+; Thomas M. Pryor,
"Spiegel and U.-I. Back Kazan Film," *New York Times* (June 13, 1953), included in Spiegel
clipping file, New York Public Library, Lincoln Center.

Outside of financial support, Spiegel's contribution was limited to casting, which itself followed a circuitous route. Kazan evidently had Frank Sinatra in mind for both the Malloy and Father Barry parts, but Spiegel wanted to save the Malloy part for Montgomery Clift. Clift was unavailable and Sinatra reportedly demanded $900,000, a sum far beyond the film's modest budget. Undecided, Kazan turned to his frequent associate, Marlon Brando, who signed a contract worth $100,000. Kazan wanted Laurence Tierney for the Charles Malloy role, but Tierney was occupied, and so the part went to another member of Kazan and Strasberg's Actors Studio, Rod Steiger.[23]

In June 1953, Lee J. Cobb, another Group Theatre graduate who had just finished acting in the New York City revival of *Golden Boy,* appeared before the House Committee on Un-American Activities and gave extensive testimony concerning Party operations. In his statement, Cobb struck a special theme which matched the developing ideas for *The Golden Warriors:* "I would like to thank you for the privilege of setting the record straight, not only for whatever subjective relief it affords me, but if belatedly this information can be of any value in the further strengthening of our Government and its efforts at home as well as abroad, it will serve in some small way to mitigate against whatever feeling of guilt I may have for having waited this long."[24] The theme of guilt and confession, implicit in the Schulberg and Kazan testimonies, was now explicit, and it merged easily with the waterfront story. In the film with the neo-gothic church hovering behind him, Terry confesses his culpability in Joey's murder to Father Barry; prodded by the priest, he next confesses to Edie Doyle as they wander outside the metal fence which encircles the waterfront community like the wire cage enclosing Terry's pigeons. But these private confessions give Terry little satisfaction, and the priest reminds him that confession before a public tribunal will better serve his "brothers." Thus Cobb's indirect suggestion that dispensation for social transgressions can be granted only by the institutions abused blended smoothly with the motivations Father Barry was to implant in Terry's mind. Shortly after his Washington appearance, Cobb joined the film project.

Eva Marie Saint had appeared on television for two and one-half years in *One Man's Family.* A member of the Actors Studio, she had her Broadway debut in 1953 opposite Lillian Gish. Kazan and Spiegel saw her perform and sent Anna Hill Johnstone, Kazan's costume designer, to see

---

[23] Sidney Skolsky, "Hollywood is My Beat," *New York Post* (Aug. 26, 1954), 29.

[24] Lee J. Cobb, testimony, *Hearings Before the Committee on Un-American Activities,* House of Representatives, 83d Cong., 1st sess., June 2, 1953, 2356.

the show. Johnstone agreed with their choice, and Saint was hired. Other characters were cast with considerably less confusion. Karl Malden, because of previous work with Kazan and the Group Theatre, was hired as Father Barry, and Tony Galento and Tami Mauriella were hired as Friendly's thugs because of their careers in the boxing world which Schulberg knew so well.[25]

After their successful collaboration on *A Streetcar Named Desire*, Kazan selected Richard Day as the new film's art director. Spanning more than thirty years in Hollywood, Day's distinguished career included six Academy Awards.[26] As supervising art director at Twentieth Century-Fox and later as a freelance set designer, his creations always captured a sense of psychological as well as physical condition. The result of his involvement in the dockside environment, *On the Waterfront* became an urban drama depicting the American city as threatening and confining. Closed spaces, dark caverns, alleyways with lights piercing open spaces and blinding the viewer, laundry hanging on clothes lines creating diagonal intrusions into the human space, underground passages which swallow automobiles and entrap unsuspecting people, and a foggy dankness which oppresses human emotions and obscures perceptions—these are the visuals which menacingly accompany Terry Malloy's futile attempt to assess his situation.

Day's carefully selected sites for location shooting in Hoboken, New Jersey, injected physical power into the dockside cityscape. The riverside piers, with Manhattan looming like a foreign country beyond the longshoremen's reach, as well as the enclosed apartments and barroom, reinforced the general theme of corruption and degradation. These physical settings were complemented beautifully by the photography of Boris Kaufman, whom Kazan hired based upon documentarist Willard Van Dyke's recommendation.[27] Kaufman was the younger brother of Dziga-Vertov and Mikhail Kaufman, both of the Soviet Kino-Pravda film group. During Boris Kaufman's early days in the Soviet film industry, he learned the photographic trade from his brothers. In 1928, he left the Soviet Union with his parents and soon collaborated with Jean Vigo on *À Propos de Nice* (1930), *Zéro de Conduite* (1932), and *L'Atlante* (1934). Arriving in the United States in 1942, Kaufman began his American career as a documentarist for the United States government and eventually as a free-

[25] George Lait, "Eva Marie Saint," *Columbia Pictures Publicity Release* (Feb. 1954), n.p.; "Waterfront Film Dramatizes the Real," *Business Week* (Aug. 7, 1954), 94–98.
[26] "Obituary," *Variety* (May 31, 1972), 68; also, several unpaginated clippings are in the Richard Day file, New York Public Library at Lincoln Center: *Variety* (Aug. 20, 1952) and *New York-World Telegram* (Dec. 29, 1937).
[27] Skolsky, "Hollywood"; Kazan and Van Dyke were both members of Frontier Films.

lance cinematographer in New York City. From these early experiences he developed his style. He preferred black and white to color because mood and overall conception or "idea" could be more directly communicated. He liked early morning and late afternoon shooting because light sources naturally modeled three-dimensional objects and because soft shadows on dimly lit objects could exploit the black and white hues in the film stock. Finally, he preferred clear days for distant shots because aerial perspective could naturally affect and smoothen hard edges. For human, close-up work, Kaufman waited for cloudy days when diffused light better exposed facial features.[28]

Kaufman believed that image and theme should be united and that cinematographers should be concerned primarily with visual continuity from scene to scene. These interests affected his work for *On the Waterfront*. Since the film was shot in story sequence, Kaufman's greatest worry involved constancy in lighting. To solve this nagging problem, which was compounded by New York City winter weather, he burned trash fires in the area while shooting. The result was an evenly diffused light, although the film contains a few mismatched takes which do break the continuity. This simple solution to a technical problem added meaning to the *mise-en-scene* and helped coordinate atmosphere with character development. Due to a pressing shooting schedule, many shots, including the entire final scene, were taken at night. To insure visual continuity, Kaufman complemented the artificial lighting with a sprayed mist, which helped disperse the concentrated light.[29] Blurred lines defining closed spaces and an incessant fog obscuring open vistas visualized correctly the moral confusion which the characters exhibited in words and actions.

Kaufman's work matched Day's dingy sets, and the tight spaces and cramped camera angles offer immediate clues to the theme of ambivalence. The closeness of the objects and characters suggests intimacy, as when Terry and Edie actually communicate within a crowded frame at close range (on the roof, in the saloon, in the corner of her apartment). But tight shots and cramped compositions also suggest entrapment (inside the birdcage, the Friendly bar pay-off scene, the ship's hold, Edie's terrified face as she hears Terry's confession). Open spaces with distant views appear only on the rooftop, suggesting a romantic image of impossible or at best temporary escape from the streets and work below.

---

[28] Christopher Baffer, "From Poland with Love: Tribute to Boris Kaufman," *Backstage* (Nov. 12, 1976), 30. For Dziga-Vertov and the Kino Eye, see Richard Meran Barsam, *Nonfiction Film: A Critical History* (New York: E. P. Dutton, 1973). Also, Jay Leyda, *Kino: A History of the Russian and Soviet Films* (London: Allen and Unwin, 1960).

[29] Edouard L. de Laurot and Jonas Mekas, "An Interview with Boris Kaufman," *Film Culture*, 1 (Summer 1955), 4–6.

Other elements of the film help frame social and moral ambivalence as the central theme of *On the Waterfront*. Speaking about his HUAC testimony, Kazan confided: "I don't think there is anything in my life towards which I have more ambivalence." He compared himself to his filmic counterpart: "Terry Malloy felt as I did. He felt ashamed and proud of himself at the same time. He wavered between the two. . . . He felt like a fool, but proud of himself. . . . That kind of ambivalence."[30] Terry's actions do reveal ambivalent feelings. Attracted and repulsed by "cops" and "crime investigators," Malloy reluctantly moves away from the vulgarity of the boxing-mobster world and toward the respectability of established institutions. The mobsters have derailed Terry's boxing career, leaving him nothing but vague memories of fights he should have won, but he continues to aid their efforts to frighten and control the frustrated longshoremen; in so doing, he remains "a bum." The situation comes into focus when Charley offers Terry a foreman's job in return for silence and support at the Crime Commission hearings. Acknowledging his indecisiveness, Terry blames his brother for not protecting him from the city's "hawks." He leaves, trying to resolve the conflict between attachment to his brother, a mobster, and to his laboring "brothers," whose lives are dominated by the mob. Charley also faces dual allegiances, but his criminal past is beyond redemption. When he tries to convince Friendly that his younger brother just needs time to free himself from the preachments of Father Barry and Edie, Friendly, reflecting Arthur Miller's world of clear choices, gives Charley his options: "You can have it his way or you can have it your way, but you can't have it both ways. . . . On your way 'deep thinker.'" Charley chooses to break with mobster dogma and acts out of personal concern for his brother; having acted out of "conscience," he is eliminated.

In a morally expedient world, actions often militate against personal feelings, creating ambivalent reactions. As Terry and Edie stroll through a neighborhood park, they talk cautiously, wanting both to stay together and to separate. He feels guilty because of Joey's murder and is worried she will discover his crime; she is repelled by Terry's friends but wants to talk to him. According to Kazan, the glove which Edie drops and Terry retrieves offers them the needed excuse to remain together.[31] The social environment pulls them apart, but their feelings bring them together with the help of a personal object. Terry tries on her glove, almost as if he were about to "try out" her moral values. He had worn boxing gloves for the mobsters, and he will now try to fit into the white glove of virtue. After he has

[30] Kazan, cited in Ciment, *Kazan*, 110.
[31] Ibid., 45.

Edie's glove on his hand, he comments jokingly about her childish appearance. He acknowledges that she has grown from an ugly kid with braces and braids to an attractive woman. However, his physical features have remained the same, and he seemingly confronts adult responsibility and even sexuality with ambivalent feelings. As they stand next to the park's cage-like fence, he reminds her how the Catholic sisters tried "to beat an education" into him, and she comments that human understanding would have worked better. Later, outside the constricting fence, Edie wears the same white gloves and listens painfully as Terry confesses his role in Joey's murder. The extra-tight close-up of her horrified expression and the blaring dockside noises emphasize Edie's shocked reaction to the ugly truth. As in *Golden Boy* and *A Streetcar Named Desire*, the physical and the spiritual are at odds.

When Terry and Edie confront each other in her apartment, ambivalent feelings surface again. The Richard Day set is white, mindful of Edie's association with virtue, but the walls are badly discolored. Blond-haired Edie in her white slip cowers in the corner below a crucifix. When Terry knocks, she primps her hair, moves toward the door, and then shouts, "Go away"; the actions and the words contradict each other. Terry, disregarding the words, breaks down the door; she retreats, making assertions about his responsibility. Shaking in rage, he yells to her to stop talking about "conscience; that's all I've been hearing about." He then insists, "You love me, Edie," pleading in a manner quite different than his door-breaking act would suggest. Reemphasizing the split between actions and feelings, she responds: "I didn't say I didn't love you. I said leave me alone." Throughout the scene, she retreats deeper into her apartment, and he follows, finally forcing her into a corner and into a passionate and contorted embrace. Unlike Stanley Kowalski's rape of Blanche DuBois, the effect of this mannerist fusion of bodies is to join opposing forces. Violence and love, brutality and tenderness, the physical and the spiritual are finally brought together. Edie and Terry have forsaken their antithetical extremes and moved to a middle ground where moral decisions are left to the individual.

The final artist brought into the collaborative effort, composer Leonard Bernstein, received the finished print in the spring of 1954. As a student at Harvard University, Bernstein had studied with Walter Piston, but after graduating he undertook advanced study with Aaron Copland, an American composer who found film work satisfying. Between concert performances, Bernstein had penned the music for two Broadway musicals and a modern ballet piece for Jerome Robbins called "Fancy Free" (1944). Repeatedly cited as a communist dupe by the House Committee on Un-American Activities, Bernstein never suffered from the publicity, and his career continued its steady rise through the 1950s. Confronted with the opportunity to write a film score, Bernstein at first balked, thinking the finished piece would be submerged beneath actors' voices and on-location noises. But the visual power of the film overwhelmed his resistance, and he joined the collaborative effort. "I was swept by my enthusiasm," he later wrote, "into accepting the writing of the score . . . although I had thereto resisted all such offers on the grounds that it is a musically unsatisfactory experience for a composer to write a score whose chief merit ought to be its unobtrusiveness. . . . But I heard music as I watched; that was enough." [32]

Because Bernstein composed the music after the actual filming had been completed and because he did not know personally any of the other collaborators, the score for *On the Waterfront* can be studied not only as an essential part of the film but as commentary on the story as well. Schulberg wanted harmonica music to emanate from instruments played within the camera's eye, thereby controlling the composer's freedom to weave dramatic complexity into the material of verbal and visual images. Kazan wanted music which would unobtrusively support the lines spoken by specific characters, thereby avoiding generalizations drawn from musical allusions. Both seemed interested in music which would not challenge the primacy of their ideas. The score which Bernstein delivered to them complemented the film's theme of ambivalence and even made clearer certain aspects of character development.

Bernstein screened the film over 50 times, selecting and timing scenes which seemed to need music, and created a highly consistent, thematic score. Rhythmic flourishes and haunting melodic passages enliven the story's development and add nuance and density to each character's actions. Interestingly enough, the final score's thematic lines, instrumentation, extended *crescendi*, and dissonance resemble techniques Aaron Copland used in his score for *The Quiet City*, the ill-fated Irwin Shaw play which Kazan directed for the Group Theatre in 1939.[33] The major slow themes in the Bernstein score are the "Waterfront Theme" (which opens the film, appears in segments throughout, and reappears in altered form during the final scene) and the "Edie/Love Theme" (which announces

---

[32] Leonard Bernstein, "Notes Struck at 'Upper Dubbing,' California," *New York Times* (May 30, 1954), II, 5. For score analysis, see Hans Keller, "On the Waterfront," *The Score and I. M. A. Magazine* (June 1955), 81–84, and William Hamilton, "On the Waterfront," *Film Music*, 14 (Sept.–Oct. 1954), 3–15.

[33] Harold Clurman, *The Fervent Years: The Story of the Group Theatre and the Thirties* (New York: Knopf, 1945), 80. A concert piece of the Copland score is available: Aaron Copland, "Quiet City," *Four American Landscapes,* Everest 3118; Bernstein also salvaged a concert suite from his film score: Leonard Bernstein, *Bernstein Conducts,* Columbia Masterworks, MS 6251.

Edie's entrances onto the waterfront stage). The two themes are played together during the "dead pigeons" scene on the roof, offering a musical "reprise" of the mannerist kiss which had momentarily united Terry and Edie—and the values they represent. After the kiss, Charley's body is discovered; after these two melodies appear intertwined, Terry confronts Johnny Friendly and gains personal revenge for his brother's murder. Thus, Bernstein's score attributes motivation to Terry's actions. Without such commentative musical statements, the causal connections between characters' thoughts and actions might be missed.

Aggressive and assertive themes etch an acoustic portrait of the corrupted, urban environment. The "Murder Theme," marked *presto barbaro* in the sheet music, is first heard as the Friendly gang emerges from its dingy waterfront shack. The percussive three-voice fugato with its rhythmic irregularity, creates an unsettling atmosphere and hauntingly presages Joey Doyle's murder. Bernstein wanted the "Murder Theme" played before each of the three murders, thus creating a formal allusion to the tripartite plot structure, but the music was cut from the sequence preceding Dugan's murder. During a tense dubbing session, Bernstein's position was overruled because Kazan and Schulberg thought the street sounds and muted dialogue of location shooting were more important.[34] A dirge-like version of the murder theme, however, does accompany Dugan's rise out of the ship's hold.

Each of the three major themes is attached to one of the contending factions of the waterfront story. The violent and corrupt mobsters are identified with the murder theme; the spiritual and incorruptible Edie is associated with the love theme; and the environment in which these two antithetical forces collide is represented by the waterfront theme.

Atmospheric unity, like that gained from Kaufman's misty photography and Day's dismal sets, is communicated in the music through a fourth, independent "Snap Theme." Even though this agitated passage is the most pervasive musical theme in the film, it is not used for literal commentary on characters or plot. At the opening of the film, the "Snap Theme" is interwoven with the "Murder Theme" during Joey Doyle's murder, but it soon disappears leaving the more aggressive theme predominant. This unique combination of melody and rhythm is heard again in Edie's apartment just prior to the kiss and again during the attack on the basement church meeting; later it is given a honky-tonk rendering for the saloon scene. After Terry discovers his brother's dead body, the "Snap Theme" replaces the "Murder Theme" as Terry goes to "take it out on their skulls." The theme is played rapidly during the fight scene between Terry and Johnny Friendly with a slower rendition heard after the fight

---

[34] Bernstein, "Upper Dubbing."

when Terry's body is discovered lying half in the water. A complex metric pattern—5/4 and 6/8 combined—animates the "Snap Theme," and the ascending and descending eighth note pattern gives the theme an active, disturbing sound. This added musical touch accents the dramatic peaks in the story and contributes to the film's overall aesthetic unity.

*   *   *

Contributions of the various collaborators are synthesized in the final scene of *On the Waterfront*. The Kaufman camera continues to frame a blurred image of the waterfront site with special attention to the dingy floating shack where hoodlums bet on horses and dispense with human lives. Longshoremen line the pier overlooking Friendly's headquarters; angry but unmoved they resemble an immense Greek frieze of noble figures incapable of action. The dockside fog, the burning trash cans, and the cold air which quickly converts each breath into mist all conspire, as the environment has throughout the film, to constrain longshoreman rage and to blur the connection between power and oppression. In such a setting, only personal rebellion is possible. When Pop casts the evil Johnny Friendly into the hellish water below, the act balances his son's fall from the rooftop at the outset of the film. But Pop's conversion to social rebel will require more than a single spontaneous act. Here Terry Malloy must act alone rather than as a proletarian hero, because—like Norman Cousins' liberal—Terry has changed his mind "slowly, painfully, and by his own volition."

But even Terry's conversion seems incomplete. Early in the story, Edie visits Terry on the roof. As she looks down on the "original golden warrior" and his loyal retinue, the camera catches her standing next to a rough-hewn, rooftop antenna. The intersecting lines of the wooden structure form an identifiable cross, which visually foreshadows Father Barry's eulogy to Dugan. During a later visit to the roof, Edie brings Joey's jacket to Terry. Unlike Edie's glove which symbolically allowed Terry to "try on" a new morality, Joey's jacket brings with it a heavy responsibility; Joey testified and Dugan testified. Each owner of the jacket was forced to subordinate self-interest to a higher social good. "There's more to this than I thought, Charley," Terry finally admits to his brother. With Edie and her cross intruding into Terry's barren world and with Father Barry peppering the reluctant crusader with visions of a better world, Terry, like an anti-Faust, is being dragged—kicking and screaming—out of hell into heaven.

In the final scene, these visual and verbal references come into play. As Terry staggers to the warehouse door to meet the awaiting gray-haired man, he carries the longshoreman's hook, a suggestion of the cross Christ carried as well as the burden placed on the shoulders of longshoremen. Terry wears a sacred cloth, the coat worn by previous martyrs. He is bleeding about the head, a visual allusion to the crown of thorns, and is enervated from the beating (flagellation) he has just received. Edie, who has by now fused the contradictory roles of lover and saint, tries to help Terry, but is restrained by Father Barry, who urges Malloy forward to his duty. He leads the longshoremen—the rejuvenated flock—to work while the scarred and evil figure of Johnny Friendly remains outside the closing doors.

Kazan has insisted that the final scene is not utopian: "I never meant that when they go back to work at the end of the film there isn't going to be that same corruption starting up a month later."[35] But with the dockside Gates of Heaven mercifully enclosing the laboring faithful and casting out the malevolent oppressor, Kazan's anti-utopian comment seems inappropriate. Actually, the Christian symbolism deceives the casual viewer. For one moment, individual revenge and Christian brotherhood seem united; but undoubtedly they will separate again.

An accurate reading of this scene requires attention to film language. In the final walk, camera point of view shifts abruptly from omniscient to first-person; looking through Terry's battered eyes, we see the blurred and unstable perspective he has on the goal being sought. This is not the first time subjective camera has been employed; it appears earlier in the film after a truck nearly kills Terry and Edie. From Terry's viewpoint, we see Charley's limp body hanging from a partially-lighted alley wall. A slow zoom to Charley's face helps the audience anticipate Terry's emotional response. Thus, in the final scene when the first person camera returns, the audience should recognize that Terry is motivated more by vengeance than by altruism. The film's structural argument, an admixture of ideas borrowed from Johnson's book and HUAC testimony, exposes demeaning labor conditions, explains the reason for these conditions, and suggests a legal solution. After the structural argument ends with the Crime Commission testimony, the film changes perspectives, permitting Terry, like John Proctor in *The Crucible,* to demand his self-respect. From the social perspective, which included clear moral choices, the point of view shifts to the participant's perspective, where outlines are less clear. All the Christian imagery points to a better world, but Malloy's perceptions suggest otherwise.

The facts of the longshoreman struggle prove that little substantially changed after this fleeting victory. "Mr. Upstairs," the man who appeared in the photograph which Terry smashed prior to testifying, and who flicked off the television set just as Terry named the corrupt officials,

---

[35] Kazan, cited in "Grand Illusions," 24.

remained in power. As mentioned earlier, the film's "Mr. Upstairs" could have been financier "Big Bill" McCormick, but it also could have been ILA president Joseph P. Ryan, who still held power when the film was released. Nonetheless, his actual identity remained with mobster John Dunn who died in the electric chair. Regardless of his name, some central figure still dominated the lives of longshore workers, and Johnny Friendly correctly boasts: "I'll be back." As the warehouse door closes behind the victorious workers in the last shots of *On the Waterfront,* the image of caged pigeons should return to the viewer's mind. The warehouse symbolizes both protection and entrapment. The workers, having for the moment regained control of their union, must face the problem which originally brought unions into existence: how can the laborer maintain autonomy and dignity in a capitalist society? To Kazan and Schulberg the problem was similar for the modern liberal whose situation they made analogous to the film's labor rebel: how can liberals eradicate the social problems which the Communist Party exploited? With its ambivalent ending, the film suggests that the challenges require constant vigilance. The structural argument blamed corrupt individuals for the failure of a workable institutional structure; the ambivalent ending with its suggestion of continued corruption posited the idea that oppression is inherent in the institutional system. The two positions—the viability of liberal institutions and ambivalence toward individual action—contradict each other. Thus, the film is a curious mixture of assertions favoring social reform and suggestions as to the futility of such reforms.

The musical score accentuates the tenuous nature of a reformer's victory. Avoiding a strong, tonic cadence, Bernstein's closing musical passages, which are derived from the "waterfront theme," are riddled with dissonance (fourths and flatted ninths), rhythmic snaps (sixteenth-note attacks from one-half step below the sustained note), and moving intervals which are severed quickly with hard accents. The final note of the score is not a sustained tonic which would imply a stable resolution. Instead, the last note is a staccato, accented eighth note marked quadruple *forte,* and spread over a chord which is saturated with half-step dissonance. The visuals, the music, and the dialogue tell of temporary victories, fragile successes which will again be threatened by corruption. These cinematic elements accurately reflect the historical situation. Even the sanguine Rev. John Corridan commented that "the arrest, prosecution and conviction of a few waterfront criminals will improve the situation on the docks only temporarily."[36]

*   *   *

[36] Corridan, cited in Johnson, *Labor Front,* 227.

Interest in and disagreement over *On the Waterfront* started shortly after its release in July 1954. *The Saturday Review* predictably called it "one of the most exciting films ever made in the United States," but *Harper's Magazine,* slightly more critical of certain liberal positions, described it as "a safely sterilized and hygienic slumming expedition," explaining that the story was "false to the longshoremen whose lot it purports to depict, false to the dedicated individuals who have tried to improve that lot, and ultimately false to itself." *The New York Times,* after pointing out that valuable background material was missing, went ahead to call the film "the most violent, graphic and technically brilliant job of movie-making to be unveiled this year." *The Morning Telegram* (New York) characterized the drama as a "rough, tough baby with the simple passions of mankind stripped bare." *Commonweal* said the film was a "simplification of the waterfront mess," but allowed that "the final scenes have the quality of making a saint." *Time* insisted the film maintained "the old sentimental prejudice that ordinary people are wonderful no matter what they do." *Life* magazine accurately reflected the dichotomy of critical reactions by explaining that *On the Waterfront* "is the most brutal movie of the year, but it also contains the year's tenderest love scenes." Perhaps to confuse further the connection between historical event and fictional presentation, Anthony (Tony Mike) de Vincenzo, whose life inspired the character of Terry Malloy, sued Columbia Pictures and Sam Spiegel for $1,000,000 for invading his right to privacy. He won a smaller settlement, as did Frank Sinatra who sued the same people for $500,000, a sum he said had been promised him when he was offered the part. From Chicago to San Francisco, local longshore unions, both corrupt and honest, sued the film's backers for libelous assaults on the honor of longshoremen.[37]

While critical and legal controversy surrounded the film, the Academy of Motion Picture Arts and Sciences made its position clear. *On the Waterfront* received Oscars for Best Production, Best Screenplay, Best Direction, Best Actor, Best Supporting Actress, Art Direction, Black and White Photography, and Editing (Gene Milford). The New York Film Critics showed similar approval by awarding the film their three best awards: Best Movie, Best Director, and Best Actor. Even the most disparaging critic (*Harpers*) conceded the film "was beautifully acted, beautifully directed and beautifully photographed."

---

[37] *Saturday Review* (July 24, 1954), 25; *Harper's Magazine* (Aug. 1954), 93–95; *New York Times* (Aug. 1, 1954), 18; *Morning Telegram* (Sept. 6, 1954), 2; *Commonweal* (Aug. 20, 1954), 485–86; *Time* (Aug. 9, 1954), 82; *Life* (July 19, 1954), 45–46; "Sinatra Sues 'Waterfront,'" *New York Times* (Dec. 22, 1954), 54; "Union Sues 'Waterfront,'" *New York Times* (Mar. 18, 1955) in *On the Waterfront* folder, New York Public Library, Lincoln Center.

The theme of ambivalence in *On the Waterfront,* especially with its partially obscured purpose of personal aggrandizement, elicited blistering critiques from some writers. An exasperated Lindsay Anderson blasted the film's final scene as "implicitly (if unconsciously) Fascist." In an article which seemed to plead for populist melodrama, Anderson complained about the "horrid vulgarity" of the story and the "deep human falsity and demagogic dishonesty of argument." He was most disturbed that the ignorant and befuddled longshoremen transferred loyalties so easily from one oppressor (Johnny Friendly) to another potential oppressor (Terry Malloy) without experiencing some "sense of liberation." They seemed to accept fascist control as their condition in life. Aroused and confused over the ambivalent message, Anderson insisted that the final scene could be taken in only "two ways: as hopelessly, savagely ironic; or as fundamentally contemptuous, pretending to idealism but in reality without either grace, or joy, or love." [38]

Anderson noticed correctly that the actual conditions which created the oppressive "system" were missing: how did the rackets become so effective; with whom did the racketeers deal; how did they come to power? Although answers to such queries were sprinkled throughout the film, detailed descriptions of social causes, usually the most compelling feature of realist drama, were curiously lacking. Even Budd Schulberg acknowledged this omission: "After years of prowling the New York waterfront, roaming the West Side and Jersey bars across from the docks, drinking beer with longshore families in the kitchens of their $26.50 per month railroad flats, and talking to harbor union leaders, waterfront priests, and Irish and Italian rank-and-file 'insoigents,' our film *On the Waterfront* left me with an irresistable conviction that there was still far more to say than could be included in my screenplay." Anderson attributed the film's superficiality to director Kazan, but Schulberg adduced technical reasons. Not an indifference to the subject, but "the tyrant, the ninety-minute feature film" was to blame. "The Film is an art of high points," Schulberg explained, "I think of it as embracing five or six sequences, each one mounting to a climax that rushes the action onward. . . . A successful film must go from a significant episode to more significant episode in a constantly mounting pattern." What weakened the film's description of waterfront corruption was attention to the individual, moral struggles of Terry Malloy. "The film's concentration on a single dominating character brought close to the camera's eye made it aesthetically inconvenient—if

[38] Lindsay Anderson, "The Last Sequence of *On the Waterfront,*" *Sight and Sound,* 24 (Jan.–Mar. 1955), 127–30.

not impossible—to set Terry's story in its social and historical perspective."[39]

As if responding to Anderson's criticism Schulberg wrote a novel, *Waterfront* (1955), which made much clearer the problems and attitudes of New York's longshoremen. The essential difference between *On the Waterfront* and Schulberg's novel is the difference between conceptualization and dramatization. In *Waterfront*, the shipping company, under the direction of an ex-German army officer, Captain Schlegel, is made culpable along with the mobsters for longshore oppression; the mobster connection to the mayor's office is made explicit, and police complicity becomes obvious; the church hierarchy shows concern over losing large contributions from wealthy backers whose lives are negatively affected by Father Barry's investigations; the pigeon metaphor is greatly expanded, making their slaughter at the book's end a much more significant event; Peter Panto, the murdered longshoreman who inspired Arthur Miller's waterfront script, is mentioned, and like Panto, Runty Nolan ("Kayo" Dugan in the film) is dumped in the river. Most important, the rebellion reaches beyond one character, as several longshoremen testify at the hearings and wildcat union meetings attract more dissidents as the movement gathers momentum. But ultimately, Terry's heroic actions bring little change, and the mob isolates the troublemaker from the workers and then drowns him in the river. Even though the background material which Lindsay Anderson demanded figures prominently in the novel, the desired "sense of liberation" never materializes. The nuns accept Katie (Edie in the film) back into the fold, church officials reassert control over Father Barry, the Friendly gang silences Terry Malloy, the Golden Warriors murder the defenseless pigeons, and Johnny Friendly continues to run his operation from jail after receiving a mild scolding from his boss. As apathy and anger intermingle, calming the beleaguered docks, Father Barry and Katie contemplate "the way evil often intertwines itself with good, and the way life had of rubbing some of the quality of one on to the other." Ambivalence still blurs the distinctions between right and wrong, denying rebellion the clearly-defined cause upon which revolutionary zeal depends. In such an environment, progress, as Father Barry resolves, is not measured in "hundred yard dashes, but in mere centimeters, painfully crawling forward."[40]

In the past decade, comments about *On the Waterfront* have continued to vary as widely as they did when the film first reached the public.

[39] Budd Schulberg, "Why Write It When You Can't Sell It to the Pictures?" *Saturday Review* (Sept. 3, 1955), 5–6.
[40] Budd Schulberg, *Waterfront* (London: W. and J. MacKay, 1955, 1956).

Placing the film in an existentialist mold, John M. Smith explained that
"the real force of the film's ending is the ending of self-pity and the
assertion of the fundamental importance of effort." Andrew Dowdy
commented that the waterfront exposé represented "a covert reply to
contempt for the informer." Renee Penington, narrowing the focus of the
film, described it as a public expression of Kazan's "agony" over inform-
ing on his former Communist Party associates. Peter Biskind, attempting
to stem the rising tide of pro-Kazan criticism, analyzed the film in terms of
power, suggesting that the physical bullies (mobsters) were replaced by
moral bullies (Edie and Father Barry). Neil Hurley found On the Waterfront to be boldly revolutionary in illustrating the process of "conscienti-
zation," the psychological path which leads a rebel to revolution. Hurley
thought the politically-charged story was "one of the greatest social
realism films to emerge from Hollywood." In a similar tone, Laurence
Kardish called "this stark, uncompromising and often brutal film . . . one
of the high points of the decade." [41] The variety of material included in the
waterfront story—organized crime, Communist Party membership,
House Committee testimony, political corruption—engendered conflict-
ing responses depending on which element of the film most rankled or
delighted the viewer. But more directly, the parallel arguments—the
sanctity of liberal institutions and the ambivalence of human actions—
invited, indeed encouraged, controversy.

While comments about the original work continue to reflect different
perspectives on society as well as on the film, the waterfront story itself
continues to resurface in different forms. In 1972, Budd Schulberg returned to the boxing world of The Harder They Fall and wrote Loser and
Still Champion: Muhammad Ali. The sentiment expressed in that title
reached the screen indirectly when the film Rocky (1976), which borrowed
liberally from On the Waterfront, swept the country. Even though the film
satirized Muhammad Ali, depicting him as a droll and foolish "golden
boy," the duality between materialism and love was revived. Instead of
corrupt mobsters, Rocky had to survive a beating from purely greedy
capitalists. In the spring of 1977, Muhammad Ali himself was reported
negotiating with Columbia Pictures for a remake of On the Waterfront
with Ali as Terry Malloy. [42] Although nothing developed after the initial

---

[41] John M. Smith, "Three Liberal Films," Movie (Winter, 1971–1972), 21; Andrew
Dowdy, The Films of the Fifties: The American State of Mind (New York: William Morrow,
1973, 1975), 39; Renee Penington, "The Agony of Kazan's Informer," The Thousand Eyes
Magazine (Jan. 1976), 8; Peter Biskind, "The Politics of Power in On the Waterfront," Film
Quarterly, 29 (Fall, 1975), 25–38; Neil Hurley, The Reel Revolution: A Film Primer on
Liberation (Maryknoll: Orbis Books, 1978), 59; Laurence Kardish, Reel Plastic Magic: A
History of Films and Filmmaking in America (Boston: Little, Brown, 1972), 208.
[42] "Ali's Revenge," New York Post (Mar. 1, 1977), 6.

contacts, it is interesting to note the difference between Kazan, who submitted to government pressure in part to protect his career, and Ali, who resisted government claims and nearly had his career destroyed. Clearly, the conflict between authority and individual conscience remains alive. Moreover, resistance to government control of quite another sort has also shaped the life of Michael Clemente, boss of I.L.A. Local 968 (called both Michael J. Skelly and Johnny Friendly in *On the Waterfront*). On March 6, 1979, the 71-year-old Clemente and another member of the Vito Genovese "family" were indicted on charges of attempting "to corruptly control and influence the waterfront industry in the Port of New York." [43] When the apparently defeated Johnny Friendly defiantly bellowed, "I'll be back," not even the most cautious director or screenwriter could have known the haunting accuracy of the boast, and no one could have predicted that the criminal's words would be heard around the docks twenty-five years later. As the film's ending suggested, the waterfront story is not yet over.

[43] Arnold H. Lubasch, "Five Indicted in Dock Inquiry; Two Linked to Crime 'Family,'" *New York Times* (Mar. 7, 1979), B1.

CHAPTER 10

Dr. Strangelove (1964): Nightmare Comedy and the Ideology of Liberal Consensus

CHARLES MALAND

DR. STRANGELOVE OR: HOW I LEARNED TO STOP WORRYING AND LOVE THE BOMB (Stanley Kubrick, 1964) is one of the most fascinating and important American films of the 1960s. As a sensitive artistic response to its age, the film presents a moral protest of revulsion against the dominant cultural paradigm in America—what Geoffrey Hodgson has termed the Ideology of Liberal Consensus.[1] Appearing at roughly the same time as other works critical of the dominant paradigm—*Catch 22* is a good literary example of the stance—*Dr. Strangelove* presented an adversary view of society which was to become much more widely shared among some Americans in the late 1960s. This essay will examine the Ideology of Liberal Consensus, demonstrate how *Dr. Strangelove* serves as a response to it (especially to its approach to nuclear strategy and weapons), and look at how American culture responded to its radical reassessment of the American nuclear policy in the early 1960s.

The American consensus to which *Dr. Strangelove* responds was rooted in the late 1930s and in the war years. When Americans in the late 1930s began to feel more threatened by the rise of foreign totalitarianism than by the economic insecurities fostered by the stock market crash, a previously fragmented American culture began to unify. A common sys-

---

[1] *America in Our Time* (New York: Doubleday, 1976), 67. Besides Hodgson's book, the following have aided my understanding of the American consensus, its roots in the late 1930s, and American Cold War nuclear policies: Richard Pells, *Radical Visions and American Dreams* (New York: Harper, 1973); Robert Skotheim, *Totalitarianism and American Social Thought* (New York: Holt Rinehart, 1971); Lawrence S. Wittner, *Cold War America* (New York: Praegar, 1974); and Norman Moss, *Men Who Play God: The Story of the H-Bomb and How the World Came to Live With It* (New York: Harper, 1968).

tem of belief began to form, a paradigm solidified during World War II, when American effort was directed toward defeating the Axis powers. Fueled by the success of the war effort and the economic prosperity fostered by the war, this paradigm continued to dominate American social and political life through the early 1960s.

The 1950s are commonly remembered as an age of conformity typified by the man in the gray flannel suit, the move to suburbia, and the blandness of the Eisenhower administration. There were, of course, currents running counter to the American consensus in the 1950s—C. Wright Mills challenging the power elite and the era's "crackpot realism"; James Dean smouldering with sensitive, quiet rebellion; the Beats rejecting the propriety and complacency of the era—yet most people remained happy with America and its possibilities. Much more than a passing mood or a vague reaction to events, this paradigm—the Ideology of Liberal Consensus— took on an intellectual coherence of its own. According to Geoffrey Hodgson, the ideology contained two cornerstone assumptions: that the structure of American society was basically sound, and that Communism was a clear danger to the survival of the United States and its allies. From these two beliefs evolved a widely accepted view of America. That view argued its position in roughly this fashion: the American economic system has developed, softening the inequities and brutalities of an earlier capitalism, becoming more democratic, and offering abundance to a wider portion of the population than ever before. The key to both democracy and abundance is production and technological advance; economic growth provides the opportunity to meet social needs, to defuse class conflict, and to bring blue-collar workers into the middle class. Social problems are thus less explosive and can be solved rationally. It is necessary only to locate each problem, design a program to attack it, and provide the experts and technological know-how necessary to solve the problem.

The only threat to this domestic harmony, the argument continued, is the specter of Communism. The "Free World," led by the United States, must brace itself for a long struggle against Communism and willingly support a strong defense system, for power is the only language that the Communists can understand. If America accepts this responsibility to fight Communism, while also proclaiming the virtues of American economic, social, and political democracy to the rest of the world, the country will remain strong and sound. Hodgson sums up the paradigm well when he writes: "Confident to the verge of complacency about the perfectability of American society, anxious to the point of paranoia about the threat of Communism—those were the two faces of the consensus mood."[2]

[2] Hodgson, 75–76.

These two assumptions guided our national leadership as it attempted to forge social policy in an era of nuclear weapons. After the Soviet Union announced in the fall of 1949 that it had successfully exploded an atomic bomb, President Truman on January 31, 1950 ordered the Atomic Energy Commission to go ahead with the development of a hydrogen bomb. By late 1952 the United States had detonated its first hydrogen bomb, 700 times more powerful than the atomic bomb dropped on Hiroshima. Less than a year later, on August 8, 1953, the Soviets announced that they, too, had a hydrogen bomb. The arms race was on.

About the time that Sputnik was successfully launched in 1957—leading to national fears about the quality of American science and education—some American intellectuals began to refine a new area of inquiry: nuclear strategy. Recognizing that nuclear weapons were a reality, the nuclear strategists felt it important to think systematically about their role in our defense policy. Henry Kissinger's *Nuclear War and Foreign Policy* (1957), one of the first such books, argued that the use of tactical nuclear weapons must be considered by decision makers. More widely known was the work of Herman Kahn, whose *On Thermonuclear War* (1960) and *Thinking About the Unthinkable* (1962) presented his speculations on nuclear war and strategy, most of which stemmed from his work for the RAND Corporation during the 1950s. Kahn was willing to indulge in any speculation about nuclear war, including such topics as the estimated genetic consequences of worldwide doses of radioactive fallout, the desirable characteristics of a deterrent (it should be frightening, inexorable, persuasive, cheap, non-accident prone, and controllable), and the large likelihood of vomiting in postwar fallout shelters.[3]

Though the professed intent of the nuclear strategists was to encourage a rational approach to foreign policy in a nuclear age, the mass media seemed intent on making the public believe that thermonuclear war might be acceptable, even tolerable. A few examples illustrate that some mass magazines believed that nuclear war would not really be that bad. *U.S. News and World Report* carried a cover article, "If Bombs Do Fall," which told readers that plans were underway to allow people to write checks on their bank accounts even if the bank were destroyed by nuclear attack. The same issue contained a side story about how well survivors of the Japanese bombings were doing. *Life* magazine placed a man in a reddish fallout costume on its cover along with the headline, "How You Can Survive Fallout. 97 out of 100 Can Be Saved." Besides advising that the best cure for radiation sickness "is to take hot tea or a solution of baking soda," *Life* ran an advertisement for a fully-stocked, prefabricated fallout shelter for only $700. The accompanying picture showed a happy

[3] *On Thermonuclear War,* 2nd ed. (Princeton: Princeton Univ. Press, 1961), 45–54, 86, 148.

family of five living comfortably in their shelter. I. F. Stone suggested in response to this kind of writing that the media seemed determined to convince the American public that thermonuclear warfare was "almost as safe as ivory soap is pure." While all this was going on, a RAND corporation study released in August 1961 estimated that a 3000 megaton attack on American cities would kill 80 percent of the population.[4]

This paradoxical, bizarre treatment of the nuclear threat can be explained in part as an attempt by journalists to relieve anxiety during a time when the Cold War was intensifying. A number of events from 1960 to 1963 encouraged this freeze in the Cold War. Gary Powers, piloting a U-2 surveillance plane, was shot down over the Soviet Union in May 1960. In 1961, the Bay of Pigs fiasco occurred in May, President Kennedy announced a national fallout shelter campaign on television in July, and in August, the Berlin Wall was erected and the Soviet Union announced that they were resuming atmospheric testing of nuclear weapons. Worst of all, the Cuban Missile Crisis of October 1962 carried the world to the brink of nuclear war, thrusting the dangers of nuclear confrontation to the forefront of the public imagination. Though the crisis seemed to be resolved in favor of the United States, for several days nuclear war seemed imminent.

One result of this intensification was to erode the confidence of some Americans in the wisdom of American nuclear policy. Though there had been a small tradition of dissent regarding American nuclear policy in the 1950s—led by people like J. Robert Oppenheimer, Linus Pauling, Bertrand Russell, and C. Wright Mills, and groups like SANE (the National Committee for a Sane Nuclear Policy)—these people were clearly a minority, prophets crying in the wilderness. But Edmund Wilson's warning in 1963 that our spending on nuclear weapons may be one of mankind's final acts, and H. Stuart Hughes' impassioned challenge to deterrence strategy and his support of disarmament in the same year, were both symptomatic of a growing dissatisfaction of some Americans with the federal government's nuclear policy.[5] Judged from another perspective, outside the assumptions of the Ideology of Liberal Consensus, the threat posed by the Soviet Union did not at all warrant the use of nuclear weapons. In the same vein, the realities of America itself—as the defenders of the Civil Rights movement were pointing out—did not live up to the rhetoric about the harmonious American democracy so prevalent in

[4] See *U.S. News and World Report*, 5 (Sept. 25, 1961), 51–55; *Life*, 51 (Sept. 15, 1961), 95–108; I. F. Stone, *The Haunted Fifties* (New York: Vintage, 1969), 314–17.
[5] See Wilson's *The Cold War and the Income Tax* (New York: Farrar, Strauss, 1963), and H. Stuart Hughes, *An Approach to Peace* (New York: Atheneum, 1962), especially "The Strategy of Deterrence," 52–67.

the 1950s. By 1962 and 1963, when *Dr. Strangelove* was being planned and produced, the Ideology of Liberal Consensus seemed increasingly vulnerable. In fact, it is not unfair to say that an adversary culture opposed to the hypocrisies and inconsistencies of the dominant paradigm was beginning to form.

Stanley Kubrick, director of *Dr.Strangelove,* played a part in extending that adversary culture. Born in 1928 to a middle-class Bronx family, Kubrick was from an early age interested in chess and photography. It is not hard to move from his fascination with chess, with the analytical abilities it requires and sharpens, to the fascination with technology and the difficulties men have in controlling it which Kubrick displays in *Dr. Strangelove* and *2001: A Space Odyssey.* Photography became a pastime when Kubrick received a camera at age thirteen, and a profession when *Look* magazine hired him at age eighteen as a still photographer. From there Kubrick became interested in filmmaking and made a short documentary on middleweight boxer Walter Cartier called *Day of the Fight* (1950). He followed this with a second documentary for RKO, *Flying Padre* (1951), after which he made his first feature film, *Fear and Desire* (1953). From then on Kubrick was immersed in making feature films.[6]

In his mature work Kubrick has returned constantly to one of the gravest dilemmas of modern industrial society: the gap between man's scientific and technological skill and his social, political, and moral ineptitude. In Kubrick's world view, modern man has made scientific and technological advances inconceivable to previous generations but lacks the wisdom either to perceive how the new gadgetry might be used in constructive ways or, more fundamentally, to ask whether the "advance" might not cause more harm than good. Kubrick first faced this problem squarely in *Dr. Strangelove.*

Kubrick's films before 1963 do hint at interests which he was to develop more fully in *Dr. Strangelove. The Killing* shows a group of men working toward a common purpose under intense pressure and severe time limitations. *Paths of Glory*—one of a handful of classic anti-war films in the American cinema—vents its anger at the stupidity of military leaders,

---

[6] Biographical information on Kubrick is available in Alexander Walker's *Stanley Kubrick Directs,* rev. ed. (New York: Harcourt, 1972), probably the best book on Kubrick's work. Since *2001,* the literature on Kubrick's films has proliferated. Jerome Agel's anthology, *The Making of 2001* (New York: Signet, 1970) started the list of books on Kubrick's work. Other volume-length studies are Daniel Devries, *The Films of Stanley Kubrick* (Grand Rapids: Eerdmans, 1973); Norman Kagan, *The Cinema of Stanley Kubrick* (New York: Grove, 1972); and Gene Phillips, *Stanley Kubrick: A Film Odyssey* (New York: Popular Library, 1975), which includes a discussion of *Barry Lyndon.* A thoughtful essay defining Kubrick's artistic vision is Hans Feldmann's "Kubrick and His Discontents," *Film Quarterly,* 30 (Fall 1976), 12–19.

their callous disregard for other human lives, and their own lust for power. Released in 1957 in the midst of the Cold War, *Paths* was a courageous film made slightly more palatable for audiences because of its setting and situation: World War One and the evils of French military leaders.

It is not totally surprising, then, that Kubrick should make a film about military and civilian leaders trying to cope with accidental nuclear war. Actually, Kubrick had developed an interest in the Cold War and nuclear strategy as a concerned citizen in the late 1950s, even before he thought of doing a film on the subject. In an essay on *Dr. Strangelove* published in mid-1963, a half year before the release of the film, Kubrick wrote: "I was very interested in what was going to happen, and started reading a lot of books about four years ago. I have a library of about 70 or 80 books written by various technical people on the subject and I began to subscribe to the military magazines, the Air Force magazine, and to follow the U.S. naval proceedings."[7] One of the magazines he subscribed to was the *Bulletin of the Atomic Scientist,* which regularly published articles by atomic scientists (Oppenheimer, Edward Teller, and Leo Szilard) and nuclear strategists (Kahn, Bernard Brodie, and Thomas Schelling). The more he read on the subject, the more he became engrossed in the complexities of nuclear strategy and the enormity of the nuclear threat:

> I was struck by the paradoxes of every variation of the problem from one extreme to the other—from the paradoxes of unilateral disarmament to the first strike. And it seemed to me that, aside from the fact that I was terribly interested myself, it was very important to deal with this problem dramatically because it's the only social problem where there's absolutely no chance for people to learn anything from experience. So it seemed to me that this was eminently a problem, a topic to be dealt with dramatically.[8]

As his readings continued, Kubrick began to feel "a great desire to do something about the nuclear nightmare." From this desire came a decision to make a film on the subject. In preparation, he talked with both Thomas Schelling and Herman Kahn, gradually coming to believe that a psychotic general could engage in what Kahn termed "unauthorized behavior" and send bombers to Russia.[9]

Kubrick found the literary work upon which his film was based almost by accident. When he requested some relevant readings from the Institute of Strategic Studies, the head of the Institute, Alastair Buchan, suggested

---

[7] "How I Learned to Stop Worrying and Love the Cinema," *Films and Filming,* 9 (June 1963), 12.

[8] Kubrick, 12.

[9] See Lawrence Suid, *Guts and Glory: Great American War Movies* (Reading, Mass.: Addison-Wesley, 1978), 194; and Kahn, 467.

Peter George's *Red Alert,* a serious suspense thriller about an accidental nuclear attack. The book contained such an interesting premise concerning accidental nuclear war that even a nuclear strategist like Schelling could write of it that "the sheer ingenuity of the scheme . . . exceeds in thoughtfulness any fiction available on how war might start." Kubrick, likewise impressed with the involving story and convincing premise, purchased rights to the novel.[10]

However, when author and screenwriter started to construct the screenplay, they began to run into problems, which Kubrick describes in an interview with Joseph Gelmis:

> I started work on the screenplay with every intention of making the film a serious treatment of the problem of accidental nuclear war. As I kept trying to imagine the way in which things would really happen, ideas kept coming to me which I would discard because they were so ludicrous. I kept saying to myself: "I can't do this. People will laugh." But after a month or so I began to realize that all the things I was throwing out were the things which were most truthful.[11]

By trying to make the film a serious drama, Kubrick was accepting the framework of the dominant paradigm, accepting Cold War premises and creating the gripping story within these premises. This was the approach of *Red Alert* as well as of *Fail Safe,* a popular film of late 1964 adapted from the Burdick and Wheeler novel. But after studying closely the assumptions of the Cold War and the nuclear impasse, Kubrick was moving outside the dominant paradigm. Kubrick's fumbling attempts to construct a screenplay provide an example of what Gene Wise, expanding on Thomas Kuhn, has called a "paradigm revolution" in the making: a dramatic moment when accepted understandings of the world no longer make sense and new ones are needed.[12]

Kubrick describes in an interview how he resolved his difficulties with the screenplay: "It occurred to me I was approaching the project in the wrong way. The only way to tell the story was as a black comedy, or better, a nightmare comedy, where the things you laugh at most are really

[10] "Meteors, Mischief, and War," *Bulletin of the Atomic Scientist,* 16 (Sept. 1960), 293. In the late 1950s and early 1960s, the possibility of accidental nuclear war was widely discussed and considered plausible. Joel Larus, in his *Nuclear Weapons Safety and the Common Defense* (Columbus: Ohio State Univ. Press, 1967), 34, lists ten representative essays and books published between 1958 and 1962 which consider the problem. See also Peter George, *Red Alert* (New York: Ace, 1958).

[11] *The Film Director as Superstar* (New York: Doubleday, 1970), 309.

[12] Wise discusses the paradigm revolution occurring in America from the late Thirties to the Fifties in his *American Historical Explanations* (Homewood, Ill.: Dorsey Press, 1973), 129–32, 233–95.

the heart of the paradoxical postures that make a nuclear war possible."[13] After deciding to use nightmare comedy in approaching his subject, Kubrick hired Terry Southern to help with the screenplay. This decision connects Kubrick to the black humor novelists of the early 1960s. Writers like Southern, Joseph Heller (*Catch 22*), Kurt Vonnegut (*Mother Night*), and Thomas Pyncheon (*V* and *The Crying of Lot 49*) shared with Kubrick the assumption of a culture gone mad, and responded to it with a similar mixture of horror and humor. Morris Dickstein's comment that "black humor is pitched at the breaking point where moral anguish explodes into a mixture of comedy and terror, where things are so bad you might as well laugh," describes quite accurately the way Kubrick came to feel about the arms race and nuclear strategy.[14]

The premise and plot of the film are, paradoxically, quite realistic and suspenseful, which in part accounts for why the nightmare comedy succeeds. At the opening of the film a narrator tells us that the Russians have built a Doomsday device which will automatically detonate if a nuclear weapon is dropped on the Soviet Union, destroying all human life on the planet—a case of deterrence strategy carried to the absurd. A paranoid anti-Communist Air Force general, unaware of the Russian's ultimate weapon, orders a fleet of airborne SAC B-52s to their Russian targets. The President of the United States finds out, but soon learns that the jets cannot be recalled because only the general knows the recall code. Moving quickly into action, the President discusses the problem with his advisors, calls the Russian Premier, and assists the Russians in their attempts to shoot down the B-52s. Finally, all the planes are recalled but one, which drops its bombs on a secondary target, setting off the Russian retaliatory Doomsday device. *Dr. Strangelove* concludes in apocalypse.

After the narrator's initial mention of a Doomsday device, Kubrick subtly begins his nightmare comedy by suggesting that man's warlike tendencies and his sexual urges stem from similar aggressive instincts. He does this by showing an airborne B-52 coupling with a refueling plane in mid-air, while the sound track plays a popular love song, "Try a Little Tenderness." The connection between sexual and military aggression continues throughout the film, as when an otherwise nude beauty in a *Playboy* centerfold has her buttocks covered with a copy of *Foreign Affairs*, but it is most evident in the names given the characters by the screenwriters. Jack D. Ripper, the deranged SAC general, recalls the sex murderer who terrorized London during the late 1880s. The name of Army strategist Buck Turgidson is also suggestive: his first name is slang

[13] Gelmis, 309.
[14] *Gates of Eden: American Culture in the Sixties* (New York: Basic Books, 1977), 92–127.

for a virile male and his last name suggests both bombast and an adjective meaning "swollen." Major King Kong, pilot of the B-52, reminds viewers of the simple-minded beast who fell in love with a beautiful blonde. Group Captain Lionel Mandrake's last name is also the word for a plant reputedly known for inducing conception in women, while both names of President Merkin Muffley allude to female genitals. Appropriately, Ripper and Turgidson are hawks, while Muffley is a dove. Other names—Dr. Strangelove, the Soviet Ambassador De Sadesky, and Premier Dmitri Kissov—carry similar associations. These sexual allusions permeate the film, providing one level of the film's nightmare comedy.[15]

More important than these sexual allusions, however, is *Dr. Strangelove's* frontal assault on the Ideology of Liberal Consensus. Above all else, *Dr. Strangelove* uses nightmare comedy to satirize four dimensions of the Cold War consensus: anti-Communist paranoia; the culture's inability to realize the enormity of nuclear war; various nuclear strategies; and the blind faith modern man places in technological progress.

The critique of American anti-Communist paranoia is presented primarily through General Ripper, played by Sterling Hayden (see Figure 1). Kubrick portrays Ripper as an obsessed member of the radical right.[16] Convinced that the Communist conspiracy has not only infiltrated our country but also, through fluoridation, contaminated our water, Ripper decides to take action by sending the B-52s to bomb Russia. Cutting off all communication to the outside world, he then orders his men to fight anyone attempting to capture the base.

The most grimly ominous character in the film, Ripper dominates its action in the first half, and Kubrick underlines this action stylistically, often shooting Ripper from a low camera angle. But Ripper's words also characterize his paranoia. Kubrick once agreed that whereas *2001* develops its focus visually, *Dr. Strangelove* does so much more through its dialogue. Early in the film, Ripper reveals his fears to Mandrake (Peter Sellers, in one of his three roles):

Mandrake, have you ever seen a Communist drink a glass of water? Vodka, that's what they drink, isn't it? Never water—on no account will a Commie

[15] The sexual allusions of *Dr. Strangelove* are developed more fully and systematically in Agel, 136–37, and Anthony F. Macklin, "Sex and *Dr. Strangelove,*" *Film Comment*, 3 (Summer, 1965), 55–57.

[16] The portrayal was probably influenced by the activities of such radical right groups as the John Birch Society and the Christian Anti-Communist Crusade, active in the late 1950s and into the 1960s. Birch leader Robert Welch sounds much like Ripper in his comment that President Eisenhower is "a dedicated, conscious agent of the Communist conspiracy" (Wittner, p. 231).

Figure 1. Anti-Communist Paranoia: Colonel
Ripper (Sterling Hayden) ponders the dangers of
fluoridation. (Courtesy of Cinemabilia)

ever drink water, and not without good reason . . . Mandrake, water is the
source of all life: seven-tenths of this earth's surface is water. Why, do you
realize that 70 percent of you is water? And as human beings, you and I need
fresh, pure water to replenish our precious bodily fluids. . . . Have you never
wondered why I drink only distilled water or rain water and only pure grain
alcohol? . . . Have you ever heard of a thing called fluoridation? Do you realize
that fluoridation is the most monstrously conceived and dangerous Communist
plot we've ever had to face?[17]

Later Ripper mentions that fluoridation began in 1946, the same year as
the postwar international Communist conspiracy. By portraying this
paranoid officer willing to obliterate the world because of fluoridation,
Kubrick lays bare the irrational American fear of Communism as one
source of the cultural malaise of the early 1960s.

The second object of attack through satire—the failure to realize how
nuclear weapons have changed the nature of war—is carried out primarily
on one of General Ripper's B-52s. The pilot of the plane, Major King
Kong (Slim Pickens), gives evidence of outmoded notions about war in his
pep talk to the crew after they have received the "go" code:

[17] Dialogue has been transcribed from the film (Distributor: Swank).

Figure 2. Failure of Liberalism: President Muffley
(Peter Sellers)—the well-intentioned but ineffectual
Stevensonian liberal. (Courtesy of Cinemabilia)

Now look boys—I ain't much of a hand at makin' speeches. . . . I got a fair idea
of the personal emotions that some of you fellas may be thinkin'. Heck, I
reckon you wouldn't even be human bein's if you didn't have some pretty
strong feelin's about nuclear combat. But I want you to remember one thing.
The folks back home is a-countin' on you and, by golly, we ain't about to let
'em down. I'll tell you something else: if this thing turns out to be half as
important as I figger it just might be, I'd say you're all in line for some important
promotions and personal citations when this thing's over with. And that goes
for *every last one* of you, regardless of yer race, color, or yer creed.

Such a pep talk might be appropriate for a World War II film—in fact,
most films about that war contained some such scene—but Kong's blindness to what he is being asked to do is almost complete. The fact that
Kong wears a cowboy hat while making the speech, connecting him to the
frontier heritage, and that "When Johnny Comes Marching Home"—a
patriotic American war tune—plays on the soundtrack in the background,
reinforces the conception of Kong as a dangerous anachronism.

To drive this point home, Kubrick has Kong go through the contents of
a survival kit. It includes, among other items, a pistol, nine packs of
chewing gum, several pairs of nylon stockings, a miniature combination
Bible and Russian phrase book, and, of course, an issue of prophylactics.

Besides parodying what every soldier shot down over enemy territory
might need, the scene reasserts that Kong is fighting another war at
another time, never having realized that if his bomber goes down after
dropping its atomic load, the crew will not have to worry much about
survival, to say nothing of survival kits. Kubrick, perhaps responding to
the media articles which made light of the nuclear threat, attacks the
shortsightedness of those who think nuclear war may not actually be that
bad.

National strategies also come under attack. Here the satire is particularly pointed; the various strategic positions taken by characters in the
War Room correspond quite closely to positions taken by military and
civilian strategists.

General Turgidson (George C. Scott) is a "hardliner." His position is
even more severe than that of John Foster Dulles, who announced the
policy of "massive retaliation" in 1954.[18] Turgidson secretly favors a
first-strike policy—he would like to see the U.S. obliterate the Russians
offensively. After learning that the planes have been accidentally sent to
their Russian targets, Turgidson urges the President to intensify the attack
with even more planes:

T: It is necessary now to make a choice, to choose between two admittedly
    regrettable but nevertheless distinguishable postwar environments.[19] One,
    where you got twenty million people killed and the other where you got 150
    million people killed.

M: (Shocked) You're talking about mass murder, general, not war.

T: I'm not saying we wouldn't get our hair mussed. But I do say no more than
    ten to twenty million killed, tops—depending on the breaks.

M: (Angrily) I will not go down in history as the greatest mass murderer since
    Adolph Hitler.

T: Perhaps it might be better, Mr. President, if you were more concerned with
    the American people than with your image in the history books.

Scott delivers these lines with zestful enthusiasm, and his animated features suggest that he can hardly wait for the annihilation to begin. In
rhetoric distressingly similar to the arguments occurring occasionally in
the journals, Turgidson advises "total commitment," sacrificing a "few
lives" for what he believes would be a more secure and satisfactory
"post-war environment."

[18] Moss, 106–11.
[19] Here Kubrick borrows language and ideas from Herman Kahn. Table 3 on p. 20 of *On
Thermonuclear War* is headed "Tragic But Distinguishable Postwar States," and it esti-
mates the time for "Economic Recuperation" if anywhere from two million to 160 million
Americans are killed in a thermonuclear exchange.

President Muffley's position is the most reasonable of any in the War Room. He is neither a fanatic nor a warmonger. Unfortunately, he's also nearly totally ineffectual as he tries to implement his goal: attempting to avoid catastrophe at all costs through communication with the Soviets. Peter Sellers plays this role with a bald wig, in part to differentiate himself visually from his other two roles, in part to remind audiences of Adlai Stevenson, the quintessential liberal of the 1950s, twice-unsuccessful candidate for the Presidency (see Figure 2).[20] When Muffley negotiates with Premier Kissov over the hot line to Moscow, he appears ridiculous. After Kissov says Muffley should call the People's Central Air Defense Headquarters at Omsk, Muffley asks, "Listen, do you happen to have the phone number on you, Dmitri? . . . What? . . . I see, just ask for Omsk information." Muffley argues with Kissov about who is sorrier about the mistake, insisting that he can be just as sorry as Dmitri. Such small talk amidst the enormity of the crisis is ludicrous. By appearing both ridiculous and ineffectual, Muffley furthers Kubrick's nightmare comedy. For if the person who has the most rational strategy (and who also happens to be the commander in chief) is unable to control nuclear weapons and his military advisors, citizens really have something to worry about.

Although Dr. Strangelove does not speak until the last third of the film, the creators seem to have taken a great deal of care in creating Strangelove as a composite of a number of pundits in the new "science" of nuclear strategy. As a physicist involved in weapons research and development, he invites comparisons to Edward Teller. Not only was Teller involved in the creation of the atomic bomb, but he was also a strong anti-Communist who pushed hard for the development of the much more powerful hydrogen bomb in 1949 and 1950.[21] In his background, accent, and some of his dialogue, Strangelove suggests Henry Kissinger. Like Kissinger, Strangelove came from Germany in the 1930s and still speaks with a German accent. With his wavy dark hair and sunglasses, he also bears a physical resemblance to Kissinger. Even his definition of deterrence—"the art of producing in the mind of the enemy the fear to attack you"—sounds remarkably like the definition Kissinger offered in his *Nuclear Weapons and Foreign Policy* (1957).[22] Finally, Herman Kahn

[20] When Stevenson suggested a test ban on nuclear weapons during the 1956 presidential election, Vice-President Nixon blasted the suggestion as "catastrophic nonsense" (Moss, p. 155).
[21] Moss, 64–84, has a long profile on Teller. In the late 1950s and early 1960s, Teller was a strong opponent of test-ban treaties, and wrote articles in the popular press which deemphasized the threat of fallout.
[22] Kissinger, 96, defines deterrence as "the attempt to keep an opponent from adopting a certain course of action by posing risks which will to him seem out of proportion to any gains to be achieved." The definition is a little more elegant than Strangelove's, perhaps, but the thrust is the same.

plays a part in the Strangelove composite, primarily as related to the Doomsday device. Strangelove tells the President that he recently commissioned a study by the Bland corporation (Kahn worked for RAND) to examine the possibility of a Doomsday device. The study found the device technologically feasible; it would be hooked to a computer and programmed to detonate under certain prescribed circumstances. However, Strangelove found the machine impractical as a deterrent because it would go off even if an attack was accidental. All these details are similarly discussed in Kahn's *On Thermonuclear War,* with Kahn similarly concluding that though the device would contain most of the characteristics of a deterrent, it would not meet the final characteristics of being controllable.[23] As a mixture of Teller, Kissinger, Kahn, and probably a number of others (Werner Von Braun is another possibility), Strangelove becomes a significant symbol (see Figure 3). Essentially, he is the coldly speculating mind, not unlike one of Nathaniel Hawthorne's calculating and obsessed scientists. Like them, Strangelove is devoid of fellow feeling. He proves this near the end of the film: even after the American B-52 gets through to bomb its target, Strangelove has ideas. He offers a plan to take all military and political leaders (along with attractive women at a ratio of ten women to one man) into a mine shaft in an effort to survive the virulent radioactivity produced by the Doomsday device. Clearly, none of the strategic postures presented by Kubrick—Turgidson's militarism, Muffley's tender-minded rationality, or Strangelove's constant speculations—are able to control the inexorable march of nuclear holocaust.

Although *2001* is more famous for its exploration of technology, Kubrick shows a fascination with machines in *Dr. Strangelove.* Most prominent is the simulation of the B-52 cockpit, which Kubrick—after the Air Force denied him any assistance in making the film—had built from an unauthorized photograph he discovered in an aviation magazine.[24] Throughout the B-52 scenes, Kubrick keeps viewer interest by alternating close-ups of various panel controls with shots of crew members expertly carrying out their orders. Besides those in the B-52, many other machines—telephones, radios, the electronic wall chart in the War Room—play important parts in the film.

Kubrick develops his attitude toward technology in *Dr. Strangelove* by making use of both machines of destruction and machines of communica-

---

[23] Kahn reported in his RAND study of the Doomsday device that most people he talked to rejected the idea of constructing such a weapon. Some scientists and engineers, however, told him that it was a great idea. In a masterful understatement, Kahn wrote that he found this enthusiasm "disquieting" (p. 148).

[24] Kagan, 112.

Figure 3. Nuclear Strategist: Dr. Strangelove (Peter Sellers)—the calculating and obsessed strategist, devoid of any fellow feeling. (Courtesy of Movie Star News)

tion; the problem in the film is that while people handle the machines of destruction with great alacrity, the more neutral machines of communication are either ineffectual or turned toward destructive purposes. Through a misuse of radio codes, Ripper sends the B-52s on their destructive mission; DeSadesky uses a camera to take pictures of the War Room, presumably for purposes of intelligence. When people try to use the neutral machines to prevent destruction, however, they prove to be ineffective. During President Muffley's call to Kissov, for example, social amenities and small talk hinder attempts to stop the B-52s, as does the slowness of the process. Likewise, when Mandrake tries to call the President after he has discovered the recall code, he cannot because he does not have a dime for the pay phone.

Though people can't use neutral machines effectively, they handle the machines of destruction with deadly efficiency. This includes not only the conventional weaponry at the Air Force base, where Army infantry and artillery attempt to take over the base, but also, more distressingly, the nuclear weapons. The whole crew of the B-52 expertly manipulate their machines, even after the explosion of an anti-aircraft missile damages the plane. Kong, to the dismay of the audience, shows great ingenuity in repairing damaged circuits in time to open the bomb doors over the target. Kubrick is not really suggesting that machines are dominating men. Rather, he seems to perceive a human death instinct. Arising from a nearsighted rationality, this death instinct leads man first to create machines, then to use them for destroying human life (see Figure 4). In questioning the "progress" inherent in technology, Kubrick was challenging a fundamental assumption of the dominant paradigm. This challenge to technology—both to the stress on technique in society and to the increasing importance of machines in modern life—was to become a dominant theme in the late 1960s, important in several works of social criticism during that era, including Theodore Roszak's *The Making of A Counter Culture* (1969), Lewis Mumford's *The Myth of the Machine: The Pentagon of Power* (1969), and Philip Slater's *The Pursuit of Loneliness* (1970).

The film's final scene underlines Kubrick's attack on the Ideology of Liberal Consensus. Mushroom clouds billow on the screen, filling the sky, exuding both an awesome power and a perverse beauty. Simultaneously, a light, sentimental love song from the late 1940s—Vera Lynn's "We'll Meet Again"—provides a contrasting aural message in an excellent use of film irony. Its opening lines are: "We'll meet again, don't know where, don't know when, but I know we'll meet again some sunny day." If we go on with the world view of the postwar era, Kubrick ironically suggests, we will never meet again, because there will be no one left on earth.

Figure 4. Technological Expertise, Political Ineptitude: In the War Room, leaders watch the progress of the B-52s on "the Big Board" and debate policy. (Courtesy of Cinemabilia)

Retaining the conflict between image and sound throughout the final credit sequence, Kubrick hopes to prod his viewers to reflect on all that they have seen.

Taken as a whole, *Dr. Strangelove* fundamentally challenges the Ideology of Liberal Consensus by attacking anti-Communist paranoia, American adherence to outmoded notions of heroism, various nuclear strategies, and faith in social salvation through technological expertise. The Cold War foreign policy so strongly supported by Americans in the late 1940s and 1950s rested on the belief that America was a fundamentally just society threatened only by the germs of "Godless" Communism. *Dr. Strangelove,* though it certainly does nothing to imply that the Soviet leaders are any wiser than their American counterparts, suggests that no nation-state has a monopoly on foolishness and that the backstage strategies of military and political leaders are simply exercises in paranoia. The nightmare comedy presented a disturbing and deeply wrought challenge to America in 1963 and 1964.

The film would not be so important were it not so *un*characteristic in the way it treated the Cold War. The House Un-American Activities Committee investigated Hollywood in two waves, once in 1947 (resulting in the infamous Hollywood Ten trials) and later in the early 1950s.[25] Hollywood responded not by fighting government interference—as it had in the mid-Thirties censorship controversies—but by cooperating, blacklisting people who were suspected of leftist affiliations in the Thirties and making a spate of films which overtly or covertly supported the dominant paradigm.

The paradigm was overtly supported by a good number of anti-Communist melodramas from the late 1940s and early 1950s, of which *My Son John* (1952) may be the most famous example. These films were most popular between 1948 and 1953; in 1952 alone, twelve of them were released. Films about World War II, portraying the Nazis or the Japanese as villains, tended also to divide the world into good (the Allies) and evil (the Axis powers) and thus to support the dominant paradigm. Here Kubrick's anti-war *Paths of Glory* (1957) was clearly an anomaly. Even science fiction films, like *The Thing* (1951) or *War of the Worlds* (1952), by using threats from outer space as a metaphor of the Communist threat, covertly supported this conventional way of looking at and understanding the world.[26] More directly related to *Dr. Strangelove* are a series of films through the 1950s and into the 1960s dealing with the bomb and especially with the Strategic Air Command.

Dr. Strangelove seems all the more amazing when one contrasts its iconoclasm and sharp satire with *Above and Beyond* (1952), *Strategic Air Command* (1957), *Bombers B-52* (1957), *A Gathering of Eagles* (1963), and *Fail Safe* (1964). The first of these films concerns the story of Paul Tibbetts, commander of the group which actually dropped the first atomic bombs on Hiroshima and Nagasaki. Much of the story concerns Mrs. Tibbetts' gradual acceptance of her husband's secret yet important work. *Strategic Air Command* follows much the same vein. In it a major league baseball star and former World War II pilot, played by Jimmy Stewart, gives up the last years of his prime to return to active duty. Stewart's wife, at first upset at her husband's decision, realizes that it is necessary for the peace and well-being of the nation. Produced in the same year, *Bombers B-52* concerns a sergeant who resists the temptation to take a higher paying civilian job, and thus retains his wonderful existence as an enlisted man.

Both *A Gathering of Eagles* and *Fail Safe* were released about the time of *Dr. Strangelove*, yet their approaches to their subjects are light years

[25] On HUAC investigations of Hollywood, see Robert Sklar, *Movie-Made America* (New York; Random, 1975), 256–281; John Cogley, *Report on Blacklisting* (New York: Arno, 1972); and Eric Bentley, ed., *Thirty Years of Treason* (New York: Viking, 1971). The last book is primarily made up of transcriptions of testimony.

[26] On anti-Red films, see Andrew Dowdy, *The Films of the Fifties* (New York: William Morrow, 1973), 38.

from that of *Strangelove*. General Curtis LeMay, commander of SAC, took a personal concern in *A Gathering of Eagles*: he stressed the need to explain how many safeguards had been created to prevent accidental war. The film concerns a young colonel who takes over a SAC wing that has failed a surprise alert and gradually trains his men so they are ever ready to go to war if the necessity arises. LeMay was pleased with the film, judging it "the closest any of [the Air Force films] ever came to showing the true picture of what the military was all about."[27]

Fail Safe, released less than a year after *Dr. Strangelove*, at first seemed quite similar to *Dr. Strangelove* in that in both films, nuclear weapons are detonated by accident. But *Fail Safe* does nothing to suggest, as *Strangelove* does, that national policy is ridiculous. Instead it portrays the President (Henry Fonda) as a responsible and competent man caught in a tragic, yet controllable circumstance. His decision—to obliterate New York City in exchange for the accidental destruction of Moscow—prevents the destruction of the world and is powerfully rendered without a touch of irony: in the final moments, we see freeze frames of people on New York streets just before the bomb explodes. Despite its powerful cinematic ending, the film is, as Julian Smith has suggested, "a morally and intellectually dangerous film because it simplifies and romanticizes the issues of national responsibility."[28]

All these films present a common respect for national and military leaders. Though bad apples may show up occasionally, though accidents may cause some difficulties, each film ends with control being reestablished, the viewer reassured that the American way is the best course and that the military is doing the best job possible to shield us from the Communist menace. None hint, as does *Dr. Strangelove*, that we may need protection against ourselves.

A look at how reviewers and the public responded to *Dr. Strangelove* can give us some indication of how Kubrick's adversary views were accepted. Since a feature film most often must reinforce the cultural values and attitudes of its viewers if it expects to be popular, it is understandable that neither critics nor the public were swept away by the film. Though few critics of mass magazines or political journals panned the film, a number of them, thinking within the bounds of the dominant paradigm, came up with strange interpretations. The critic for the right-wing *National Review*, for example, suggested that *Dr. Strangelove's* theme was that all ideology should be abandoned. He went on to defend American

---

[27] Suid, 170. This discussion is indebted to Suid, 187–215, and Julian Smith, *Looking Away: Hollywood and Vietnam* (New York: Scribners, 1975), 178–203.
[28] Smith, 198.

ideology "with its roots thrust deep in Greek political thought," closing curiously with a hope that Kubrick might make a film criticizing Stalinism. *Saturday Review's* Hollis Alpert gave a generally favorable review, concluding with these comments: "No one thinks our ingeniously destructive world-destroying bombs are a laughing matter. Certainly director Kubrick doesn't. But on some fairly safe planet out of view, maybe this is the way they would view our predicament." Alpert seems to miss Kubrick's point. No one accepting the dominant paradigm would see nuclear weapons as a laughing matter, but Kubrick, after studying the arms race, the Cold War, and the idea of deterrence carefully, realized the insanity of the situation and found that the only way he could possibly approach the material was through the satirical thrust of nightmare comedy. By having his audience laugh at the situation, he hoped not that they would realize its seriousness but rather that they would perceive its absurdity. Alpert, evidently, misunderstood the social rhetoric.[29]

Two observers who thought highly of the film were Stanley Kauffmann and Lewis Mumford. Writing for *The New Republic,* Kauffmann—a critic notoriously harsh on most American films—thought *Dr. Strangelove* the best American film in fifteen years. The film showed "how mankind, its reflexes scored in its nervous system and its mind entangled in orthodoxies, insisted on destroying itself." This is a keen analysis: the entangling orthodoxies were those of the Liberal Consensus. Mumford's response to the film came in a letter to the *New York Times* defending the film, and he was as perceptive as anyone about the film's thrust when he wrote: "What the wacky characters in *Dr. Strangelove* are saying is precisely what needs to be said: this nightmare eventuality that we have concocted for our children is nothing but a crazy fantasy, by nature as horribly crippled and dehumanized as Dr. Strangelove himself. It is not this film that is sick: what is sick is our supposedly moral, democratic country which allowed this policy to be formulated and implemented without even the pretense of public debate." In a particularly acute comment, Mumford went on to argue that the film represented "the first break in the catatonic cold war trance that has so long held our country in its rigid grip." [30] It is no surprise that Mumford, who had been a perceptive cultural critic of America at least since *The Golden Day* (1926), would later offer one of the most articulate criticisms of America's worship of technology in *The Pentagon of Power* (1969), still one of the most sensitive and persuasive studies of America to emerge during the late 1960s.

Like the critical observations, the box-office figures on *Dr. Strangelove* suggest a mixed response. Though figures for film rentals are notoriously

---

[29] W. H. von Dreele, "Satirist With Astigmatism," *National Review,* 16 (Mar. 10, 1964), 203–04; "What's in a Title?" *Saturday Review,* 47 (Jan. 25, 1964), 24.

[30] Kauffmann, *The World on Film* (New York: Harper, 1966), 14–15. Mumford's letter is quoted in Kauffmann's second review of the film, 19.

rough, they seem to indicate that after doing a very strong business in
New York and some other large cities, *Dr. Strangelove* slowed down and
failed to live up to its early returns. It opened at•the Victoria and the
Baronet in New York, setting house records in the Baronet (an "art"
theater) and providing the best business in years for the first week at the
Victoria. Business remained strong at both theaters for at least nine
weeks, yet when the final box-office tabulations were in for 1964, *Dr.
Strangelove* ranked 14th, after such films as *The Carpet Baggers, It's a
Mad . . . World, The Unsinkable Molly Brown, Charade, Good Neighbor
Sam,* and *The Pink Panther*. Right above *Dr. Strangelove* in the 1964
box-office ratings was the Beatles/Richard Lester Production, *A Hard
Day's Night,* which is at least symbolically significant. For what was
beginning to happen in the film industry in the 1960s was that the audience
for films was getting younger and more iconoclastic. Since *Dr.
Strangelove* did very well in New York—the center for our cultural
trendmakers—and not so well in smaller cities, the box-office figures
seem to indicate that the adversary attitude toward dominant values expressed in films like *Dr. Strangelove* was still puzzling to many people in
1964. Nevertheless, this attitude was strangely attractive to those becoming disaffected with American society.[31]

Dr. Strangelove is a watershed film. By rejecting the Ideology of Liberal Consensus through the iconoclastic perspective of nightmare comedy, it established a stance which was to become widespread in American
movies in the late 1960s. Its alternating tone of comedy and horror was to
reappear in *Bonnie and Clyde* and *Little Big Man*. Its critical attitude
toward dominant social values was to be expanded in *The Graduate, Easy
Rider,* and *Five Easy Pieces*. Its disdain for military leaders and war found
its way to *M*A*S*H*. Its notion that technological change was not necessarily social progress appeared in such diverse films as *Butch Cassidy and
the Sundance Kid, McCabe and Mrs. Miller,* and *A Clockwork Orange*.
Its importance as a groundbreaking film in the history of American movies
can hardly be overestimated.

Yet the film is also important in a broader cultural sense. Lionel Trilling
once wrote that at its base, art is a criticism of life. *Dr. Strangelove,* in the
way it attacks the "crackpot realism" of American culture in the 1950s
and early 1960s, is as important a cultural document as the Port Huron
Statement of 1962, Martin Luther King's "I Have a Dream" speech at the
March on Washington in 1963, Herbert Marcuse's *One-Dimensional Man*
(1964), or Malcolm X's *Autobiography* (1965). Anyone seeking to understand the breakdown of the American consensus in the early and mid-
1960s, and the new iconoclasm which was challenging it, can learn a good
deal from the nightmare comedy of *Dr. Strangelove*.

---

[31] Box-office figures are from *Variety's* section on box-office grosses, 234 (Feb. 5, 12, 19,
26, Mar. 4, 11, 18, 25, and Apr. 1, 1964), and 237 (Jan. 6, 1965).

CHAPTER 11.

A Test of American Film Censorship:
Who's Afraid of Virginia Woolf? (1966)

LEONARD J. LEFF

AMERICAN FILM CENSORSHIP IS ALMOST AS OLD AS AMERICAN FILM ITSELF. Municipal censorship boards were first formed in 1907, state boards in 1911. Their constitutionality was upheld by an influential 1915 United States Supreme Court decision that regarded motion pictures as "a business pure and simple . . . capable of evil, having power for it, the greater because of their attractiveness and manner of exhibition."[1] In 1922, film industry executives, seriously threatened by legislation pending against them, turned almost desperately to self-regulation. Representatives of the major Hollywood studios created the Motion Picture Producers and Distributors of America (now called the Motion Picture Association of America) and hired Will H. Hays, Harding's Postmaster General, as its president. Largely through Hays's influence, the industry successfully lobbied against the passage of federal censorship laws. Still, critics continued to inveigh against the corruptive potential of American films.

To satisfy their critics, studio heads in 1930 adopted a set of guidelines that would restrict film content. The Motion Picture Production Code contained sections on crime, sex, vulgarity, obscenity, religion, and profanity.[2] Prohibitions affected the treatment of certain subjects (for example, abortion, adultery, childbirth) and the use of specific words (for example, "chippie," "fairy," "son-of-a"). Once they adopted the Code, however, the producers ignored it. Violations were common and, in Mae West's films, egregious. But in 1934, when Catholic bishops created the Legion of Decency, studio heads recognized that they must either observe their own Production

---

[1]Justice Joseph McKenna, as quoted in Richard S. Randall, *Censorship of the Movies: The Social and Political Control of a Mass Medium* (Madison: University of Wisconsin Press, 1968), p. 19.
[2]The Motion Picture Production Code and its predecessor, the "Don'ts and Be Carefuls," are reprinted in Garth Jowett, *Film: The Democratic Art* (Boston: Little, Brown and Co., 1976), pp. 465-472.

Code or face the loss of millions of Catholic patrons. The Production Code
Administration, formed in direct response to pressure from the Legion of
Decency, put teeth into the 1930 Code: violations of its guidelines became
punishable with a $25,000 fine. Powerful censorship agencies were now in
place. Together, the Production Code Administration and the Legion of
Decency influenced the language, tone, and themes of American cinema
from the mid-1930's to the mid-1950s.

Complaints against the Production Code Administration and the Legion
of Decency were voiced privately and publicly: under the Production Code,
producer Walter Wanger said in 1939, "it was—and is—almost impossible
to face and deal with the modern world."[3] Yet rather than individual complaints, social and artistic forces within a changing society at last challenged
these two groups. *The Moon Is Blue* (1953) and *The Man with the Golden
Arm* (1956) were early tests. Both were directed by Otto Preminger, released
by United Artists, and exhibited without Code Seals. The Production Code
Administration (PCA) denied approval to both films because of their
themes, adultery in *The Moon Is Blue* and drug addiction in *The Man with
the Golden Arm.* The works' commercial success illustrated that major productions could survive—even prosper—without a Seal and that the Code
was no longer invulnerable. Responding to pressure, in 1956 and 1961, re-
spectively, the PCA did ease its prohibitions against the treatment of nar-
cotics and homosexuality. But the 1960s brought still other challenges with
the wider distribution of European films. *L'Avventura* (1960), *The Virgin
Spring* (1960), and *Jules and Jim* (1962) were mature works for mature
audiences; condemned by the Legion and not even brought before the PCA,
they demonstrated the agencies' weaknesses in dealing with adult subject
matter.

By 1964 the stress was internal as well as external. Within the PCA and
the Legion, some argued that fixation on the rules blinded administrators to
worthwhile, if controversial films. *The Pawnbroker* revealed this internal
tension. The story of a German emigrant haunted by memories of the holocaust, the film was honored at the 1964 Berlin Film Festival yet, because of
its brief shots of a bare-breasted woman, it encountered PCA and Legion
disapproval. The Legion's "Condemned" rating sparked a public controversy among Catholic intellectuals, and the PCA's decision to deny a Code
Seal was overturned by its own Review Board. Neither organization could
long survive intact. Within two years, the Legion had recognized its deficiencies and effected a major reform; in turn, as the Legion had done thirty
years before, it directly influenced the PCA. But what specifically occurred
during this crucial period from 1964 to 1966 has remained obscure. For var-

---

[3]Wanger, as quoted in Paul W. Facey, *The Legion of Decency: A Sociological Analysis of
the Emergence and Development of a Social Pressure Group,* Diss. Fordham 1945 (New York:
Arno Press, 1974), p. 179.

ious reasons the PCA and, to a lesser extent, the Legion have rarely disclosed the details of their actions on individual Hollywood films of this or any era. In his otherwise well-documented book on censorship, Richard S. Randall occasionally resorts to conjecture because "the PCA has never made public its decisions or their rationalizations. Information that has become public . . . has usually been supplied by dissatisfied film proprietors."[4]

For research on this essay, however, both the PCA and the Legion opened their files to the author.[5] As primary evidence now demonstrates, one film played a pivotal role in defining the philosophy, structure, and operation of these agencies following their evaluation of *The Pawnbroker.* The watershed that demonstrated the Legion's new commitment to mature works and forced the industry to abandon the Code was the most expensive nonspectacle film of its time, Warner Brothers' *Who's Afraid of Virginia Woolf?* With the appropriately brash "screw you," Martha and George not only ushered in Nick and Honey but dispatched a whole era of film censorship.

When Edward Albee's *Who's Afraid of Virginia Woolf?* opened on Broadway in October 1962, its disturbing theme, vivid characters, and caustic dialogue generated considerable controversy. "Whether such a dramatic ordeal will be successful may be questionable," *Variety* wrote; likewise, "whether it would be suitable for the road or pictures may be dubious."[6] Six weeks after its premiere, though, it had already begun showing a profit.[7] Despite its length, despite its problematic theme, and despite its blasphemous and profane dialogue, it thus became an attractive property not only for the road (its first touring company grossed almost $1.5 million) but for motion pictures.[8] In March 1963 Jack Warner, who had recognized the play's commercial possibilities and apparently optioned it, sent the PCA a copy of the text for its review and comment. The PCA responded promptly: the text was unacceptable. In a brief letter, PCA director Geoffrey M. Shurlock advised Warner that to earn a Code Seal he must "remove all the profanity and the very blunt sexual dialogue." Shurlock acknowledged that such action "would considerably reduce the play's impact" but concluded

[4]Randall, p. 202.

[5]The author wishes to thank the Motion Picture Association of America; the Division for Film and Broadcasting, U.S. Catholic Conference; Ernest Lehman; and the Hoblitzelle Theatre Arts Library, Humanities Research Center, The University of Texas at Austin, for their gracious assistance during the research phase of this essay.

[6]"Hobe.," rev. of *Who's Afraid of Virginia Woolf?,* by Edward Albee, *Variety,* 17 October 1962, p. 54, col. 4.

[7]"'Woolf' Has Earned $750,000 Profit; Includes Coin from 500G Pic Sale," *Variety,* 18 March 1964, p. 60, col. 1.

[8]"Subscription Is A Must on Tour, Sez Nancy Kelly," *Variety,* 3 June 1964, p. 81, col. 4. Now, as then, "pre-sold" properties, especially celebrated ones like *Virginia Woolf,* attracted motion picture producers.

that "under the circumstances" the PCA could render no other judgment.[9] Five days later, Walter MacEwen and Steve Trilling, two Warner Brothers executives, met with Shurlock to discuss the objectionable words, phrases, and actions.

Shurlock's decision was based on two explicit sections of the Motion Picture Production Code, "Obscenity" and "Profanity." "Obscenity in word, gesture, reference, song, joke, or by suggestion (even when likely to be understood only by part of the audience) is forbidden." Though "damn" and "hell" could be used in historical or Biblical contexts, "pointed profanity and every other profane or vulgar expression, however used, are forbidden." The PCA had recently bent the Code for *Hud* (1963), which contained "bitch" and "bastard," but it did not intend to break the Code for *Virginia Woolf*.[10] In addition to over seven "bastards" and five "sons-of-a-bitch," the PCA's required deletions included over twenty "goddamns," thirteen references to Christ, and assorted anatomical phrases such as "right ball," "monkey nipples," and "ass." At first, Warner Brothers seemed ready to comply. In March 1963, Steve Trilling wrote to Albee's agent that, with the playwright's help, Warners could film *Virginia Woolf and* observe the code. The studio was confident that "Albee is sufficiently inventive and creative to substitute potent and pungent dialogue that could prove highly effective, even though possibly reducing somewhat the 'shock' impact of this highly regarded play."[11] Albee declined.

Meanwhile, limited pre-production activities continued. In November 1963, screenwriter Ernest Lehman was sent a script "to see whether [he] thought it was possible movie material" (ELC, 2). No doubt aware of Warner's increasingly serious interest in *Virginia Woolf,* Shurlock publicly reaffirmed the PCA's position. Shurlock saw *Virginia Woolf* on Broadway in December 1963. Afterwards he expressed hope that "nobody brings the script to me—I wouldn't want to be the one to butcher it." Speaking to a *Variety* reporter but indirectly to Warner, he said that an MPAA member company that attempted *Virginia Woolf* would be in for "some major headaches."[12] Yet in March 1964, in spite of unresolved problems regarding the

[9]Geoffrey M. Shurlock, Letter to Jack L. Warner, 20 March 1963, *Virginia Woolf* papers, Motion Picture Association of America, New York City. Unless otherwise indicated, subsequent references to the Motion Picture Association of America (MPAA) and the Production Code Administration (PCA) are taken from materials in unnumbered file folders pertinent to *Virginia Woolf* at the MPAA, New York City.

[10]"Rough Language, Still Moral Picture; Some Angles of Marty Ritt on 'Hud,'" *Variety,* 22 May 1963, p. 4, col. 1.

[11]Steve Trilling, Letter to Abe Lastfogel, 29 March 1963, Box 19, *Virginia Woolf* papers, The Ernest Lehman Collection, Hoblitzelle Theatre Arts Library, Humanities Research Center, The University of Texas at Austin. The Lehman Collection contains twenty-six boxes of uncatalogued materials pertinent to *Virginia Woolf.* All further reference to the Collection will appear in the text. "(ELC, 19)," for example means that information is drawn from the Ernest Lehman Collection, Box 19.

[12]"Likes the Play, Hates the Problem," *Variety,* 18 December 1963, p. 5, col. 1.

dialogue, Warner Brothers announced that it had purchased the play for $500,000. Since the sale price and the selection of key artists (over which Albee had no control) would give some approximation of the film's projected budget, speculation immediately centered on the choice of a director. A Warner Brothers spokesman told the *New York Times* that Fred Zinnemann would direct. Both the *Hollywood Reporter* (in a front page story) and the *Los Angeles Times* confirmed Zinnemann's selection.[13] According to Lehman, however, Zinnemann was "never even discussed" (ELC, 26). Zinnemann's involvement would have connoted a substantial budget, and at this point, because of the film's controversial nature and certain battle over a Code Seal, Warner Brothers seemed unready to make such a financial commitment.

Throughout 1963 and 1964 the studio explored distribution channels outside Code jurisdiction. An obvious solution would have been to produce *Virginia Woolf* for the "art theaters." The "art film" (often an import) was released under the name of a major studio's subsidiary. Since only member companies of the Motion Picture Association had to submit their films to the PCA, a work with a subsidiary's name on it was not bound to Code guidelines. (By 1965, this practice had become a focus of industry critics.) Because such films were exhibited in only one or two theaters in large metropolitan areas, however, they had reduced commercial potential. Warner Brothers, furthermore, had no established subsidiary. Thus in spring 1964, discussion turned to the "theatrofilm," which was also not regulated by the PCA. Richard Lederer, Warner Brothers' vice-president in charge of advertising and publicity, had alerted the PCA to this possibility; accordingly, PCA executive Michael Linden suggested that the Administration consider its response to an alternative release pattern for *Virginia Woolf*.[14]

As a "theatrofilm" *Virginia Woolf* would have been handled like Warner Brothers' then-forthcoming *Hamlet* with Richard Burton—a two-day-only booking in 971 United States and Canadian theaters. *Hamlet* continued the studio's experimentation with a kinescope-like process called Electronovision. On June 30 and July 1, 1964, Electronovision, in which Burton was a stockholder, brought seven cameras into a Broadway theater to film two performances of *Hamlet.* Cut primarily during production, the "negative" was ready a few days later. Jack Warner must have then observed what reviewer Bosley Crowther noted when the film opened: "the photography is fuzzy, especially in the long shots; the lighting is poor and distractingly uneven, the recording of the voices allows for . . . annoying vibration or

[13]"Movie Rights to 'Virginia Woolf' Sold to Warners for $500,000," *New York Times,* 5 March 1964, Sec. 1, p. 37, col. 2; the Ernest Lehman Collection contains the *Hollywood Reporter* (7 April 1964) and *Los Angeles Times* (n.d.) stories (ELC, 22).

[14]Michael Linden, Memorandum to Ralph Hetzel (MPAA Acting President), 1 July 1964.

echo."[15] Based on the poor cinematic quality of *Hamlet* and the candid advice of Electronovision president William Sargent, Warner decided that the
process was too risky for a $500,000 property.[16] By fall 1964, with "theatro-
film" rejected, it was clear even to the public that *Virginia Woolf* was going
to be a Hollywood blockbuster.

In September 1964, the *Hollywood Reporter* told Patricia Neal and
Henry Fonda to "go on hoping," but that Jack Warner wanted Elizabeth
Taylor and Jack Lemmon to star (September 8, 1964, p. 4) and John
Frankenheimer to direct (September 17, 1964, p. 4; ELC, 26). Towards the
end of the year, negotiations with Taylor, Richard Burton, and Mike
Nichols, the film's director, had begun. Sandy Dennis tested in February
1965, and when Robert Redford refused the role of Nick, George Segal was
cast.[17] By spring, the major artists had all been signed, Lehman had finished
a working screenplay, and filming was set to start in mid-August. During
that six-month period, Warner Brothers had vacillated about how to handle
Albee's language. In early screenplay drafts, Lehman tried such substitutions as "Make the Hostess"/"Hop the Hostess" (ELC, 1), "For cry sake!"
(ELC, 3), and (for "Jesus Christ") "oh my God" (ELC, 16). Lehman recognized their limitations, and in the third draft (March 14, 1965), he restored
most of the original dialogue. When Jack Warner read this script, he still
was not committed to film an unexpurgated *Virginia Woolf*. Most of his
marginalia supported the compliment he gave Lehman near the end of the
script: "Best writing/reading in years" (p. 149). But throughout, he either
circled references or dog-eared pages that he obviously wanted Lehman to
review: words like "sons of bitches," "goddamn," "bastard," "stud," and
"chastity belt" as well as phrases like "with your melons bobbling" and
"mount her like a gd dog" (ELC, 6). With "theatrofilm" rejected and thus
the PCA still to be considered, Warner remained undecided about the language. His decision was finally made for him by the director, Mike Nichols.

---

[15]"The Screen: Stage 'Hamlet' With Richard Burton," rev. of *Hamlet*, by William Shake-
speare, *New York Times,* 24 September 1964, Sec. 1, p. 46, col. 2.
     [16]Information on the Electronovision *Hamlet* was gleaned from the following articles in the
New York Times: A.H. Weiler, "Broadway 'Hamlet' to Be Filmed For Short Run in 1,000
Houses," 27 June 1964, Sec. 1, p. 14, col. 1; Sam Zolotow, "Stage's 'Hamlet' Becomes a
Film," 3 July 1964, Sec. 1, p. 13, col. 1; Peter Bart, "Filmed 'Hamlet' Gets Costly Push," 19
September 1964, Sec. 1, p. 19, col. 4; "Broadway 'Hamlet' Grosses $3 Million in Movie
Houses," 30 September 1964, Sec. 1, p. 34, col. 7; telephone interview with William Sargent,
20 May 1980.
     [17]Segal inherited parts in two works that Redford turned down, *Virginia Woolf* and a tele-
vision production of *Death of a Salesman* (Roderick Mann, "Segal Is Being Sued and Loving
It," *Calendar, Los Angeles Times,* 24 February 1980, p. 29). Relating an anecdote about an un-
named film that he scripted (its subject is "a famous screen drama of marital strife"), Ernest
Lehman says that "a now celebrated actor" was offered a role but "had to say a reluctant no,
because of his gut feeling that his wife would never see him with the same eyes after he played a
man whose masculinity was humbled" (Lehman, "Nobody *Tries* to Make a *Bad* Picture,"
American Film, 3 [March 1978], 7).

The whimper that Dustin Hoffman uses in *The Graduate* originated with Nichols. "I was told that I used to do that in meetings with Jack Warner," Nichols told an interviewer. "Somebody said, 'When Mr. Warner is telling his jokes, you must stop whimpering.'"[18] Nichols could afford to whimper. Hand-selected by the Burtons to direct, he was paid handsomely (the budget for "Direction and Supervision" was over $350,000, his fee reportedly $250,000 [ELC, 19]). Though he was young and inexperienced, his Broadway reputation—as well as Hollywood's shifting artistic climate—gave him virtually total control. He worked on the screenplay with Lehman for eight weeks during spring 1965, and together, with Warner's reluctant approval, they permanently restored most of Albee's dialogue. Rudi Fehr, head of editing at Warners in 1965, said that Nichols was "the domineering force on the picture": what he wanted, Warner gave him. The reverse did not hold true; Warner wanted "protection" footage for the stronger language, but he was afraid to alienate Nichols by pressing for it. According to Fehr, Nichols filmed no alternative scenes.[19]

Midway through production, Warner Brothers sent the PCA the *Virginia Woolf* shooting script. As Shurlock wrote Warner on October 9, 1965, few differences existed between the text the PCA read in March 1963 and the script it received in October 1965. "We note that [the script] still contains a good deal of the profanity, the blunt sexual references, and the coarse and sometimes vulgar language which we noted in the original playscript when we first commented on it." Interestingly, Warner Brothers, the PCA, and even the public knew that the language was in not only the script but also the film. On October 9, 1965, a *Saturday Evening Post* feature article reported that the filming left "the play's salty dialogue . . . virtually intact."[20] Later, Shurlock was chastised for not having taken a firmer stand about the filming; yet he told Warner clearly, if not firmly, that the script remained "unapprovable under Code requirements" (ELC, 23). The way had now been cleared for the final confrontation between *Virginia Woolf* and the PCA.

The filming itself, on a closed set, was relatively uncomplicated and, though ultimately thirty-six days behind schedule, not grossly overbudget by Hollywood standards.[21] Once finished, *Virginia Woolf* was locked in the

---

[18]Joseph Gelmis, *The Film Director as Superstar* (Garden City, N.Y.: Doubleday, 1970), p. 291.

[19]Telephone interview with Rudi Fehr, 22 June 1979.

[20]C. Robert Jennings, "All for the love of Mike," *Saturday Evening Post,* 9 October 1965, p. 86.

[21]The $7.5 million negative cost resulted in part from the principals' six- and seven-figure salaries combined with the schedule slippage. According to a proposed contract (15 January 1965: ELC, 19), Elizabeth Taylor was entitled to $100,000 for each week the film was overschedule; both she and Burton "voluntarily settled for a sizeable reduction, reportedly so as not to penalize director Mike Nichols in his film debut" ("Four Actor 'Woolf' Cost $7,500,000; Liz-Dick Gesture to Mike Nichols," *Variety,* 4 May 1966, p. 215, col. 5).

ELIZABETH TAYLOR · RICHARD BURTON
N ERNEST LEHMAN'S EDWARD ALBEE'S **WHO'S AFRAID OF**   PRESENTED BY WARNER BROS. WB
PRODUCTION OF   **VIRGINIA WOOLF?**

(Courtesy of Museum of Modern Art/Film Stills Archive)

studio's vault; Warner had denied access to the press, exhibitors, and even high-ranking studio personnel.[22] Though the studio and the PCA did not communicate between the time the script was rejected in October 1965 and the film was submitted, the PCA finally saw *Virginia Woolf* on May 2, 1966. The following day Shurlock telephoned Warner that the picture was unacceptable. According to the *New York Times,* the West Coast PCA denied the film a Code Seal because the studio had refused to make certain cuts.[23] Shurlock, however, urged Warner to appeal the PCA's decision "in the hope that [the Review] Board would see fit to give this picture an exemption."[24]

If Warner lost the appeal, he had two alternatives: he could cut the film or resign from the Motion Picture Association. Cutting the film, practically impossible without "protection" footage, would have subjected Warner Brothers to "a good deal of criticism for 'knuckling under to the blue-

[22]"Hold 'Virginia Woolf' From Tradeshowing Until Eve of Preem," *Variety,* 18 May 1966, p. 4, col. 4.
[23]Vincent Canby, "Valenti Is Facing First Film Crisis," *New York Times,* 28 May 1966, Sec. 1, p. 12, col. 6.
[24]"Notes of Meeting of Production Code Review Board on Friday, June 10, 1966. . . ," *Virginia Woolf* papers, MPAA, New York City.

noses'" in mutilating its "'class' offering"; the play, after all, had won the New York Drama Critics Circle citation, received a Tony Award, and even contended for (and controversially been denied) the Pulitzer Prize.[25] Ironically, the other alternative would have subjected the industry at large to "a good deal of criticism"; major films exhibited without a Code Seal, like *The Moon Is Blue,* jeopardized the legitimating effect of the Seal and invited renewed anti-industry censorship legislation.

Meanwhile on May 24, 1966 the Advertising Code Administration of the MPAA approved *Virginia Woolf* promotional materials conditional upon the PCA Review Board's favorable action on the film itself. The ACA formally required two changes: with an orange crayon, it indicated on a one-sheet how far Warner Brothers should raise Elizabeth Taylor's dress to eliminate her "excessive exposure," and it deleted from a one-minute radio spot George's line, "Shove it." Though it made no comment, it must have noted with considerable interest the prominent announcement in the ads: No admission of anyone "under the age of 18 unless accompanied by his parent." In its front page story of May 26, 1966 the *Hollywood Reporter* best summed up the significance of Warner's unexpected action: "In an unprecedented move that literally forces the movie industry into classification of films, something strongly opposed in the past, Jack L. Warner . . . yesterday announced he would insist on an 'Adults Only' policy for the presentation of 'Who's Afraid of Virginia Woolf?' by including a clause in all contracts with exhibitors."[26]

Throughout his presidency of the Motion Picture Association (1945-63), Eric Johnston had strongly opposed film classification. To Johnston, it was economically disadvantageous to the industry. A film unsuitable for children often played only a downtown run; managers of neighborhood theaters, carefully attuned to community opinion and more susceptible to criticism than downtown exhibitors, rarely booked adult films that had been widely publicized *as* adult films. Also, such films were often restricted from the occasionally lucrative double bill. The Motion Picture Association (MPAA) believed, finally, that voluntary classification could evolve into mandatory censorship. In sum, to most producers, distributors, and exhibitors, classification meant reduced box office revenue.

Ralph Hetzel, Johnston's successor and acting MPAA president from 1963 to 1966, was no more sanguine about classification. With Warners' *Virginia Woolf* policy, however, classification had become a reality. The MPAA puzzled over the implications. In Dallas, "adults" were sixteen and

[25]"MPAA Nixes Its Seal for 'Woolf'; Puts WB, Sans 'Art' Subsidiary, In Possibly Awkward Position," *Variety,* 8 June 1966, p. 4, col. 2.

[26]Clipfile, Academy of Motion Picture Arts and Sciences. Previous films "recommended for adults only" included *Elmer Gantry* (1960), *Lolita* (1962), and *Darling* (1965); rather than "recommend," Warner Brothers' contract with exhibitors mandated "adults only" and further specified that children be admitted only with their *parents.*

older, an MPAA internal memorandum noted; should, then, "Warner's include in the contract an exemption for kids younger than the company age
limit in those areas already covered by a more liberal governmental censorship law? Or should Dallas and other censorship cities (or states) amend
their laws to ban kids under 16, 'or an age determined by a distributor,
whichever is higher?'"[27] Though the tone of the memorandum was whimsi-
cal, Jack Valenti, new head of the MPAA, told the press that Warner
Brothers' action had "effected broad discussion of film classification possibilities, now under study."[28] Since the advent of adult films, the American
Catholic hierarchy had urged the MPAA to develop a policy of self-censor-
ship based upon voluntary classification; *Virginia Woolf* gave the Church
the opportunity to reiterate its point.

    Like the PCA, the Legion of Decency encountered challenges in the
1950s. *The Miracle,* Roberto Rossellini's short film about a girl who believes she has given birth to the Messiah, became the focus of a controversy
that Catholic churchmen helped stir. When the New York City commis-
sioner of licenses tried to block exhibition of the film in 1950, the church
lent its moral support by not only publicizing its condemnation of *The
Miracle* but actively crusading against its subsequent exhibition throughout
the country. Some Catholic intellectuals felt that their leadership had over-
reacted to the film; however, Francis Cardinal Spellman continued to exco-
riate "those who would profit financially by blasphemy, immorality and
sacrilege."[29] Yet in deciding that New York had exceeded its censorship authority, the Supreme Court in 1952 widened the freedom of expression allowed in film. The Legion soon realized that demonstrating pickets and inflammatory rhetoric would not stem the flow of adult films.

    The Legion's liberalized approach to mature films may be dated from the
mid-1950s. Following Pius XII's "Remarkable Inventions" encyclical in
1957, the pledge regarding film attendance became more positive, the number of categories for film classification increased, and the organization became more sympathetic to adult subject matter. The Legion also accelerated
its lobbying effort for an MPAA classification advisory service. In November 1961, a Catholic bishops committee predicted "'an understandable popular demand for mandatory classification should the industry refuse to regulate itself.'" Twelve months later, with the MPAA still adamantly opposed
to classification, the church committed itself to support legislation for advisory film classification, legislation that the MPAA had continuously
fought, particularly in New York.[30]

[27]Tim Clagett, Memorandum to Ralph Hetzel, 3 June 1966.
[28]"Valenti and Nizer Handle Selves Expertly in First Hollywood Press Row," *Variety,* 22
June 1966, p. 3, col. 1.
[29]Spellman, as quoted in Richard Corliss, "The Legion of Decency," *Film Comment,* 4
(Summer 1968), p. 43.
[30]"Catholic Bishops Foresee Mandatory Classification If Showmen Uncurbed," *Variety,*

The Legion, though, hoped to influence by example as well as political pressure. It boasted that by persuading producers to use advisory labels, it had been able to award more lenient ratings to *Elmer Gantry* (1960), *La Dolce Vita* (1961), *Lolita* (1962), and *Long Day's Journey Into Night* (1962). Furthermore, its annual awards, begun in 1965, honored and thus promoted distinguished films for "Youth," "General Audiences," and, significantly, "Mature Audiences." On the Legion's thirtieth birthday (1964), an *America* editorial praised the organization's broad-minded purpose: not to censor, but to give "an intelligent and discriminating moral guide to moviegoers."[31] The following year, as a fitting climax of "the broad transformation that [had] taken place in the functions and services of the Legion during its eight-year period of renewal," the American Bishops gave the Legion of Decency a new name, The National Catholic Office for Motion Pictures (NCOMP).[32]

Yet from the beginning, Jack Warner was fretful about how the Catholic organization would receive *Virginia Woolf*. Although the Legion had dealt leniently with serious works of quality, it had its limits.[33] *Virginia Woolf*, with its plethora of abusive and profane dialogue, would surely test those limits. And if *Virginia Woolf* was condemned, it would suffer at the box office; in 1966, few major theater chains would book "C"-rated films. Both from inside and outside the studio, Warner had been cautioned about the effect of the play's text on the Legion of Decency. "It might be well to obtain Catholic technical advice," Shurlock wrote Warner on March 26, 1963, "in order to avoid anything offensive regarding the Latin prayers in [George's Dies Irae]." The characters' blasphemy concerned Rudi Fehr, Warner's head of editing. Shortly before filming began, Fehr read a screenplay peppered with the word "goddamn." "The Legion of Decency will object to its use," he predicted to Walter MacEwen; "I have the same concern in regards to the use of the name 'Jesus.' It is not approved when used lightly" (August 4, 1965; ELC, 19). Warner, however, was showman enough to know that without its caustic dialogue, *Virginia Woolf* would

29 November 1961, p. 5, col. 5; "Bishops Insistent on 'Classifying'; Refute Arguments of Hollywood That Labels Invite Full Censoring," *Variety,* 5 December 1962, p. 11, col. 4.

[31]"Legion of Decency," Editorial, *America,* 9 May 1964, pp. 624-25. Since 1963, the classification categories have been as follows: A-I, morally unobjectionable for general patronage; A-II, morally unobjectionable for adults and adolescents; A-III, morally unobjectionable for adults; A-IV, morally unobjectionable for adults, with reservations; B, morally objectionable in part for all; C, condemned.

[32]Editor's foreword to Msgr. Thomas F. Little, "The Modern Legion and Its Modern Outlook," *America,* 11 December 1965, p. 744. Hereafter, I have used the name "Legion of Decency" to refer to the organization's actions before 1966 and the name "NCOMP" to refer to its actions immediately thereafter.

[33]*Jules and Jim,* for example, exceeded the Legion's guidelines. After condemning the film, it noted: "This story of an unconventional 'household-for-three' arrangement is developed in a context alien to Christian and traditional natural morality" ("Janus Films Fights Legion Ratings of 'Jules and Jim' by Plugging 'C' Tag," *Variety,* 12 September 1962, p. 11, col. 5).

have less commercial appeal. He was likewise astute enough to realize something equally important: he could protest to NCOMP that he retained the text not to generate ticket sales but to preserve the integrity of a contemporary classic.

In spring 1966, as the meeting with the Catholic organization neared, Warner grew increasingly anxious. "Don't worry," advertising vice-president Richard Lederer reassured him, "the film's artistic."[34] But Legion action—as Warner certainly knew—was difficult to predict. Though in philosophy the Legion was liberal, in practice it often acted conservatively. The guiding principles of the Legion group that actually rated films predated not only the "moral guide" of 1964 but the "Remarkable Inventions" of 1957. This screening body was the International Federation of Catholic Alumnae. IFCA applied to films "*traditional* standards of morality upon which the sanctification of the individual, the sacredness of the home and ethical foundation of civilization necessarily depend."[35] Characterized by one NCOMP executive as "little old ladies in tennis shoes," these middle-aged women took their task seriously, if inflexibly. Their liberalism was questionable: they condemned the major work for "mature viewers" in 1964, *The Pawnbroker*. To the Alumnae, fleeting shots of a black woman's breast proved inflammatory; could they, Warner might have pondered, condone the "bobbling melons" of *Virginia Woolf*? Fortunately for the studio, in 1966 IFCA no longer screened films alone.

NCOMP knew that, given its principles and history, IFCA was unlikely to offer "positive backing to films of superior artistic and spiritual value."[36] But because of the women's long, faithful service, NCOMP could not simply dismiss them. Its solution was to dilute their strength. In the early 1960s, NCOMP assembled a board of consultants—film teachers, scholars, and graduate students; business people; writers—to assist in the evaluation of problematic films. By 1965, the number of consultants and their frequency at screenings had increased; conversely, the number of IFCA members had decreased since those who had died or resigned had not been replaced. By the time *Virginia Woolf* came before NCOMP, the ratio of the consultants to IFCA was 3:1. William Mooring, a new addition to the board and a conservative, resigned early. Forced out by a majority of liberals, he urged NCOMP to return to a policy of "realistic guidance" and to drop "its emphasis upon ideological, ofttimes antireligious drama as superior 'art'

[34]Telephone interview with Richard Lederer, 22 June 1979.
[35]Mrs. James F. Looram, Chairman of the IFCA Motion Picture Dept., as quoted in Harold C. Gardner, S.J., *Catholic Viewpoint on Censorship* (Garden City, N.Y.: Hanover House, 1958), p. 99.
[36]Little, p. 746. In the eight years following the encyclical, the Legion cited forty films for their notable value, Little said; but (as will be demonstrated) IFCA's standards regarding the depiction of alternative modes of expression, physical and verbal, were more conservative than those of the Legion generally.

for mature sophisticated people."[37] Mooring notwithstanding, the newly constituted screening board was conservative on some points. For example, it still discouraged nudity. In his 1965 review of Legion modifications, Msgr. Thomas Little frankly admitted that "in the last two years 34 films, of which 20 were major American productions, would have been released with scenes employing nudity had not the producers realized that they would then have been condemned."[38] With *Virginia Woolf* the problem was language, not nudity; still, "friendly persuasion" was to be NCOMP's method.

Two days after Warner Brothers announced its "Adults Only" policy for *Virginia Woolf, Variety* reported that the studio's decision to classify its film was the result of a "'recommendation' from [the] National Catholic Office for Motion Pictures."[39] Father Patrick Sullivan, Msgr. Little's associate, later confirmed that the Legion was "directly instrumental" in Warner Brothers' admittance policy.[40] The determining factor was clearly the screening body's recent addition of consultants who apparently felt that, properly restricted, *Virginia Woolf* could be approved for certain Catholic filmgoers. IFCA disagreed. The voting distribution shows that even with Warner Brothers' concession, IFCA acting alone would have "Condemned" *Virginia Woolf*:

Consultants			IFCA		
A-II	1	2%	A-II	—	0.0%
A-III	7	10%	A-III	2	11.0%
A-IV	40	61%	A-IV	3	15.5%
B	11	17%	B	3	15.5%
C	7	10%	C	11	58.0%

[37]*Motion Picture Daily,* 1 September 1965, p. 1; as quoted in Randall, p. 191. Parishioners also sensed changes in the church and were moved to object. When one man wrote to NCOMP to complain about its action on *Virginia Woolf,* the Office assured him that its rating resulted from a consensus of ninety-one reviewers. The correspondent returned the letter with a marginal note: "Are these all 'big city' liberals?" (*Virginia Woolf* papers, National Catholic Office for Motion Pictures, New York City). Unless otherwise indicated subsequent references to NCOMP are taken from materials in unnumbered film folders pertinent to *Virginia Woolf* at NCOMP, New York City.

[38]Little, p. 746. Though Little seemed proud of his accomplishment, some Hollywood filmmakers objected to NCOMP's having the final cut. Directors like Elia Kazan railed at NCOMP, but the major studios usually negotiated quietly and accepted a rating without comment. After all, they met NCOMP week after week. Antagonism and protest over one film might adversely affect the organization's treatment of future ones.

[39]"Catholic Office's A-4 Rating to 'Woolf'; Industry's Own Seal Still Not Bestowed," *Variety,* 1 June 1966, p. 7, col. 1.

[40]Many Catholics protested NCOMP's action on *Virginia Woolf* (see nn. 37 and 41); on 28 June 1966, Father Sullivan wrote to one of the organization's critics that "this office was directly instrumental in having Warner Brothers restrict patronage of the film. . . ."

Acting together, however unwillingly, the new screening board awarded *Virginia Woolf* an A-IV.[41] On June 9, 1966, one day before Warner Brothers' appeal came before the PCA Review Board, NCOMP announced its decision.

Like NCOMP's, the MPAA's dilemma was clear: "How do we preserve our obligation to the society in which we live," Valenti asked, "and at the same time widen creative dimensions?"[42] In its rating of *Virginia Woolf*, confidently predicted by the trade press over a week before its public announcement, NCOMP had answered the PCA's question. More important, by "recommending" that Warner Brothers voluntarily restrict its film, NCOMP had vigorously endorsed the classification system that the MPAA had long opposed. Neither course open to the MPAA was attractive to it: if it exempted *Virginia Woolf* from Code restrictions, it involuntarily supported classification; if it denied Warner Brothers' appeal, it demonstrated its weakness in dealing with a film that even NCOMP had found artistic and thus acceptable for its clientele. To complicate matters further, *Virginia Woolf*—as the Review Board knew and was again reminded at the hearing—was not just a movie but a $7.5 million investment, "near a high for a non-spec[tacle] studio film."[43]

The Review Board met in Warner Brothers' New York screening room at 10:00 a.m., June 10, 1966. Following the film's exhibition and a luncheon, the Board reconvened in a private suite at the St. Regis.[44] After Valenti

[41]A "Legion of Decency Inter-office Memo" (25 May 1966) contains this distribution. A total of 90 persons voted (the total given elsewhere is 91, but the distribution accounts for only 90); five persons were undecided about a specific category. Of 67 Consultants, 33 were clergy; of those, 65% voted for "A-IV," 3% for "C." 34 Consultants were laity; of those, 55% voted for "A-IV," 15% for "C." NCOMP files on the *Virginia Woolf* rating contain two folders of correspondence, much of it critical of the rating, the screening body, or the Office leadership. Most of the mail was generated by a *Life* article entitled "A surprising Liz in a film shocker" (10 June 1966, pp. 87-98). Prominent in the piece was a production still of Martha/Liz "scorching, sexual frug with Nick" (p. 88) and samples of the film's "earthy, uninhibited dialogue" (p. 92). The article, which also included a photograph of Msgr. Little and Father Sullivan, explained how NCOMP had arrived at its rating. Writing to *Life* (15 June 1966), Little protested that the article's concentration on a "relatively brief sequence" gave the impression that *Virginia Woolf* was an obscene exercise." Such coverage was unfair to both the film and NCOMP. But what undoubtedly irritated the Office's critics most was seeing a provocative Martha/Liz and a drunken George/Dick pictured in the same article as Little and Sullivan. Little's final comment to *Life* touched on this sensitive area: NCOMP bases "its evaluation only on the film itself and not upon the personal lives of anyone associated with the production." (*Life* deleted the portions cited above when it published two paragraphs from the letter on 1 July 1966, p. 21.)

[42]"Notes . . . ," p. 14.

[43]"Four Actor 'Woolf' Cost $7,500,000," p. 1, col. 5.

[44]Unless otherwise indicated, the account of the meeting is taken from the "Notes of Meeting . . ." (see n. 24); page numbers are given in parentheses following specific references. The "Notes" preserved by the PCA were subsequently reviewed and, at some point, silently altered by participants in the discussion. Though only this amended, formal version was made available, it gives a sufficient idea of the content, if not the tone of the discussion and, more important, a clear indication of the voting.

(Courtesy of Museum of Modern Art/Film Stills Archive)

opened the meeting, Shurlock summarized the PCA's previous communication with Warner Brothers, including his recommendation that the studio appeal his decision. Both the Legion and *Life* had recognized the film's merit, Shurlock said; the PCA must also find a way to recognize quality "in making exemptions on our own and approving a picture without having to call this entire Board into session" (p. 3). Speaking for Jack Warner, Richard Lederer highlighted the serious, artistic purpose of the film, the voluntary classification, and the studio's general responsibility to its public.

(Courtesy of Museum of Modern Art/Film Stills Archive)

He also noted that Warner had "a lot of money invested in [*Virginia Woolf*]" (p. 3). Valenti then rehearsed his own "lonely soul-searching" and subsequently recommended an exemption for the film. He enumerated five reasons: (1) *Virginia Woolf* was "a superior picture"; (2) Warner Brothers' classification had limited it to mature audiences; (3) the MPAA's request for two deletions ("screw you" and "frigging") had been honored; (4) exemption would apply only to *Virginia Woolf*, not films of lesser quality; and (5) NCOMP had given the film an A-IV rating (pp. 4-6).[45]

The objections to Valenti's recommendation came from Sherrill Corwin, representing 15,000 theater owners, and Spyros Skouras, former head of Twentieth Century-Fox. The former maintained that exhibitors had successfully handled mature films in the past with no mandatory "adults-only" clause inserted in the contract: "We feel we can police our theatres for pictures that need policing" (p. 8). He feared what Eric Johnston and the

[45] *Variety* later reported the deletions, though it named neither word. "There has been some puzzlement about why these changes were thought necessary, since those who might be offended by strong language are hardly likely to be mollified by only two small deletions" ("Two Phrases Cut From Soundtrack Of 'Who's Afraid of Virg. Woolf?'" 13 July 1966, p. 1, col. 1).

MPAA had always feared: classification. But he must have realized that classification was inevitable. Moments before, Valenti had said, almost ominously, that he knew little about classification, yet "speaking confidentially, I intend to know more" (p. 4). Skouras objected on moral grounds. He praised the film's artistry but sought to remove "God damn," "son of a bitch," and "Hump the Hostess" from its soundtrack. Their retention, he argued, would not only make Code enforcement impossible but injure society. During the voting that followed, all endorsed exemption except Skouras. Valenti then spoke directly to him. The new MPAA president explained that, according to Warner Brothers, the film's text was unalterable without some reshooting, but in the future the Association was "going to be stronger and tougher . . . to get scripts, dialog, etc., before a picture is completed and before a lot of money is invested" (p. 10). Skouras blamed Shurlock and Warner: Shurlock should have communicated more often with the studio, Warner should have made "replacement scenes for the ones that the Code Authority was bound to oppose." As a result of their joint negligence, the studio head concluded, the floodgates were open (p. 11).

In the press release that announced the Board's decision to grant *Virginia Woolf* a Code Seal, Valenti noted that *Virginia Woolf* had been granted an exemption because of its quality and the studio's classification; he emphasized that the exemption applied only to "a specific important film." But the Code itself was obviously under fire. Ten days later in Hollywood, Valenti spoke to three hundred studio executives, directors, and performers about the "adoption of a 'revised Code,' actually a new Production Code."[46] When it appeared three months later, *Newsweek* greeted it disparagingly: like the old, the new streamlined code is "a glittering diadem of hypocrisy."[47] Ultimately, it served as a temporary resource to be used until the industry could accept classification. Codes had clearly become obsolescent. Martin Quigley, Jr., whose father had coauthored the original Production Code, said in a caustic *Motion Picture Herald* editoral that "it is pointless to consider whether the Code expired when the decision was made to film *Virginia Woolf* without regard to the Code, or when the decision was made by the Review Board to grant the picture an 'exemption' from the Code." The film was of "high quality" and "great cost"; both triumphed over its "torrent of blasphemy, profanity and obscenity."[48] Quigley's title said it all: the Code was dead.

Forces both outside and inside the industry had hastened the Code's death. In the fifteen years before *Virginia Woolf*, changes in communica-

[46]Vincent Canby, "Public Not Afraid of Big Bad 'Woolf,'" *New York Times,* 25 June 1966, Sec. 1, p. 21, col. 1.

[47]"Hollywood: Three-and-a-half Square," *Newsweek,* 30 October 1966, p. 22.

[48]"The Code is Dead," 6 July 1966; Clipfile, Academy of Motion Picture Arts and Sciences.

tion, knowledge, and the law had so altered America's cultural perspectives that the censor's task had become difficult, if not impossible. Perhaps the external forces at work on the Warner Brothers' film and its regulatory agencies are best understood simply by highlighting important Supreme Court actions. *The Miracle* suit in 1952 was of course the first, for it recognized film as a "significant medium for the communication of ideas." The Roth decision, the result of two companion cases in 1957, awarded protection to writers, artists, and filmmakers in the depiction of sex: a work was not obscene unless "to the average person, applying contemporary standards, the dominant theme of the material taken as a whole appeals to the prurient interest." Five years later, in another decision, the court added that the work in question must be "so offensive as to affront current community standards of decency."[49] The result was that in the public sector, works like *Virginia Woolf* were constitutionally protected against censorship.

Within the industry, as Valenti must have known, *Virginia Woolf* had indeed opened the floodgates. Motion picture classification was implemented within two years of the premiere of *Virginia Woolf,* and films became increasingly more outspoken in theme, content, and language.[50] But *Virginia Woolf* was not an intentionally political weapon. Warner did not make the film to effect a decisive change in the way the MPAA mediated between the industry and its public. Albee's play was a good commercial property, the price of Mike Nichols was the preservation of its text, and with or without a Seal the film would have been distributed. However much it advocated film classification, NCOMP did not force Warner Brothers to restrict *Virginia Woolf* in order to bring about a comparable practice industry wide. In all likelihood, the consultants sought assurance that a film "morally unobjectionable for adults, with reservations" (A-IV) would be seen only by adults; with Warner Brothers' concession, NCOMP could more easily defend an unpopular rating against its critics.

Finally, after three years with an "acting president," the MPAA was being led by events; implicit in Shurlock's urging the Board to discover a way to recognize quality was a plea for leadership. Valenti offered it. He promised "new ideas, new objectives, new programs."[51] One member of the MPAA staff found his leadership "inspiring": Valenti "used words like 'loyalty' and 'energy' and 'vigor'—words, said the staffer, 'that all of us

[49]Randall, "Censorship: From *The Miracle* to *Deep Throat,*" in *The American Film Industry,* ed. Tino Balio (Madison: The University of Wisconsin Press, 1976), pp. 432, 439-440.

[50]Two Supreme Court decisions, each announced on 22 April 1968, hastened the industry's adoption of a classification system. *Interstate Circuit v. Dallas,* the more important one, implied that local and state censorship boards could operate unchallenged by constitutional tests. In an attempt to prevent a proliferation of such boards, the industry established a national classification system (Stephen Farber, *The Movie Rating Game* [Washington, D.C.: Public Affairs Press, 1972], p. 14).

[51]Ronald Gold, "Ex-LBJ Aide's Film Vision," *Variety,* 1 June 1966, p. 52, col. 4.

needed to hear.'" [52] Valenti quickly grasped the ineffectiveness of the Code and the futility of trying to preserve it. He spoke with Warner for three hours about the language of *Virginia Woolf* and concluded that "it seemed wrong that grown men should be sitting around discussing such matters." [53] NCOMP had allowed Valenti to assume a leadership position both morally and politically opportune. His Washington experience, the "historical inevitability" of *Virginia Woolf* irrespective of the Board's decision, and the obvious need for strong leadership at the head of the MPAA earned him the support of his Board.

No one had conspired to kill the Code, no one was capable of saving it. Warner Brothers' commitment to film *Virginia Woolf* largely as written, internal changes at the National Catholic Office for Motion Pictures, a concentrated fiscal, social, and political pressure on the Production Code Administration—these cohered at one moment in history to change the face of American film censorship.

[52]"Valenti Meets Manhattan Press," *Variety*, 25 May 1966, p. 18, cols. 2-3.
[53]Valenti, *The Movie Rating System: How It Began, Its Purpose, How It Works, The Public Reaction* (New York and Washington, D.C.: Motion Picture Association of America, n.d.), p. 2.

CHAPTER 12.

Apocalypse Now (1979): Joseph Conrad and the Television War

WILLIAM M. HAGEN

IN HIS INTRODUCTION TO THE PROGRAM NOTES OF *APOCALYPSE NOW,* Francis Coppola states the dual intention of his film, implying, through use of the journey archetype, the role Joseph Conrad's *Heart of Darkness* was to play:

> The most important thing I wanted to do in the making of *Apocalypse Now* was to create a film experience that would give its audience a sense of the horror, the madness, the sensuousness, and the moral dilemma of the Vietnam war. . . . I tried to illustrate as many of its different facets as possible. And yet I wanted it to go further, to the moral issues that are behind all wars. [In making the film,] I, like Captain Willard, was moving up a river in a faraway jungle, looking for answers and hoping for some kind of catharsis.

But the film suffered at the hands of critics because it did not fulfill expectations of what a Vietnam film should be. Like *The Deer Hunter* (1978), it was measured by realistic-political standards precisely because the war was still recent, vivid, and ideologically charged for many viewers.

At the time, any battlefield film about Vietnam would have found less acceptance for its visual interpretation since the American experience of the war was so visual. Nor would the filmmaker be working against the beautifully framed and composed black-and-white imagery of a *Life Magazine.* That vision of war, static and even orderly helped create the aesthetic backgrounds for the obviously staged, thematically simple films about World War II. On the other hand, the Vietnam war was an intimate, loosely framed, on-the-run cinema verité experience. The immediacy, the emotion, the cumulative parataxis of this experience, the sense that things happen but do not connect, had undercut any attempts to interpret or put in perspective, whether from a visual artist, a president or a Senate Foreign Relations Committee opponent. Under the visual-aural onslaught, reason and order lost much of their authority.

There was a Walter Cronkite, "the war's narrator,"[1] accepted as both credible and rational. His popularity, however, probably had more to do with his function as a masterful moderator of images than as a profound commentator.[2] Eric Sevareid, who had the role of commentator on CBS, was quite good at it. But even those of the audience who wanted to believe that the horrific and endlessly repeated off-focus action or in-focus blood and pain could be enfolded by his reasonableness must have finally come to view those wrapups as feats on a par with Johnny Carson's nightly monologues.

Those who remember anything of the many interviews and press conferences about the war, probably remember the tone and tenor of the questions more than any of the answers. The questions grew increasingly skeptical and even cynical, all too plainly communicating to the television audience that no subsequent answers were to be trusted. The cumulative impact of such questions suggested that there were no answers that had not been "tried" before. A distrust in answers, a distrust in answering and the use of the logic, authority, and language involved in answering,[3] a sense that experience itself was unavoidably fragmented, leading to what R.D. Laing had earlier called a "politics of experience": these were all part of the legacy of the "television war."[4]

In this context, then, any film about Vietnam that followed the traditions of realistic narrative filmmaking (especially of war films) would be working against a collective sensibility that had arrived at different preconceptions of what was authentic. The panoramic shots of an omniscient camera, in-focus shots with a foreground and background, painterly attention to image and color tones, expertly edited, rhythmic alternation of shots, a story that follows various individuals through a plot with episodes that begin, peak and have an end or pause, clearly heard dialogue, music: all these elements of a carefully produced feature film were counter to the war that was pre-

---

[1]Larry Lichty's "The Night at the End of the Tunnel," *Film Comment* 11 (July-August, 1975), 35.

[2]Mark Crispin Miller and Karen Runyon, in a summation of Cronkite's career, agree that his presence, his "quality of restrained benevolence," contributed more to his appeal than what he actually said. "And That's the Way It Seems," *New Republic* 185 (February 14, 1981), 22.

[3]The weariness with explanations and language itself was occasionally expressed directly by the newscasters. At the end of a 1972 report during which viewers saw women and children killed by road mines, Bob Simon was moved to say, "By evening government spokesmen are saying another grand victory has been won in Quang Tri province, the situation has once again been stabilized. But there will be more fighting and more words. Works spoken by generals, journalists, politicians. But here on Route One, it's difficult to imagine what those words can be. There's nothing left to say about this war. There's just nothing left to say." Quoted in Lichty, p. 33.

[4]Michael J. Arlen, in such books as *Living-Room War* (1969) and *The View from Highway 1* (1976) has written perceptively and critically of television's coverage of Vietnam. Two of the contributors to this volume, Peter Rollins and David Culbert, have completed a film on the subject, *Television's Vietnam: The Impact of Visual Images,* available from Oklahoma State University's Audiovisual Center.

sented to the American people by television. Many reviewers were never quite able to get this television war out of their minds when they viewed Vietnam films. Ironically enough, the superior quality of the picture on the big screen—which *seems* more real for all of its detail—also tended to draw many into a consideration of how well the films imitated what *really* went on in Vietnam.[5]

Coppola attempted to use and confront viewers with the fact that their experience of the war had been shaped by the media. His film features a structure which has radical disjointures of tone and action from episode to episode and a script that repeatedly enforces a view of the war as a disorganized, futile exercise moving to the beat of Wagner and hard rock. Nonetheless, viewers were all too aware that an auteur-director and, in the latter half of the picture, a star had control of the script and the necessary organization of technology to bring off the best lines and the most spectacular scenes. The *Heart of Darkness* elements were apparently meant to move the viewers away from vicarious involvement in the experience toward "the moral issues." These elements were regarded by many, however, as aesthetic self-consciousness or overcontrol, an unnecessary self-reflexivity that, along with the voice-over narration, book titles, and quoted lines, made the film much too "literary." In fact, those critics who avoided judging the film as realistic mimesis often ended up judging it as literary mimesis. The film was neither Vietnam nor *Heart of Darkness* and it was so much the worse for that indeterminancy.

In a sense, the most negative critics were right: the film was neither and it had meant to be both. Setting aside the issue of whether any carefully wrought film about Vietnam could have struck the audience of 1979-80 as being fully authentic, the contradictions between realism and "literary effects," experiential disorder and imposed moral lessons inherent in this film undercut its unity. A possible theme, enunciated by Willard, stresses the search for an orderly way to prosecute this war. The unsettling implication of his encounter with Kurtz is that at the center or around the chaos there may be a calm, meditative buddha or nature that can contemplate any destruction, including its own. Unfortunately, the implication is not developed enough during the whole film experience of the war up to Kurtz's compound; too, Conrad's world is hardly Coppola's. Hence, Kurtz's final utterance, "the horror," is neither a complete summation of the film nor a point where Conrad's theme joins Coppola's.

Like Coppola's film, *Heart of Darkness* is a highly personalized journey

---

[5]I would qualify this statement with an impression: most young people I have talked to seem less bound by mimetic questions, except as they assert that *Apocalypse Now* or *The Deer Hunter* portray events similar to what "really happened" or capture the "feel" of combat in Vietnam. Of course, we already have a generation of young adults whose primary memory of Vietnam *is* films, not newsreels.

through a particular setting. It does not seek, as its primary aim, to document and analyze the typical operations of imperialism. Indeed, based as it is on Conrad's brief contact with those operations in one extreme situation (King Leopold's Congo), it tends to portray them more through isolated confrontations and hearsay than through direct description. Marlow may glimpse the soul of Kurtz, but he fails to explore the inner workings of the Company. Nor is he really interested in such details, since he can judge the whole affair by its waste of human lives, black and white. A more precise detailing of the company's typical methods or agents would hardly clarify or alter Conrad's conclusions. Quite the contrary. To make an indirect brief for the film, it would be analogous to those futile attempts to make sense of the Vietnam war from the kill ratios released by the Defense Department. Moral conclusions must ultimately rise above such facts. On the basis of Marlow's experience, it would be fair to say that the more one becomes enmeshed in the details of company operations, the more one is mentally and morally endangered. Marlow chooses Kurtz as his nightmare against the spectre of a "sane" station manager, so professionalized and dehumanized by his administrative position that he can only judge Kurtz in terms of how his methods will affect company profits. What, then, causes the moral and psychological degeneration of those who enter this dark continent? For all of the observed inefficiency and stupidity, Marlow finally stresses unmeasurable and mysterious causes—a certain lack of inner restraint, a loss of civilized values, and the force of a brooding natural environment.

By the same token, *Apocalypse Now* does not really attempt to document the course of the Vietnam war or even many of its typical features. If anything, it bypasses documentation to confront our media-fed memory of the war and our armchair moralisms about its futility with scenes which push us to the extremes of vicarious participation (the air assault) and gut-level revulsion (the carnage at Kurtz's compound). The first scene, in Willard's hotel room, challenges our very sense of reality and prepares us for some of the surrealism in the last third of the picture, reminding the Conrad reader, perhaps, of the way the listening sailor characterizes Marlow and his style of tale-telling in the beginning of *Heart of Darkness*. In an excellent article, "The Power of Adaptation in *Apocalypse Now*," Marsha Kinder analyzes the scene to show its importance in defining important structural elements for the whole film: the subjective point of view, a surrealistic or dream-like war, a dispassionate voice-over narration, a mad ritual of violence, and simultaneous layers of experience that tend to dissolve into obsessive images of heads, helicopters, fire and smoke.[6]

There are some problems, however, in Kinder's contention that this scene immediately conditions the viewer to perceive all of the subsequent ac-

[6]*Film Quarterly,* 33 (Winter 1979-80), 12-20.

Under helicopter cover, U.S. patrol boats stage an amphibious landing on a coastal village under Viet Cong control, in *Apocalypse Now,* a United Artists release. (Courtesy of the Museum of Modern Art/Film Stills Archive)

tion as a kind of dream. With the arrival of the two soldiers to sober Willard up and the next briefing scene, filmed and acted in slow, nondramatic, documentary fashion, the first scene becomes quite unique, a kind of localized hallucination. The layering of experience, the simultaneous realities of the dream, for instance, don't recur in the same way until the ritual killing of Kurtz and the final scene. This is not to deny the importance of the first scene in defining stylistic elements; it is to realize what Coppola realized when he confronted the large task of editing—that the style of the film tends to change from scene to scene.[7]

For my own more modest purposes, the first combat scene "declares" Coppola's anti-documentary intentions more effectively for the viewer. In fact, the director himself appears in the scene as part of a television camera team. "Don't look at the camera. Just go by like you're fighting. . . . Move! Move! Keep on going. . . . Don't look at the camera," he yells to soldiers slogging ashore into a village which is being "liberated" by an Air Cavalry unit. The viewer who realizes that the director is in the picture perhaps accepts this appearance as another self-conscious auteur gesture, in the tradition of Alfred Hitchcock. Those who know of Coppola's agony of process in making his overbudget project, may see the appearance as another assertion by the director that Willard's journey and Kurtz's conflicts were also *his.*

[7]Eleanor Coppola, *Notes* (New York: Simon and Schuster, 1979), p. 233.

On the realistic level, however, the television camera and, later, the many Nikons strapped to Dennis Hopper should remind the viewer that the Vietnam war was the most photographed, reported, and even staged war in history. In that first battle scene, the director's own cameras move with the soldiers, away from the fixed television perspective, to the apparent confusion of mopping up. It is a reality that overwhelms the viewer's eyes and ears, quite in contrast to the contained "reality" on the small screens of our television sets. A bellowing cow being lifted by helicopter sling, houses burning or being bulldozed, a church service in progress, smoke rising, villagers being herded into a landing vehicle, bodies lying all over, all shot in ground-level pans which capture foreground action while passing over planes of background activity that cannot be included at the same time: the television icons of war are all there, but in much more threatening deep focus. This is a reality that one cannot stabilize, a reality that juxtaposes glimpses of kindness towards villagers with devastation of their village, perceptual disorder with the order of an operation being carried out as planned, even down to the unit "signature" in the playing cards left on the dead. The film initiates the viewer into a Vietnam outside the television screen, a place and a war that cannot be framed and parcelled out in nightly newscasts. It encompasses and passes by so much that it becomes simultaneously complete and fragmentary, real and unreal.

The style of filming moves the viewer toward what had seemed only the hallucination of Willard's overwrought mind in the opening scene. Although sometimes sacrified for a more "omniscient" style of rendering—as in the later air assault—the approach to reality in this scene defines the way Coppola will approach the Vietnam war. It will be a personal, involved view that tends to sacrifice moral distance for perceptual overload. Unlike Conrad's Marlow, one will not be able to focus on surface necessities as a way of staying disengaged.

The scene provides access to the psychological plot of the film. As in *Adventures of Huckleberry Finn,* the river keeps the plot moving, providing more or less traumatic encounters that represent the war as a series of massive incoherencies which test the stability and resourcefulness of the participants. In literary terms, it tends to graft the episodic plot and amoral world of the picaresque tradition to the stream-of-consciousness style of Michael Herr's *Dispatches.* As Willard travels up the river, beyond the Do Lung Bridge, the script becomes increasingly Conrad-through-Coppola, focusing more on the psychological-moral effects of the madness. Perceptual disorder increasingly becomes physical and mental disorder, until we reach Kurtz, whose apparent order of mind and manner are belied by the actual disorder around him.

In the original Milius script, Willard was converted by Kurtz. So much so that he and Kurtz were "firing up at the helicopters that are coming to get him, crying crazily. A movie comic."[8] A later version, mentioned in Eleanor Coppola's *Notes,* had Willard die in a bomb strike as the result of a double-cross by headquarters.[9] This finale, which may be the footage that appears behind the credits in the 35-mm version, gave way to the alternate post-murder scene shown to "test audiences," in which Willard seemed to accept command of Kurtz's army. As he worked with Willard, however, Coppola slowly moved away from the film as the story of his journey, temptation and conversion. "In no way could he get in the way of the audience's view of what was happening, of Vietnam."[10] In fact, Harvey Keitel was released from the role, after filming began, because he projected too strongly. Quite obviously then, Willard was conceived at some distance from Marlow, first as a person who became what he sought to eliminate, later as a person who provided a neutral point of view for the unfolding of the war. As the latter version began to prevail, with the presence of Martin Sheen, Coppola had to return to the original conception somewhat to make Willard interesting: "Marty's character was coming across as too bland; I tried to break through it."[11] The result was the insertion of the first crazy scene—which does not prepare the viewer for the neutral witness—and, more subtly, the sense of guilt, the disdain for the way the war is being run, and the growing sense of kinship with Kurtz.

The interior elements are communicated through a voice-over narration, written by Michael Herr, which was added after all of the on-location shooting was finished. One assumes that this method too was to make Willard more interesting, psychologically, without letting his character get in the way of any important action. Kinder suggests that Sheen's poor health, after his heart attack, may have necessitated this monotone method of characterization.[12] The irony is that many critics seized the narration sections as borrowed and bungled Conrad, when, in fact, the two modes of narration are strikingly different in purpose and effect. Marlow's whole story is filtered through his matured consciousness, with each event valued and sometimes displaced so that the reader actually gets two "stories"—one of an adventuring self which is reactive and feels alternately fascinated and threatened by all that is around him; the other of a reflective self which characterizes, judges, and carefully shapes into words the earlier self and what was encountered. In contrast, Willard's narration is more interior monologue, the reactive thoughts of someone involved in the action, who, in effect, does not think during the most intensely dramatic scenes. Often, Willard's comments seem more self-protective than analytic. The net effect is that while Marlow's commentary tends to deepen and extend the significance of his ex-

[8]"An Interview with Francis Coppola," *Rolling Stone* (Nov. 1, 1979), p. 53.
[9]*Notes,* p. 241.
[10]*Rolling Stone,* p. 53.
[11]*Rolling Stone,* p. 53.
[12]Kinder, p. 15.

perience, Willard's narration tends to flatten his character even more than the low-key acting style. His neutrality can be interpreted as a professional pragmatism which positions him nearer to the disorder of the war than to any set of values by which it can be judged. This is particularly interesting, when we remind ourselves that Willard, like Marlow, is supposedly narrating his story after the fact. In the opening scene, the narrator tells us, "There is no way to tell his story without telling my own. His story is really a confession and so is mine." If so, it is a confession without much self-revelation or reflection, unless you assume that the filmed action is somehow selected and shaped by Willard's consciousness. As indicated above, I believe his sensibility is not present enough in the visual style for most of the plot up to the encounter with Kurtz. The consciousness of Willard frames the experience, without enclosing it. His consciousness, like the river, is the means by which we get to the major episodes, but the episodes themselves are unmeditated. Thus, the necessary shifts back and forth between image and voice create problems. Each time the viewer leaves an episode he has experienced with overwhelming directness, the returning voice "expects" him to accept a reductive moralism. Coppola, perhaps, thought such banalities as "We cut them in half with a machine gun and give them a bandaide." would help his audience put Vietnam behind them.

A major difference between Marlow and Willard is that Marlow is an idealistic young man, who tends to judge the company's actions in terms of their humanity, whereas Willard is a professional soldier, who tends to judge the war in terms of its military efficiency. It is through Willard, in fact, that Coppola comes closest to an analysis of the military dilemma in Vietnam.

We should remember that the standard criticism of the French effort in Vietnam is that they never learned how to fight a guerrilla war in the countryside. Certainly one cannot say precisely the same about the American military. Khe Sanh was never on the verge of becoming Dien Bien Phu, in spite of some press efforts to portray it as such. American technology's ability to move the troops and concentrate fire power insured success in most sustained engagements. It was less successful in "winning the hearts and minds" and securing the land. The gigantic enclaves, whether military bases or relocation camps, symbolized the extent of American success and failure. With the superior depth and breadth of film, Coppola is able to portray this extent much better than television: Willard journeys through a series of large-scale beachheads or enclaves, each created by technology (up to Kurtz's compound), each surrounded by the jungle and the darkness where "Charlie" lives. (Whether this depiction arose from the director's "apparent sense that the world is seen most truthfully when it is seen as a spectacle"[13] or his analysis of America's military effort is perhaps beside the point.) Wil-

[13]Stanley Kauffmann, "Coppola's War," *New Republic,* 181 (Sep. 15, 1979), 24.

lard's awareness of the hostile environment and the circus-like atmosphere of each operation extends to include an indirect criticism of the culture that is so tellingly displayed in the major scenes. The few military men competent to lead find that America has given them "rock and rollers with one foot in their graves." From water-skiing to the rock show to Lance's acid trips to the electronic nightmare of Do Lung Bridge, technology's children are depicted as soft, self-indulgent, and unequal to their hidden enemy. Willard's professional dedication places him in critical opposition to the military and culture he has pledged to serve. Both create barriers to his mission.

Whereas Marlow grimly attends to the immediate necessities of running a boat up the river without breaking down or scraping bottom, Coppola's Willard withdraws into meditations on his mission and Kurtz through the dossier. What breaks in on him is not the silence of the jungle or the disorder of white men obsessed by ivory, but the crew of "rock and rollers." Like Marlow, Willard is one of the "new gang" who wants the purity of being dedicated to something apart from himself. He takes the mission, not because he has faith in its rightness, but because it is a mission. He focuses on the dossier for much the same reason Marlow focuses on his boat—to keep his mind stabilized by immediate facts so he can ignore the larger instabilities around him.

We reach the limits of similarity here because Willard possesses little of the consciousness of being psychically threatened that Marlow has. At no point before the very end does Willard feel the lure of the unleashed power around him. Viewers may be drawn to "go ashore for a howl and a dance" with the GIs in the spectacular USO sequence, but not Willard. He recognizes none of the kinship with the "natives" on shore that Marlow does. Like the tough-guy detective (another Marlow), Willard uses cynicism to keep the darkness at arm's length so he can preserve his solitary fidelity to the code of his profession. Just as in *The Maltese Falcon,* even when one doesn't trust the client who defines the mission, one can only come through whole and clean if he honors his commitment. If he violates what narrows to a personal, professional code and gives in to the jungle, the whole sense of darkness encompassing a small "light" of moral integrity—essential to the *cinema noire,* for instance—will be lost.

All three writers connected with *Apocalypse Now* seem to have been aware of the Conradean possibilities the jungle presented with regard to Willard. In the opening of the original script by John Milius, the wilderness is first seen without humans, as primeval. An ambush develops in which Americans, already changed by their environment, emerge dressed as savages, "unexplainably, out of the growth" and blast away at the camera or reach toward the camera to scalp a dead Vietnamese.[14] The exposition of

[14]"'Apocalypse Now' Script Extracts," *Film Comment,* 12 (July-August, 1976), 14.

this action, then, associates the barbarism of Kurtz's army with the jungle itself. Hence, Kurtz could begin to influence Willard through the jungle during his journey up the river. As Milius puts it, "I'd have tried to give the jungle as much personality as possible, have it be . . . as much a character as the war." [15] Michael Herr, who wrote the narration, recorded the force of the Vietnam jungle in *Dispatches*: "Forget the Cong, the *trees* will kill you, the elephant grass is homicidal, the ground you were walking over possessed malignant intelligence, your whole environment was a bath." [16]

Since Coppola decided to form his film around the quest-journey of the PBR up the river, one can hardly blame him for not showing the war of the foot soldier, where snipers and the fear of ambushes would make the jungle a kind of force. He dramatically establishes something of this aspect early in the film when Chef, the Louisiana "saucier," is scared witless by the sudden appearance of a tiger out of the forest. It demonstrates just how "tight" Chef and the rest of the crew were "wrapped" and relates that tension and the resultant craziness to the enclosing environment. Willard echoes Chef's key line,—"Never get out of the boat."—enlarging it to include what you might become if you did leave the boat: "Kurtz got off the boat. He split from the whole fuckin' program." Unfortunately, these connections are not reinforced in subsequent scenes. Instead, Willard turns again to the dossier history of Kurtz. Up to the Do Lung sequence, the jungle is merely a setting against which battles or napalm drops are staged. It is the impersonal, surrounding green or part of the darkness in the USO and bridge sequences. After the latter, a high angle long shot establishing the boat's slow progress up the snaking river and a subsequent eye-level long shot of the boat moving directly away from the camera—optically *not* moving—between high canyon walls again suggests the pressure of the environment. The two attack scenes that follow are modelled on the attack scene in Conrad that so effectively impresses Marlow as an attack of the jungle itself, with disembodied arms, legs, eyes, and spears seeming a part of some greater beast. But the context or staging of both in the film prevents a similar impression. The more dramatic machine-gun-tracer attack, which seems to explode out of the jungle, is somewhat isolated and undercut by the oddity of a long banner and the red smoke ("purple haze") that Lance spreads around. Lance, the California surfer, looks around and concludes, "This is better than Disneyland." The arrow and spear attack is somewhat comically staged, with men running on the shore and Lance making a hat of the arrows. The deaths in these incidents are further separated from the jungle by an ironic tape recording in the first case and a rather grotesque attempt to impale Willard in the second.

[15]"John Milius Interviewed by Richard Thompson," *Film Comment,* 12 (July-August, 1976), 15.
[16]Michael Herr, *Dispatches* (New York: Avon, 1978), p. 66.

Willard's statement about Kurtz, just before he kills him indicates that Coppola may have intended a brooding personality for the jungle: "Even the jungle wanted him dead and that's who he really took orders from anyway." Perhaps the superimposed faces of Kurtz and temple idols at the end are to suggest this personality. Certainly, a more continuous emphasis on the power of the jungle could have strengthened the Kurtz character and Willard's attraction to him much more than did allusions to Charlie Manson, the General's analysis, or Kurtz's own explanations.

Even if Coppola had stressed the mysterious and unconquerable power of the jungle, those who sought a realistic representation of the Vietnam war would have trouble accepting Kurtz. *Dispatches* mentions special agents who operated freely, without contact with headquarters, but no one even attained the kind of power and immunity from attack of a Kurtz. Nor does Coppola intend for the viewer to "read" him that way. Instead, he seems to have conceived Kurtz as a kind of objective correlative: "There it is. [Brando's face] And that's the way I felt about Vietnam."[17] Once we make appropriate adjustments for Kurtz's fictionality, however, we become more aware of problems with his aesthetic credibility. A major plot problem is that there is too little to discover about him. Rather than approaching him gradually, coming at him through layers of opinion and hearsay, as Marlow does, Coppola strips much of his mystery away in the briefing session. He is never the genius, the man who had ideas and, at the same time, was more successful than anyone else in the "company." Kurtz is introduced as a man who has gone "totally beyond the pale of any acceptable human conduct." This judgment is delivered by an authoritative source, quite above the self-interested bunglers who presume to judge Kurtz in Conrad's novel. Moreover, Kurtz himself witnesses to this judgment, courtesy of a Sony tape recorder: "We must kill them. We must incinerate them—pig after pig, cow after cow, village after village, army after army." The general even analyzes—in fine study guide fashion—How It Happened and What It All Means: "Out there with these natives, there must be a temptation to be God, because there's a conflict in every human heart between the rational and irrational, between good and evil. . . . Sometimes the dark side will overcome the better angels of our nature." Hence, the heart of Coppola's darkness is explained at the very beginning. Willard and the viewer are reduced to corroborating the charges with their own eyes by encountering the man and his atrocities before carrying out the sentence upon him. There was still some opportunity for an exploration of character, but given an overweight Marlon Brando, who hadn't read *Heart of Darkness* before he arrived on the set, who didn't like Coppola's original conception of his character, and who, more or less, worked up his character while the cameras

[17]*Rolling Stone*, p. 56.

Producer-director Francis Coppola discusses a scene with his star, Marlon Brando (left) on the set of *Apocalypse Now,* a United Artists release. (Courtesy of the Museum of Modern Art/Film Stills Archive)

ran, all during a stay of two weeks, it's not surprising that the photography strikes the viewer with more force than the acting.

The original beginning of Milius's script thrusts Kurtz on the viewer quite early. Few would disagree with Brooks Riley that a change was needed: "To have shown us Kurtz first, only to abandon him for the next two-thirds of the film would have proved an unforgivable betrayal of the character and a dilution of the film's carefully planned unveiling of the man behind, under, or above the myth."[18] Horror film fans will recognize the principle operating here: Don't display your monster too early in the film. As it turns out, the dossier's increasingly blurred photos of Kurtz may be more important than the information on his background. When we encounter the man, it is a powerful visual encounter. His bald head and huge body slowly emerge and melt back into the shadow, creating a drama more interesting than anything he says. Certainly Coppola felt that the character was "in place" when Brando shaved his head. The film celebrates that moment for the director: "I think it's wonderful that in this movie, the most terrifying moment is that image: just his face."[19] Kurtz's presence is primarily

[18]*Film Comment,* 15 (September-October 1979), 26.
[19]*Rolling Stone,* p. 54.

Guided by a crazed freelance photographer (Dennis Hopper), left, Capt. Willard (Martin Sheen), foreground, and Chef (Frederic Forrest) warily survey a temple compound guarded by Montagnard warriors in *Apocalypse Now,* a United Artists release. (Courtesy of the Museum of Modern Art/Film Stills Archive)

physical, a piece of the spectacle of the film, a meditative object around which everything else should form into incantation or ritual. That object, first cleansed, then blackened, then bloodied is played off against other disembodied heads, human and stone, against the tangled masses of living and dead bodies, against light, explosions of light, and surrounding darkness. It finally becomes a mental projection on the black screen of Willard's mind. This is to give Coppola his due.

But I would agree with the "majority" critical position: "the film succeeds in forcing us to experience the horror of the war and to (perhaps) acknowledge our own complicity in it, but it fails to illuminate the nature of Kurtz's horror."[20] For all of Kurtz's rationalizing and quoting, we do not really get to the moral origins of this darkness. In fact, the quotes and book titles suggest texts external to the film that make much better *sense* of Western man's loss of civilized values. At its most powerful, the film relegates words and analysis to a musical status: Kurtz's controlled fugue of literary fragments and isolated memories separates him even from his own operations and has the power of a closed, complete, paranoid structure; his disciple, the photo journalist, rambles through a romantic scherzo of enthusiasm, aspiration and pseudo-analysis which betrays his instability and im-

[20]Kinder, p. 13.

mersion in a new cult (with his old cult objects, Nikons, hung round his neck). Neither of these men explains or can explain; and Willard lacks the distance and moral intelligence to explain.

Unfortunately, perhaps, film is a moving picture. The director cannot completely reduce environment to images formed around the head of Kurtz (or Willard). Whereas the meditator needs a more or less constant sound and image so he can move his mind to new perspectives of the object and new levels of consciousness, the film supplies its own order of perspectives as it changes angle, lighting, scene, etc. This is an order which tends to disrupt or preclude the movement of the mind, at least while the film is being shown. Hence, not the most dramatic shots of heads at the end nor the echoed resonance of Kurtz's last words move us much past perception. The hard rock sound and light show that detonates behind the credits in the 35 mm version seems to ratify a state of dazed receptiveness.

In Coppola's immediately preceding pictures, *The Godfather* series and *The Conversation,* the protagonists have attempted to separate themselves from American culture while living in its midst, to seek order, stability, and fulfillment in an independent network of rules and values. Michael Corleone and Harry Caul both operate according to professional codes in a world where the rules—based on loyalty to family, religion, company, or country—have broken down. In this sense, both are "code" characters whose conflicts involve the effort to live by the code they have chosen to follow, while others—even those closest to them—often live without a code, by a different code (Kay Corleone), or violate their supposed loyalty to the main character's code (Fredo Corleone). Many viewers, especially of *The Godfather* series, found much to admire in the characters' integrity and commitment to order, as if these characters had, like their Hemingway predecessors, almost managed to separate themselves completely from the societal breakdown around them. Such viewers indicate more about the culture than about the films involved; in the cultural context of Coppola's pictures, there is no "separate peace" available. First, the creation of a separate system of professional values is, properly seen, not really a rejection of the culture. A number of artists and sociologists, from Thomas Pynchon to Theodore Roszack, have charted the breakup of a moral consensus and society itself into technocratic-professional, cultural, or ideological groups. The members have loyalty limited by such groups, whether job, life-style, or belief groups, and will often act in ways contrary to generally accepted mores and laws to gain their ends. Indeed, this is the second feature that distinguishes the characters of Coppola's films from Hemingway's code heroes: their activities actually help promote a breakdown of society's mores and loyalties. Ultimately, their own systems of value and behavior are breached and "turn on" the characters, to isolate them in a small paranoid space. The final shots of Michael alone in a room or Harry destroying his room in search of a transmitter show the extent to which each character's professional behavior has stripped him of the very things (family, order) that his profession was to secure in the first place.

Willard begins *Apocalypse Now* in a hotel room, divorced from his wife, waiting desperately for another mission, any mission so he can pull himself together. Unfortunately, his mission involves killing a man who seems to embody the very professional values he finds so lacking in the rest of the operations he encounters. What's more, Kurtz has formed his own efficient system of war, outside the American effort. He has "cut himself loose" in a way that Willard finds admirable, although his lack of method or the madness of his methods ultimately leads Willard to carry out his original mission. But Kurtz seems to have directed him since his savagery in murdering Kurtz enacts Kurtz's methods.

"The horror, the horror" hardly creates an impact comparable to Conrad's novel for several reasons. In willing his own murder, Kurtz does not seem to have reaffirmed the civilized values that the outsider has brought into his world. Instead, he has transformed the outsider into one of his own kind, presumably fitting him to either lead or destroy his whole world. Those, in fact, are the two endings that Coppola filmed—either of which would have been logical. After such premeditation are we to accept Kurtz's words that evidence of some hidden conversion, a renunciation of everything he has accomplished, including his own murder? The words echo in Willard's mind after the moment, just as they echo in Marlow's mind, but with what a difference! Unlike Marlow, Willard has not restrained himself; he has "cut himself loose" from his own professional code. Kurtz's words, as remembered, could indicate repugnance, but again there is nothing else in Willard's behavior to indicate that a conventional moral sensibility has returned. The final destruction of Kurtz's compound (in the 35mm version) would seem to indicate otherwise. Above all, the horror of Kurtz's fall from moral and professional grace is muted becaus there is no consistent, dramatic representation of those values in the film. The war, American culture in Vietnam, the behavior of those involved, especially Willard, do not represent ideals against which Kurtz can be judged.

The most dramatic sense of abysm at the end of the film is aesthetic, not moral. *Apocalypse Now* begins with personal futility and destruction and enlarges the scope in each ensuing major scene. Each scene becomes "worse," but, as in Dante's *Inferno,* not as emotionally intensifying as the first encounter. Paradoxically, each more horrible scene tends to be more spectacular and thus more exciting in visual-aural effects. Can the viewer really enlarge a sense of moral horror against the visceral impact of better and better pyrotechnic displays?[21]

[21]My attempt to reconstruct and analyze that process is entitled *"Heart of Darkness* and the Process of *Apocalypse Now," Conradiana,* 13.1 (1981), 45-54.

The pressure of the television war seems quite apparent in *Apocalypse Now*. After all of the newsreel fragmentation of experience and the disillusionment with logical explanation, any filmmaker would have been hard put to make cinematic sense of the war. For a lesser director, the spectacular battle sequences would have been enough. But the humanist in Francis Coppola would not let him simply portray the waste or futility or black humor of Vietnam. So he attempted to follow the example of Joseph Conrad, whose journey into the heart of imperialism exposed the frailty of Western cultural and moral values. Unlike Conrad's world, however, Coppola's America does not offer the stable consensus standards or ideals against which the actions of a Kurtz or Kilgore will seem horrible. The standard left is represented by Willard, the much narrower one of professional discipline. When that standard is breached, the grounds for judgment within the work of art are soon gone. One is left with an aesthetic of intensities. Contrary to the old saw, experience of a journey, of the processes of filmmaking, of a Vietnam will not always gather itself into a moral perspective.

CHAPTER 13.

Film, Television, and American Studies

PETER C. ROLLINS

CURRENT APPROACHES TO FILM
AND TELEVISION

MOTION PICTURES SHAPED OUR MINDS, AND TELEVISION IS NOW SHAPING the minds of our students. Television programming for children has been carefully scrutinized recently by such groups as Action for Children's Television. A number of scholars and affected institutions have begun to examine the practices of television news programs and documentaries. The popularity of such docudramas as *Washington: Behind Closed Doors* (1978) and *Roots* (1977-79) spurred historians to criticize the methods of a competing educator. Americanists should be alert to these developments if for no other reason than that more people watched *Roots* and absorbed its lessons about American civilization than will ever graduate from all the American Studies programs in the United States.

Developments in television have a brighter side: successful and conscientious productions such as the PBS-sponsored *American Short Story Series* (1977) and the recent adaptation of *The Scarlet Letter* (1979) have sparked student interest in the art of adaptation. *Civilization* (1970), the *Adams Chronicles* (1976), *Nova* (1974), and the *Ascent of Man* (1975) have provided similar teaching opportunities for historians and scientists.

In spite of many successes, some traditionalists have given film and television a cold shoulder. John E. O'Connor, editor of *Film and the Humanities* (New York: Rockefeller Foundation, 1977), reports that teachers with an interest in the film media have encountered hostility from senior faculty members who portray themselves as defenders of what is sanctimoniously called "the Word" (pp. 2, 13). Motivated more by fear than understanding, the old guard claims that the humanities must resist all encroachments by the media. On the other hand, teachers who have actually used media in the classroom know that their students, as a result of increased discrimination, watch less film and television. Based upon experience, these innovators suggest that the best way to defend "the Word" is to expand the concept of literacy to include facility with verbal and visual languages: our students and fellow citizens will be truly educated only if they are able to "read" both forms of communication.

As History and English departments across the country begin to use film seriously, scholars of the American Studies persuasion should be especially interested, for the study of film in a social context requires interdisciplinary skills: film is laden with metaphors and symbols and affects and reflects contemporary consciousness, so that Americanists trained to discern the interrelationships among intellectual, aesthetic, and institutional forces should provide insight and leadership.

This essay will attempt to provide a bridge to film and television for students of American culture. Some of the questions that are currently being asked about film will be described in the first section. Next, the professional associations and periodicals which devote attention to film will be surveyed. Concluding remarks will offer some practical suggestions about how to order and research films. A few basic reference works on a variety of film and television topics will then be listed.

Threat of the Hidden Persuaders

Propaganda analysis has been most active during wartime. During World War II, Siegfried Kracauer exposed the cinematic tricks of Nazi newsreel and propaganda films in "Propaganda and the Nazi War Film," a visual analysis which still teaches much about how filmmakers and their editors sway masses (in his *Caligari to Hitler* [Princeton: Princeton Univ. Press, 1971], 275–332). American attempts to counter German propaganda are described in *An Historical and Descriptive Analysis of the "Why We Fight" Series* (New York: Arno, 1977) by Thomas Bohn. Like Kracauer, Bohn is attentive to both content and cinematic language. Although the Korean war marked a low point for all forms of documentary, Peter C. Rollins, *"Victory at Sea: Cold War Epic"* reveals that documentaries for television often peddled foreign policy nostrums (*Journal of Popular Culture*, 2 [1973], 463–82). Critiques of Vietnam documentaries are few in number, but *Big Story: How the American Press and Television Reported and Interpreted the Crisis of Tet 1968 in Vietnam and Washington* (Boulder, Colo.: Westview, 1977) by Peter Braestrup suggests so many projects that it is a library in itself. Braestrup follows up

Big Story with "Vietnam as History," *The Wilson Quarterly*, 2 (1978), 178–88, a survey of fiction and nonfiction dealing with our most recent war.

Lawrence H. Suid provides a scholarly examination of America's war films in *Guts and Glory: Great American War Movies* (Reading, Mass.: Addison-Wesley, 1978), a work whose use of primary sources should serve as a model for film scholars. More limited in focus and more subjective is *Looking Away: Hollywood and Vietnam* (New York: Scribner, 1975) by Julian Smith.

Raymond Fielding, in *The American Newsreel* (Norman: Univ. of Oklahoma Press, 1972) reveals that the falsification of evidence which we associate with recent documentaries has been a hallowed tradition of the genre since 1898 when an ambitious American photojournalist sank the *Maine* in his bathtub. Two excellent overviews of documentary and newsreel history are Richard M. Barsam, *Nonfiction Film: A Critical History* (New York: Dutton, 1973) and Eric Barnouw, *Documentary: A History of the Non-Fiction Film* (New York: Oxford, 1974). Barsam's book contains film summaries; Barnouw's slim volume is more valuable for interpretations; both cover the same ground although each has a distinct perspective. Lewis Jacobs, *The Documentary Tradition: From Nanook to Woodstock* (New York: Hopkinson and Blake, 1971) provides a massive set of readings to complement the narratives by Barsam and Barnouw.

The power of television documentaries has been of concern in recent days. Falsification of materials by Peter Davis for *The Selling of the Pentagon* dramatized the need for critical viewing, although Spiro Agnew may have been an ill-chosen spokesman for media critics. ABC's *Youth Terror* (1977) demonstrated that even advocates of *cinema verité* are not averse to reconstructing scenes (Robert Sklar, "Network Verité," *American Film* [Jan. 1979], 18–23). William Bleum recounts the early days of television documentary in *Documentary in American Television* (New York: Hastings House, 1965). Alan Rosenthal, in *The New Documentary in Action* (Berkeley: Univ. of California Press, 1971), and C. Roy Levin, in *Documentary Explorations* (New York: Doubleday, 1971), interview contemporary practitioners. Stephen Mamber, in his *Cinema Verité in America* (Cambridge: MIT Press, 1974), closely examines major films of those interviewed by Rosenthal and Levin.

A number of studies of television examine economic and institutional factors affecting the content and form of network news. Although Edward Jay Epstein's *News From Nowhere* (New York: Random House, 1973) has drawn much negative criticism, it is still the most provocative study of how institutional factors determine what stories reach the public. Among the best "gatekeeper studies" is Lawrence W. Lichty and George A.

Baily, "Rough Justice as a Saigon Street: A Gatekeeper Study of NBC's Tet Execution Film," *Journalism Quarterly*, 41 (1972), 221–29. William Adams, Fay Schreibman, and others delineate and apply methods currently available for the study of television in *Television Network News: Issues in Content Research* (Washington, D. C.: George Washington Univ., 1978). This anthology is an excellent starting place because every article closes with an extensive bibliography.

In his *Public Opinion* (1922; rpt. New York: Macmillan, 1970), Walter Lippmann opened the contemporary discussion about how the media shape our perceptions, but Lippmann was concerned primarily with the written word. Daniel Boorstin's popular volume, *The Image: A Guide to Pseudo-Events in America* (New York: Atheneum, 1972) tries to bring Lippmann's analysis up to date. As yet, we have no synthesis, but Richard Adler in "What is Visual Literacy?" argues persuasively that a culture increasingly dependent upon electronic media needs to be literate in both verbal and visual languages (*American Film* [June 1978], 22–27).

Film as Historical and Cultural Document

Films can serve the student of American culture in a far more interesting way than simply as a record of visual reality, for films register the feelings and attitudes of the periods in which they are made. Andrew Bergman, in *We're in the Money: Depression America and Its Films* (New York: New York Univ. Press, 1971), concludes that classic genre films of the Depression era taught lessons about the American Dream, the benevolence of government, and the role of the individual—lessons which mollified the frustrations of citizens during difficult times. Robert Sklar evinces a broad understanding of the cultural forces affecting both the production and reception of movies in *Movie-Made America: A Cultural History of American Movies* (New York: Random House, 1975). Sklar appears to contradict many of the assertions in his book in "Windows on a Made-Up World," *American Film*, (July 1976), 60–64, an article which claims that, rather than speaking for national attitudes, the Dream Factory created "a screenworld that reflected its own—its personal, corporate, and communal ambitions and feelings" (p. 60). Both approaches, although apparently contradictory, may identify valuable topics for study. Charles J. Maland, *American Visions: The Films of Chaplin, Ford, Capra, and Welles, 1936–1941* (New York: Arno, 1977) looks at films of the Thirties as "symbolic universes" which helped Americans to deal with the problems of the Depression era. Maland's emphasis on specific directors distinguishes his book from other interdisciplinary surveys.

Garth Jowett, *Film: The Democratic Art* (Boston: Little, Brown, 1976) is another "must" for Americanists. With the belief that motion pictures are "a major socializing agency in the first half of this century" (p. ix), Jowett looks at the process by which films have become symbols of change. He also traces how special interest groups (e.g., civic, religious) have striven to exploit or retard this power. Because Jowett is more concerned with attitudes toward movies than with film content, his study complements Sklar's. Michael Wood, in *America In the Movies, or "Santa Maria It Had Slipped My Mind"* (New York: Basic Books, 1975), supplies a highly subjective reading of American films as "scrambled messages from waking life." With a lively imagination, Wood attempts to decode film messages concerning the success ethic, individualism, and the role of women. Wood's readings are always interesting, even when they are only tenuously documented. Martin Jackson, John O'Connor and others discuss specific films in *American History/American Film* (New York: Ungar, 1979): feature films (1920–1976) are examined at four-year intervals with emphasis equally distributed between texts and contexts. Topics considered are women in film, the war film, minorities in film, American humor in film, and the West in film; each discussion focuses upon a specific production.

Methodology is discussed by Paul Smith in *The Historian and Film* (Cambridge: Cambridge Univ. Press, 1976), a book which stresses the documentary film, a genre ignored by Sklar, Jowett, Maland, and Jackson. More practical in its focus is John E. O'Connor and Martin A. Jackson, *Teaching History With Film* (American Historical Association, 1974), an overview which identifies the opportunities and pitfalls of this new area of research and teaching. Charles F. Altman attempts to synthesize the factors involved in film/American studies research into a compact statement in "Towards a Historiography of American Film," *Cinema Journal*, 16 (1977), 1–25. More highly specialized looks at film preservation, research, and the use of film archives are Eileen Bowser, "Symposium on the Methodology of Film History," *Cinema Journal*, 14 (1974), 1–80, and William T. Murphy, "The National Archives and the Historian's Use of Film," *The History Teacher* 6 (1972), 119–34.

In addition to obvious elements of content, documentary films can be studied for their reflection of social and political forces. Richard D. MacCann, in *The People's Films: A Political History of U.S. Government Motion Pictures* (New York: Hastings House, 1973), presents a pioneering study of public information activities of the U.S. Government. He examines British precedents, the experience of Pare Lorentz and his Film Service, World War II propaganda, and postwar USIA film activities. Robert L. Snyder focuses exclusively on the *oeuvre* of the American Film

Service, 1936-41, in *Pare Lorentz and the Documentary Film* (Norman: Univ. of Oklahoma Press, 1968). Peter C. Rollins and Harris J. Elder concentrate on two controversial New Deal productions in "Environmental History in Two New Deal Documentaries: *The Plow That Broke the Plains* (1936) and *The River* (1937) (*Film and History*, 4 [1974], 11–13). *The March of Time* (New York: Oxford Univ. Press, 1978) by Raymond Fielding, is a long-awaited study of America's most important newsreel from 1935–1953. Many of the strengths and weaknesses of our current photojournalism can be traced back to *March of Time*. William Alexander considers the biases of this series in *"The March of Time* and *The World Today,"* *American Quarterly*, 29 (Summer 1977), 182–93.

Movie censorship and the attempts of pressure groups to influence content are discussed in a few works already cited—at length by Jowett and to a lesser degree by Sklar. Two special studies of equal thoroughness are Richard S. Randall, *Censorship of the Movies: The Social and Political Control of a Mass Medium* (Madison: Univ. of Wisconsin Press, 1968) and Ira H. Carmen, *Movies, Censorship and the Law* (Ann Arbor: Univ. of Michigan Press, 1966). Paul W. Facey, a member of the Society of Jesus, gives a sympathetic portrait of a Catholic censorship group in *The Legion of Decency: A Sociological Analysis of the Emergence and Development of a Social Pressure Group* (New York: Arno, 1945). No one studying film censorship should be denied the hilarity of *See No Evil: Life Inside a Hollywood Censor* (New York: Simon and Schuster, 1970) by Jack Vizzard, the personal narrative of a Motion Picture Production Code administrator.

Minorities and women have not fared well in American films. The only scholarly works on blacks in film are Daniel Leab, *From Sambo to Superspade: The Black Experience in Motion Pictures* (Boston: Houghton Mifflin, 1975) and Thomas Cripps, *Slow Fade to Black: The Negro in American Film*, 1900–1942 (New York: Oxford Univ. Press, 1977). Ralph and Natasha Friar, in *The Only Good Indian: The Hollywood Gospel* (New York: Drama Book Specialists, 1972) suggest subjects of value for further study by those concerned about the image of the Native American.

Examining the images of women in films has wisely been seen as a necessary part of the women's movement. Molly Haskell, *From Reverence to Rape: The Treatment of Women in the Movies* (New York: Holt Rinehart and Winston, 1973) is a crusading book in which the crusader wins out over the scholar. In Marjorie Rosen's *Popcorn Venus: Women, Movies, and the American Dream* (New York: Avon Books, 1973), chapter titles such as "The Twenties—Wet Dreams in a Dry Land" may increase sales, but they reflect a rhetoric which inhibits historical and social insights. More insightful is Brandon French, *On the Verge of Revolt: Women in American Films of the Fifties* (New York: Ungar, 1979). Joan Mellon looks at the male image in *Big Bad Wolves: Masculinity in the American Film* (New York: Pantheon, 1977).

Studies of film genre are not without interest to Americanists. John G. Cawelti, *The Six-Gun Mystique* (Bowling Green: Bowling Green Univ. Press, 1971) has been an extremely influential model for a number of scholars interested in the Western; Cawelti's notion of "formula" has been applied fruitfully to other genres. Perhaps too ambitious in its desire to reach commanding syntheses is Ralph and Donna Brauer, *The Horse, the Gun, and the Piece of Property: Changing Images of the TV Western* (Bowling Green: Bowling Green Univ. Press, 1975). Will Wright, *Six Guns and Society: A Structural Study of the Western* (Berkeley: Univ. of California Press, 1975), is a book whose clarity distinguishes it from most structuralist writings. Jack Nachbar, *Focus on the Western* (Englewood Cliffs, N. J.: Prentice-Hall, 1974), gives examples of approaches to the Western along with extensive bibliography.

American comic films are dealt with in the surveys by Sklar and Maland. A lengthy cinematic study of the comic film is Gerald Mast, *The Comic Mind: Comedy and the Movies* (New York: Oxford, 1973). With so few books available on film comedy, *Movie Comedy* (Grossman, 1977), an anthology of reviews arranged to follow the chronology of film history, fills a necessary gap. Two articles by Peter C. Rollins, "Will Rogers: Symbolic Man, Journalist, and Film Image," *Journal of Popular Culture,* 9 (1976), 851–77 and "The Relevance of Nostalgia: Will Rogers in *Steamboat Round the Bend,*" in *American History/American Film,* 77–96, attempt to link a film comic's work to contemporary issues—even for films which appear escapist. We need works on film comedy that match existing studies of American humor.

Other genres have received varying attention from cultural historians. Jack Shadoian, *Dreams and Dead Ends: The American Gangster/Crime Film* (Cambridge: MIT Press, 1977) relates changes in historical events to the evolution of a popular genre. The musical, science fiction, and horror genres have yet to be treated with equal seriousness. Two film genre textbooks which provide basic orientation and bibliography are Stuart Kaminsky, *American Film Genres: Approaches to a Critical Theory of Popular Film* (New York: Dell, 1977), and Stanley J. Solomon, *Beyond Formula: American Film Genres* (New York: Harcourt, Brace, 1976). Kaminsky is attuned to historical developments, while Solomon is attentive to cinematic elements. Barry Grant's *Film Genre: Theory and Criticism* (Metuchen, N. J.: Scarecrow, 1977) is an anthology which includes essays by major students of film genre.

Period studies abound. Although superficial, an A. S. Barnes series (*Hollywood in the Twenties, Hollywood in the Thirties*, etc.) has the virtue of collecting productions of a decade by genre; these books can prove useful to the scholar who wants to know what else was under production while the film which interests him was being made. Bibliographies by period conclude the major interpretations by Sklar, Jowett, Maland, Wood, and Jackson.

Institutional and genre histories of television are of recent vintage. Erik Barnouw, *Tube of Plenty: The Evolution of American Television* (New York: Oxford Univ. Press, 1975) is an essential history of the industry with useful chronologies and bibliographies. The only serious examination of the genre of television is *TV: The Most Popular Art* (New York: Anchor Books, 1974), a study by Horace Newcomb which inventively applies Cawelti's concept of "formula." Newcomb's notion of "a television aesthetic" will interest those who believe that television can become an artistic medium. Newcomb's anthology, *Television: The Critical View* (New York: Oxford Univ. Press, 1976) amplifies his survey. *About Television* (New York: Harper and Row, 1972) by Martin Mayer takes a journalistic approach to the business side of the medium, although chapters dealing with genre are also rewarding. For example, Mayer's reconstruction of *The Selling of the Pentagon* (1971) controversy is a model for those who wish to apply investigative reporting to the film media. *Remote Control: Television and the Manipulation of American Life* (New York: New York Times Books, 1978), by Frank Mankiewicz and Joel Swerdlow, is a searing indictment of the television "business."

The *Journal of Popular Culture*, the *Journal of Popular Film and Television*, and the *Journal of the University Film Association* have all carried special issues dealing with television's history, aesthetics, and research. "Television News Archives: A Guide to Major Collections" by Fay Schreibman is an essential map to original materials (in *Television Network News*, 86–97). At the present time, original materials should be sought through the Vanderbilt Television Archives; the Museum of Broadcasting (East 53rd St., New York, N. Y. 10022); the Motion Picture Division, U.S. Archives; and other sources described by Schreibman. One of the few reference works available is Les Brown, *The New York Times Encyclopedia of Television* (New York: New York Times Books, 1977). Studies of television are truly in their infancy.

In 1947, Siegfried Kracauer proclaimed that historians erred in ignoring the film record. Over the last five years, Kracauer's notion that films reflect the mentality of a nation has come of age. With far more subtlety than pioneer Kracauer ever displayed, historians have shown that feature films and television programs originally designed to entertain can be valuable cultural records and effective teaching tools.

Film and Literature

Film and literature have had a symbiotic relationship since the origin of the newer medium. Sergei Eisenstein and D. W. Griffith freely admitted that they borrowed from literary sources such innovations in film technique as fast cutting and parallel action. Robert Richardson discusses this germinative process in *Literature and Film* (Bloomington: Univ. of Indiana Press, 1972). Many of the "classics" on the aesthetics of film should be avoided. Rudolf Arnheim, *Film as Art* (Berkeley: Univ. of California, 1957); Siegfried Kracauer, *Theory of Film: The Redemption of Physical Reality* (New York: Oxford Univ. Press, 1960); and Raymond Spottiswood, *A Grammar of the Film* (1935; rpt. Berkeley: Univ. of California Press, 1950) are all such "classics" possessing antiquarian interest only.

The search for a method of decoding film styles and "film language" has been of special concern over the last five years. Andrew Sarris popularized the auteur approach to Hollywood films ("Notes on the Auteur Theory in 1962," *Film Culture*, 27 [1962], 35–51). Peter Wollen's *Signs and Meaning in the Cinema* (Bloomington: Univ. of Indiana Press, 1972) further spread the auteur theory, while adding to a growing interest in semiotics in film. The original source for semiotic theories is Christian Metz, *Film Language: A Semiotics of the Cinema* (New York: Oxford Univ. Press, 1974). An American philosopher's "ordinary language" speculations on the process of perceiving film is Stanley Cavell, *The World Viewed: Reflections on the Ontology of Film* (New York: Viking, 1971). Two excellent books will usher beginners to seats in the darkened theater of film theory. J. Dudley Andrew, *The Major Film Theories: An Introduction* (New York: Oxford Univ. Press, 1976) is the more lucid overview because it applies the same questions to all theorists examined. In *Theories of Film* (New York: Viking, 1973), Andrew Tudor examines the strengths and shortcomings of formalist, realist, auteur, genre, and semiotic schools. The spectrum of American film critics has been categorized by Edward Murray, *Nine American Film Critics: A Study of Theory and Practice* (New York: Ungar, 1975). A scholarly survey is Myron Lounsbury, *The Origin of American Film Criticism* (New York: Arno Press, 1973).

Two anthologies serve the audience for film theory. Gerald Mast and Marshall Cohen, eds., *Film Theory and Criticism: Introductory Readings* (New York: Oxford Univ. Press, 1974) is the most comprehensive textbook available. In addition to sections on traditional film theories, Mast and Cohen also devote attention to literature in film and Shakespeare in film. Bill Nichols, ed., *Movies and Methods: An Anthology* (Berkeley: Univ. of California Press, 1976) clusters articles around major contemporary schools. Countless collections of film criticism exist; Richard Heinzkill's *Film Criticism: An Index to Critics' Anthologies* (New York: Scarecrow, Press, 1975) provides an index to 41 volumes.

A succinct guide to film language is Harry M. Geduld and Ronald Gottesman, *An Illustrated Glossary of Film Terms* (New York: Holt, Rinehart, and Winston, 1973). Novices with a literary background will appreciate John Harrington, *The Rhetoric of Film* (New York: Holt, Rinehart, and Winston, 1973), for Harrington approaches films as acts of communication and then at every point refers to familiar terms of literature and language. Lee Bobker's *The Elements of Film* (New York: Harcourt, Brace, 1974) is a textbook which has improved with each new edition.

Adaptations have become topics for research and teaching. The acknowledged classic on adaptation is *Novels Into Film* (1957; rpt. Berkeley: Univ. of California Press, 1971) by George Bluestone, a work whose early chapters discuss the similarities and contrasts between the two media. Geoffrey Wagner, *The Novel And The Cinema* (Madison, N. J.: Fairleigh Dickinson Univ. Press, 1975) explores similar ground. Reversing the normal process, Claude-Edmonde Magny, in *The Age of the American Novel: The Film Aesthetic of Fiction Between the Two Wars* (1948; rpt. New York: Ungar, 1972) studies the influence of film upon American fiction. Gerald Peavy and Roger Shatzkin have edited two useful anthologies of reviews and articles which throw light upon adaptations. The first, *The Classic American Novel and The Movies* (New York: Ungar, 1977) focuses upon thirty classic American novels (1826–1929); the second, *The Modern American Novel and the Movies* (New York: Ungar, 1978) continues the survey (1930–1975). Both volumes have selected bibliographies and filmographies. Bruce F. Kawin, *Faulkner and Film* (New York: Ungar, 1977) and Phillip Gordon, *Fitzgerald and Film* (New York: Ungar, 1979) are the first of what will soon become a freshet of individual author studies. John Harrington's *Film and/or Literature* (New York: Holt, Rinehart, and Winston, 1977) is a textbook containing articles about film in relation to the literary arts (theater, novel, poetry).

Because short story adaptations always have been classroom favorites, a recent television series for PBS is sure to be used heavily in the future. *The American Short Story* (ed. Calvin Skaggs, New York: Dell Publishing, 1977) brings together under one cover the stories by Bierce, Crane, James, Hemingway, and Fitzgerald from which films were adapted for

PBS during 1977. The films are available for sale from Perspective Films (369 W. Erie, Chicago, Illinois, 60610), but many municipal and university libraries now rent the series. The convenience of this "package" for teaching literature will be difficult to match. The paperback anthology includes, in addition to the stories, interviews with filmmakers, examples of scripts, and shot analyses, all of which illuminate the process of adaptation. A second series is currently being planned.

The relationship between theater and film is explored in a thoughtful—if elementary—way in Allardyce Nicoll, *Film and Theatre* (1936; rpt. New York: Arno, 1972). James Hart, *Focus on Film and Theatre* (New York: Prentice-Hall, 1974) offers a sampling of perspectives through the writings of actors, playwrights, directors, and scholars. Maurice Yacowar, *Tennessee Williams and Film* (New York: Ungar, 1977) is a study by a leading film scholar. The most fruitful work in stage and screen studies is currently being accomplished in the area of Shakespeare studies: The *Literature/Film Quarterly* has published three issues dealing exclusively with Shakespeare; a *Shakespeare On Film Newsletter* carries information about film sources and film scholarship. Charles Eckert, ed., *Focus on Shakespeare and Film* (New York: Prentice-Hall, 1972) is a useful starting point. Colleagues unanimously report that Jack Jorgens' *Shakespeare on Film* (Bloomington: Indiana Univ. Press, 1977) is the most useful single volume on the subject. These studies may deal with a seventeenth-century British bard, but insights about word and image relationships can be applied by Americanists to native materials.

A continuously updated reference work which includes most adaptations is A. Enser's *Filmed Books and Plays: A List of Books and Plays From Which Films Have Been Made* (London: Andre Deutsch, 1971). Douglas G. Winsten, in *The Screenplay as Literature* (Madison, N. J.: Fairleigh Dickinson Univ. Press, 1973) argues that the screenplay should be studied as a distinct literary genre. Interviews with major Hollywood screenwriters are assembled in *The Screenwriter Looks At The Screenwriter* (New York: Macmillan, 1972). Scripts are difficult to find. Authorship can be determined by consulting *Who Wrote The Movie And What Else Did He Write? An Index of Screenwriters And Their Film Works, 1936–1969* (ed. Leonard Spiegelgass, Los Angeles: The Academy of Motion Picture Arts and Sciences, 1970), a source which indexes screenwriters and lists their film and literary works. Ernest Hemingway and William Shakespeare here take their place with Joseph Hoffman, scriptwriter for *Sex And The Single Girl,* and William P. McGovern, scriptwriter for *The Big Heat.* There are a number of published filmscripts. Navigation to the right one is aided by Clifford McCarty, *Published Screenplays: A Checklist* (Kent, Ohio: Kent State Univ. Press, 1971) and by G. Howard

Poteet, *Published Radio, Television, And Filmscripts: A Bibliography* (Troy, N. Y.: Whitston, 1975). As anyone who has conducted film research knows, possession of a script saves hours of time and pounds of pencil lead.

In the spirit of the visual literacy movement, Harris J. Elder, *Writing About Film* (Dubuque: Kendall/Hunt, 1977) presents a short orientation to film language, explains how to organize notes taken at a screening, and provides rudimentary guides to research. Any teacher who plans to use films as topics for composition should adopt this compact text.

The *Literature/Film Quarterly* (Salisbury State College, Salisbury, Maryland, 21801) began publication in 1973. Since then, this journal has devoted attention to traditional topics such as Shakespeare in film, and has also published a number of articles on adaptations. The film and book review sections are useful for the novice who needs help keeping afloat in the flood of new publications on film and literature.

ASSOCIATIONS AND JOURNALS

American Culture Association

In 1978, Russel B. Nye and others formed the American Culture Association "to promote and facilitate the study of American Culture in the broadest sense of the term, from 'elite' to popular and folk culture as a continuum." Since then, the *Journal of American Culture* (101 University Hall, Bowling Green University, Bowling Green, Ohio, 43403) has been publishing articles along the full spectrum of its declared interests. Future issues of *JAC* will contain sections on television and movies. The first annual meeting of the American Culture Association was held in Pittsburgh in April 1979.

American Film Institute

The American Film Institute was founded in 1967 to preserve the national film heritage and to bring together leading artists of the film industry, educators, and aspiring artists. *American Film: Journal of the Film and Television Arts* (JFK Center for the Performing Arts, Washington, D. C., 20566) is a magazine from AFI for general readers, which will be of interest to Americanists for interviews and articles on current trends. The popularity of this attractive publication has helped develop broad support for the American Film Institute.

Under the leadership of Sam L. Grogg, Jr. (1973–79) and Peter Bulkalski (1979–) AFI's National Education Services has undertaken a number of projects. The AFI *Factfile* series provides basic information about organizations, programs, events, books, and periodicals related to film and television. Current titles of interest are "Guide to Classroom Use of Film," "Women and Film/Television," "Children and Film/ Television," "Movie and TV Nostalgia," "Film Music," "Animation," "Film/Television, A Research Guide." AFI now conducts an annual summer workshop in film and television documentation. Anyone who plans to conduct original research from materials in university or industry archives should seriously consider this workshop. *Motion Pictures, Television, and Radio: A Union Catalogue* (Boston: G. K. Hall, 1977), by Linda Harris Mehr, is a guide to manuscript collections for those who cannot attend the AFI workshop.

Two National Education Services programs respond to individual teacher and researcher needs. The NES Information Services section has proven consistently helpful for bibliographical information (202-828-4088). The NES Curriculum Advice Service has model course syllabi which have been contributed by teachers who are members of AFI. Specific questions are also invited by this service. The AFI *Education Newsletter* is a bi-monthly publication with current information about articles and resources, as well as the usual announcements concerning film festivals and conferences. A "Course File" section has carried model syllabi on "New Film Theory," "The History of Animation," "The Art of Alfred Hitchcock." The *Newsletter* and *American Film* are free to AFI members. Many academics have complained that AFI has been insufficiently solicitous of the needs of film researchers; some have observed that AFI reflects Hollywood's commercial point of view. All those who wish film studies well—both within and outside AFI—hope that a growing popular base will allow this useful institution to achieve independence from Hollywood patrons.

American Historical Association

At the Boston meeting of the AHA in 1970, an independent group of interested historians created the Historians Film Committee. The stated goals of the committee were "to further the use of film sources in teaching and research; to disseminate information about film and film use to historians and other social scientists; to work for an effective system of film preservation." The organization meeting also called for "a journal of film and social sciences . . . to facilitate the exchange of information among scholars and others concerned with film." The Historians Film Committee has been extremely active: while it has scheduled panels on film at the AHA national meetings, it has also sent representatives to a number of conferences on film both in and outside the United States.

Of greatest interest to teachers, however, is the journal which blossomed from the committee's newsletter. Appropriately titled *Film and History*, the journal is both pleasurable and rewarding to read. Every issue has an essay on film and history methodology. Some recent titles include: William T. Murphy, "John Ford and the Wartime Documentary" Kenneth Hey, "Automobile Consciousness and the American Film"; Leonard Quart, "Altman's Metaphoric America"; and Richard Oehling, "Hollywood and the Image of the Oriental, 1910–1950." Teachers will find the "History Through Film" section to be the most useful portion of this magazine. Here teachers describe courses in which they have actually used film. The professor whose syllabus appears provides an introductory statement describing the goals and objectives of the film history course. Because *Film and History* is as new as the historian's interest in film, its editors solicit letters, articles, and reviews. To subscribe or to submit ideas, write to the editors, Martin A. Jackson and John E. O'Connor, the Historians Film Committee, c/o The History Faculty, New Jersey Institute of Technology, Newark, New Jersey, 07102.

A movement advocating that historians make their own films began in the early 1970s. Richard Raack, in "Clio's Dark Mirror: The Documentary Film in History," *The History Teacher*, 6 (1973), 109–18, criticizes the failings of documentaries made for television. Raack and others set a high standard for films made by historians in three award-winning productions. *Goodbye Billy: America Goes to War, 1917-18* (1969) is a model for non-narrative compilation; *Will Rogers' 1920s: A Cowboy's Guide to the Times* (1976) is somewhat more didactic but has received three major awards; *Storm of Fire: World War II and the Destruction of Dresden* premiered at the 1978 annual meeting of the American Historical Association and drew such a large audience that the program was repeated. Two articles describe the goals and methods of historians as filmmakers: Patrick Griffin's "The Making of *Goodbye Billy*," *Film and History*, 2 (1972), 6–8, provides insights into some of the special problems related to using old sound and image sources; Peter C. Rollins, "The Making of *Will Rogers' 1920s*," *Film and History*, 7 (1977), 1–5, discusses the combined use of documentary and fictional materials.

American Library Association

The *Film Library Quarterly* is published by the Film Library Information Council (Box 348, Radio City Station, New York, New York, 10019). While this periodical is aimed at librarians responsible for the purchase and rental of film, it goes beyond such a specialized objective. Articles of interest to Americanists have ranged from "Paul Strand as a Documentary Filmmaker,'' ''Chaplin and the American Avant Garde,'' and ''Interviews with Emil de Antonio.'' Current films are regularly and intelligently reviewed. It is easy for academics to forget that municipal libraries have become increasingly involved in the circulation of films. The local library may not only have films available for use; the librarian may even be a film scholar or buff.

American Studies Association

The American Studies Association conventions in San Francisco (1973), San Antonio (1975), Boston (1977), and Minneapolis (1979) included formal sessions, workshops, and screenings which dealt with film.

An ad hoc ASA Film Committee was formed in 1976 to give focus to research and teaching concerns. During the fall semester, Richard Oehling (Assumption College), John Munley (Boston College), Leslie Fishbein (Rutgers University), John O'Connor (New Jersey Institute of Technology), and David Culbert (Louisiana State University) met on a number of occasions to shape a syllabus entitled ''American Studies and Film.'' The experimental course was taught at Boston College by Peter C. Rollins (Oklahoma State University) during the spring semester. The annotated syllabus deals with issues of American Studies and is available at no charge from the National Endowment for the Humanities, Education Programs Division, Washington, D. C. 20506.

Modern Language Association

The annual meetings of the Modern Language Association frequently list seminars on film topics. A special section for Film and Literature is now provided in the annual bibliographical survey, *The Modern Language Association International Bibliography of Books and Articles on the Modern Languages and Literature.*

National Film Society

The National Film Society was founded in 1975 ''to preserve and honor film's past—and to bring film ownership to the average citizen via home video (legally).'' At its annual meeting in Hollywood, the society brings together fans, collectors, scholars, and Hollywood practitioners. A number of actors and technicians share experiences with members after film screenings.

During the early years of the National Film Society, *American Classic Screen* (7800 Conser Place, Shawnee Mission, Kansas, 66204) catered to collectors and buffs. In the near future, this audience will be provided with a newsletter of its own, while the society's magazine becomes a showplace for interviews and articles by scholars. Editor John Tibbetts hopes that *American Classic Screen* will eventually attract a readership which includes both specialists and fans—a goal aimed at by many film journals but attained by none.

Popular Culture Association

Since 1969, many scholars have become involved in the activities of the Popular Culture Association, which has taken a continuing interest in film studies.

The *Journal of Popular Film* was founded in 1972. Following both media realities and the precedent of other journals, the scope of the journal broadened and is reflected in a new title. The *Journal of Popular Film and Television* proclaims on its subscription page that movies and television "are the mirrors by which American culture surveys its mottled complexion . . . a movie says as much about its audience as it contributes to the development of its art form." Some recent titles of interest to students of American culture are Thomas Cripps, "The Movie Jew as an Image of Assimilationism, 1903-27"; Gary K. Wolfe, "*Dr. Strangelove, Red Alert,* and Patterns of Paranoia in the 1950s"; Peter Rollins, "Ideology and Film Rhetoric: Three Documentaries of the New Deal Era"; and Kathleen McCarthy, "Wicked Vice and Virtue: Movie Censorship in Chicago, 1907–1915." The *Journal of Popular Film and Television* frequently appends bibliographical essays. Some recent examples are Daniel J. Leab, "The Black in Films"; Gretchen Bataille and Charles L. Silet, "The Indian in American Film"; and Larry Landrum, "Science Fiction Film Criticism in the Seventies." To subscribe or to submit articles to any of the Popular Culture Association's periodicals *(Journal of Popular Culture, Journal of Popular Film and Television, Popular Music and Society),* write to the editors of the relevant journal: (Title of Journal), 101 University Hall, Bowling Green University, Bowling Green, Ohio, 43403.

University Film Study Center

The University Film Study Center (18 Vassar St., Cambridge, Massachusetts, 02139) is a consortium of Northeastern colleges and universities responding to the growing interest in film. MIT, Brandeis, Dartmouth, Harvard, Amherst, Hampshire, Bowdoin, and other schools are all involved in this group, whose general offices are located at MIT.

The UFSC conducts an intensive summer session on a New England campus each year. The UFSC also conducts seminars, festivals, and contests during the academic year. The UFSC *Newsletter* carries information about these events as well as helpful essays on films, books, and problems of financing film projects. Members have the privilege of studying films at the center at no charge. Participating schools are given preferential rental rates.

HOW TO FIND FILMS

Film Rentals

Most schools have an audiovisual center where rental catalogs may be obtained and questions answered. Most will have a large number of catalogs from both university and commercial distributors around the country, and will help to place orders. This service is especially useful where university bookkeeping is complex.

The Audio-Visual Center, Indiana University, Bloomington, Indiana 47401, is the largest distributor of "educational" films; its catalog runs over 1200 pages. A catalog of the Federal Government's films for sale and rental can be obtained by writing to The National Audiovisual Center, National Archives and Records Service, General Services Administration, Washington, D. C., 20409.

The next most important noncommercial distributor of film is the Museum of Modern Art. MOMA's collection includes almost all of the classic documentary and fiction films of the Western world from the origin of the art form until fairly recently. The newsreel and documentary collections are especially useful to the student of film and history. For a MOMA catalog, write to Circulation Director, Department of Film, The Museum of Modern Art, 11 West 53rd Street, New York, New York 10019.

Commercial distributors will send catalogs to anyone who plans to rent films. Audio-Brandon Films is the major distributor of "art" films on 16mm. Audio-Brandon's offerings cover practically every developed nation in the world for both silent and sound eras. Its *International Cinema Catalog* can be obtained from Audio-Brandon Films, 3 MacQuesten Parkway South, Mt. Vernon, New York 10550. Films Incorporated carries a full line of "entertainment" films which are often of interest to those who plan to analyze feature films as cultural documents. For a catalog, write to Films Incorporated, 440 Park Avenue South, New York, New York 10016. A special catalog from Films Incorporated entitled *Rediscovery of the American Cinema* organizes relevant films under a number of useful categories.

Because the commercial film business is fragmented into a multitude of competitive units, it is difficult to determine which distributor has the desired film at the cheapest rate. *Film Programmer's Guide to 16mm Rentals* (ed. Linda Artel and Kathleen Weaver, Berkeley, California: Reel Research, 1976) is an inexpensive reference tool. Much more expensive but only slightly more informative is *Feature Films on 8 mm and 16mm: A Directory of Feature Films Available for Rental, Sale, and Lease in the United States* (ed. James L. Limbacher, New York: R. R. Bowker, 1976). Both sources include the offerings of the 90 or more film distributors in the United States. Films are classified by title in one section and by filmmaker in another. A list of distributors with their addresses is at the back of the volume. These books are indispensable guides through the maze of individual film catalogs.

My experience has been that journals such as *Film and History, The History Teacher,* and the *Journal of Popular Film and Television* have been the most fruitful sources of ideas about what films to use and how to get them into the classroom. The overviews edited by Artel and Limbacher together with the individual catalogs have provided specific information about price and location. However, teachers should first become familiar with school film libraries and should ask film programmers to schedule films that could be coordinated with their courses. Suggestions to student union and film series committees a year in advance might help make a small budget go a long way. In addition, teachers in metropolitan areas should be alert to public library film programs and to television offerings as well.

Videorecorders and Videodiscs

Recent technological changes have affected the availability of film materials. Off-the-air recording of classic films is possible with RCA Selectavision and SONY Betamax cassette systems. Videodisc playback systems are also now on the market. The RCA machine operates on a needle principle; more exciting for researchers and teachers is the Magnavox system, which, because it operates by laser beam, will allow a viewer to examine any portion of a disc for any length of time without damage to equipment. Every frame of a disc is numbered and the entire disc can be scanned by a "search mode" which finds a desired scene or shot. Once the segment of interest is reached, the image can be frozen on the screen indefinitely, or the frames advanced at any rate desired, be it one, two, three frames at a time. Teachers and researchers in film will be excited by the obvious opportunities for the close analysis of cinematic texts.

The studio collections of Universal, Warner Brothers, Paramount, and Walt Disney are all partially represented in the disc offerings as are some Britannica Films and a few selections from the American Film Theater series. Obviously, more films will become available as the market grows. Anyone interested in teaching opportunities associated with the videodisc should be reminded that the disc machines, while less expensive than videorecorders, do not have an off-the-air recording capacity. Like record players, they play back what has been recorded by studio equipment.

RESEARCH TOOLS

Reader's Guide to Periodical Literature does not index many film periodicals. New bibliographical tools have become available in the last few years to guide researchers to reviews, articles, and books of importance.

Film Reviews

Film reviews are usually of interest as evidence of contemporary responses to new releases rather than for their insights. *The New York Times Film Reviews, 1913-76* (New York: Arno Press, 1976) provides eight volumes of facsimile printed reviews in chronological order; a ninth volume supplies an index to materials by film title, personal name, and corporate name. Using the personal name index, a scholar can see at a glance all of the film reviews by the *Times* for John Ford or Will Rogers or any other actor, producer, or director. Each review is preceded by a list of basic credits.

A number of guides help the researcher to locate film reviews. James M. Salem, *A Guide to Critical Reviews* (Metuchen, N. J: Scarecrow, 1971) lists 12,000 films in alphabetical order with review citations under each title entry. Stephen E. Bowles, *Index to Critical Film Reviews in British and American Periodicals* (New York: Burt Franklin, 1974) is also useful.

Finding recent reviews can be a problem. David M. Brownstone and Irene M. Franck's *Film Review Digest Annual* (KTO, 1976) surveys reviews of major releases. In each case, credits are supplied, followed by 150 to 200 word excerpts from reviews by the *Village Voice, Los Angeles Times, Commentary,* and other periodicals. *Access* (Syracuse, N. Y.: John G. Burke) is a very new index which will guide the researcher to reviews in *Playboy* (Bruce Williamson), *New York Magazine, TV Guide* (Judith Crist), *Rolling Stone,* and the *Village Voice* (Andrew Sarris).

General and Scholarly Articles

Magazine and scholarly articles have been indexed in a number of sources. Harold Leonard, ed., *The Film Index* (New York: Arno, 1941) is an annotated bibliography covering English language sources from 1907 to 1935; books, films, and magazine articles are listed under subject categories. Picking up where *The Film Index* left off is *The New Film Index,* edited by Richard D. MacCann and Edward S. Perry (New York: Dutton, 1975). Categories such as "Film and Society," "Nonfiction Films," and "Film Theory and Criticism" will be of special interest to Americanists. Also organized by topic is *The Critical Index: A Bibliography of Articles on Film in English, 1946-73,* (ed. John C. and Lana Gerlach, New York: Teachers College Press, 1974). Entry 450, "Social Groups," is representative of the collection; here listed as subcategories are "Blacks," "Women," "Youth," "Children," "American Indians," "Jews." Although *The New Film Index* and *The Critical Index* overlap, they should both be consulted.

In the last few years, a number of serially published indexes have become available. *Film Literature Index,* edited by Vincent Aceto and Fred Silva (Albany: Filmdex, 1973) begins coverage in 1971 and surveys 240 periodicals using both title and subject categories. An effort has been made to include general readership magazines (*The Atlantic, Harpers*) as well as journals dealing with broad cultural trends (*American Scholar, Partisan Review*). *Retrospective Index to Film Periodicals, 1930-71,* edited by Linda Batty (New York: R. R. Bowker, 1975) overlaps with other indexes, but should be checked. Less useful for the Americanist, but providing an international perspective, is *The International Index to Film Periodicals*, edited by Karen Jones (New York: R. R. Bowker, 1972). This work is an outgrowth of efforts by the International Federation of Film Archives (FIAF) to tabulate everything written on film. Unfortunately, many of the international periodicals listed are not on library shelves.

Books

Bibliographies abound in the recent surveys by Sklar, Jowett, and Maland. Peter Bukalski, *Film Research: A Critical Bibliography* (Boston: G. K. Hall, 1972) is a list of the major books dealing with film. I. C. Jarvie, *Movies and Society* (New York: Basic Books, 1970) concludes with a massive, annotated bibliography dealing with social science studies of the film industry and film impact. George Rehrauer, *Cinema Booklist* (Metuchen, N. J.: Scarecrow, 1972) is a chatty, but comprehensive, annotated bibliography containing 1,500 entries.

BASIC TEXTS

Film History

Gerald Mast, *A Short History of the Movies* (2nd ed., Indianapolis: Bobbs-Merrill, 1976) is more comprehensive than its title denotes. In "Film History and Film Histories," Mast reflects upon the difficulties of writing a synoptic history. He also comments on other histories now competing with his for the textbook market (*Quarterly Review of Film Studies,* 1 [1976], 297–314).

Film Terminology

Harry M. Geduld and Ronald Gottesman, *An Illustrated Glossary of Film Terms* (New York: Holt, 1973) is an extremely helpful introduction to the vocabulary of film. Lee Bobker, *Elements of Film* (New York: Harcourt, 1974) devotes chapters to image, sound, direction, and acting.

Dictionaries and Companions

Complementary reference works of constant usefulness by George Sadoul are *Dictionary of Filmmakers* (Berkeley: Univ. of California Press, 1972), which provides basic data at a glance as does *Dictionary of Films* (Berkeley: Univ. of California Press, 1972). Since most Americanists are interested in older films, these works do not date quickly. *The Oxford Companion to Film,* edited by Liz-Anne Bawden (New York: Oxford Univ. Press, 1976) has been excoriated by *cognoscenti,* but it is nevertheless a very helpful volume to have on the shelf.

Guides

Guidebook to Film: An Eleven-in-One Reference (New York: Holt, 1972) by Ronald Gottesman and Harry M. Geduld contains an extensive annotated bibliography, a list of theses and dissertations on film topics, and the addresses of major film distributors. The *Guidebook* also contains a four-page list of "Hollywood Novels." Frank Manchel, *Film Study: A Research Guide* (Madison, N. J.: Farleigh Dickinson Univ. Press, 1973) supplies annotated filmographies and bibliographies, but also has sections dealing with film genres, major film themes, film history, and film study. Both works are now dated.

Special Publishers' Series

The Frederick Ungar Publishing Company has been responsible for the books by Jackson, Kawin, Peary, French, Magny, and Murray cited in this essay. More volumes are planned.

The Prentice-Hall *Focus* series edited by Ronald Gottesman and Harry M. Geduld is extremely valuable. To date there are *Focus* anthologies on the following films: *Citizen Kane, Blow-up, Birth of a Nation, The Seventh Seal, Bonnie and Clyde, Rashomon,* and *Shoot the Piano Player.* The following genres have been examined: *The Horror Film, the Science Fiction Film,* and *Shakespearean Films.* Selected directors (D. W. Griffith, Alfred Hitchcock, Howard Hawks) have also been placed under the critical light of the *Focus* series. The Indiana University Press has a series of Film Guides on specific films which include *The Grapes of Wrath, La Passion de Jeanne d'Arc, 2001: A Space Odyssey, Psycho, The General, Rules of the Game, The Battle of Algiers, Henry the Fifth.* The Viking Press has a Film Script series covering *Ninotchka, North by Northwest, Adam's Rib, A Night at the Opera, A Day at the Races, Singin' in the Rain.*

An Appleton-Century-Crofts *Film Scripts* series has produced a number of useful texts: *Film Scripts: One* (1972) contains scripts for *The Big Sleep* (1946) and *A Streetcar Named Desire* (1951); *Film Scripts: Two* has *High Noon* (1952), *Twelve Angry Men* (1957), and *The Defiant Ones* (1958); *Film Scripts: Three* holds *The Apartment* (1960), *The Misfits* (1961), and *Charade* (1963). More volumes are planned.

Industry Studies

United Artists: The Company Built by Stars (Madison: Univ. of Wisconsin Press, 1976) by Tino Balio is an administrative history of a major studio, 1919-51. In *The American Film Industry* (Madison: Univ. of Wisconsin Press, 1976), editor Balio has collected a number of fascinating studies concerned with the ways in which " the realities of economics, changing legal restraints, technological advances, studio organization and procedures, trade practices . . . have influenced the form and content of movies" (p. vii). Much more work is needed in this area. Hortense Powdermaker, *Hollywood: The Dream Factory* (Boston: Little, Brown, 1950) looks at the Hollywood community from the perspective of an anthropologist visiting a primitive tribe. Most of the insights of this entertaining book are still valid.

The Future of Film

Warhol, Mekas, Brakage, and others are discussed in Gregory Battcock, *The New American Cinema* (New York: Dutton, 1967). *The Film Culture Reader,* edited by P. Adams Sitney (New York: Praeger, 1976) contains groundbreaking articles by members of the new American cinema group. Computer films, multiscreen films, and other innovations are extolled in Gene Youngblood, *Expanded Cinema* (New York: Dutton, 1970). *Abstract Film and Beyond*, by Malcolm Le Gice (Cambridge: MIT Press, 1977) is indebted to other studies, but his discussions are flavored by the interests of a practicing filmmaker.

Teaching Film

Dennis Bonenkamp and Sam L. Grogg, Jr., eds., *The American Film Institute Guide to College Courses in Film and Television* (Princeton: Peterson's Guides, 1978) surveys the use of film in American universities, although many exciting developments in American Studies, English and History are not reflected. Richard Maynard, *The Celluloid Curriculum: How to Use Movies in the Classroom* (Rochelle Park, N. J.: Hayden, 1971) is a chatty, unpretentious book aimed at elementary and secondary school teachers; nevertheless, reports on courses dealing with film and such topics as the Western, blacks, the Depression, and the McCarthy era will be of interest to those about to experiment with a new medium. John E. O'Connor and Martin A. Jackson, *Teaching History With Film* (Washington, D. C.: American Historical Association, 1974) is the only systematic attempt to integrate film into a humanities area. John E. O'Connor, ed., *Film and the Humanities* (New York: Rockefeller foundation, 1977) contains one sample syllabus each for American Studies, Literature/Film, Philosophy, and Anthropology. "American Studies and Film," a model syllabus assembled by Peter C. Rollins with the help of the ASA Film Committee, is available at no charge from the National Endowment for the Humanities, Education Programs Division, Washington, D. C. 20506.

Anthropological Films

Anthropologists are using cameras to record ethnographic information; some experiments have encouraged "natives" to film their world as they see it. *Principles of Visual Anthropology*, edited by Paul Hocking (The Hague: Mouton, 1973) is a rich collection of conference papers by Margaret Mead, Jean Rouch, Alan Lomax, and Edmund Carpenter. More recently, Karl G. Heider, in *Ethnographic Film* (Austin: Univ. of Texas Press, 1976), assesses the future prospects for the camera eye as a recorder of culture. Appalshop Films (Box 743, Whitesburg, Kentucky, 41858) and the Center for Southern Folklore (P.O. Box 4081, Memphis, Tennessee, 38104) are producing films which record the native crafts and customs of Appalachia. Most of these productions are listed and described in *American Folklore Films and Video Tapes*, edited by Bill Ferris and Judy Peiser (Memphis: Center for Southern Folklore, 1976).

FILM JOURNALS

American Cinematographer
1782 North Orange Drive
Hollywood, California 90028

Articles focus on technical problems, but the detailed attention to film language will be appreciated. For example, the July 1976 issue carries articles by Alan Pakula on the making of *All The President's Men;* it also discusses the technical innovations introduced by *Bound For Glory.*

American Classic Screen: Journal of America's Film Heritage
7800 Conser Place
Shawnee Mission, Kansas 66204

A new journal which hopes to appeal to both the buff and the scholar.

American Film: Journal of the Film and Television Arts
JFK Center for the Performing Arts
Washington, D. C. 20566

This is a general reader periodical of special interest for current trends and interviews.

Cinema Journal
Film Division
Northwestern University
Evanston, Illinois 60201

Always carries articles of merit, although the focus is not principally American. (This is the journal of the Society for Cinema Studies.)

Film and History
c/o History Faculty
New Jersey Institute of Technology
Newark, New Jersey 07102

Carries special studies, examples of film/history courses, reviews of individual films of interest to historians.

Film Comment
Box 686 Village Station
Brookline, Massachusetts 02147

Often contains articles of interest to Americanists, although its focus is contemporary cinema.

Film Heritage
University of Dayton
Dayton, Ohio 45409

A scholarly journal with a special interest in American film.

Film Library Quarterly
17 West 60th Street
New York, New York 10023

Not as specialized as the title appears to indicate.

Film Quarterly
University of California Press
Berkeley, California 94702

Interviews, scholarly articles, and reviews, often on American topics.

Filmmaker's Newsletter
41 Union Square West
New York, New York 10003

Interviews with technicians and directors are especially interesting.

The History Teacher
California State University
Long Beach, California 90840

Has an excellent media section in which teachers with convictions about the use of film in the classroom review new productions.

Journal of Popular Film and Television
101 University Hall
Bowling Green University
Bowling Green, Ohio 43403

A colorful and useful journal which often carries filmographies, bibliographies, checklists.

Journal of the University Film Association
University of Houston
Houston, Texas 77004

Aimed at those who teach in film departments; as a result, emphasis is divided between film production and film scholarship.

Literature/Film Quarterly
Salisbury State College
Salisbury, Maryland 21801

Simply a "must" for anyone interested in the relationship between film and literature.

Quarterly Review of Film Studies
Redgrave Publishing Co.
Pleasantville, New York 10570

Attempts to be the *New York Review of Books* for film. Many extended reviews are of interest to Americanists.

Shakespeare On Film Newsletter
Department of English
University of Vermont
Burlington, Vermont 05405

Provides helpful information about film rentals and recent productions.

Velvet Light Trap
Old Hope School House
Cottage Grove, Wisconsin 53527

Carries studies of classic American directors, films, and studios.

Wide Angle
University of Ohio Press
Athens, Ohio 45701

A new journal with a major interest in American film history and film genre studies.

Film Data and Rental Sources

1. *The Birth of a Nation* (1915), 100 minutes, black and white, silent, with Henry B. Walthall and Mae Marsh, directed by D.W. Griffith. Rental: Kit Parker Films.

2. *The Jazz Singer* (1927), 89 minutes, black and white, silent/sound, with Al Jolson and Warner Oland, directed by Alan Crosland. Rental: MGM/UA Entertainment Co.

3. Thirties Documentaries:
The Plow That Broke the Plains (1936), 28 minutes, directed by Pare Lorentz. Rental: Oklahoma State University Audio-Visual Center; National Audio-Visual Center; many state and university sources.
The River (1937), 30 minutes, black and white, sound, directed by Pare Lorentz. Rental: Oklahoma State University Audio-Visual Center; National Audio-Visual Center; many state and university sources.
Native Land (1942), 85 minutes, black and white, sound, directed by Leo Horwitz and Paul Strand. Rental: Radim Film Images.

4. Charles Chaplin:
City Lights (1931), 81 minutes, black and white, silent, with Charles Chaplin and Virginia Cherrill, directed by Charles Chaplin. Rental: Films Incorporated.
Modern Times (1936), 89 minutes, black and white, silent/music, with Charles Chaplin and Paulette Goddard, directed by Charles Chaplin. Rental: Films Incorporated.
The Great Dictator (1940), 128 minutes, black and white, sound, with Charles Chaplin and Jack Oakie, directed by Charles Chaplin. Rental: Films Incorporated.

5. *The Grapes of Wrath* (1940), 115 minutes, black and white, sound, with Henry Fonda and Jane Darwell, directed by John Ford. Rental: Films Incorporated.

6. *Wilson* (1944), 154 minutes, black and white, sound, with Alexander Knox and Charles Coburn, directed by Henry King. Rental: Films Incorporated.

7. *The Negro Soldier in the Army* (1944), 40 minutes, black and white, directed by Stuart Heisler. Rental: Kit Parker Films.

8. *The Snake Pit* (1948), 108 minutes, black and white, sound, with Olivia de Havilland and Celeste Holm, directed by Anatole Litvak. Rental: Films Incorporated.

9. *On the Waterfront* (1954), 108 minutes, black and white, sound, with Marlon Brando and Eva Marie Saint, directed by Elia Kazan. Rental: Kit Parker Films.

10. *Dr. Strangelove* (1964), 93 minutes, black and white, sound, with Peter Sellers and George C. Scott, directed by Stanley Kubrick. Rental: Swank.

11. *Who's Afraid of Virginia Woolf?* (1966), 129 minutes, black and white, sound, with Elizabeth Taylor and Richard Burton, directed by Mike Nichols. Rental: Swank.

12. *Apocalypse Now* (1979), 153 minutes, color, sound, with Marlon Brando and Martin Sheen, directed by Francis Ford Coppola. Rental: MGM/US Entertainment Co.

DISTRIBUTOR ADDRESSES

Films Incorporated
440 Fifth Avenue
New York, New York 10016

Kit Parker Films
Carmel Valley, California 93924

MGM/United Artists Entertainment Co.
1350 Ave of the Americas
New York, New York

National Audiovisual Center
National Archives and Records Service
Washington, D.C. 20409

Oklahoma State University
Audiovisual Center
Stillwater, Oklahoma 74078

Radim Film Images
1034 Lake St.
Oak Park, Illinois 60301

Swank Motion Pictures
60 Bethpage Road
Hicksville, New York 11801

Contributors

Ray B. Browne is a founder of the popular culture studies movement. His Popular Culture Center (Bowling Green State University, Bowling Green, Ohio 43403) is a hub for scholarship which reports the findings of scholars through such innovative publications as the *Journal of Popular Culture, Journal of American Culture,* and *Journal of Regional Cultures.* Scholars concerned with the popular arts are brought together each year by annual meetings of the Popular Culture Association and the American Culture Association, both of which are based at the Popular Culture Center. Many authors in this collection—indeed, many readers of these essays—have been influenced by or have strong feelings about this dedicated scholar-leader whose publications are so diverse and extensive that a list is unnecessary.

Everett Carter is a professor of English and teaches at the University of California, Davis. He has written *Howells and the Age of Realism, The American Idea: The Literary Response to American Optimism,* has edited works by William Dean Howells and Harold Frederic, and has contributed articles on American literature to various periodicals. In May 1982 he was awarded the degree *Docteur Honoris Causa* by the University of Bordeaux III.

Thomas Cripps is professor of history and coordinator of the graduate program in popular culture at Morgan State University. He has written *Black Shadows on a Silver Screen,* a prize-winning film; two books on blacks in film; and many articles, the most recent of which won the Charles Thomson Prize for 1981.

David Culbert is associate professor of history at Louisiana State University. He teaches courses in American history and the history of mass media. He has published *News for Everyman: Radio and Foreign Affairs in Thirties America* (1976) and *Mission to Moscow* (1980). His most recent work is a 90-minute documentary film essay (with Peter Rollins), *Television's Vietnam: The Impact of Visual Images.*

Leslie Fishbein is associate professor of American Studies at Rutgers, The State University of New Jersey. Her articles on American radicalism, film and history, and women's history have appeared in *American Quarterly, The Historian, Film and History,* and *Women's Studies.* Her book *Rebels in Bohemia: The Radicals of "The Masses," 1911-1917* (1982) treats the attempts of prewar Greenwich Village rebels to resolve the conflicts among feminism, Freudianism, radicalism, and bohemianism that shaped their lives.

Douglas Gomery is associate professor of communication arts and theatre at the University of Maryland and teaches courses in broadcasting and film. He has published numerous articles on the economics and history of the mass media in such journals as *Screen* (UK), *Quarterly Review of Film Studies, Cinema Journal,* and *Yale French Studies.* He is currently at work on a book about the Hollywood studio system for Macmillan.

William M. Hagen is an associate professor of English at Oklahoma Baptist University where he heads the department and teaches courses in Western Civilization, fiction and film. He has published on modern fiction, American film, and related subjects in such journals as *Conradiana, World Literature Today, Studies in the Novel,* and *Cineaste.*

Kenneth R. Hey is chairman of the film department at Brooklyn College and teaches courses in history, theory, and criticism. He has lectured and written on topics in American studies and film and has published essays in *American Quarterly, Michigan Quarterly, Film and History, Archives of American Art Journal* and others. He is film critic for USA Today magazine and has just completed a book-length manuscript entitled "Out of Touch: Hollywood Culture and Hollywood Films from 1908 to 1944."

Ira S. Jaffe is associate professor of film at the University of New Mexico, where he directs the film program in the College of Fine Arts. His articles and papers explore cinematic and cultural aspects of the work of various filmmakers, including Welles, Flaherty, and Bunuel, as well as Chaplin.

Thomas J. Knock is a lecturer in American history at Princeton University. He specializes in twentieth-century American political and diplomatic history and maintains a strong interest in film history. He has published articles in *American Quarterly* and *Political Science Quarterly* and is presently engaged in a major critical study of Woodrow Wilson and the League of Nations.

Leonard J. Leff teaches screenwriting and film aesthetics in the Department of English at Oklahoma State University. An earlier version of his essay on *Who's Afraid of Virginia Woolf?* and the course of American film censorship was published by *Cinema Journal.* More recent essays have appeared in *Journal of Popular Film and Television* and the *Quarterly Review of Film Studies.* He is currently in preproduction on a film about American poet Theodore Roethke.

Charles Maland is associate professor of English at the University of Tennessee, where he teaches courses in film and American literature. Besides a number of articles on film and American culture, he is the author of two books: *American Visions: The Films of Chaplin, Ford, Capra, and Welles, 1936-41* (1977) and *Frank Capra* (1980). In 1981-82 he was a Fulbright Senior Lecturer of American Studies at the University of Bergen, Norway.

Peter C. Rollins is associate professor of English at Oklahoma State University where he teaches courses in film and American studies. His many articles on film/history as well as film/literature have appeared in such journals as *Film and History, Journal of Popular Film and Television, Literature/Film Quarterly,* and *American Classic Screen.* His work with Will Rogers materials in Oklahoma has led to the publication of many articles, one book, *Will Rogers: A Biobibliography* (1983), and a film, *Will Rogers' 1920s: A Cowboy's Guide to the Times* (1976). He has recently completed a 2.5 hour documentary entitled *Television's Vietnam: The Impact of Visual Images* (Humanitas Films, 1983). Both productions are available through the Audiovisual Center, Oklahoma State University, Stillwater, Oklahoma 74078.

Vivian C. Sobchack teaches film studies at the University of California, Santa Cruz. She has published *The Limits of Infinity: The American Science Fiction Film,* coauthored *An Introduction to Film,* and published articles in *Literature/Film Quarterly, Millennium Film Journal, American Quarterly,* and *Journal of Popular Film and Television* (of which she is associate editor). Her cinematic interests are eclectic and interdisciplinary. Currently, she is completing *The Address of the Eye: A Semiotic Phenomenology of Film Experience.*